DATE DUE

RENEW BY CALLING EXT. 3225			
SEP 0 1 1995			

D1172817

ABANDONED

The Betrayal of the American Middle Class Since World War II

ABANDONED

The Betrayal of the American Middle Class
Since World War II

William J. Quirk and R. Randall Bridwell

MADISON BOOKS
Lanham • New York • London

Published by Madison Books
4720 Boston Way
Lanham, Maryland 20706

3 Henrietta Street
London WC2E 8LU England

Distributed by National Book Network

The paper used in this publication meets the minimum
requirements of American National Standard for
Information Sciences—Permanence of Paper for
Printed Library Materials, ANSI Z39.48–1984. ∞™
Manufactured in the United States of America.

Library of Congress Cataloging-in-Publication Data

Quirk, William J., 1933–
Abandoned : the betrayal of the American middle class
since World War II / William J. Quirk and R. Randall
Bridwell.
p. cm.
Includes index.
1. Middle classes—United States. 2. Intellectuals—
United States. 3. United States—Social conditions—
1945– 4. United States—Economic conditions—1945– 5. United States—Politics and
government—1945– I. Bridwell, R. Randall.
II. Title.
HT690.U6Q57 1992
305.5'5'097309045—dc20 92–5166 CIP

ISBN 0–8191–8459–4 (cloth : alk. paper)

British Cataloging in Publication Information Available

To my daughter, Augusta — WJQ

*To my wife, Susan, my daughter, Sarah Margaret,
and my son, Philip — RRB*

Contents

ACKNOWLEDGMENTS

We would like to thank John Montgomery, dean of the School of Law, University of South Carolina, who encouraged us at every stage of this undertaking. We are indebted to the following former students who gave valuable help with the research on this book: Rivers Jenkins, Greg Bryant, Mike Brittingham, Mel Williamson, and George Miller.

Several good friends were kind enough to read the entire manuscript and provide many indispensable suggestions: John Hughes Cooper, Ron Matthias, Dennis Nolan, Dick Simmons, Arthur Sporn, Howard Stravitz, and Paul Weaver. Howard Stravitz made essential contributions to Part II.

Similarly, Professor and Mrs. Thomas M. Lowry, Jr. both read the manuscript and gave the authors much appreciated help in its preparation.

A number of friends gave their time to read parts of the manuscript and offer helpful suggestions: Jim Berry, Elizabeth Currier, John Eichner, Morris Handel, Rick Handel, Jonathan Harvey, Tracy Herrick, Steve Hu, Neal Hurwitz, Dan and Phil Lacy, John McClaughry, Alan Medlin, J.B. Ness, Larry Nirenstein, Doug Parsons, Pat Quealy, Joel Stoudenmire, and Belton Zeigler.

Special thanks to Tom Cherubini and Harvey Lincoff of the New York Hospital.

Also special thanks to Arthur and Holly Magill for advice and friendship over the years.

Rhonda Jennings, a third year student at the law school, was very helpful in the final preparation of the manuscript.

Finally, we wish to thank the staff at the law school for their dedicated efforts in the preparation of the manuscript, particularly Laura Long, DeAnna Sugrue, Frances Donnelly, Nancy Shealy, and Belinda Davis. Laura Teets also helped with the manuscript.

William J. Quirk
R. Randall Bridwell
December 1991

PROLOGUE

On Sunday, September 2, 1945, under gray skies, the U.S. Third Fleet crowded Tokyo Bay—carriers, battleships, cruisers, and destroyers. The U.S. flag flying above the USS *Missouri* was the same that had flown over the Capitol when Japan struck Pearl Harbor without warning on the morning of December 7, 1941. Theodore H. White was on the foredeck of the *Missouri* as the Japanese foreign minister and army chief of staff came on board shortly before 9:00 a.m. General Douglas MacArthur appeared a few minutes after 9:00; the Japanese signed the surrender; MacArthur signed and made a short magnanimous speech; and then our allies signed. MacArthur then announced, "These proceedings are closed." At that moment, White reports, "We heard a drone and looked up." Four hundred B-29s had taken off hours earlier from Guam and Saipan to arrive precisely at that moment. "They stretched across the rim of the horizon, and their heavy droning almost instantly harmonized with a softer buzzing as 1,500 fleet aircraft from our flattops joined them." The planes circled low over the fleet and then "still very low, they disappeared across the sky, over two cities they had left in ruins, first Yokohama, then Tokyo, as if brandishing our power over the people who had dared, without warrant and with planned deceit, to attack and bloody us at Pearl Harbor."

Four different systems are competing for a win today. The American, Japanese, European and Russian. Recently, Russia seems to have faded out of the race at least as much as a great nuclear power can. Europe, led by a unified Germany, is moving up fast. The two leaders—the U.S. and Japan—depend on each other for trade and have large areas of agreement but have such different values that they were at war not that long ago. The issue now is whose values will prevail in the 21st century.

In 1944, the Consolidated Vultee Plant at Fort Worth, Texas, symbolized the creative and productive energies unleashed by the war: a new B-24 rolled off the assembly line every hour. The plane was called the "Liberator." The U.S. and English constitutional and political traditions were based on the individual. The enemy held a communal, collective and anti-individualistic view of society. Ideologically, the war was a conflict as old as Athens and Sparta. Winston Churchill characterized the conflict, not as one of purely national objectives, but as between two different ways of life. People asked Churchill: "What are we fighting for?" He said: "If we stop, you'll find out."

Following World War II, Americans enjoyed four things:

First, they had more money. More and more people had a level of prosperity that was undreamed of in the 1930s.

Second, they had a sound legal system, which commanded the respect of the majority. People felt the courts would give them a fair deal if they had to use them and that criminal laws would be enforced.

Third, they had more and better education. The country had excellent primary and secondary schools. The average citizen was able to go on from high school to college.

Fourth, the political system had withstood the strain of Depression and war and was working fine. People believed in democracy and its potential for good.

In his *Constitutionalism in America*, Arthur E. Sutherland, the constitutional historian, wrote that the basic plan of Western constitutional democracy is simple. Essentially it is the development, through the last seven centuries, of five "aspirations in human government":

(1) majority rule;
(2) government subject to justice;
(3) equality of man;
(4) diffusion of governmental power lest it be too strong for liberty; and
(5) statement in a written compact of fundamentals of decent rule.

These aspirations, he said, rest on "an ancient theory, that the basis of governmental power is a contract between the governor and the governed." Citizens should be free "acting through an organized majority, to control their own political and economic fate."

The great eighteenth century democratic revolutions, according to R.R. Palmer, professor of history at Princeton, were based on "a new feeling for a kind of equality," a discomfort with social stratification and formal rank. Palmer writes, in his *The Age of Democratic Revolution*, that politically, the revolutionary movement "was against the possession of government, or any public power, by any established, privileged, closed, or self-recruiting group of men." It denied that "any person could exercise coercive authority simply by his own right, or by right of his status." Authority had to be delegated by the people and officials had to be removable. No special elite, created by custom and inheritance, could rule. Similarly, "history," in a dialectical sense unknown to the eighteenth century, could not "give some special elite or revolutionary vanguard a right to rule."

Who are the middle class? About 80 percent of Americans describe themselves as middle class meaning they work for a living and are not rich and not poor. The group defines itself by its expectations rather than by any particular income level. That's the way we use the term in this book. Economically we mean the "non-poor/non-rich" (i.e. above the 15 percent poverty level and below the 1 percent wealthy).

World War II was a middle-class war; it was fought with middle-class blood and gold. Following World War II, the American middle class increased dramatically in size and prosperity. The U.S. economy was the most powerful in history, home ownership was widespread and, helped by the GI Bill, the middle class started going to college.

The term "middle class" implies a certain state of mind. It suggests dedication to work as the primary means of subsistence and success. The middle class does not inherit much wealth and believes people should work to live. Economists say the middle class has a high or long "time preference," meaning its members look to the long run. In the long run, merit, thrift and hard work will be rewarded. Predictability, stability and fairness are essential to make the system work. The short run offers excitement and immediate gratification. The middle class rejects it. A belief in the family—as opposed to temporary alliances—is part of the same thinking. Stability comes from the family and the traditions every family has. Middle-class values aren't based on a grand dream of an ideal social order; they are prosaic, they are geared to survival—of the individual, his family and his country.

The middle class is also the only group that cares what happens to the country. They have what Jefferson called a "stake" in the society. The rich are always poised for flight to sunny climes if things start to get rough; the underclass could care less. The strength of the country is its middle class, what we call the "typical American."

The typical American was described in the writings of Eric Hoffer. Hoffer, after he had worked alongside longshoremen and field hands during the Depression, wrote a series of brilliant books on political philosophy. In 1964, he wrote of Americans:

> Imagine an American writing about America and not mentioning kindness, not mentioning the boundless capacity for working together, not mentioning the unprecedented diffusion of social, political as well as technological skills, not mentioning the American's ability to do the world's work with a minimum of supervision and leadership, not mentioning the breathtaking potentialities which lurk in the commonest American.

Americans are democratic, not elitist; they believe in practical solutions to problems rather than social experiments designed to prove the truth of a theory. Writing in 1856, Jefferson's granddaughter, Ellen Randolph Coolidge, recalled Jefferson's "obstinate propensity to think well of mankind, of human nature, to trust largely the good sense and good feeling of the mass." America is the country of the common man, not the intellectual.

Beginning in the 1960s, intellectuals in government, the media, and the universities started to undermine the democratic premise. The intellectuals were themselves part of the economic middle class, but they hated it. They ridiculed middle-class values. They joined forces with the wealthy upper class who always disdained the middle class. To end-run democratic control, the new allies moved power to the courts; the judges started imposing basic social and economic doctrine. The courts ordered quotas and other benefits based on group membership. They no longer judged each citizen on his own merits by neutral principles. They casually overrode local government. The country set off on a 25-year experiment with non-democratic government.

Hoffer wrote that the new intellectuals—in government, the media and universities—scan the daily newspapers for "evidence of the depravity and perversity of American life." They "want power, lordship, and opportunities for imposing action" which the central government, if they can control it, can give them. Intellectuals hate the middle class.

Intellectuals believe in what they construct in their minds. They are disinterested in facts and the real world. Like Lenin, they create a theory, or dream, of what society should be like. Ordinary people, however, don't share the intellectual's dream. They know it means they will get pushed around to make them fit in. The intellectual, if he can, will impose his dream with extreme callousness. Hoffer reports Gandhi once saying "the hardness of heart of the educated" was what worried him most about the future.

What drives the new intellectuals crazy, Hoffer finds, is the "mass of the American people" and their accomplishments. What the intellectuals hate, what they "cannot stomach is the mass of the American people—a mindless monstrosity devoid of spiritual, moral and intellectual capacities." The new intellectuals project upon America what they know about one another: the "infighting, mistrust, envy, malice, conformity, meagerness, and staleness of the cliques and sects." They "do not trust each other, but their deepest mistrust is of the common people." They are unified by disdain for the majority and the institutional and social arrangements the majority prefer. They are as biting as they can be when they speak of what they call the "bourgeoisie" and "bourgeois" values.

Americans look at Russia and its former satellites and see revolution in action. In fact, the changes occurring in the United States since 1965 have been just as revolutionary as those in Eastern Europe—we have just been going in the opposite direction. In Eastern Europe the intellectual system based on concepts of Karl Marx has been overthrown in favor of individual freedom and democracy. As Boris Yeltsin says, Russia has ended its 74 year experiment with communism.

In America, the new intellectuals contrived a vastly intrusive system. The individual—according to their new system—is a bundle of prejudices and attitudes that need adjusting. He should be redesigned into something better. The individual, of course, did not think he was so bad. He didn't want to be redesigned, and as long as he had any power, was not going to be redesigned. The ordinary citizen was guilt-free, as Hoffer wrote in 1964: "My kind of people does not feel that the world owes us anything, or that we owe anybody—white, black, or yellow—a damn thing." No group, or individual, has any "special claims on us, and no valid grievances against us."

To overcome this attitude problem, the new intellectuals felt obliged to reduce individual freedom and power. Beginning in the 1960s, intellectuals in government, the universities, and the media, began to attack the critical premise of the democracy—the power of the individual. They began to end-run the democracy by extensive reliance on:

(1)   The Judiciary—The country started letting an unelected group impose basic social and economic doctrine.

(2)   Debt—Congress made debts which it had no intention of repaying. The unrepresented future had to pay. The guy who was supposed to pay didn't even have a seat at the table. And, of course, because of the debt burden, the future could not do what it wanted. It had to pay for what the past did.

We had judges and debt, of course, when the country was still an effective democracy. But we then looked to judges to decide cases, not impose values on us. We looked to borrowing to cover some extraordinary cost, not to finance the everyday operation of government. But, beginning in the 1960s, judges and debt started to dominate the country. The Supreme Court-led Revolution attacked the majority's values and interests. The Revolution denied the majority will on social issues ranging from crime to newly created individual rights. Similarly, the Revolution overrode majoritarian restraints on economic matters such as debt, public spending and taxes.

The collapse of American democracy reversed the gains which followed the war. For the average American, the reality is now less money, a busted criminal justice system, a pitiful education system, and fading political rights. The middle-class world has collapsed with a shocking suddenness. No one, in 1965, gave any serious thought to the danger that the rights of the unorganized majority would be subjugated by a tyranny of the minority.

Both political parties abandoned the middle class. The Republicans actually represent the upper end of the socio-economic spectrum—the top 5 percent at most. The Democrats drifted to the lower end, the minorities and some traces of organized labor—altogether maybe 15 percent. The 80 percent middle is unrepresented; the Republicans disdain them because they believe they are economic failures, they earn less than $85,000 per year; the Democrats hate them because they think they are racist. The Republicans win all the national elections because they are able to use rhetoric the middle-class believes in. The Democrats can't use middle class rhetoric because it would offend their real constitutency. But, once in office, the Republican policies don't follow the middle-class rhetoric. The real Republican policies benefit their upper end constituents; they don't have to cater to the middle class because the middle class has no place to go. The point is, in a one-party system, the voters don't have much influence.

The end-runs around democracy and the one-party system overthrew the idea that government derives its just powers from the consent of the governed. This created a fatal schism between what the government was doing and what the majority of the people believed it should be doing. A country where the government has one mission, and the people another, of course, won't move the ball down field. The failure of democracy consequently also caused the economic failure of the middle class. Since 1972 workers' average real wages have run steadily down. A rising tide gets all the boats home but the tide has not been rising for a long time. Families have kept up the appearance of prosperity by a tremendous increase in borrowing and by having two bread winners instead of one. But, right now, the children of the middle class are falling out of it and the parents can't help because they're just hanging on themselves.

Government, once it overthrew the democracy, was able to pursue policies its allies in the universities and media liked but that the people hated. A government at war with its people, however, cannot ask too many sacrifices of them. The government can not, for example, ask the people to pay taxes to support the programs they hate. Once government stops representing the people, the people stop feeling any responsibility for it. The government has to borrow to pay for programs the people don't support. The national debt is now $3.5 trillion and costs almost $300 billion in interest annually, which is about 60 percent of income tax collections. A government at war with its people leads to national bankruptcy.

America has always had a very wealthy upper class. The wealthiest half of the top 1 percent of American families own 24.3 percent of the net worth of the country. This group, about 500,000 families, is out of the middle class; they hold very substantial liquid assets—about 50 percent of the privately held stocks and bonds. They don't need to work to live. Their share of the national wealth, however, has not changed much over the years; the figures only go back to 1922 but they run pretty consistently around 25 percent. Americans, unlike Europeans, have never really resented the rich. The American Dream, after all, was that you could join them. Chrysler used to advertise its Town and Country convertible saying there was an "air about this glorious convertible—a whisper of country clubs and moonlight rides."

The top 10 percent of American families earn good incomes. The top 1 percent, about 1 million families, averages a surprising $617,214 of income from all sources; the next 4 million families average $132,553; and the next 5 million families average $85,664. Since 1977 the income of the top 1 percent has almost doubled. The top 1 percent receives more of the country's pre-tax income than the bottom 40 percent of families. The top 1 percent probably has a fair amount of savings and is in good shape. The rest of the top 10 percent—the $85,664 and the $132,553 families—are another story. Politicians, when they aim taxes at what they call the "rich," always go after this group; they are the "Bubble" people of the 1986 Tax Act. But its not true: they're not rich; they are upper middle class. They have good salaries but probably not a lot of savings.

Which brings us to the bottom 90 percent of American families. It is hard to see how they are getting by. Their average income is $31,669. *Since 1977, the bottom 90 percent have seen their average wages and salary drop by 3.5 percent.* Tracy G. Herrick of Jefferies & Co., Inc. (San Francisco) points out there have been three periods in the nation's history when middle-class living standards declined for more than a decade: (1) 1804-1821; (2) 1852-1882; and (3) 1972-present. "Each of the two previous periods," Mr. Herrick writes, "was accompanied by a political revolt of the middle class, war, and ended with the emergence of a major new political party."

The economic failure of the middle class means that fundamental change is coming. The country can't function if it has no confidence in its future opportunities. If further deterioration is to be avoided, a new constitution has to be formed to close the breach that has opened between the people's beliefs and the government's beliefs.

Eastern Europeans know very well it was the intellectuals who were pushing them around, whom they have thrown over and whom they have to keep out of power if they want to keep their freedom. In 1990, Czechoslovak Finance Minister Václav Klaus, told a meeting in Munich: "People could not afford once more to put their fates into the hands of irresponsible intellectuals."

The new intellectual needs power in society because he has no clear socially useful role. He doesn't work with his hands, he doesn't make anything, he cannot, like a man of action, organize a great undertaking. The intellectual is a man of words and paper. His "uncertain status," as Hoffer puts it, and his "lack of an unquestionable sense of social usefulness" require that the intellectual gain power or attach himself to someone who has. The intellectual's justification for gaining power is the "realization of a grandiose design," he "needs the sanction of ideals and the incantation of words."

Since any stick will do to beat a dog, the intellectuals champion cause after cause to beat the middle-class American. The causes, in rough historical order, include: socialism, the Vietnam War, nuclear bombs and power, racism, environmentalism, radical feminism, AIDS, and homelessness. The overriding cause is hatred of the middle class.

The new American intelligentsia, as Charles Krauthammer points out, is working to "undermine a social system it cannot abide." Its members attack the country's two central values: "the idea of a common Western culture" and "the idea of a common American citizenship." Its members proclaim support for a new oppressed, "no longer the bloated and ungrateful working classes, but a new class of carefully selected ethnic and gender groups. Blacks, Hispanics, women, homosexuals, Native Americans." Their attack on the idea of common American citizenship "consists of the division of Americans into a hierarchy of *legally preferred* groups based on race and gender." Setting one group against another—the destruction of the American idea—"poses a threat that no outside agent in this post-Soviet world can hope to match."

What will the world look like for our children? One kind of world has a few strong nations which generally agree on the shape of things and whose edicts are enforced by the United States. The citizen will not have a lot of control or liberties. Another kind of world is made up of a lot of constitutional democracies. "Nothing is clearer today," wrote Al Smith in 1923, "than that the only type of government which is stable and lasting in the long run is that which receives its sanction from the majority of the people."

The difference between the two worlds is the presence or absence of a middle class. Every effort to get a constitutional democracy going —without a middle class—has failed. Jefferson saw the middle class as critical to the democracy because it is the point where politics and economics meet. You can't have a constitutional democracy without a middle class and you can't have a prospering middle class unless it has the power and liberty provided by constitutional limitations on government. Ultimately, political power must be based on economic strength. A citizen who has lost his economic sovereignty will lose his political sovereignty.

From 1787 to the mid-1960s, the country flourished under what amounted to a series of "constitutions." There was the official Constitution of the United States drafted in Philadelphia, there was the unwritten common law "constitution" which supported and elaborated it, there was the economic and financial "constitution," the education "constitution," and the political "constitution." The various constitutions provided the political stability and predictability essential to the efficient operation of an industrial economy. The constitutions established the people's basic understanding of what the country was trying to do; of the individual's relation to the country and its relation to him.

Beginning in the 1960s the intellectuals in government, the media, and the universities started to undermine each of these constitutions. A revolution, Palmer writes, is a "conflict between incompatible conceptions of what the community ought to be." The country's old constitutions—its concept of what the community ought to be—have been overthrown by our 25-year experiment with nondemocratic government. The citizen, however, has not accepted the overthrow of his various constitutions. It is unlikely that he will.

This leads us to what Palmer calls a "revolutionary situation," meaning one in which "confidence in the justice or reasonableness of existing authority is undermined; where old loyalties fade, obligations are felt as impositions, law seems arbitrary . . . where existing sources of prestige seem undeserved, hitherto accepted forms of wealth and income seem ill-gained, and government is sensed as distant, apart from the governed and not really 'representing' them." In 1794, a group of Sheffield workingmen demanded: "What is the constitution to us if we are nothing to it."

The crisis, at this point, Palmer continues, "is a crisis of community itself, political, economic, sociological, personal, psychological, and moral at the same time. Actual revolution need not follow, but it is in such situations that actual revolution does arise. Something must happen if continuing deterioration is to be avoided; some new kind or basis of community must be formed."

As the American middle class fades away, so, of course, does America. Does that make a difference? Why not cede economic dominance and the political dominance that goes with it to Japan and Europe? There is one reason. De Tocqueville said this country is great because its people are good. It will be a better world, fairer, and more democratic, if the U.S. leads. The authors can't prove that. That's our bias, the way we were brought up.

In 1963, Hoffer wrote in *The Ordeal of Change*:

> Only here, in America, were the common folk of the Old World given a chance to show what they could do on their own, without a master to push and order them about. History contrived an earth-shaking joke when it lifted by the nape of the neck lowly peasants, shopkeepers, laborers, paupers, jailbirds, and drunks from the midst of Europe, dumped them on a vast, virgin continent and said: "Go to it; it is yours!"

Is it worth a fight to keep the American middle class? Does it make a difference whether or not the U.S. leads the world? As Churchill said when asked what we were fighting for in World War II: "If we stop, you'll find out."

Thus, it is manifest that the best political community is formed by citizens of the middle class, and that those states are likely to be well-administered in which the middle class is larger, and stronger, if possible, than both other classes.

Aristotle, *Politics*, Book IV, chapter 11

PART I

THE MONEY ABANDONMENT

She [the U.S.] must guard her solvency as she does her national frontiers.

> Dwight D. Eisenhower, making his first political speech after resigning as head of NATO, in a plastic raincoat in the rain at Abilene, Kansas on June 4, 1952.

[U]ltimately they [expanding debt and deficits] are both politically and economically unsustainable.

> Paul A. Volcker, Federal Reserve Chairman, to House Subcommittee on Telecommunications, Consumer Protection and Finance of the Committee on Energy and Commerce, April 23, 1986, speaking of the rapid growth of debt in the country.

The promise of America, Washington pointed out in his "Farewell Address," was tied to common American citizenship: "The union of government which constitutes you one people . . . is a main pillar . . . of your real independence, the support of your tranquility at home, your peace abroad, of your safety, of your prosperity, of that very liberty which you so highly prize." Washington warned against divisiveness based on sectional attachment and the "baneful effects of the spirit of party." He concluded: "The name of AMERICAN, which belongs to you, in your national capacity, must always exalt the just pride of patriotism more than any appellation derived from local discriminations."

Jefferson believed the American Revolution was part of a larger revolution—the revolution of the human spirit against oppression. America offered the first opportunity, free from European despotism, aristocracy and mobs, to build a nation on a particular idea of the dignity of man. The U.S. is the only country formed on a set of ideas agreed to by the people after debate.

"Social mobility, the prudential virtues, and universal education, land, free government, free thought, and human dignity; economic plenty and industrial power," writes John Morton Blum, professor of history at Yale, "all these sometimes contradictory elements were reconciled within one over-arching edifice, that of the American nation, the United States." The elements merged, Blum writes, "to form the promise of American life." This offered opportunity to men of diverse ambitions and diverse ideals. The American promise was often realized, making it a "revolutionary promise, exciting new expectations in men everywhere, equating those expectations with the successful American revolution."

"This middle-class country had got a middle-class president, at last," wrote Ralph Waldo Emerson upon the election of Abraham Lincoln. Lincoln was self-made, self-taught and his sympathies were middle class. As he told the Ohio troops, "I am living witness that any one of your children may look to come here as my father's child has . . . that each of you may have, through this free government . . . an open field and a fair chance for your industry, enterprise, and intelligence." The people he most admired, Lincoln wrote, were "the attorney in a country town; the merchant at the cross-roads store; the farmer who toils all day."

Following the Civil War, the industrialization of the country strongly developed one element of the American promise—economic growth. But, the "latitude large industry enjoyed," as Blum puts it, endangered the other elements of the promise. Equality of opportunity is not compatible with great discrepancies of wealth and poverty. Middle-class reformers, at the turn of the century, "urged the use of the Sherman Antitrust Act to restore equitable competition, the construction of public regulatory agencies to discipline industrial power, and the increase of funds available for business loans at moderate rates."

The Progressive movement, led by Theodore Roosevelt, was the middle-class reaction to industrialization. The middle class believed that extremes of wealth and poverty and the war raging between management and labor would sooner or later destroy the American promise, and the country.   Roosevelt used the Sherman Act to break up great concentrations of economic power and tried to regulate its future use.

Roosevelt thought his "natural allies" were the same as Lincoln's—"the farmers, small businessmen and upper class mechanics." Blum, who edited *The Letters of Theodore Roosevelt*, writes:

> Patrician though he was, Roosevelt had a genius for reaching the average voters, for endowing his deliberately commonplace statements of middle-class virtues with the drama of his own exuberance. For all the superficial differences between himself and his electorate, he contended, down at bottom they had the same ideals.

The middle-class political compromise fashioned by Roosevelt and the Progressives has been the country's foundation in the twentieth century. In the 1950s, based on this firm foundation, we were at the height of our stature and justified self-confidence on the world scene. On January 21, 1954, the world's first atomic submarine, the *Nautilus,* was launched at Groton, Connecticut. Later that year, on May 17, 1954, the United States Supreme Court declared that legally required racial segregation of public schools was unconstitutional. The air force announced, on December 29, 1951, that run-up tests were being started at Seattle on the B-52 *Stratofortress*. On April 12, 1955, ten years to the day after the death of President Franklin D. Roosevelt, the polio vaccine invented by Jonas Salk was released to the public. On March 15, 1956, *My Fair Lady* opened at the Mark Hellinger Theatre in New York City for a run that lasted till September 29, 1962. In June of 1957, American ground combat forces left Japan after twelve years of military occupation. During July and August of 1958, the *Nautilus* was joined by her newly launched sister ship, the *Skate,* for a sail beneath the northern polar ice cap. On April 25, 1959, the St. Lawrence Seaway was opened, realizing the two-hundred-year old dream of North American explorers.

America was the financial clearing house to the world. The majority of international monetary transactions were conducted at The Federal Reserve Bank of New York on Liberty Street. In April 1957, the Bank held 200 million ounces of gold. America was the world's largest producer of petroleum, steel and agricultural commodities.

By the end of President Dwight Eisenhower's second term, January 20, 1961, America was routinely accomplishing unheard of things. From the Northwest Passage to the North Pole, the American presence was seen and felt. Inflation, during the Eisenhower years, averaged 1.4% percent per year. His budgets were balanced or close to it. The national debt, in 1960, was $291 billion and we had to pay $9 billion in interest on it.

America is now smothered under an almost incalculable avalanche of debt. The financial cornerstones of responsible government—from the Social Security system to the Federal Deposit Insurance Corporation—are in shambles. It takes 60 cents of every tax dollar collected from every citizen just to pay the interest on the national debt—*interest is rolling along at $32 million an hour*. The national debt is growing *over $1 billion each day*. In 1991 we paid *$283.1 billion in interest* on the national debt. You can't run the country on borrowed money. What happened?

The American Revolution against Britain and its constitution was largely rooted in tax and economic issues. The British Crown imposed taxes and other financial burdens without American consent. After Independence, the founding fathers set out to create a constitution which would guarantee they would never be subject to that kind of governmental power again. The framers thought that with a written constitution limiting the power of government—federal and state—they could ensure political and financial stability.

Now, obviously, things have not turned out the way they thought. Both political parties have united to end-run the democratic checks on debt and tax policy. We start the story with the New York City crisis of 1974-75, since it was the first major experiment with debt and tax policies at odds with the constitutional rules established by the majority. The New York constitution was bypassed by the use of clever abstract theories which the courts accepted. The government, as a result, operated without limits, and the constitutional democracy was broken.

Subsequently, the same methods were applied at the national level with the same results—national insolvency and the collapse of law and order. The authors believe that financial collapse could not have happened without abandonment of the democratic constitutional principles which were set up to prevent exactly what happened. We also believe that we are not going to come close to correcting any national problems until we restore those democratic constitutional principles.

We will look first at what happened to America's economic constitution (Part I). Then we will look at the destruction of the various constitutions which supported it: the Political Abandonment (Part II), the Legal Abandonment (Part III), and the Academic Abandonment (Part IV).

As it existed in 1965, the Economic Constitution of America was basically Jeffersonian, and had the following characteristics:

1.   It was driven by economic growth, which produced an expanding middle class and a rising standard of living.

2.   Individuals enjoyed increasing upward social and economic mobility based on merit.

3.   The U.S. was self-sufficient; we had a favorable balance of trade, and U.S. individuals and companies owned the U.S. means of production.

4.   The U.S. market was 65-70 percent of the world market and was largely served by U.S. business.

5.   The country enjoyed close to full employment at good-paying jobs.

6.   The dollar was sound as a dollar was supposed to be; there was minimal inflation; interest rates were low and the financial future seemed predictable.

7.   We had a sound and solvent banking system and the S&Ls were doing their job.

8. We were committed to a strong dollar which was internationally tied to gold.

9. The Tax Code favored manufacturing and investment and exempted those with the lowest income.

10. We had an affordable Social Security system; Social Security took a maximum of $174.00 from a worker's paycheck and provided a small pension to the disabled and those over 65.

11. Antitrust laws were enforced against conspiracies in restraint of trade and anti-competitive mergers.

12. The national government came close to balancing its budget; deficits were small.

13. The national debt was no higher than the present generation could pay and intended to pay; debt service was never more than 20 percent of income tax collections.

14. The line separating the public sector from the private sector was clear and understood by both sides.

Are we better off without those 14 provisions of the old Economic Constitution? No reader thinks that. Well, what has happened? The nation's resources and people haven't changed; we haven't been conquered. What *has* changed? The Jeffersonian Constitution—which protected the rights of the unorganized majority—was undermined by the intellectual minority. Since 1965, the average citizen has been playing against a stacked deck. This is the story of how the deck was stacked.

CHAPTER ONE

New York City Fiscal Crisis - 1974-1975 - A Dry Run And Some Characters Introduced

During the 1970s and 1980s the country lost its general atmosphere of security and confidence. Looking back, the warning of what was to come, the dead canary in the mine shaft, was the New York City fiscal crisis of 1974-75. In many ways, the City's troubles were a preview of where the nation was headed in the 1980s and 1990s. The majority, in New York, had expressed its will in detailed constitutional provisions governing debt, spending and taxes. The constitution prohibitied deficits and assured the fiscal solvency of state and local government. Could a small group end-run these majoritarian restraints? Absolutely, first to run up huge deficits by illegal borrowing and then to cover up their chicanery. The cover up was so successful and the media and courts so cooperative that the people did not realize the extent of the damage till 1991.

The current story is that New York City went through a fiscal crisis in the 1970s but was saved just as it was about to go over the cliff. The problem has been treated as if it was caused by impersonal forces like a volcano or tidal wave. There hasn't been any interest in finding out if identifiable people caused the City's bankruptcy, and, of course, no interest in assigning blame and punishment.

The "impersonal forces approach" is now the basic model for explaining the national bankruptcy. The only new variant the politicians, media and academics have thought up is to say that if anyone is to blame, it is the middle-class American. He is lazy, inattentive and wants benefits without paying for them. The leaders, in short, found the only innocent party in the whole deal, the only one who was doing his job, and put the blame on him. The New York City fiscal crisis also first

ABANDONED

demonstrated that the governmental attitude toward debt was the surest barometer of the health of the democracy.

There were two main explanations for what went wrong in New York City. One, the City had been inundated by a "great tide" of some sort, by impersonal forces beyond the control of anyone. The second theory was that the deed had been committed by people, real people who on specific dates made decisions that had predictable consequences. To figure out the correct interpretation, you have to go back to a debate between Thomas Jefferson and James Madison and see the way our constitutional government was designed to stabilize both politics and economics.

On December 20, 1787, Jefferson wrote to Madison on the necessity of a bill of rights: "[A] bill of rights is what the people are entitled to against every government on earth, general or particular, and what no just government should refuse or rest on inference." Its provisions would be enforced by an independent judiciary. Madison was unenthusiastic: "Wherever there is an interest and power to do wrong, wrong will generally be done." Further, "experience proves the inefficacy of a bill of rights on those occasions when its control is most needed." These "parchment barriers" cannot restrain government.

These observations apply with equal force to individual liberties and fiscal matters. As Jefferson pointed out, a government cannot get into financial trouble unless it goes in for recurring deficit financing. If additional costs are paid for by increased taxes, the issue is forced to a head and will be fully debated. The only way government can accomplish deficit financing, of course, is by borrowing. For this reason, all state constitutions limit the state's power to borrow. The federal Constitution does not limit the federal government's power to borrow. The Framers thought they had handled the problem because they gave the national government such limited taxing powers that it would not be able to borrow much. That is, since any borrowing had to be repaid with tax revenues, and the taxing power was restricted, the government could only borrow small amounts. Jefferson was anti-debt because debt cast the burden on a future unrepresented generation.

Public finance has a short menu. Programs, wars, and welfare can be paid for in two ways: (1) what is called "pay-as-you-go," which means the government program is paid for by current taxes, or (2) by borrowing. A debt or, in the old phrase, "funding policy," means we are going to borrow and spend the money today and someone else is going to pay it back—with interest—tomorrow. Debt separates the spending from the cost which—as everyone with a credit card knows—makes all the difference in the world.

Popular and necessary programs are traditionally financed "pay-as-you-go." Twenty-five percent of the cost of World War II was financed on a pay-as-you-go basis. The people, however, resist paying taxes to support unpopular programs, such as the Vietnam War and the Great Society experiments. Properly so. In a democratic society, unpopular programs are not supposed to go forward. Debt enables government to go ahead with a policy or program even though the people are not willing to pay for it and the government knows they are not willing to pay for it. For this reason, the control and management of debt is necessary for the success of the democracy.

The political tendencies of public debt were outlined in a 1895 study by Henry C. Adams. Borrowing, Adams pointed out, was opposed to the full realization of self-government and constitutional government. Debt allows government to veil the true meaning of its acts, permitting it to enter upon great enterprises without bringing all the facts fully to the knowledge of the public. As Adams put it, "A loan calls for no immediate payment from the people, but produces vast sums for the government." A direct tax, however, demands immediate payment from the people. Indirect taxes raise the prices of consumer products which people notice; a loan does neither. Adams wrote:

> The funding system stands opposed to the full realization of self-government . . . Any method or procedure, therefore, by which a public servant can veil the true meaning of his acts, or which allows the government to enter upon any great enterprise without bringing the fact fairly to the knowledge of the public must work against the realization of the constitutional idea. . . .A loan calls for no immediate payment from the people, but produces vast sums for the government. It requires a certain degree of thought to recognize that debts imply burdens, and for this reason a government that resorts to borrowing may for a time avoid just censure. Loans do not, like direct taxes, demand a visible payment from the people; nor, like indirect taxes, raise the price of consumed articles. They address themselves rather

to the interests of those who have control over capital, and by the promise of a perpetual annuity induce the holders of money to intrust it to the state. *The administration is satisfied, since its necessities have been relieved without exciting the jealousy of the people; the lenders are satisfied, since they have secured a good investment for their capital and are not bothered with its management; while the people are not dissatisfied because of their profound ignorance of what has taken place. Herein lies the danger of permitting a government freely to mortgage its sovereign credit.* (emphasis added)

The states learned the destructive power of debt and compound interest through hard and bitter experience. Back in 1846, the state of New York's free borrowing policies—for canals and railroads—had brought it to the edge of bankruptcy. Comptroller Flagg reported the state was pressed "to the very brink of dishonor and bankruptcy." Flagg said the state's bad loans had "inflicted lasting evils on all who labor and pay taxes." Taxpayers were incensed at the thought they would have to shoulder the burden of the state's bad loans. The people said "Never again." The 1846 Constitutional Convention was called to restrain the power of the governor and legislature to borrow. The convention, applying Jeffersonian principles, decided that the people's direct approval, by referendum, must be given before any debt could be incurred.

One leader at the convention, Michael Hoffman, explained, that the "greatest infirmity" of free governments was their disposition to contract debt; a bad law can be repealed but a bad debt cannot be:

> If we look at home, at the neighboring states, or to foreign representative governments, we shall be obliged to acknowledge that their greatest infirmity is their disposition to contract debts. The freest government on the other side of the water has contracted the largest debt known to history. . . . [I]t behooves those who were desirous of securing free and republican government to find some limitation safe in practice to this most dangerous power. In almost any case if a bad law is passed by the legislature it can be repealed—the legislature have few temptations to pass a bad one. It is not so in relation to the subject of debts and compound interest. *It is silent, creeps along, gets into the State, and when the act is once passed, the debt incurred, the obligation is as strong as death for its payment. That can only be*

wrung from the industry of the people, by taxes, indirect or direct.
This being the case, and being so entirely different from almost all
subjects on which legislation can act, it requires an especial remedy.

In support of the Hoffman proposal, Mr. Arphaxad Loomis
pointed out that debt was essentially anti-democratic because it restrained
the freedom of future generations without their consent: "[T]he
legislature and the people . . . never had the right to legislate for the
future, to enthrall and bind down those who came after them, either by
debt or any other system of legislation which would prevent them from
a perfect freedom of action." In the course of the debates, Hoffman
gave the most concise statement of the committee proposal:

> [I]t was saying that we will not trust the legislature with the power of
> creating indefinite mortgages on the people's property.. . .And . . . that
> whenever the people were to have their property mortgaged for a State
> debt, that it should be done by their own voice, and by their own
> consent.

In all of economic theory, debt is one of the simplest concepts,
and the implications of public debt for democratic government are
equally clear. Debt, since it binds the unrepresented, is essentially anti-
democratic. To the extent one generation burdens another with a
perpetual debt—a debt that cannot be paid—it is deeply immoral.

The power to contract debt is the most dangerous power a
constitutional democracy has. The democracy is often *able* to borrow
large sums and it generally *wants* to. A lender, before he will part with
his money, requires some assurance he is likely to get it back. He needs
a rule of law and a stable society, e.g., America since the Revolution or
England since the eighteenth century.

A country with strong credit has an obvious advantage when it is
competing against a country which has limited credit. For example,
England and France in the eighteenth century competed for world
supremacy. In England, the royal prerogative had already been
destroyed by the rise of Parliament. Parliament took over the power of
the purse from the Stuart kings. Borrowing was in the name of the
country, made by the people's representatives, and protected by the

constitution. England enjoyed very strong credit. In 1688 her national borrowing was 660,000 pounds. In 1784 it was 246,000,000 pounds.

France was quite another picture. Louis XIV, the Sun King, like any king, was a very poor credit risk. The problem, aside from his capriciousness, was that he held absolute power. He might, at will, lower the interest rate or lengthen the term of a loan. No intelligent person would lend money to someone who has an absolute power over the law, including the law governing the debt. The French kings also had a long history of calling in royal creditors for trial on vague charges which were dismissed as soon as the creditor decided to forgive the king's debt. The practice was called *chambre de justice*.

Similarly, since World War II, the United States, a country with the strongest credit, has had an obvious advantage in competing against the Soviet Union, a country with limited credit. During the 1980s, the U.S. went heavily into debt to finance tremendous defense spending. The Soviet Union tried to keep up with the U.S. but, because of its weak credit, did not have the resources. It would not quit the race with the U.S., however, until it had spent itself into bankruptcy and dissolution.

On September 6, 1789, Jefferson wrote to Madison from Paris saying the country should get straight, "at the threshold of our new government," how we are going to keep debt from eating up the democracy. Jefferson's premise, which he believed "self evident," was that one generation cannot bind another. It followed that "No generation can contract debts greater than may be paid during the course of its own existence." The *"earth belongs in usufruct* [trust] *to the living* . . . the dead have neither powers nor rights over it." (emphasis added) If one generation can charge another for its debts, "then the earth would belong to the dead and not to the living generation." Jefferson continued: "The conclusion then, is, that neither the representatives of a nation, nor the whole nation itself assembled, can validly engage debts beyond what they may pay in their own time."

Beginning in 1965, one administration after another poured debt onto the heads of future generations. For the first time in our history, the debt was far beyond what the living generation intended to pay, or could pay, in its time. The post-1965 administrations, in Jefferson's words, ate "up the usufruct of the lands for several generations to come," breaching his basic moral principle that the "public debts of one generation" cannot "devolve on the next." Jefferson gave the example of Louis XV:

> Again suppose Louis XV and his contemporary generation had said to the money-lenders of Genoa, give us money that we may eat, drink, and be merry in our day; and on condition you will demand no interest till the end of 19 years you shall then for ever after receive an annual interest of 12-5/8 per cent. The money is lent on these conditions, is divided among the living, eaten, drank, and squandered. Would the present generation be obliged to apply the produce of the earth and of their labour to replace their dissipations? Not at all.

The Founders all believed the democracy could not tolerate a perpetual public debt. Washington, on November 19, 1794, urged Congress to provide "a definitive plan for the redemption of the Public Debt." Hamilton proposed getting rid of it over 30 years with surplus tariff revenues and a special excise tax. Madison said 30 years was too long: "a debt which will require more than 30 years (the term calculated) [by Hamilton] to pay it off, *will never be paid.*" (emphasis added) New emergencies will add to it faster than the debt is reduced. Madison recommended a direct property tax apportioned among the states. However, a federal property tax was not imposed and the country did not get out of debt until Andrew Jackson's administration. The object of the debate remained: how to confine the debt-making power so that it does not contradict democracy by binding future unrepresented generations.

Madison believed war to be the most dreaded public enemy since it led to debt. He wrote, in 1795, "of all the enemies to public liberty, war is, perhaps, the most to be dreaded, because it comprises and develops the germ of every other. War is the parent of armies; from these proceed debts and taxes; and armies, and *debts, and taxes are the known instruments for bringing the many under the domination of the few.*" (emphasis added)

Jefferson, a few years later, concluded that our Constitution contained a critical flaw which could lead to its overthrow. He wrote to John Taylor, on November 26, 1798: "I wish it were possible to obtain a single amendment to our Constitution. I would be willing to depend on that alone for the reduction of the administration of our government of the genuine principles of its Constitution: *I mean an additional article, taking from the federal government the power of borrowing.*" (emphasis added)

The New York City crisis presented—in starkest terms—the question Jefferson and Madison debated: Can you, by a written constitution, limit the power of government?   New York's constitution required the City to operate on a pay-as-you-go basis in order to prevent debt from destroying democracy.   The constitution, following the thought of Jefferson and Madison, imposed strict limits on the City's power to borrow.

The means of financing government operation is critical to the democracy.   In a democracy you have to agree on what you want to do and how to pay for it.   A pay-as-you-go system demands immediate taxes to cover all government spending.   There are two sides to the bargain.   The executive proposes the program and the legislature is asked to pass the taxes to pay for it.   The legislature must restrain executive exuberance or it will be answerable at the next election.   The requirement of immediate payment for government programs acts as an efficient brake on governmental enthusiasm.   Debt, since it requires no immediate taxes, removes the fundamental limitation on popular government.   The limitation is that to fund a program for the benefit of one group, the money has to be taken from a different group.   Under a pay-as-you-go approach, what the payees will currently receive the payors must currently pay.   The payors are apt to resist—the issue must be discussed—and some compromise reached.   That is how a democracy works.

With a borrowing policy, as Jefferson saw, the rules are entirely different.   The executive again proposes, but now he meets no effective opposition.   The viciousness of the borrowing policy is that the future taxpayer, who will pay, is not represented by any of the current parties. Legislative accountability is undermined.   The burden is easily cast upon the unrepresented future.   Pay-as-you-go, as Lyndon Johnson was well aware, would never finance a Vietnam War.   The cost had to be hidden by a borrowing policy and related depreciation of the currency.

Borrowing, the state's experience showed, is an easy way for government to get money, much too easy.   The constitution's fiscal provisions, based upon sound economic principles, limited a city's borrowing power. A city may borrow only for capital projects. Further, its capacity to borrow is limited in order that future generations not be unduly burdened. Even for capital projects, it may not borrow more than 10 percent of the value of its taxable real estate. The interest burden, consequently, must stay in a reasonable relation to the tax base. If a city borrows, it must pledge its full faith and credit—its commitment to pay must be clear and unambiguous so that the future burden may be understood. Finally, and most importantly, the city must maintain a balanced budget—it must have income to cover its expenses. Deficit financing is illegal.

Had the constitution been obeyed, New York City's fiscal crisis would never have occurred. Had the law been enforced it could not have happened. It all started in 1960 with John Mitchell and his "moral" obligation bond. "Moral" was not the right word for it. The constitution, since 1846, had required a referendum before the state could issue any debt. A proposed project must be put on the ballot, and the people must vote to authorize it; otherwise, it could not be undertaken. This constitutional system had worked smoothly for over 100 years. In the late 1950s, the people turned down several pet housing projects of Governor Nelson Rockefeller. In 1960, Rockefeller and his lawyer, Mitchell, decided that the people didn't know how to vote right, and there was just no sense asking them anymore. The Mitchell scheme permitted borrowing without a referendum. What he devised was the use of a newly created public corporation to issue the debt. Thus was born the Housing Finance Agency (HFA), and later, the Urban Development Corporation (UDC). But, since no one would lend to a corporation with no productive assets, some inducement to lend had to be created. The result was the fiction that the state is "really" behind the borrowing, it is "morally" obligated to make good on the HFA or UDC debt. With the Mitchell device in place, the state cranked out some $10 billion of debt, and never asked the people anything.

The trouble was that it had all been done before. A similar scheme had been floated in the 1920's. When New York's Constitutional Convention met in 1938, members of the convention considered a device like Mitchell's at length. Robert Moses was there, and he said it was a good thing to have an "implied" State liability. However, the convention went against him. The convention decided that if people really wanted the state credit behind debt, the state must hold a referendum. And if they don't hold a referendum, there is no way the state can be made liable, whether by legal obligation or by "moral" obligation. Therefore, a specific provision was added to the constitution to expressly outlaw moral obligation debt.

When the "moral obligation" debt went sour, Mitchell was asked by the Moreland Commission in December 1975 why he had rolled over specific constitutional provisions:

> COMMISSIONER HERSHMAN: It didn't trouble you, for example, in the case of HFA, that the moral obligation bond was used really to avoid the verdict of the public, that they didn't want the housing that was to be produced by these bonds?
> JOHN MITCHELL: It became incumbent, upon the public official, the bond attorneys and so forth to find ways of issuing bonds to avoid those constitutional restrictions [a vote of the people], in the public good, of course . . . . It wasn't the verdict of the people. It was providing a different type of housing and was doing it within the constitution under the mandate of the state legislature.

In "the public good, of course," is what the people thought *they* were supposed to decide, not Mitchell. The fact that the moral obligation bonds were a fraud on the public was quickly clear to all involved. The state comptroller, Arthur Levitt, later recalled: "I remember back in 1960 going to lunch with John Mitchell at the Bankers Club. It was set up by Nelson Rockefeller. Mitchell was going to persuade me that moral obligation bonds were a bold new imaginative financing tool." Levitt continued: "Mitchell was a bond lawyer in those days, but he was just as he was when he was with Nixon. Smoking a pipe, soft-spoken, but very tough."

After Mitchell's law was passed, Levitt called the bankers together. He told them "'You should be the first to decry these bonds. It was wrong.' The banks said to me, 'Yes, it's wrong. But since the governor and legislature are determined to embark on such financing, we're in business to make money on such financing.'"

One of the authors of this book wrote an article about the Mitchell bonds and sent it around. Most people said it was kind of interesting but "a little boring, you know." "What's a referendum requirement?"

"What's a debt?" Only the late Senator Sam Ervin of North Carolina got the point. He wrote back, on July 14, 1971: "I certainly agree with you that it is only a short step from the corruption of the financial provisions of a state constitution to corruption of the Bill of Rights. The Nixon administration has demonstrated, time and time again, its insensitivity to the great constitutional principles upon which our nation is founded."

Ervin saw that it was a basic error to view the crisis as purely fiscal in nature. It was a fiscal crisis, to be sure, but cities had gone bankrupt before and it was not unique in that. At its heart, it was a constitutional crisis—a moral crisis for democracy. In 1975, the banks, because of their imprudence, found themselves holding billions of valueless state and city debt. As a result, for the next three years the political establishment had only one basic policy—how to get the loss off of them and onto the public at large. Of course, if anyone told the public that, the scheme wouldn't work, so secrecy became the guiding premise of the effort.

The basic question, as noted above, was, and is, simple: "Can you, by a written constitution, limit the power of government?" The Framers of the American federal and state constitutions thought they could ensure both political and fiscal stability with written compacts. Indeed, the written constitution was the unique contribution of the American Revolution. The English constitution was unwritten, and the colonists thought they had been very badly treated under it. The colonists thought that the king and Parliament had simply made up the rules as they went along. The written constitution was designed so that prohibitions on government action were written in the clearest language possible. And an independent judiciary was created to enforce its terms.

The Declaration of Independence noted King George's history of "repeated injuries and usurpations, all having in direct object the establishment of an absolute tyranny over these states." The "injuries" directed by the king toward the colonial legislatures were prominent in the Jefferson's mind: (1) "He has refused his assent to laws"; (2) "He has called together legislative bodies at places unusual, uncomfortable, and distant from the depository of their Public Records"; (3) "He has dissolved Representative Houses repeatedly"; and (4) "He has refused for a long time, after such dissolution, to cause others to be elected."

The king's actions had made the legislatures futile and, as a result, "the Legislative Powers, incapable of Annihilation have returned to the People at large for their exercise." The country began, then, with the premise that the legislative power resided in the "people at large."

The Revolution established the basic ideas for the country—the consent of the governed and the sovereignty of the people—but how were you supposed to implement those ideas? This was a very hard problem. Napoleon, for example, agreed that sovereignty was in the people but, upon becoming emperor, said "I am the constituent power." The American solution was to make the people, acting in constitutional convention, the constituent power. As R.R. Palmer writes in *The Age of the Democratic Revolution*: "The constitutional convention in theory embodied the sovereignty of the people." Palmer points out that this was nothing peculiarly American in the basic revolutionary ideas of natural liberty and equality but the use of the constitutional convention as the constituent power was distinctive. The theory, Palmer writes, was made up of a few simple principles:

(1) "The people chose [the convention] for a specific purpose, not to govern, but to set up institutions of government."

(2) "The convention, acting as the sovereign people, proceeded to draft a constitution and a declaration of rights."

(3) "The constitution and accompanying declaration, drafted by the convention, must, in the developed theory, be ratified by the people."

(4) "The convention thereupon disbanded and disappeared, lest its members have a vested interest in the offices they created. *The constituent power went into abeyance, leaving the work of government to the authorities now constituted.*" (emphasis added)

(5) "The people, having exercised sovereignty, now came under government. Having made law, they came under law."

(6) "At the same time, they put restraint upon government. All government was limited government; all public authority must keep within the bounds of the constitution and of the declared rights."

In sum, there were two levels of law: (1) "a higher law or constitution that only the people could make or amend"; and (2) a statutory law "to be made and unmade" by the legislature.

The people, acting in convention, had unlimited power. At New York's 1821 Constitutional Convention a delegate attacked a proposal by Mr. Livingston, saying, "We were not sent here . . . [to interfere] with vested rights." Livingston replied:

> Sir, the people are here themselves. They are present by their delegates. No restriction limits our proceedings. What are these *vested* rights? Sir, we are standing upon the foundations of society. The elements of government are scattered around us. All rights are buried; and from the shoots that spring from their grave we are to weave a bower that shall overshadow and protect our liberties.

The early state constitutions recited that governmental power was derived from the people. The early constitutions vested broad power in the legislature. Later, as abuses showed up, the constitutions were amended to place limitations upon the legislature. The constitutions were the people's grant of power to government. The government had to exercise the grant in the precise manner prescribed by that instrument. In the absence of an express, or necessarily implied, limitation upon the grant, the power of the legislature is complete. However, if the legislature exceeded its grant, its action, according to the Supreme Court in *Norton v. Shelby County*, 118 U.S. 425 (1886)

> is not a law; it confers no rights; it imposes no duties; it affords no protection; it creates no office; it is, in legal contemplation, as inoperative as though it had never been passed.

The heart of the American approach was to institutionalize the Revolution. This meant that nothing was to be beyond the control of the people. The constitution described the structure and function of the government and established the basic Bill of Rights' protections. But these basic policies could be changed. The Constitution could be amended to permit the recall of judges or anything else. To alter the Constitution, other than by the established amending process, was revolution. The overthrow of the Constitution—to the minds of its Framers—could only be done by violence.

In the American system, the written constitution is the foundation for the rule of law. All lawful authority is traceable to it. A constitution, however, is only words on "a scrap of paper." It is not self-enforcing. The Founders believed that the men in the executive and legislative branches would be honorable. They would act in accord with their grant of delegated power. Of course, men of good faith might disagree as to how the grant should be interpreted in a particular case. Certainly, however, if the Constitution clearly prohibited certain conduct, that was the end of it. No one acting under the Constitution could be a party to such conduct. The Founders' second premise was that, if men were not as honorable as they might be, the courts would enforce the Constitution. Judges were given extraordinary privileges—such as tenure for life—only to protect them in the exercise of this high power.

The New York Constitutional Convention of 1846 brought the state's fiscal policy—its approach to debt and taxes—under the control of the written constitution. Debt and taxes were limited by the constitution. Money issues were tied to democracy to implement Jefferson's ideas.

The New York City crisis of the 1970s was the first successful large-scale overthrow of the fiscal limits imposed by constitutional government. Let's look at the men who ran the crisis, and how they managed to end-run the New York constitution. Many went on to national careers. They include the inventor of the junk bond and major members of the Japanese brain trust. Some dabbled in S&Ls. They include people who assisted President Richard Nixon in revolutionizing executive power.

John Newton Mitchell

John Mitchell was born in Detroit in 1913 to comfortable, middle class parents; he grew up in suburban Long Island. He attended public schools in Blue Point and Patchoque, and was graduated from Jamaica High in 1931. Mitchell considered going to Harvard Law School but decided on Fordham in the belief that it was advantageous to attend a New York law school if you intended to practice in New York. At Fordham, he went to classes at night so that he could work during the day. Mitchell was an undergraduate at Fordham from 1932 to 1934 and received his law degree in 1938. He was admitted to practice that same year.

In 1937, while still attending law school, Mitchell secured a job clerking at the Wall Street law firm of Caldwell & Raymond. After graduation, Mitchell went with the firm as an associate. Within four years, when Mitchell was 29, the firm became Caldwell Trimble & Mitchell. The firm was a bond firm, the type of firm that had developed after the Civil War when many western cities and towns came to New York's capital markets to borrow money for a railroad or other project. Unfortunately, in some cases the city would borrow the money, and then later say that there had been a technical flaw in the bond authorization, and therefore the debt was void and did not have to be repaid. The New Yorkers found this deplorable, and the practice arose of having a New York law firm act as "bond counsel" to look carefully at the local proceedings and then give an opinion as to the legality of the borrowing. Although paid by the issuer, the law firm in fact represented the purchasers. Several law firms became recognized as specialists in this practice. Underwriters would not bid on a debt issue unless the city provided an opinion letter from one of these firms.

Old "Judge" James H. Caldwell, the senior partner in Caldwell & Raymond, went back into the early days of the business. In the 1930s, cities began to issue a new kind of security—public housing bonds. Caldwell was unfamiliar with this new type of issue and turned it over to his young associate, John Mitchell. Says Mitchell, "Soon I was getting a percentage of the fees on this specialty and was making more money than the partners. So just before I went into the service they made me a partner."

From 1943 to 1946, Mitchell served in the navy as commander of a motor torpedo boat squadron. Lieutenant John F. Kennedy served under him. After the war, Mitchell returned to his firm and resumed his successful career. In 1967 his firm was merged, with Richard Nixon's, to produce Nixon, Mudge, Rose, Guthrie, Alexander & Mitchell. Mitchell was campaign manager for Nixon in 1968, and became attorney general in 1969 at the age of 56.

In 1960, Mitchell, at the request of Nelson Rockefeller, invented the "moral obligation" bond. In addition to the moral obligation bond, Mitchell is credited with inventing the "lease-financing" device which made the Albany Mall possible. Under this scheme, the state called its debt a "lease" rather than a bond. If it was labeled a bond, there had to be a referendum according to the constitution. Under the "lease-financing concept," the state was not borrowing—it was just entering into a 40-year lease which Albany County (the referendum requirement did not apply to a county) may borrow upon—for $1.5 billion or so. The bond purchasers, of course, looked to the state's obligation as lessee, not Albany County, for payment. In fact, the assessed value of all the taxable property in Albany County did not equal the lease amount. In the event of foreclosure, bondholders would take over all the public and private property in the county. When queried by friends about these constitutional evasions, Mitchell always said it was the only way to get things built. Nervous Nellies never got things done.

Mitchell, although he was doing very novel things, never explained to the bar what he was about, either in a law review article or speech. This was the genesis of the "stone wall." It was better to let the dogs sleep and issue the debt. The stone wall is a good legal tactic. Any potential critic first has to figure out for himself what is going on and then what is wrong with it. The critic has to provide all the facts and analysis. The Mitchell technique was to keep quiet and do it big, and to get billions of dubious bonds out as quickly as possible. He understood a great truth: If the evasion was done on a big enough scale, the courts would never declare the bonds void.

Mitchell's friendship with Nixon began around 1963. Nixon had come to New York after he lost his campaign for governor of California. He was a senior partner at Mudge Stern, a large, old firm which had been experiencing something of a decline. Nixon also bought a cooperative apartment at 810 Fifth Avenue for $100,000. (Nixon's sale of this apartment for $312,500 in 1969 later became part of his tax problems during his impeachment hearings.) Nixon and Mitchell met originally on a professional basis. In a series of transactions, Mitchell acted as bond counsel to the bond issuer, and Nixon represented the underwriters who were buying the bonds. The men got along well, and later agreed to merge the two firms.

Nixon Mudge was about a 100-man firm (23 partners) while Mitchell's had 10 lawyers (4 partners). The firm is currently known as Mudge Rose, and is now a major advisor to the Japanese. Following the merger, Nixon and Mitchell had adjoining offices. They saw each other constantly, generally lunching together and frequently playing golf.

On March 22, 1973, President Nixon urged Attorney General Mitchell to "stonewall it" and "plead the Fifth Amendment" to the Ervin Committee. The President said:

> I don't give a s_ _ _ what happens. I want you all to stonewall it, let them plead the Fifth Amendment, cover up or anything else if it'll save it—save the plan. That's the whole point.

Later in the conversation the President told Mitchell: "We can't have a complete cave-in and have people go up there and testify. You would agree on that?" Mitchell said: "I agree." The above quoted material was omitted from the edited White House transcript released to the public on April 30, 1974. The Mitchell tape, together with a June 23, 1972, Haldeman tape (directing use of the CIA to block the FBI investigation of the Watergate burglary), are "widely regarded," the *New York Times* reports, "as the evidence that ended Mr. Nixon's presidency."

On April 14, 1973, Richard Nixon had one last clear chance to avoid impeachment. If John Mitchell would come forward and take the rap for Watergate, it was possible that it would end with him. The attorney general was high enough to have authorized the Watergate burglary on his own initiative. People could believe that. There were no other good options available. If Nixon couldn't get out of Watergate quickly, his position would deteriorate at a steady rate. But if Mitchell would be a good soldier and take the heat, Nixon might stay clear.

Nixon had no moral compunction about selling out his old friend, but did not want to do it personally. As he told Haldeman and Erlichman: "You know its a pain for me to do it—the Mitchell thing is damn painful." Instead Nixon delegated the job to John Erlichman. Mitchell toyed with Erlichman, an old enemy, and the whole thing went up in smoke.

To those familiar with John Mitchell's evasions of the New York constitution his later career and felony conviction came as no surprise. As attorney general, of course he would ride over the U.S. Constitution, placing illegal wiretaps, suppressing dissenters, and pushing through "affirmative action" over the express limitations in the 1964 Civil Rights Act. Mitchell served 19 months in prison for conspiracy, obstruction of justice and perjury.

Thus, one of the central architects for the legal and executive abandonment carried out under President Nixon already had experience in overthrowing constitutions. In New York, Mitchell had set the stage for judicial abandonment. If he could get the New York courts to sign on to his obvious constitutional subterfuges, the road was open to public spending outside the restraints of democracy.

Mitchell died in 1988, but not before he witnessed the success of his constitutional tricks at both the local and national level.

Donald Trump

The old New York expression, a "Commodore Hotel ride," derives from the out-of-towner coming into Grand Central Station, (when people did) rushing out onto Vanderbilt Avenue and asking a cab driver to take him to the Commodore Hotel (now the Hyatt Regency). The cab driver would start out, run up a large tab on the meter and, after a meandering ride, deliver the visitor to the door of the Commodore Hotel, about 100 yards from where he started. By 1976, Donald Trump thought the City's fiscal crisis had so weakened it that he could take it for a $150 million "Commodore Hotel ride."

The deal was that the 30-year-old Trump would buy the Commodore Hotel for $10 million from the trustee for the bankrupt Penn Central Company. Trump would immediately turn around and sell it to the Urban Development Corporation (UDC) for $1. UDC was a Rockefeller constitution-evading corporation which had gone bust in 1973. What was old UDC doing here? Where did it get the $1? Why did Trump sell something for $1 that he had just paid $10 million for? It would all become clear later. UDC turned right around and leased it back to Trump for 99 years.

The trick was that UDC, while it had no credit and no assets, still had statutory powers and privileges. One of these privileges was that property owned by UDC was exempt from city taxes. UDC's paper ownership made Donald's hotel tax-exempt. The City would lose at least $150 million in future real estate taxes by the end of the Trump deal. With the City cooperating, UDC was selling its statutory powers like tomatoes by the roadside. The government of New York gave Donald a $150 million handout to get him started in life.

The constitution, of course, said you couldn't do that. The city or state could not contract away its taxing power. The constitutional policy was simple—without a limitation one administration could come in, give everybody tax contracts, and disappear. The next administration comes in and finds it's supposed to run the government with no taxes. One generation could bind the next just as it could with debt. So the constitution said that you could not burden the future in that way. You can give a tax exemption, but it has to be revocable.

The 1938 draftsman of the constitutional prohibition pointed to the Chrysler Building. The Chrysler Building exemption from taxes dated back to 1857 and the property has paid no taxes since. In 1938, the constitution was specifically written to prohibit tax contracts made after 1938. Yet, in 1976, the City created a new tax contract—right across the street—for Donald and his Commodore Hotel. The court of appeals upheld the imaginative plan against a taxpayer's action, saying it would prevent "urban blight," the "grim realities of urban decay," and "combat otherwise inevitable urban blight." All of this blight, the court thought, was taking place at 42nd Street and Park Avenue. No one could write a constitution limiting governmental power clearly enough for them. They could always find an ambiguity—a way to end-run the constitution. Donald easily prevailed over the future taxpayer who would have to pick up the tab. The constitution did not restrain the court. Thus, the Donald was launched.

Trump was the prototype of the successful businessman in the post-democratic era. He had been born in 1946 to Fred Trump, a major New York real estate developer. He graduated from Peekskill Military Academy, a school that no longer exists, and received a B.A. degree from Wharton in 1968. The New Age businessman postures as a hard dealing free market man, but what he really loves is getting the government to give him some special privilege. In 1979 Donald paid $10 million for the Bonwit Teller department store at 57th Street and Fifth Avenue. Trump demolished the department store replacing it with the Trump Tower, a 59-story building with 18 floors of retail and commercial space which was retained by Trump. The next 38 floors contained 266 luxury condominium units that were sold to the jet set for $155 million at prices ranging from $407,000 to $3,150,000. The sales of the condominiums recovered Trump's cost in the project. Condominiums were sold to Paul Anka, Sophia Loren and Steven Spielberg.

All this sounds pretty glittering; it did not sound like property that should be given tax exemption to keep away the "grim realities of urban decay." But Donald and his attorney, Roy Cohn, thought they were entitled to a tax exemption worth $50 million. The law, section 421 of the New York Real Property Law, authorized tax exemption for new multiple dwellings built on land which, on October 1, 1971, was "vacant, predominantly vacant or under-utilized." Bonwit Teller, in 1971 was not "vacant"; it was not "predominantly vacant"; was it "under-utilized"? The City rejected Donald's application saying it did not see anything "under-utilized" about a 12-story operating department store. Donald and his attorney took his case to the court of appeals three times. Each time the court of appeals agreed with them, they were entitled to tax-exemption. That gave Donald a perfect 4 for 4 in his dealings with the court of appeals. Donald's empire collapsed in June, 1990 under the weight of interest payments due on $3.5 billion of debt. At the time of the collapse, the old Commodore and the Trump Tower were the only two Trump properties showing a positive cash flow.

Donald's run exemplified the way people made money in the 1980s. He never made anything; his projects never showed much profit (the Plaza Hotel, even charging customers $2.00 to check a coat, only makes about $20 million, a year which doesn't cover half the debt service on the $407 million Donald borrowed to buy it); and it is unclear if he ever sold anything at a great profit (he claimed a 400-percent profit on the sale of the St. Moritz to Australian financier Alan Bond, but that was clearly inflated, and the collapse of Bond's empire—he had to return Van Gogh's *Irises* to Sothebys—raised doubts as to what exactly Donald had been paid). So where did all the money come from? He did a couple of successful greenmail operations, but you couldn't run the *Trump Princess* for long on that stuff.

Donald made money the way all the 1980s entrepreneurs did. Donald's deals, the LBOs, RJR-Nabisco, were all the same—they turned on finding the dumb lender. The dumb lender—bank or junk bond buyer—would loan more than the project was worth and the entrepreneur would pocket the excess. The excess borrowing paid for the *Trump Princess* and Donald's fabulous lifestyle.

The practice of pocketing excess borrowing is an old real estate game known as "shaving." Huge borrowing also meant huge fees for investment bankers and lawyers. Donald's bankers, who provided $2 billion, included Citibank ($990 million), Chase Manhattan ($290 million) Manufacturers Hanover ($160 million) and Bankers Trust ($100 million). They never insisted that Donald provide them with an audited financial statement. Of course, neither did his other big lender—the Junk Bond buyers ($1.3 billion). The bankers and junk bond buyers were both sure that Donald was fabulously wealthy. If you made him mad with embarrassing questions he'd just get the money someplace else.

What made the lenders so dumb? They believed what they read in the papers. Donald had used the media to create an illusion—that he was fabulously wealthy. The press believed—and reported—any puffed-up figures Donald fed them. The illusion was taken as a fact by the lenders; for the bankers it substituted for audited financial statements. But it just wasn't true; it was never true. Donald had done well on the original government give-away deals (the Commodore Hotel and Bonwit's) but he was never the large money he pretended to be. The balloon popped when the press turned on Donald in a May 19, 1990 *Forbes* cover story written by John Connolly.

Well, so what? It is certainly perfectly okay in a free market system to take advantage of dumb lenders. It is; but the problem in the 1980s was that all the lenders were playing with some kind of taxpayer guarantee. The commercial bankers and the junk bond buyers (S&Ls, insurance companies and pensions) all had some kind of government guarantee. They were playing with the middle-class taxpayer's money. If they won, they kept the profits. If they lost—as they tended to do over the long run—it was too bad for the taxpayer.

The 1980's were widely touted as a business boom, like the 1920's. But it wasn't true; it was a credit boom, not a business boom. Limitless credit was available for almost any project. The middle-class taxpayer, although he did not know it, was guaranteeing the credit through bank deposit insurance. Lending transactions work best when both the lender and the borrower are at risk, they work okay when one party is at risk, but they don't work at all when neither party is at risk. Government put all the risk on the middle-class taxpayer who was not represented by either party at the table and about whom neither party cared a bit. Obviously, this system had to lead to disaster.

In April 1991, Donald's bankers began to liquidate the Trump empire that their dumb loans had built. Bankers Trust took the Grand Hyatt (Commodore); Citicorp took most of the Trump Shuttle and Trump's 27 percent of Alexander's Department Store; and Manufacturer's Hanover took an interest in the Trump Plaza Casino in Atlantic City. Trump apparently would keep the Trump Tower (Bonwit's). It was unclear where the Taj Mahal casino and Plaza Hotel would end up. The bankers released Donald from liability on his personal guarantees of loans. The bankers refused to disclose the exact amount of the forgiven loans but said they were in the "hundreds of millions."

William Edward Simon

In 1982, a Bill Simon investment group put up one million dollars and borrowed $79 million to take over Gibson Greetings. In 1984, Simon took the company public for $290 million. His personal stake of $300,000 grew to $60 million in 18 months. The Simon-Gibson deal was the prototype—it did what all junk bond deals then sought to imitate. Another abandonment tool was successfully tested.

Bill Simon was born in Paterson, New Jersey in 1927. He graduated Lafayette College in 1952. From 1952 to 1957, he was with Union Securities Co. in New York City; from 1957 to 1964 he was a Vice President of Weedon & Co.; from 1964 to 1972 he was a senior partner of Salomon Brothers. In 1973 he became a deputy secretary of the treasury, and in 1974 he became secretary.

When the City fell apart and ran to Washington for help, Simon took a generally uncharitable view despite his many years in New York. On May 14, 1975, he said, "We're going to sell New York to the Shah of Iran. Its a hell of an investment." In September, he thought federal aid would, "contravene the constitutional principal of federalism." It was not, in another of his statements, "appropriate." On "Meet the Press," September 7, 1975, he said the City must assure that welfare goes "to the needy, not the greedy."

After the fiscal crisis had blown up, some confidential minutes were disclosed that showed that all the parties had known exactly what was going on all along. The minutes were those of the Comptroller's Advisory Technical Debt Management Committee, a group of nine bankers and investors formed in 1970 to advise the City of New York. (In 1970-71, as a partner in Salomon Brothers, William Simon was a member of the committee.) The minutes showed, that at least as early as April 1974, the banks were fully aware of the coming disaster. On December 17, 1974, the committee had a breakfast meeting with the Mayor at Gracie Mansion:

WALLACE SELLERS (Merrill Lynch): Borrowing to finance deficits is no longer a viable procedure.
MAYOR BEAME: I can't commit myself or the City to a discontinuance of the practice . . . W want to work with the financing community . . .

the banks can and should help sell the city and should not just sit by
and tell the City to reform.

FRANK SMEAL (Morgan Guaranty): The position of the city is different
from that of the federal government in that the latter prints the money.
The City needs the institutional market. With the evergrowing militan-
cy of the unions with which the City must deal, a question arises as to
whether debt is really a first lien on revenue.

WALLACE SELLERS: On the last city bond sale the banks lost $50
million. It is important for the City that the banks survive.

MAYOR BEAME: The only really new borrowing the City will engage
in is the $520 million to be borrowed by the Stabilization Reserve
Corporation. . . . All other City borrowing is against expected
revenues, as it always has been.

COMPTROLLER GOLDEN: What the banks are saying is that in their
present weakened condition the sheer magnitude of our borrowing
makes it impossible for the capital markets to absorb the quantity of
debt we are issuing.

MAYOR BEAME: The reaction of the layman is that the debt is weak,
not that the banking system is capital short . . . How does the current
proportion of the city debt in the market compare to prior years?

THOMAS LABRECQUE (Chase Manhattan): It is now double.

GEDALE HOROWITZ (Salomon Brothers): The City has lost its
institutional market. Although the City's banks will continue their
support, the out-of-city banks have stopped buying the City's obligations. It is that market that we must recapture.

MAYOR BEAME: The banks are the City's best buttress for supporting
municipal debt and they must therefore sell the City to the rest of the
country.

COMPTROLLER GOLDIN: The problem is one of supply and demand.

FRANK SMEAL: You cannot run the City on borrowed money.

MAYOR BEAME: We are borrowing against firm receivables. It is the
financial community and the capital markets that have not carried out
their responsibility.

FRANK SMEAL: The market has just suffered the greatest losses in
history in its support of the City's debt.

RICHARD NYE (The First Security Company): The whole system could
come tumbling down.

MAYOR BEAME: The question is will the banking community sell the
City.

The federal government, as Frank Smeal pointed out, was different from the City because the federal government could print money.

The House Committee on Banking and Currency, on October 30, 1975, questioned Secretary of the Treasury Simon. Congressman Rees was skeptical about Simon's lack of knowledge. He asked about his tenure on the Comptroller's Advisory Technical Debt Management Committee as follows:

> MR. REES: Now, you were, as I understand it, adviser to Comptroller Beame for a while in 1969-70 and 1971, at a time when the City started increasing the use of capital budget funds for operating purposes. . . .
> SECRETARY SIMON: The function of the technical committee for debt management in New York City was to advise them on the technicalities, the timing and the instruments that could be financed at the lowest possible interest rate. Our involvement as to their fiscal business in New York was unwanted and unwelcome, but I can assure you, Congressman Rees, that not only did I express my personal opinions—and you can imagine what they are—but also, in my many luncheons at Gracie Mansion, and talking to Mayor Lindsay at the time, warned him of what was going to happen one day, down the road, if they continued to do this. And like everything else, people never worry about anything beyond the next election.

That the technical committee was not always concerned with "technicalities" is clear to the reader from the above quoted transcript of the December 17, 1974, Gracie Mansion breakfast meeting. Congressman Tsongas of Massachusetts asked a follow-up question in which he referred to Simon as an "adviser" to the City. Simon objected strongly:

> SECRETARY SIMON: But I will correct, very strongly, your suggestion that I was an adviser. My advice was asked on technical management, technical, mechanical management of debt. My advice on fiscal responsibility, which was often given, was most unwelcome.
> MR. TSONGAS: Could you supply for the record those public statements you made during that period of time advising the people of New York City as to the consequences of the current fiscal mismanagement that you advised?

SECRETARY SIMON: I never made public statements; I was not sought to make any, and I did not seek to make any public statements. In my capacity, I was not a self-appointed adviser to New York City; when given the opportunity, I was pleased to present what I thought of the situation to the officials involved.
MR. TSONGAS: So there are no public statements made by yourself during that period of time?
SECRETARY SIMON: That is correct.
MR. TSONGAS: I do not think, Mr. Chairman, that anyone is convincing anyone else during this testimony.

Mr. Simon became secretary of the treasury. After leaving the Treasury, Simon became a director of Citicorp, the inventor of junk bonds, and a very wealthy man.

Felix George Rohatyn

If a Democrat ever gets elected president again, Felix Rohatyn is likely to be secretary of the treasury or chairman of the Federal Reserve. Rohatyn became a public figure as the financial advisor to Governor Hugh Carey during the New York City fiscal crisis. Bob Strauss, then chairman of the Democratic National Committee, told Carey about Rohatyn. President Bush nominated Strauss as ambassador to the Soviet Union in June 1991.

In 1975, when the fiscal crisis struck, Felix Rohatyn was a general partner in the investment banking firm Lazard Freres earning "in six figures." In May 1975, Governor Carey, acting on the Bob Strauss recommendation, invited him to solve the crisis. Within a few months Rohatyn was transformed from a rich successful businessman into a celebrity. The society pages recorded his constant appearances at fêtes and charity balls. It was hard to get through the daily papers without coming across Rohatyn in black tie. It was, in fact, Rohatyn's familiarity with Manhattan night spots that cemented his relationship with Carey, the former congressman from far away Brooklyn. The Manhattan night spots were so popular with Carey that they became the seat of government. Rohatyn later spoke with what the *New York Times* called "wry nostalgia" of those "crazy days" when "we were running the city from a table at Elaine's, with Woody Allen sitting at the next one."

Rohatyn was born in Vienna, Austria, in 1928. The family owned a small credit bank, Rohatyn & Company, which failed in the depression. Consequently, in 1934, his father moved the family to Orleans, France where he managed a family brewery. Later, the family fled the Nazis and came to the United States. In 1940, Andre Meyer, the senior partner of Lazard Freres, came to New York from the Paris branch. In France he had known Rohatyn's stepfather. Rohatyn graduated Middlebury College in 1948 where he majored in physics. That same year he went to work for Lazard Freres, where he has spent his entire career. He became a naturalized citizen in 1950. He married in 1956, had three children, and separated in 1972. He married again in 1979. He became a partner in Lazard Freres in 1964 at age 33. His office is at 1 Rockefeller Plaza, and he is a member of the Finance Committee of Rockefeller Brothers Fund. In November, 1990, Rohatyn advised MCA on the sale of MCA to Matsushita for $6.13 billion. It was Bob Strauss—who recommended Rohatyn to Carey in 1975—who "guided," as the *Washington Post* put it, the Matsushita MCA forces "past antitrust and communications regulators and an American public increasingly wary of Japanese investors." Strauss represented both sides in the negotiations—the *Post* calls that "highly unusual"—and earned his law firm, Akin Gump Strauss Hauer & Feld, $8 million in fees from MCA and an undisclosed sum from Matsushita. Strauss said his $8 million fee was "on the low side." He added: "I don't work by the hour anymore. I don't do windows."

During the 1960s Rohatyn developed a reputation as a master of mergers. His credentials were impressive: Kinney and Warner Brothers; Lockheed and Textron; Loews Theater and Lorillard; Gulf and Western and Kayser-Roth; and ITT and the Hartford Fire Insurance Company; the last, of course, led to trouble. Rohatyn was called, along with John Mitchell, to explain to a Senate committee why the Justice Department suddenly dropped its anti-trust case in July, 1971. There were also persistent questions as to how ITT had secured a tax ruling from the IRS. The affair left a taint and a label that Rohatyn, understandably enough, is said to abhor: "Felix the Fixer."

The question in the ITT deal was whether the Justice Department had settled the antitrust case because of an ITT pledge of $400,000 to help finance the 1972 Republican Convention. John Mitchell testified to a Senate committee that the case had been handled in the regular course of business, that President Nixon was in no way involved in the settlement. The truth though, according to Nixon tapes released by the National Archives on June 4, 1991, was that Nixon had personally called Richard Kleindienst and ordered him to drop the case. A tape of March 30, 1972, records Charles W. Colson, a White House aide, warning the president that he had seen documents which tied the president to the settlement and that "it scares the living daylights out of me." H. R. Haldeman, White House chief of staff, added that "it's a hell of a problem" because John Mitchell had told the opposite story under oath.

At the 1972 Senate hearings Rohatyn was modest in describing his influence on the Justice Department. Senator Bayh thought that Rohatyn was underestimating his persuasiveness.

SENATOR BAYH. I asked Mr. Kleindienst[1]—I suppose I should have asked you first—why, after Mr. Kleindienst had made clear, he says he did, and I ask you if he did and why he did, he made it very clear that Mr. McLaren[2] was making the decisions in antitrust, why was it you kept coming back to him? Why did you not use your influence and persuasiveness on Mr. McLaren?

MR. ROHATYN: My influence and persuasiveness was obviously wasted on both, Senator. I only went back twice, Senator; after the June 17 telephone call outlining the proposed settlement. I went to see Mr. Kleindienst once more because again, the settlement seemed to me so vast and so harsh and smacking so much of dismemberment of the company, that I was very much concerned, again on the basic policy issue. Mr. Kleindienst absolutely refused to reopen the issue and turned it back to Mr. McLaren.

---

[1]Deputy Attorney General who was acting attorney general on ITT matters since John Mitchell had removed himself because of Nixon Mudge's representation of an ITT subsidiary.

[2]The Assistant Attorney General in charge of the Anti-Trust Division.

SENATOR BAYH: Is it a fair assessment of your value to ITT to say your influence was wasted when the one divesture that was going to do the most damage to the company, Hartford, was not successful?
MR. ROHATYN: I would hope I did play a good part, Senator, because I think it was the right thing to do.
SENATOR BAYH: So you cannot say your influence went to waste?
MR. ROHATYN: No, sir, I amend that statement.

The real story of the New York City fiscal crisis was, however, far different from the great rescue our cast of characters said it was.

The Abandonment

"If you elect a matinee idol as Mayor you get a musical comedy administration."

> Robert Moses, after meeting John Lindsay for the
> first time, January 1966.

Frank Smeal of Morgan Guaranty, at the Gracie Mansion breakfast meeting, had put his finger on the problem when he told Abe Beame: "The position of the city is different from that of the federal government in that the latter prints the money." The city had to find buyers for its debt while the federal government did not—in the last analysis the federal treasury could always print what it needed. That was the critical difference. It explained why the federal government could (1) act more irresponsibly than New York City ever thought of acting and (2) could do so over and over again, while New York City got caught way back in 1975.
John Lindsay did not have a printing press, but he did have recurring deficits, about $1 billion or so per year. He paid for his deficits by borrowing. On June 30, 1966, the City's total debt—in bonds and notes—totaled $5.5 billion. By June 30, 1974, Lindsay's last fiscal year in office, the debt had risen to $11 billion. In those eight years, the debt had more than doubled, rising $5.6 billion, or about $700 million per year. That was the annual revenue shortfall that was papered over with debt.

Lindsay thought his borrowing policy worked wonderfully well. It was so much simpler than taxes. Taxes always got people mad. He had learned that in 1966 when his administration imposed the first personal income tax in the City's history.

With debt no one got mad. There were no irate taxpayers or businesses threatening to leave the city. The City got the cash to spend and no one was upset. Someday someone might have to repay the debt but that was tomorrow's—and some other administration's—problem.

Lindsay wondered why no one else had ever thought of this "borrow now, let the next guy pay later" notion. Of course, someone had. His name was William Marcy Tweed, the nineteenth century boss who got control of the financial affairs of the city and bilked it out of many millions. Lindsay did not invent profligacy: he only reinstituted it.

Indeed, the fall of Tweed (he died in jail) had led to constitutional limitations on the power of the city to borrow. The 1846 constitution limited state borrowing but not local government borrowing. In 1884, after Tweed, the constitution was amended to limit local government borrowing. The people adopted these provisions to prevent any repetition of his profligate borrowing policy. "Never again," said the people. The constitution prohibited any borrowing in excess of 10 percent of the value of taxable property in the city. That was the debt limit. Any borrowing in excess was void. In addition, borrowing could only be done for capital projects—not for deficit financing. Further, the term of the debt could not extend beyond the probable useful life of the project. (A version of Jefferson's idea that the current generation could not borrow beyond what it intended to pay in its time.) Those were the rules for the city's long term debt—its bonds.

The city was also allowed to do some short term borrowing. The purpose of this was to even out cash flow; if you expected a large amount of taxes in April, you could anticipate that receipt by borrowing in, say, January. But this exception was hedged with restrictions. Short-term notes had to be repaid within one year, and could only be issued in anticipation of real revenue or taxes. In sum, the New York constitutional provisions governing city debt were, and are, the toughest in the country. They were carefully and thoughtfully designed to prevent excessive borrowing, to prevent any New York City Mayor from piling the debts so high they must topple and crush the City—to prevent, in other words, exactly what happened.

Lindsay believed the constitutional limits were too binding, he called them "archaic." In our modern world, he said, we need more flexible standards to enable us to grapple with our complex problems. So he set out to evade the "archaic" constitution.

First came the Capital Budget Raid, which meant that bond proceeds were used to pay for ordinary operating expenses rather than capital projects. The constitution, as noted above, provided that no borrowing can be for longer than the probable useful life of a project. In 1968, the legislature amended the Local Finance Law to provide a 30 year useful life for "job-training." A 30-year bond could then be issued to finance a job training program. The city counsel said that borrowing was permissible for this purpose because it was a *social* capital item—an investment in people rather than bricks. The mayor thought that was a grand theory: If you can build buildings, you can build human beings. That was all very nice, but clearly the state had to adopt a different constitution before you could do things like that.

The second major Lindsay evasion of the constitution was the Great Rollover. The objective here was to abuse the constitutional requirements limiting short-term borrowing. Beginning around 1970, the debt quickly snowballed to $6 billion by 1975, when the city finally lost its credit. The constitution said that all short-term borrowing must be based on real revenues or taxes and must be repaid within one year. The gimmick Lindsay used was to repay the old notes, and then immediately reborrow twice as much. In year one (1970-71), the city secured $1 billion by short-term borrowing. In year two, the city borrowed $2 billion, $1 billion of fresh money and $1 billion to rollover the due debt. In year three, the city had to borrow $3 billion, $1 billion for fresh money and $2 billion to rollover the debt. And so on. It collapsed when they had rolled it up to $6 billion in outstanding short-term debt. The notes were supposed to be issued against real anticipated taxes or revenues, but Lindsay issued them against the clear blue sky.

Madison had warned Jefferson about "parchment barriers" and that when "there is an interest and power to do wrong, wrong will generally be done." As the Great Rollover was getting under way, one of the authors wrote a letter to the *New York Times*. It was published

March 16, 1972, under the heading "A Dying City Drowning in Debt."
It read:

> The proposed new city expense budget contains a startling 48 percent
> increase in the cost of debt service. Debt service for the year 1972-73
> is estimated to cost $1.023 billion, an increase of $330 million over the
> current figure of $693 million. . . . Debt is different from ordinary
> legislation because a bad law can be repealed, but a bad debt cannot.

The Great Rollover, undisturbed, rolled on.

Lindsay piled the debts higher and higher. In addition to the huge
accumulated debt, he left the city an operating deficit of some $2 billion
a year. Obviously, no reasonable person would lend money to such a
failing entity. In March 1975, after Lindsay had escaped to Majorca and
left poor Abe Beame holding the bag, the Banks cut off the city's credit
line; it could not borrow at any price.

The Fix

> *The Legislature is not bound to continue to impose the sales tax
> or to make appropriations from such tax to the corporation.
> The corporation has no taxing power and the MAC bonds do not
> constitute an enforceable obligation, or a debt, of either the
> State or the City and neither the State nor the City shall be
> liable thereon. Neither the faith and credit nor the taxing power
> of the State or the City is pledged to the payment of principal of
> or interest on the bonds.*
>
> MAC Prospectus, June 1975.

Felix Rohatyn, the financial wizard, came up with the idea of the
non-hamburger Big MAC. He said look, the city can't borrow any more
but the city continues to collect revenues. The city sales tax alone
brings in about $1 billion a year. We will take that stream of revenue
from the city and place it in a new corporation: (MAC, or the Municipal
Assistance Corporation). The new corporation, with revenues of $1
billion, and no expenses, should easily be able to borrow $8 or $10

billion on 20 year bonds. The $8 or $10 billion would then be funneled back to the city which could then, once more, pay its recurring operating deficit and also pay off the outstanding short-term debt.

The music would play again. And after a while, the people would forget the recent difficulty. The City could go back to borrowing as it had before. There was no cost to the state. No new taxes were imposed. The City's alter ego would borrow for it now. There was no cost to anyone and it solved all the problems. It was pure wizardry.

Before talking about a few constitutional problems with the wizard's scheme, you have to understand what problem he was trying to solve—the problem of loss allocation. When the banks shut off the City, it had $12 billion of debt outstanding. The debt of a bankrupt city is, of course, worthless, or close to it. A tremendous loss was coming. The largest holders of the city debt were the same New York city banks who had cut off the credit. Felix's problem was to get that loss off the banks and on to someone else, say, the holders of MAC bonds.

Well, was there any constitutional question about setting up a new corporation to "assist" the City? Could the City—assuming anyone would buy its debt, do the borrowing directly? Clearly, it could not. First, the city was prohibited from any further borrowing. Its past borrowings and other liabilities, such as unfunded pensions, had used up all of its ten percent debt limit. Second, the constitution only authorized borrowing to construct capital projects not to fund deficits. Third, any debt of the City had to be backed by its full faith and credit and could not be limited to a particular tax source.

The theory of the MAC Act is that the dummy corporation is free of all constitutional restraint. The constitution, Rohatyn's lawyers said, only prohibits "the City" from doing things. It makes no mention of a dummy corporation called MAC funded with taxes and borrowing on behalf of government. Is, then, the dummy free of all constitutional restraints, of the restraints that bind government itself? In honesty, the question can hardly be considered serious. Of course, the constitutional restraints apply to the alter-ego dummy operated by the city. A contrary view makes the constitution a trivial and foolish document. It binds the legislature only as long as it wishes to be bound. When it no longer wishes to be bound, it will set up a dummy that is free of all constitutional restrictions.

Previously all public corporations in New York had possessed some capacity to generate revenues. The older authorities, such as the Port Authority or the Triborough, held an important bridge or tunnel which was a strong revenue producing asset. The users paid tolls and no recourse was made to governmental funds. Even the ill-fated UDC had a theory as to how it would get revenues. But, with MAC there arrived the distilled essence of the public corporation—a fiscal gimmick in its pure state. All pretext of a self-supporting venture was gone. The debt could only be paid with taxes. Finally, a public corporation had been created which had no purpose other than to evade the constitution.

On July 9, 1975, at the height of the MAC silliness, Aleksandr I. Solzhenitsyn came to the Americana Hotel to speak to an AFL-CIO luncheon: "Is it possible or impossible to transmit the experience of those who have suffered to those who have not suffered? Is it ever possible to warn anyone of oncoming danger? How many witnesses have come to your country, how many waves of immigration, all warning you of the same experiences and the same dangers? Yet these proud skyscrapers still stand, and you go on believing that it will not happen here. Only when it happens to you will you know it is true."

No one thought to ask Solzhenitsyn his opinion of MAC. It might not have been explainable: "Well you see Lexy, we have this City that can't borrow anything so what we do is we set up this new corporation, see, and it goes out and borrows money and then it turns the money over to the City that can't borrow anything."

The Sell-Out

> We should not strain ourselves to find illegality in such
> programs. The problems of a modern city can never be solved
> unless arrangements like these, used in other states, too, are
> upheld, unless they are patently illegal.

New York Court of Appeals, upholding MAC
Prototype Act (1975)

The moral atmosphere surrounding the final passage of the MAC
bill may be conjectured from Mayor Beame's plaintive question to Felix
Rohatyn wondering whether "what we are doing is legal or in our
authority." Rohatyn smiled, put his arm around Beame's shoulder and
said "Don't worry, Abe, you've done it plenty of times before." Was
it possible the courts would sign on to this moral bleakness?

The court did sign on in a 4-3 decision saying that "we should not
strain ourselves to find illegality in such programs." The court found
arrangements "like these" should be upheld "unless they are patently
illegal." *Wein v. City*, 36 N.Y.2d 610 (1975). No one had asked them
to strain themselves. In a later decision, the court found it is "apparent
that the state in avoiding violation has been driven to the brink of valid
practice." *Wein v. State*, 39 N.Y.2d 136 (1976). In a still later
decision, the Court expressly ruled that just because debt was issued in
violation of the constitution didn't mean it didn't have to be paid. *Wein
v. Carey*, 41 N.Y.2d 498 (1977). That rounded it out nicely.

The court simply let the constitution go. The court's failure
marked the end of constitutionalism in New York. If the clearest
language and spirit of the constitution could be overrun, no amount of
words or clarity of expression would help. The citizen, with no constitution to protect him, is vulnerable to any attack upon him. Madison
had said: "Wherever there is an interest and power to do wrong, wrong
will generally be done."

In 1991-92 the state and city faced a combined budget gap of $10
billion. The question was: How could they close the $10 billion gap
without reducing spending or raising taxes? The federal government for
years had been doing just that. But Governor Mario Cuomo often said,

"The state's position is different from the federal government because the federal government prints the money." Morgan Guaranty's Frank Smeal made the same point to Abe Beame at the December 17, 1974, Gracie Mansion breakfast meeting. But since the 1975-77 court of appeals decisions, it was no longer really true. Technically, the state still could not print money but it could do the next best thing: it could now issue debt, without a referendum, for any purpose, including papering over a deficit. Governor Cuomo exploited the court of appeals' opening with a series of Rube Goldberg deals that made the most hardened citizen wince.

Attica Prison, for example, was built and paid for by the people of New York in 1931. Attica, in 1991, was sold by the state to the Urban Development Corporation (UDC) (see discussion under Donald Trump) for $200 million. The Attica deal raises at least three interesting questions:

(1) *Why did UDC want to buy Attica?* It didn't. It turned right around and leased it back to the State for 30 years. A prisoner would never know that the title to the land had shifted under his feet.

(2) *Where did UDC get the $200 million to buy Attica?* It borrowed it.

(3) *How can you borrow to buy a prison?* You can't. It has no income stream. But you can borrow on the State's promise to pay "rent" in an amount sufficient to cover principal and interest on the UDC bonds.

The taxpayer, over the next 30 years, will pay, in "rent," $200 million in principal and $290 million in interest for Attica, which was bought and paid for by his grandparents in 1931.

This outrageous deal was possible because the court of appeals had destroyed the Jeffersonian constitution created by the convention of 1846. Under that constitution, the state could not borrow to pay for a deficit. A debt had to (1) be for a capital project, like a building, with a reasonably ascertainable useful life, and (2) win approval by a popular vote. A deficit, of course, has no useful life. So the state could not do it even if the people were willing to vote for it, which they were not.

But, by the court of appeals' decisions, a dummy corporation, like UDC, is free of the constitutional limits that bind the state itself. So it could go out and borrow $200 million to give the state pursuant to a phony sale and leaseback—at a $490 million cost to the taxpayer.

In 1991, the state, inspired by the Attica model, planned to sell Aqueduct Race Track to the Port Authority and a stretch of Interstate 287 to the Thruway Authority. The court of appeals had said they didn't want to strain themselves to find illegality in such imaginative programs. The state was consequently able to take pre-existing, debt-free, public property and borrow on it to fund a deficit. The state could sell its assets to itself and live on the proceeds. In November 1991, the state doubled its previous estimate of the coming budget gap. The new estimate, $3.6 billion, was more than 10 percent of the total budget. Analysts blamed the state's past heavy use of "one shots", or non-recurring items such as Attica. On December 20, 1991 Governor Cuomo announced that New York's budget problems prevented him from running for the Democratic nomination for president. The Governor said he could not run because a "threat hangs over the heads of New Yorkers that I have sworn to put first."

The next generation could pay for Cuomo's deficits. Cuomo, in Jefferson's words, had eaten "up the *usufruct* of the lands for several generations to come." As a result, a generation of wastrels is allowed to impoverish succeeding generations. Cuomo, like Louis XV in Jefferson's example, borrows from the money lenders so that "we may eat, drink, and be merry in our day." The debt is left for the next generation. The ultimate question, as Jefferson posed it, is: Is the next generation "obliged to apply the produce of the earth and of their labour to replace [the prior generation's] dissipations?" Jefferson's answer was: "Not at all."

Epilogue

The programs which launched the crisis were allegedly necessary to avert the "grim realities of urban decay." Yet, the urban environment that followed the "rescue" of the City was something between New Delhi and Beirut. The dishonesty of the rescue effort was a corrosive acid destroying law and order in the City.

What you feel today, Rohatyn said in April 1990 "is the constant threat of something that's going to happen to you. It is not civilized life to consider yourself lucky when you've been mugged but haven't been killed." Wealth could no longer insulate a New Yorker from the horror. Said Rohatyn, "There is no part of the city where the quality of life is acceptable." Perpetual danger prevails and the citizen lives in continuous insecurity. The cost of the lawlessness was visited first upon the working class (who could afford no insulation), then upon the middle class, and then upon the wealthy.

The City, by 1991, was again facing a major fiscal crisis. Sales tax revenues, which together with inflation, had lifted it off the rocks in the 1970s and 1980s, drop very quickly in bad times. Rohatyn, in the November 8, 1990, *New York Review of Books* wrote: "New York City is facing a social, political and economic crisis far more serious than the fiscal crisis of the 1970s." During the 1970s there were "widely shared hopes that the city could provide opportunity for its citizens." Today, New York "has become a city full of anger and violence in which ethnic groups are turned against other ethnic groups, races against other races, classes against other classes."

On May 3 1991, Mayor David Dinkins announced that the City's renewed financial crisis was going to cause (1) higher taxes; (2) the lay off of 20,000 workers; (3) the turning off of 25 percent of the street lights and (4) the closing of the recently restored Central Park Zoo. The City, when the 1974-75 crisis hit, had large problems but was basically sound; when the 1991-92 crisis hit the City was already out of control with a collapsed West Side Highway, unpoliced streets, closed fire stations and a quality of life that its citizens compare to Beirut.

Under Mayor David Dinkins the City issued 20 year bonds to buy paint for bridges. Dinkins repeatedly asked Rohatyn to issue $1 billion of MAC bonds for the City. Rohatyn repeatedly refused. In November 1991 he said, "If you want to take the simplest approach to this, it is borrowing money to finance a two-year tax cut."

In 1960, when John Mitchell started tinkering with "moral obligation" bonds, the white population of New York City was 6,000,000; by 1975 it was down to 4,500,000; and by 1991 it was down to 3,000,000 and falling. The New York City experiment showed that traditional separation of powers principles could not ensure adherence to constitutional restraints.

The drafters of the 1846 New York Constitution had created a Jeffersonian mechanism for controlling the anti-democratic potential of public debt. The best way, they thought, was to give the people a vote. John Mitchell and the managers of the New York City crisis, evaded the constitutional order. Since then, debt has been both the symbol and the means of abandoning middle-class Americans by every level of government.

CHAPTER TWO

The Middle-Class Cow and the National Debt

In the 1970s and 1980s the federal government plunged down the same financial path that led New York City into bankruptcy. Just a few years ago, people thought that taxes, while certainly not wonderful, paid for defense and other common goals. Now Americans don't think their taxes do anything—every poll shows a bitter attitude toward taxes. The majority doesn't believe that paying taxes accomplishes anything they care about. Because of debt financing, the problem is worse now than people expect—the taxes we pay are increasingly going to pay interest to foreigners who have been buying up the national debt. The national borrowing policy has been bipartisan: the Republicans liked deficits because they thought they would discipline congressional spending while the Democrats didn't care about deficits because they believe the U.S. government can't run out of money. The relationship between the government's revenues (total taxes) and interest on the debt is critical.

Taxes today go largely to pay interest on the national debt—nearly *60 percent of the income taxes Americans pay go to pay interest on the national debt.* Interest on the national debt has rolled from $11 billion in 1964 to $210 billion in 1988 to $264.9 billion in 1990 and to $283.1 billion in 1991. *Interest on the national debt is now $32 million an hour.* This interest does not buy anything. Not an F-16, and not a cruller for the homeless. More and more of the interest payments go across the Pacific to the Japanese to feed their economic machine.

Table 2.1 enables the reader to see how much of his or her taxes this year go to pay interest on the national debt. (The table assumes a married couple with two children.) Sometime in the mid-1990s, assuming the continuation of present trends, *all* of the income taxes paid by people will go to pay interest on the national debt. Income tax revenues will be totally dedicated to the payment of interest, with large payments going overseas.

Clearly, we are not making a go of it if most, or all, of our cash goes to pay interest on past borrowing. Traditionally, around 20-25 percent of taxes went to pay interest on the national debt, but, in the past ten years, the figures have spiralled, as shown in Table 2.2.

Since 1975, Congress and the President have run interest from $33 billion to $283.1 billion. Now some old truths are winging home. Our leaders told us borrowing would not hurt us. And they rolled it up. *But the trouble with debt is you have to pay interest on it.* And now the national debt is so outlandish ($3.47 trillion) that the interest on it will soon eat up all of the country's individual income tax collections.

TABLE 2.1

Interest on National Debt as a Percentage of Taxes Paid

Income	Total Taxes Paid	Taxes Going to Pay Interest
$ 20,000	$ 2,100	$ 1,260
30,000	3,300	1,980
40,000	4,900	2,940
50,000	7,400	4,400
75,000	16,000	9,600
100,000	25,000	15,000

Prepared by Authors

As the debt has ballooned, it has increasingly been bought up by foreigners, primarily the Japanese. In recent years the Japanese and other foreigners bought 30-40 percent of treasury bonds and notes offered at auction. Now we don't "owe it to ourselves" anymore.

William Holstein, a senior *Business Week* editor, reports in *The Japanese Power Game* (1990), that "Japan owns about $500 billion of U.S. government debt." President Bush has just about said that any thought of being beastly to the Japanese is out since the Japanese are financing our deficits and holding up the stock market. The president was asked in a February 1989 news conference how he would reassure Americans who thought the Japanese were taking over. He answered, in part:

> I'd tell them don't get so concerned over foreign ownership that you undermine the securities markets in the country. We have horrendous deficits and foreign capital joins domestic capital in financing these deficits.

So, sure, go ahead, bash the Japs and collapse the stock and bond markets.[3]

The following chart shows the growth of the national debt. The chart only shows the official national debt; it should be increased by 25 percent to include agency borrowings not officially counted. The chart also does not include another $12 trillion for which Congress has put the taxpayer on the hook. This figure is a rough estimate of various obligations and guarantees undertaken by Congress. These include bank deposit insurance (a cool $2.9 trillion by itself), pension fund guarantees ($820 billion), mortgage insurance, direct loans, loan guarantees, actuarial deficiencies for social security and unfunded federal employee

---

[3]Official Treasury figures, for December 1989, show total foreign holdings of $392.9 billion out of total Federal securities outstanding of $2,975,537. Treasury Bulletin, May 1990. The official figures report Japanese holdings of $82.1 billion and $46.6 billion held by Germany. Letter of May 4, 1990, to William J. Quirk from Gary A. Lee, Manager, Treasury International Capital Reporting System, Office of Assistant Secretary for International Affairs, Department of the Treasury. The official figures are, of course, much too low to explain repeated statements by treasury secretaries and Federal Reserve chairmen that (1) foreigners are funding our deficits and (2) our dependence on foreign investors requires high interest rates to induce them to buy.

Several facts cast doubt on the official figures: (1) the *Financial Times* (May 8, 1990) reports that Japanese financial institutions have "routinely taken 30 to 40 percent of the issues of the [Treasury] quarterly refund;" and (2) The *Financial Times* (October 4, 1990) reports that Treasury Secretary Brady "noted that in the last year or so foreigners were buying only 15 percent of U.S. government debt issues, down from roughly a third."

and military retirement. (Richard Darman, OMB Budget Message, Part VI and *Barrons*, March 5, 1990 p. 15). The chart also does not include various unfunded liabilities, such as the $315 billion the Department of Transportation says is necessary to restore the highway system to the condition it was in 1982. Table 2.3 shows the growth of the official national debt.

TABLE 2.2

Interest Paid on National Debt 1965-1991

	Interest Paid	*Percentage of Total Taxes Paid for Interest*
1965	$ 11 Billion	22%
1975	33	26
1980	75	30
1981	96	34
1982	117	40
1983	129	45
1984	154	51
1985	179	53
1986	191	54
1987	195	50
1988	210	60
1989	227	60
1990	264.9	60
1991	283.1	60

Historical Tables, Budget of the United States - 1989 and *New York Times*

The debt will be increased by new borrowing to cover new deficits as well as to pay interest on the old. Table 2.4 sets out Congressional Budget Office figures (December 1990), which show new borrowing of $1.2 trillion to cover 1991-1995 deficits. So by 1995, the official national debt will be at least $5 trillion. At an average interest rate of 8 percent the interest cost to carry the debt is $400 billion—or about $40 million an hour.

The national debt, when we "owed the money to ourselves" was one thing, but the iron rule of human experience is that the piper calls the tune, and money means control. If you mortgage yourself to foreigners, you lose your sovereignty. Thus, a national debt owned by foreigners represents the real right of foreign creditors to claim the future products of our labor and cart them away overseas. It represents the present ability to buy up the country's choice properties.

TABLE 2.3

National Debt 1955-1991

Year	Total Debt
1955	274 Billion
1965	323 Billion
1975	544 Billion
1980	914 Billion
1984	1.6 Trillion
1987	2.4 Trillion
1988	2.6 Trillion
1991	3.5 Trillion

Historical Tables, Budget of the United States - 1989 and *New York Times*

In addition, the takeover process was made easier by the Reagan-Bush administrations' policy of intentionally destroying the value of the dollar.   Devaluation, of course, lowers the domestic standard of living—that is the point of it.   The results have been disastrous. Devaluation had the immediate effect of multiplying the value of foreign exchange which meant the Japanese and others could buy up U.S. assets more cheaply.

There is nothing hidden or mysterious about the workings of debt. A debt spiral, as some families know, starts out with spending a little beyond one's means and borrowing to cover it.   Next year, unless the family cuts its spending, it will have to borrow more—to cover the recurring spending short-fall—and also to pay the interest on last year's borrowing.   The family's cash deficit gets greater as more money goes to pay interest on debts.   In the third year the family has to borrow more to pay interest on its expanding debt and on the recurring spending short-fall.   Then the borrowing accelerates rapidly; as the spiral spins faster each new borrowing brings less relief as the money increasingly goes to pay interest on old debt.   The money-lender then owns your family.

The national debt is made up mostly of short term notes.   The notes must be constantly rolled over.   Table 2.5 describes the schedule of maturity for the "privately-held" national debt.   A whopping 68 percent is due within 5 years.   The "privately-held" debt is much lower than the total national debt because the term does not include what is called "non-marketable" debt held by Social Security and Government Pension Funds or holdings by the Federal Reserve and state and local governments.   To raise the $1.2 trillion the federal government, almost daily, is in the capital market auctioning off its debt.   This huge amount of borrowing can't be financed from domestic sources and must be sold to the Japanese and Germans.   As a result we have lost control of our own capital markets.

Table 2.6 shows what must be financed, adding (1) the rollovers of outstanding debt; (2) the 1991 deficit; and (3) the Federal Reserve holdings (which are all 3 month term).

The press thinks raising taxes will pull us out of a debt spiral, that's why they think it's "responsible." But taking 1975 as a benchmark—26 percent of tax collections went to pay interest on the national debt—for us to match that percentage today tax collections would have to be increased from $558 billion to $1.6 trillion—almost a three-fold increase. There is just not enough revenue out there to collect that kind of tax, and the people could not live under the burden. Also, the argument that raising taxes is the answer is a strange solution to a problem created by prior governmental mishandling of money.

The press often compares U.S. tax rates with those in, say, Sweden and concludes U.S. citizens are lightly taxed. They could pay much more, the press thinks, if only they weren't so selfish. Table 2.7 shows the taxes a self-employed person earning $100,000 will pay. The individual gets to keep $43,700, which the press can call a light tax if they want, but the people paying it don't.

The debt grew because democracy was bypassed by Congress and the president, just as it had been bypassed earlier by New York City officials. The federal government wanted to spend on things which the majority would not support if given a straight-up choice. So they borrowed from foreigners. The national debt has grown because Congress voted to spend, but knew people wouldn't pay the taxes to support the spending—so it borrowed more and more money. The Japanese would give us credit; they were eager to do so, just as former President Reagan said.

Programs thus went forward without upsetting the people with taxes. And then the next year Congress borrowed a little more to support some more spending the people wouldn't support and to pay the interest on what was borrowed the year before. And so on. Congress and the President had figured out a way to do what they wanted without having to ask the people. And then we were in a debt spiral, and there wasn't enough money to pay for it.

The Money Abandonment has become irreversible. The debt burden is piled so high that the debt service is all the money the middle class will ever have. The stream of revenue—future taxes on the people—which is the only support for the borrowing—is not adequate to pay it even if the people were willing.

TABLE 2.4

1991 - 1995 Deficits
(amounts in billions)

	1991	*1992*	*1993*	*1994*	*1995*
Revised Gramm-Rudman Targets[4]	$ 64	$ 28	$ 0	$ 0	$ 0
Deficits (excluding social security surplus)	$319[5]	$336	$253	$154	$143

Congressional Budget Office (1990)

Individual freedom within a constitutional framework is what explained American economic growth from 1765 to 1965. We had great physical resources, but so did a number of other countries whose economic development has not approached ours. It was the constitutional system that Washington and Madison and Jefferson set up that was

---

[4]The original 1985 Gramm-Rudman projected a zero deficit for the fiscal year beginning October 1, 1990. The 1987 revision of Gramm-Rudman projected a zero deficit for fiscal year 1993. The 1990 Budget Deal enacted October 27, 1990 projects an $83 billion deficit for fiscal 1993.

[5]On January 8, 1991 the Congressional Budget Office announced that the "recession" would add $50 billion to the Deficit which together with $30 billion for Desert Shield would bring the operating deficit to around $400 billion.

unique. The simple fact is that in a free society people develop a will to work. In a totalitarian or controlled society, they do not. From the time of Lenin, the communist world, as Eric Hoffer points out, has been designed by intellectuals. How do you build a truck in a society run by intellectuals? Government makes one giant plant, which it designs, and then dragoons people into working in it. That is the intellectual approach. Government makes a central plan and an industry—and society as a whole—is forced to conform to it. Government manages, guides and controls.

TABLE 2.5

Maturity of National Debt

Terms	Amount	
Under 1 Year	34% or	$ 597 Billion
1-5 Years	34% or	$ 613 Billion
5-10 Years	14.6% or	$ 260 Billion
10-20 Years	4.8% or	$ 85 Billion
Over 20 Years	12.6% or	$ 225 Billion
Total:		$1,780 Billion

New York Times

The plan always fails because the people won't work. Hoffer wrote in 1963 that the "chief preoccupation" of every communist government is "how to make people work." The machine does not work smoothly if "you have to deafen ears with propaganda, crack the whip of Terror, and keep pushing people around." In an individualist society, on the other hand, people do not get pushed around and they want to work. The communist world has collapsed because it couldn't make people work; economic growth requires economic freedom, which requires political freedom.

ABANDONED

TABLE 2.6

Federal Borrowing for 1991

	CATEGORY	AMOUNT
(1)	1991 Deficit	$ 400 Billion
(2)	Under 1 Year Privately Held	$ 597 Billion
(3)	Federal Reserve	$ 231 Billion
		$1,228 Billion

New York Times

TABLE 2.7

Tax Burden on Individual Making $100,000

$27,000 — Federal Income Tax
9,500 — Social Security Tax
7,000 — State Income Tax
1,300 — State Sales Tax
1,000 — Federal and State Excise Taxes on Gasoline,
        Alcohol and Tobacco
2,000 — Local Property Tax
8,500 — Indirect Taxes Passed Down to the Consumer
        on Goods and Services
$56,300 — Total Taxes Paid

Prepared by Authors

The economy in 25 years has moved from being the engine of the industrial world to what the Japanese accurately describe as a "hollowed out" economy. The economy drifted from the production of goods to the production of financial paper. Financing, which is intended to be secondary to, and assist, production, took on an existence separate and unrelated to the real world of manufacturing. What was called modern financing had nothing to do with productivity. What this new "industry" did was to find a stream of revenue somewhere, borrow as much as possible on it, and use the proceeds to finance a change of ownership in the nation's assets and pay advisors' fees. Predictably, manufacturing, as a percentage of GNP, plummeted in the last 15 years. In 1991, two-thirds of GNP is consumer spending.

The ultimate problem with this kind of economy is finding someone to sell to when no one's doing anything or making anything that's marketable. The idea that you can have an economy that rests primarily on people performing services for other people—the "service" economy—is, of course, bananas. The end of the distribution chain can't pretend that it can exist without someone up the line actually doing something—growing a potato or killing a cow. The puff-ball can collapse in an instant. U.S. business during the 1970s and 1980s should have done what the Japanese did: abandon low-wage, low-productivity industry and shift labor to more productive plants at higher capital investment per worker. Long-term investment, however, requires a reasonably stable and predictable legal system, which no longer exists.

The Economic Abandonment has set off a destructive chain reaction in which (1) Americans are heavily taxed—about 56 cents out of every dollar earned—which taxes go to (2) pay $283 billion in interest on a national debt, which debt (3) goes on forever because it is so big—$3.5 trillion—that it can't be reduced, which means (4) the interest payments go on forever to the Japanese and other foreign holders of the Debt. Because of Abandonment the Japanese will be in effective control of the U.S. economy. People in lands which previously enjoyed Japanese occupation will tell you not to count on a very high pay level. The children of the middle class will have to take low paying jobs. The children will drop out of the middle class and will have a progressively declining standard of living. The prospects for the middle class and its children, under current trends, are nil.

The new generation of Americans graduating college now are, for the most part, as the *New York Times* puts it, trapped in the impoverished middle class. College graduates have a hard time finding a job to pay more than $8 or $10 an hour. The *Times* interviewed, in November 1991, a worker on the Caterpillar line in Peoria, Illinois. The worker, 38, earned, with overtime, $45,000 a year which sounds like a solid middle class salary. But, adjusted for inflation, his salary has not gained ground since 1973. His expenses, taxes and the cost of raising four children, have risen creating the middle class squeeze. The *Times* reports that the prolonged stagnation of American incomes grew out of corporate efforts to cut labor cost to become globally competitive. However, it is now "debatable how much wage sacrifices have helped American competitiveness." The Caterpillar worker keeps his expenses down since he believes he may be laid off: "my mortage and property tax payments [$266 a month] are affordable working on minimum wage at McDonalds." He believes he is in the last generation able to expect $40,000-and-up jobs. We are, he thinks, after a generation of economic stagnation, now heading into a permanent decline. An NBC News/*Wall Street Journal* poll taken October 25-29, 1991 reported that only 25 percent of Americans think the country is "generally headed in the right direction."

Before the 1960s

On the eve of World War II, Hirohito's advisors told him "Do not wake the Sleeping Giant." Table 2.8 shows how the Giant waked up during World War II.

The war cost $270 billion. About a fourth of that ($70 Billion) was paid for by the pay-as-you-go method. The other $200 billion needed for the war effort was borrowed from the people. As a result of the war, the national debt hit a high of $270 billion in 1946; in 1991 it was $3.47 trillion.

After the war ended, defense outlays, the national debt and taxes all dropped sharply. Defense outlays dropped as the war ended—from a high in 1945 of $82.9 billion down to $9.1 billion in 1948. The national debt—which had reached $270 billion in 1946 was down to

$255 billion in 1951. Individual income tax collections reached a high of $20 billion in 1944 and were down to $16 billion in 1950. Total government receipts went from a high of $45 billion in 1945 down to $39 billion in 1950.

TABLE 2.8

Federal Expenditures (In Millions)

SUPERFUNCTION AND FUNCTION	1940	1941	1942	1943	1944	1945	1946	1947	1948
National Defense	1,660	6,435	25,658	66,699	79,143	82,965	42,681	12,808	9,105
Total Federal outlays		9,468	13,653	35,137	78,555	91,304	97,712	55,232	34,496	29,764

Historical Tables, Budget of the United States - 1989

So even the all out effort of World War II had not pushed the national debt all that high, and it was rapidly reduced in the post-war years. Interest payments in 1949 were $5 billion. In 1991 interest payments were $283.1 billion; a 57-fold increase. Table 2.9 shows the acceleration of the national debt.

TABLE 2.9

National Debt 1960-1991

1960 - $291 Billion
1980 - $914 Billion
1985 - $1.8 Trillion
1991 - $3.5 Trillion

See Table 2.3

World War II was a middle-class war and the middle class came into its own after the war. In 1950 the U.S. owned two-thirds of the world's assets and nine of the ten largest banks. With the return of the U.S. soldiers in 1945, the G.I. Bill of Rights sent many to college. The war had brought a single standard to the country as never before—merit. This impinged on privilege everywhere, for the first time the "Big Three" universities admitted students largely on the bases of SAT scores, and for the first time they took in more high school graduates than prep school graduates. Social distinctions were significantly levelled by the war. Middle-class parents could expect their children to work hard and rise higher than they themselves had risen.

There was nothing American industry could not do. We built a ship to beat the best of the English Queens across the Atlantic. The liner *United States* was launched in 1951, and set the world record on its maiden voyage. The *United States* bought 8,000 pounds of caviar a year to give away with cocktails. In 1951, the United States led the world in the production of anthracite coal, of iron ore and steel, and oil. The total value of U.S. agricultural products in 1950 was far greater than that of any other nation on earth. This included a dominant position in the production of lumber, livestock, spring wheat, winter wheat, corn, dairy products and cotton.

By the end of 1947, the United States possessed 227,679 miles of well-maintained railroad track. The average load of a railway train rose to 1,139 tons by 1944, up from 663 tons in 1931. It declined only slightly after the war. At the end of 1945, the United States merchant fleet numbered 5,745 active vessels of 1,000 gross tons or more. The gross tonnage was 41,084,190 tons. Between 1939 and 1946, 5,865 major merchant vessels were built in U.S. shipyards. These vessels carried 75% of the 268 million long tons of military supplies shipped out of the United States during the war.

The United States turned its attention to less fortunate quarters of the world—which included just about everybody. In 1946, U.S. exports totalled $9,742,000,000, comprised of products from machinery to food. U.S. imports for domestic consumption were half that amount. The excess of exports over imports in later years became even more pronounced. In 1950, the largest industrial corporation in the world by far was the United States Steel Corporation. The list could go on and on.

Russell Baker writes in *The Good Times*: "The country was so rich in the Fifties. So rich. A typical American family could afford three children, a house, two cars, three weeks at the seashore, a television set, and meat seven nights a week, all on a single wage earner's income." The Eisenhower slogan "Peace and Prosperity" described the fact. Inflation, during the Eisenhower administration, averaged 1.4 percent per year. His budgets were balanced, or close to it.

Home ownership, for the first time, became widespread. Real estate values rose—the home became the prime middle-class asset. By definition, middle-class families do not start out with much, if any, inherited wealth. Also, the cost of raising a family to "have the advantages we did not have" takes all of a paycheck that is left after taxes. Realistically, the home is the only savings device the middle class has.

The combination of low down payments, reasonable mortgage rates and rising real estate values allowed the middle class to accumulate capital. (A major Financial Abandonment in the 1980s was the attack on the middle-class home—as will be explained later, it will never be a source of wealth for the family again.) From the end of the war through the 1960s, the standard of living rose steadily. Table 2.10 shows that workers' earnings, stated in 1988 dollars, between 1947 and 1968 increased almost every year.

The middle class, during the post-war period, became much larger. The 1930s, of course, was not a time of upward mobility. Nor, for that matter, were the 1920s, when class and professional distinctions were stronger and the middle class was much smaller, probably comparable to what we would call the upper middle class today.

But the country had made some important basic decisions earlier than that. The most basic one, made during the presidency of Theodore Roosevelt, was that the U.S. would not be a plutocracy or a European-style oligarchy. Class distinctions would be muted, merit rewarded, and large discrepancies of wealth discouraged. The Roosevelt vision took a little bit of time to work out, but in the post-war period, the economic reality finally caught up with Roosevelt's ideals.

Altogether, from 1946 to 1965 the country was a pretty picture. The U.S. meant the world well and was strong. The strength of the country came from the middle class. The middle class was confident, for itself and its children.

From 1965 On

The picture, from the mid-1960s on, is very dark. The country started on a downward spiral. The political, judicial and economic leadership of the country set themselves apart from the middle class. The political and economic constitutions, under which the country and middle class had flourished, were abandoned by a new intellectual elite. The intellectual leaders were dissatisfied with the common man and set out to redesign him. The people, the leaders thought, needed a lot of managing and guiding. Government began to nag incessantly at the people. First, the government preached at the people; later, it used coercion.

The people immediately recognized government's new hostility. In 1964, 62 percent of voters said they trusted Washington to do the right thing "most of the time." Two years later, in 1966, only 48 percent thought the government would do the right thing most of the time. The leadership's contempt for the middle class was plain. The country's institutions—the government, the courts, the media, and the universities started a war against the middle class, the heart of the country. Could they get away with that?

In a sense the answer is yes, they never did get caught as such. The middle class just gave it up in the late 1980s. They just stopped listening. The unceasing nagging and spitefulness rolling out of the country's institutions simply overloaded the ordinary citizen's tolerance. When, for example, was the last time Congress did something you liked? When was the last time the Supreme Court came down with a decision—or the Congress passed a law—that anyone liked? No one can remember. The people went from puzzled (1970s) to confused (1980s) to despair (1990).

TABLE 2.10

Worker's Earnings 1947-1968
(1988 Dollars)

Year	Earnings	Year	Earnings
1947	11,516.00	1958	14,964.00
1948	11,520.00	1959	15,366.00
1949	11,811.00	1960	15,635.00
1950	12,371.00	1961	15,961.00
1951	12,313.00	1962	16,326.00
1952	12,750.00	1963	16,574.00
1953	13,330.00	1964	16,767.00
1954	13,562.00	1965	17,704.00
1955	14,042.00	1966	17,304.00
1956	14,559.00	1967	17,669.00
1957	14,753.00	1968	18,013.00

(Chart prepared by Tracy G. Herrick of Jeffries & Company, Inc. (San Francisco) based mainly on U.S. Bureau of Economic Analysis, Survey of Current Business, Table for Nonsupervisory Workers, 1989)

In October 1991, *The Philadelphia Inquirer* published a nine-part series entitled "America: What went wrong?" by Don Barlett and James Steele. The first part describes the government's role in the dismantling of the middle class: "Taken together, the myriad laws and regulations—from antitrust to taxes, from regulatory oversight to bankruptcy, from foreign trade to pensions, from health care to investment practices—form a rule book that governs the way business operates, that determines your place in the overall economy." The problem, the authors continue, is that "those who establish the rules of the game long ago ceased to represent the middle-class players. As a result, the middle-class casualties of the government rule book already can be counted in the millions."

What did the figures for this period, look like? They were awful.
The standard of living looked like it was doing okay but it was only
being held up by tremendous household borrowing. Average workers'
wages—which is what supports a sound standard of living—and which
had increased almost every year from 1947 to 1968—started down as
shown in Table 2.11.

Table 2.11 shows that there has been no income growth in the
country for 20 years. 1988 earnings were below 1968 earnings; they
were 17 percent below the 1972 high point. Home ownership, which
had risen steadily since the Depression, leveled off in the 1970s and, in
the 1980s, declined slightly. The country took on a new look; along the
highways there were endless strip malls, discount stores selling goods
from Asia and fast-food restaurants. This is the reality of the "service
economy." Jobs, in the new "K-Mart economy," were low-skill and
low-wage. A 40-hour work week at the $4.25 hourly minimum wage
works out to a yearly gross income of $8,840. Frank Levy and Richard
Michel, in their 1991 study of the vanishing middle class, *The Economic
Future of American Families (1991)*, conclude that "productivity and
general economic growth slowed considerably during the period after
1973 and that this depressed the growth of earnings and family income
relative to earlier decades." Table 2.11 shows that 1988 earnings were
below 1983 earnings and were far below 1978 under the much maligned
Carter. Table 2.12 shows, in chart form, average earnings since 1970.

Disparities of income and wealth in the U.S. are getting so great
that we may be mistaken for England before the 1832 Reform Bill or
Russia under the Tsars.   In 1988, the wealthiest 1 percent of
families—who had an average income of $617,214—received more of the
country's pre-tax income than the bottom 40 percent of families.
Average income drops sharply below the top 1 percent. There are about
100 million families in the country so there are about 1 million families
in the top 1 percent. Table 2.13 shows the average pre-tax income for
families in the designated population groups.

Realistically, only the top 1 percent can be called wealthy. These
families most likely have substantial savings and, if a financial storm
arises, they should be able to steer to a safe harbor. The rest of the top
10 percent—the $85,664 and the $132,553 family—are upper middle
class. They are doing okay, they probably still believe in the American

dream, but a serious illness or sending a child to college will certainly stretch their budget and may give them a real problem. The bottom 90 percent, with their average income of $31,669, are living on the edge; their budget cannot be stretched, they have no margin of safety.

Since 1977, Table 2.14 shows disparities of income have become much more extreme—the top 1 percent has done very well, the upper middle has improved some, but the bottom 90 percent shows a *3.5 percent loss* in wages and salary. The chart shows that the bottom 90 percent of the country's families are in a lot of trouble. They have realized virtually no increase, 0.1 percent, in real income between 1977 and 1988. Their real income from wages and salary actually fell 3.5 percent during this period. In sum, for fully 90 percent of American families the standard of living is actually falling. A true rising tide, such as we had in the 1950s and 1960s, gets all the ships home while a falling tide leaves some ships busted on the rocks and some stuck in the marsh.

The disparity of wealth is even more extreme than the disparity of income. Wealth includes financial assets (stocks, bonds, business holdings and savings accounts) and real estate assets (principal residence, vacation homes and other real estate holdings). Net worth, of course, is the sum of total assets less debt. The top half of the top 1 percent—as shown in Table 2.15—own 24.3 percent of the country's net worth. Their share of the national income is much less—5.8 percent. Clearly, any political party that says it wants to use the income tax to get the rich has got the wrong gun. The top half of the top 1 percent is not part of the middle class. They have very substantial liquid assets; they own 49.4 percent of privately held stocks and 51.1 percent of bonds. Their principal residence comprises only 4.6 percent of their gross assets. By contrast, in the bottom 90 percent, the principal residence comprises 65.3 percent of net worth.

The top half of the top 1 percent, about 500,000 families, is America's upper class. They hold the liquid wealth. Their share of the country's wealth has not changed much over the years. The most recent figures are for 1983, but Kevin Phillips has charted it back to 1922 and it is consistently around 25 percent (See Appendix B of *The Politics of Rich and Poor*).

TABLE 2.11

Worker's Earnings 1968-1988
(1988 Dollars)

1968	18,013.00	1979	18,684.00
1969	18,225.00	1980	17,956.00
1970	18,340.00	1981	17,745.00
1971	18,838.00	1982	17,899.00
1972	19,414.00 *	1983	18,186.00
1973	19,414.00	1984	18,147.00
1974	18,858.00	1985	18,071.00
1975	18,704.00	1986	18,225.00
1976	18,973.00	1987	18,032.00
1977	19,164.00	1988	17,899.00
1978	19,260.00		

*Historical high

(Chart prepared by Tracy G. Herrick of Jeffries & Company, Inc. (San Francisco) based mainly on U.S. Bureau of Economic Analysis, Survey of Current Business, Table for Nonsupervisory Workers, 1989).

So, obviously the country has, in the past, tolerated a large disparity of wealth. Today's question is whether, when the standard of living for 90 percent of the population is falling, it is any longer tolerable. And when the upper middle class—the 90-99 percentile families—is busted by college expenses and no longer has any reasonable expectation of earning a place at the top. That is, can the system work without the dream and can the dream be sustained without the reality of a rising standard of living for most of the people?

TABLE 2.12

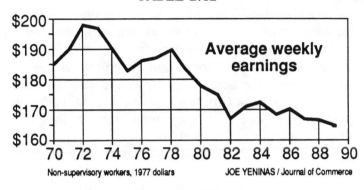

Non-supervisory workers, 1977 dollars   JOE YENINAS / Journal of Commerce

TABLE 2.13

1988 Family Income

Top 1 percent	$617,214
96-99 percentile	$132,553
91-95 percentile	$ 85,664
Bottom 90 percentile	$ 31,669

(Table 13, House Ways and Means Committee Green Book — 1991, p. 1293.)

The *Financial Times,* on September 2, 1991, editorialized that liberal societys, like F. Scott Fitzgerald's Gatsby, believe in the "orgiastic future." Freedom and growth are Siamese twins: "The energies released by freedom create growth, while the hope of growth—of an even bigger cake—underpins liberal democracy." In the absence of that hope politics is bound to focus on the distribution of what already exists. Such zero-sum politics is certain to be dismal since "liberal democracy provides no strong justification for any particular distribution of income, a difficulty that can be evaded only when there is hope of more for all."

By 1990, well-paid middle-class professionals were losing their jobs. Massachusetts officials reported that well-educated engineers, scientists, technicians and managers were the most rapidly growing group of people losing their jobs. *The American Lawyer* reports that young lawyers, with the best records from the best law schools, were fired by major New York City law firms such as Milbank Tweed, Paul Weiss and Cahill Gordon. They were eligible for 26 weeks of unemployment insurance, then welfare.

By December 1991, *The Wall Street Journal* reported that corporate staff layoffs had been running at 2,600 a day since October—the highest level since the Depression. The corporations included—the bluest of America's blue chip companies—IBM, Kodak, Xerox, GM and TRW. Executives said most of the job cuts were permanent, the jobs were not coming back. A Kodak officer said: "if it were just the recession, we would be hiring these people back again. And we aren't going to be doing that."

Maybe American business can come out of its zombie state. But the fact is that, in 1989, 61 cents of every dollar of pre-tax corporate earnings went to pay interest on debt—American business is barely keeping alive. The history of pre-tax earnings paid for interest is shown in Table 2.16.

American business is as bad off as most middle-class families. Maybe worse off. A recent study by Professor Benjamin Friedman of Harvard University reports that the net worth of American business dropped from 95 percent of GNP in 1980 to 74 percent of GNP in 1988 (*Implication of Increasing Corporate Indebtedness for Monetary Policy*, Group of Thirty, Occasional Paper 29). The huge drop is due to 2 factors: (1) physical assets (buildings, plant and equipment) slipped in value from 105 percent of GDP to 93 percent of GDP and (2) at the same time, debt rose from 29 percent of GDP to 37 percent of GDP. In other words, business went on a debt binge—not to buy physical or financial assets—but to engage in deals. American business drastically increased its debt but did not invest in the assets which could produce the income to pay off the debts.

The 1980s major financial invention, leveraged buy-outs (LBOs), was based on substituting debt for equity. An LBO is the buy-out of a company's public shareholders by a small group with borrowed money. LBOs proved what any normal person understood from the beginning: if you give a taxpayer a choice between paying taxes and not paying them he will choose to not pay. For example, in early 1989, RJR Nabisco went private in a $25 billion leveraged buy-out. Before the takeover, RJR Nabisco, as a public company, earned annually $2.6 billion of operating income and paid $682 million in taxes to federal and state treasuries. After the LBO, the new RJR Nabisco is able to deduct from its income interest payments (about $3.4 billion) on the $25 billion of takeover borrowing (bank loans and junk bonds). The new interest deduction will, of course, wipe out RJR Nabisco's income for 1989 and probably forever. The $682 million saved by not paying taxes will pay the interest on $5 billion of junk bonds. This is the taxpayer's first contribution to the deal. Also, since RJR Nabisco will probably show *losses* for a while because of the interest deduction, it will be able to carry its losses back three years. *Forbes*, in a November 28, 1988, article, estimates RJR Nabisco may receive $2 billion in tax refund checks from the U.S. Treasury for taxes paid in 1986-88. All the "profit" in an LBO, $7 billion in the case of RJR Nabisco, comes from the fact the company becomes tax-exempt and may be able to get refunds for past years. How many taxpayers knew they were contributing $7 billion to finance a change of ownership at RJR Nabisco?

The LBO depends on the availability of vast amounts of borrowed money, a lot of it in the form of junk bonds. Where did these vast sums, $25 billion in the case of RJR Nabisco, come from? They came from (1) commercial banks, (2) savings and loans, (3) pension funds, and (4) insurance companies. All of whom are playing with some type of taxpayer guarantee and are able to take a heads we win, tails the taxpayer loses, gamble. How many taxpayers knew they were on the hook for another $25 billion? Only a government that had abandoned its people would have put up with the LBO for one second.

Since 1987, business demand for money has been so low that it looks like a Depression. Private credit demand dropped from $600 billion in 1987 to $250 billion for 1991. The figures indicate U.S. business has just about given up. U.S. business cutbacks in money for

research are discussed in a May 13, 1990, *New York Times* article
entitled, "Are We Eating Our Seed Corn?"   The modern American
businessman is MBA trained; he is not technically oriented as German
and Japanese businessmen are, nor is he entrepreneurial like Henry
Ford. He is interested in financing gimmicks such as stock buy backs
which raise the stock price rather than competing with the Japanese.
They are defeatist, they ask, "Who has successfully competed against the
Japanese?"   Robert Cohen, an economist with the Economic Policy
Institute in Washington says, "Morita [Sony] is investing in the next
generation of video chips, memories and the miniaturization of devices.
If the Japanese have a breakthrough in something like magnetic levitation
trains we will be left in the dust." American business, in short, has also
abandoned the middle class, an abandonment which is certainly self-
proving.

How about American economists?   Were they trying hard to
explain to the people what had gone wrong and how to fix it? Not too
much; they seem strangely indifferent.   Harvard Professor Robert
Reich's 1991 book, *The Work of Nations: Preparing Ourselves for 21st
Century Capitalism* says America for too long has looked at competitiveness by focusing on the performance of U.S.-owned corporations.
We should look to what he calls "global webs of enterprise," which
means that a U.S. corporation which produces elsewhere is less valuable
to the country than a Japanese corporation that produces cars in
Tennessee.   Says Professor Reich: "The concern over National
Competitiveness is often misplaced. It is not what we own that counts;
it is what we do." Well, maybe, but if you don't own anything, what
you do is going to be what someone tells you to do.

One of the country's most brilliant young economists, MIT
Professor Paul Krugman, wrote *The Age of Diminished Expectations*
(MIT Press 1990). The book is sponsored by the *Washington Post* in an
effort to reach a non-professional audience on the economic problems of
the U.S.   The English financial newspaper, the *Financial Times*,
reviewed Krugman's book under the headline, "The U.S. goes out with
a whimper, not a bang." Professor Krugman believes "Japan's success
hurts our pride far more than it hurts our standard of living." The U.S.,
by 2000, will be the world's "third ranked economic power" behind
Japan and the European Community. Nobody knows, he says, why

U.S. productivity has grown so slowly since the 1970s or why income distribution deteriorated so sharply in the 1980s. Obviously, if nobody knows what's wrong it can't be fixed.

TABLE 2.14

1977 — 1988
All Income — U.S. Families
(in constant 1992 dollars)

	Wages and Salary	All Income
Top 1 Percent		
1977	107,454	314,526
1988	237,183	617,214
Percent Change	120.7	96.2
96-99 Percentile		
1977	65,864	107,945
1988	82,220	132,553
Percent Change	24.8	22.8
91-95 Percentile		
1977	58,289	76,525
1988	65,369	85,664
Percent Change	12.1	11.9
Bottom 90 percent		
1977	24,123	31,653
1988	23,281	31,669
Percent Change	-3.5	0.1

(Table 1, House Ways and Means Committee Green Book — 1991, p. 1293.)

TABLE 2.15

Net Worth — 1983

Population	*Ownership*
Top half of top 1 percent	24.3 %
Second half of top 1 percent	7.2 %
90-99 percent	35.1 %
0-90 percent	33.4 %
	100 %

Table 15, House Ways and Means Committee Green Book — 1991 at 1336.

TABLE 2.16

Corporate Pre-Tax Earnings
Paid For Interest

1950s and 1960s	-	17 cents
1970s	-	35 cents
1980s	-	57 cents
1989	-	61 cents

Journal of Commerce

Krugman correctly points out that "for the median American worker there has been no increase in real take-home pay since the first inauguration of Richard Nixon." But the point, he believes, is that no one cares. There has been what he calls a "revolution of falling expectations." People now accept being poorer. The *Financial Times*, in despair, concluded:

In sum, this is a story of an economy that does not perform, a populace that does not mind, a Congress that fails to act and a trade policy that will not work, all written by an economist who appears not to care. Read; learn; and weep.

The "populace" certainly does mind, but the rest is right.

Hardly any modern businessman has as his goal the making of a better, affordable product, built by workers making a good salary, a goal stated by Henry Ford:

> I will build a motor car for the great multitude. It will be large enough for the individual to run and care for. It will be constructed of the best materials, by the best men to be hired, after the simplest designs that modern engineering can devise. But it will be so low in price that no man making a good salary will be unable to own one—and enjoy with his family the blessing of hours of pleasure in God's great open spaces.

(Henry Ford, *My Life and Work* (1922), p. 73.)

Today's CEOs are expert at designing their own reward packages—in 1980 CEOs made 40 times the income of average factory workers—in 1989 they made 93 times as much. Drexel Burnham paid Michael Milken in 1983, $45.7 million; 1984, $123.8 million; 1985, $135.3 million; 1986, $294.8 million; and 1987, $550 million; for a 5 year total of $1.15 billion. And it was not just Milken; Time-Warner reported, for 1990, that chairman Steven Ross received total compensation of $111 million.

While the New Age entrepreneurs were raking in preposterous salaries, the traditional repositories of national wealth were going broke. The economy, of course, can't function without stable financial institutions. But, by 1991, it was clear that a lot of America's largest commercial banks were bust. In 1988, the biggest 15 banks had a 4.3 percent capital-asset ratio, meaning it had $4.30 of capital to support $100 in loans. They balanced the books (assets to liabilities) by counting all assets, including Third World loans at full book value. If their assets are "marked to market," many of them are under deep water.

In 1982, one of the authors analyzed Citibank's balance sheet for *The New Republic* in an article entitled "Busted Flat on Wall Street." He concluded that, applying conservative accounting principles, its liabilities exceeded the value of its assets. That, the author wrote, meant that Citibank was bust, adding gratuitously, that "when you're dead you're not supposed to be walking around." Citibank, unaccustomed to that kind of talk, responded that it was a crime under New York law to speak disparagingly of a bank. Crime or not, they were still bust. In 1982 Citibank ranked 1st among the world's banks. In 1988 it ranked 27th.

In the fall of 1990, Chase Manhattan fired 5,000 employees, 12 percent of its work force. Chemical Bank cut the quarterly dividend on its common stock from 68 cents to 25 cents. In September, Chase Manhattan sold bonds paying 13 percent. Citibank, on October 24, sold some preferred stock paying 12.5 percent. The same day, J.P. Morgan, a solvent bank, sold a similar issue for 6.069 percent. Short-term Treasuries were going for about 7.2 percent. Citibank and Chase, like the S&Ls before them, are paying more to get money than they are getting from lending it out—a way of doing business which, as they say, has a limited future.

As of September 30, 1990, Citibank was carrying on its books $7.8 billion of stock buy-out loans in highly leveraged transactions—what they call HLTs. Citibank was also carrying $990 million in loans it had made to Donald Trump. The bank admitted that they had never insisted that Donald provide them with an audited financial statement. By January 10, 1991, the market value of Citicorp stock had sunk to the point where you could buy all of it for $4 billion. "Toys 'R Us" would cost you $2 billion more.

On January 22, 1991, the Federal Reserve told Citicorp that it was not "appropriately capitalized," which is a nice way of saying when you're dead you're not supposed to be walking around. Citicorp announced it was going to cut jobs and other costs to save $800 million a year for the next two years. It said it intended to raise $4 billion in capital over the next several years. In October, 1991 Citicorp announced that $4.5 billion of its real estate loans were "nonperforming," i.e., more than 90 days past due. Experts said the market value of Citicorp's delinquent real estate could not be accurately determined since there was no active market. In the past year no office building worth more than $70 million has been sold in the United States. But, 60 Broad Street, the former home of Drexel Burnham Lambert, which appraised at $160 million in 1984, was sold, in October, 1991 for $57.5 million. Why did it take the Federal Reserve until 1991 to tell Citicorp it was bust when that was clear, to any casual observer, in 1982? It was a good question.

In late February, 1991, Prince al Waleed bin Talal, a 35-year-old Saudi Prince, announced he was putting $590 million into Citicorp, which, together with what he bought in late 1990, made him Citicorp's largest single shareholder, owning 14.9 percent of its common stock. The Prince, in 1979, received a degree in business administration from Menlo College in California. Some thought Prince Waleed was a front for his father, Prince Talal bin Abdulaziz, or perhaps for other members of the Saudi Royal family, but Prince Waleed said that after he graduated Menlo he had taken out a loan from a local Citibank branch and had made his money in the contracting business. How many people believe the Prince's $590 million came from his contracting business? But if not, who is the largest single shareholder of America's biggest bank?

Also in late February 1991 Citicorp announced a $382 million loss for the last quarter of 1990. On March 6, 1991, John Reed announced at a news conference in Buenos Aires that he had just completed a deal to sell $600 million of Citicorp preferred stock to what the *New York Times* described as a "broad group of investors."

In August, 1991, a top banking overseer, Representative John D. Dingell (D. Mich.) let the cat entirely out of the bag. Citicorp, he said was "technically insolvent" and "struggling to survive." Citicorp denied it was insolvent but acknowledged it needed to raise $4 to 5 billion in capital by 1993. What for?

Robert Reischauer, the head of the Congressional Budget Office, testified in January 1991 to the Senate Banking Committee that "if just one of the 10 largest banks fails, it alone could account for losses of $10 billion or more" to the FDIC. Was the failure of a big bank likely? Reischauer said: "While failure of one of the very large banks may be unlikely, it is certainly possible." On April 26, 1991, Charles A. Bowsher, the comptroller general, told the Senate Banking Committee

that his audit of the FDIC showed it was "nearly insolvent." William
Seidman, chairman of the FDIC, disagreed with parts of the audit, but
Bowsher told CNN Businessline the differences between them were not
that significant and that everyone agreed the FDIC, by year end, would
be out of money. On June 11, 1991, Bowsher told Congress, the *Times*
reports, that the S&L bailout is in "such disarray that its costs cannot be
estimated." In August, the General Accounting Office announced that
100 major banks—each with assets over $100 million—will go bust over
the next 3 years. Fifteen of the banks were already insolvent but
remained open for business.

Slowly, the truth was making its way to the surface. The big
banks were busted and operating—just as the S&Ls did for 10 years—on
governmental indulgence. The taxpayer knew another shock was on its
way.

The collapse of the U.S. banking system led to macabre jokes.
The *Wall Street Journal* reported one: Why was it inevitable that the
U.S. and Kuwait would be such close allies? Because Kuwait is a
banking system without a country, and the U.S. is a country without a
banking system. The taxpayer has no legal liability for the bank losses
beyond what is in the FDIC. With the S&Ls, however, Congress has
voluntarily assumed, on behalf of the taxpayer, to pay all the S&L
losses—usually estimated to cost somewhere between $500 billion and
$1.4 trillion. (Stanford Law & Policy Review, Spring 1990, p. 24). It
is likely though, particularly when Congress throws in the commercial
bank losses, that the cost can't be estimated at any figure. The real cost
is infinite—it is whatever the middle class has now or will have in the
future.

In the Spring of 1991 Congress turned again to what it called
"Banking Reform." The "banks are tottering," said the *New York Times*,
and Congress's "first task is to reform the system so that banks can earn
decent profits without assuming unreasonable risks." Treasury Secretary
Brady threatened Congress that a massive taxpayer bailout of the banks
can only be avoided if Congress enacts the administration bank reform
proposals. Specifically, the proposed reform would let banks go into the
securities and insurance business; let big banks branch nationwide; and
get $25 billion of taxpayer money into the busted FDIC so it can bail out
busted banks. At this point, of course, talking about reforming the

banks is like charting a different course for a Titanic long since resting on the bottom of the North Atlantic.

Congress, just before the Thanksgiving adjournment, voted $100 billion for the continuing S&L bailout and the new commercial bank bailout. The House members, fearful the vote could come back to haunt them, passed the bailout by voice vote which meant there was no record of how any member voted. The Senate also was headed for a voice vote but Senator Paul Wellstone (D. Minn.) objected which prevented the unanimous vote necessary to avoid a record vote. The bipartisan nature of the abandonment was clear in the speech of House majority leader Richard A. Gephardt (D. Mo.). "This is an unpleasant task. But I hope everyone will remember that we're not bailing out anyone but our constituents, who have their deposits in these institutions." Since 1989, Congress had already voted $80 billion for the S&L bailout. As the $100 billion Thanksgiving Bailout was going through, Comptroller General Bowsher noted that while it sounded like a lot of money, the failure of one big bank would eat up the whole thing.

Traditionally, the role of a bank in a community is to provide a safe depository and to make loans to sound local businesses. For some time now, however, the banks have deserted these historical functions. Their main source of profit today is their credit card business. As of May 1, 1991, banks were charging 19% on credit card balances while paying 6% on money market accounts. The banks also make large profits by charging customers outrageous fees such as $25 for a bounced check.

It is very hard to see any continuing taxpayer interest in the survival of busted banks. The taxpayer never shared in bank profits and is not responsible for their failure. There is no justification for Congress putting the loss on him. The government should let the market work to liquidate the failed banks.

The banks today are creating major economic problems since they won't lend to a businessman even for a sound purpose. The economy can't start to move until there is a stable banking system. We need an accounting to determine the extent of the losses and how they should be allocated. The busted banks should be shut; their floating hulks are hazards to navigation and should be cleared out to make room for our healthy banks to make business loans.

Solvency problems were not confined to the big banks. In late November 1990, the Equitable Life Assurance Society, according to Wall Street rumor, was about to file for Chapter 11 protection from creditors. The Equitable immediately denied the speculation. Increasingly, however, life insurance industry insiders spent time discussing what they call "the solvency issue." For some time, there has been concern that the property and casualty companies were writing business—which had to lose over the long run—to get immediate cash flow. The life insurance industry, with $1.3 trillion of assets, is three times the size of the property and casualty companies.

In the 1970s and 1980s, the industry partly abandoned its traditional mortality table business in favor of more "innovative" products. Equitable pioneered the Guaranteed Investment Contracts (GICs) which, in effect, were long term deposits with a fixed high rate of interest. But Equitable lost over $1 billion because it owed more on its GICs than it could earn with the money it got. Financial analysts call this a "negative spread," by which they mean paying 10% for money while you are earning 8%. The negative spread in the S&L industry is what started the trouble. Life insurers, like the S&L's were driven by the negative spread into dumb high-interest investments such as junk bonds and risky real estate loans. Equitable, in November 1990, said it was eliminating 500 jobs, 7 percent of its payroll. In 1991 consumers noticed sharply higher property and casualty rates as the companies, aided by state regulators, taxed the middle class to stay afloat, a sort of private bailout. By 1991, it was beginning to look as if all the country's major financial institutions were bust.

Median family income was also going nowhere despite the great increase of two-salary families. Family income took until 1987 to get back to where it was in 1973. The percentage of adult women working rose from 35.7 percent in 1955 to 56 percent in 1987. The percentage of men working, on the other hand, dropped from 85.4 percent in 1955 to 76.2 percent in 1987.

Citizens have been forced to borrow heavily to maintain their standard of living as real wages dropped. During the 1980s consumer borrowing took off, as shown in Table 2.17. Since the interest rates on all these debts are high, consumer borrowing is now a very heavy interest burden for the American family to pull along. To cover college and other expenses, desperate Americans have been forced to convert their main asset—the equity in their homes—into cash by borrowing against it. In 1990, because of borrowing, U.S. home equity fell by $300 billion, 16 percent of the total.

An awful lot of middle-class borrowing has been to pay for children at college. A year at Princeton cost $5,800 for the academic year 1975-76; $8,751 for 1980-81; and $20,873 for 1990-91. The cost was reduced for minorities by scholarships but any upper middle-class family earning over $60,000 could forget it. They could borrow or sell assets or send the child to a local junior college. Who cared? The colleges had discovered that America's upper middle-class families would pay any price to give their children the best start in life. They did it but the strain of doing it was a family catastrophe.

One extraordinarily depressing set of figures comes from the Bureau of the Census; they chart (Table 2.18) the increase in a person's earnings between age 40 and age 50 over the past three decades, beginning with someone who was 40 in 1953. The current fact that Americans hit their earning peak at age 40, and then drop for the rest of their lives, is dismal. Since 1965, the tax burden on the middle-class families has risen twice as fast as household income as shown in Table 2.19.

Social Security will be discussed later, but here it will just be noted as the clearest Reagan abandonment of the middle class. In 1980, a family with 2 earners paid a combined employee-employer maximum tax of *$6,350,* which was plenty. (Maximum salary of $25,900 at rate of 6.13 percent). In 1991, a family with 2 earners paid a combined employee-employer maximum tax of *$16,340* (maximum salary of $54,300 at a rate of 7.65 percent for each). Social Security added a 15 percent tax rate—up to $54,300—so for most middle-class taxpayer's the federal tax burden was 45 percent (30 percent income and 15 percent Social Security), not exactly a low rate. 74 percent of Americans pay more Social Security tax than they pay income tax.

Since income above $54,300 is free of social security, the more income you make the less social security—as a percentage of your income—you pay. For example, the $54,300 couple paid 15 percent of their income for the social security tax; a $205,000 couple paid 3.7

percent; Michael Milken, on his 1987 $550 million salary, would not notice it.

Family income, as we've noted before, is only holding up because of the tremendous increase in working wives. The two-paycheck families, however, often end up with surprisingly little cash. The *New York Times*, in Table 2.20, analyzed a married professional couple living in New York City with one 4-year-old child. Table 2.20 shows the two-worker family, consequently, receives *$5,909 in cash* from the wife's $50,000 of earnings. The real beneficiary, of course, is the government, which gets *$24,313 more in taxes*.

Normally, lower workers' earnings and higher taxes yields poverty. But the country does not *seem* poverty-stricken. Consumption—and the appearance of prosperity—are maintained by (1) women working; (2) postponed marriage; (3) low birth rate and (4) borrowing and more borrowing.

By the beginning of the 1990s, the government was milking the middle-class cow as never before, and with less finesse. Government had two main beliefs about the cow: (1) that it should keep giving milk, even if government is hostile and contemptuous of it; and (2) that the cow should not worry where the milk goes—if most of it goes overseas to foreigners, that is none of the cow's business.

A political system which leads a rich country into bankruptcy is a failure. Any government will collect enough taxes to cover expenses if it can. If it doesn't, it means it can't. A legitimate government, one resting on the consent of the governed, can call on its people to pay for what it is providing. The U.S. government, for 25 years, has pursued programs the people did not believe in. The government, as a result, could not call on the people to pay for them. Instead, the government borrowed money to carry on its programs. The result is national bankruptcy.

Crane Brinton, in his *Anatomy of Revolution* (Prentice Hall 1952), studied four revolutions—the 17th century English, the 18th century American and French, and the 20th century Russian—to see what common elements they had. Brinton rejected the conventional theory that revolutions are caused by economic distress and deprivation; rather, he found that all four of his revolutions came in times of reasonable prosperity. One important factor is "the existence among a group, or groups, of a feeling that prevailing conditions limit or hinder their economic activity"—a feeling they are "cramped." For example, ambitious groups in America became convinced "that British rule was an unnecessary and incalculable restraint, an obstacle to their full success in life." But the material economic grievance, while necessary to the revolution, will not bring it on. As Pat Buchanan writes in *Right From the Beginning* (Little, Brown 1988), economics is not the science that sends men to the barricades and up against the king's guns; "men fight to preserve the most beautiful of the pictures in their minds." In the case of our Revolution, of course, Jefferson created the most beautiful of pictures for the mind—the freedom of the human spirit.

Another critical factor, Brinton writes, is that the old governments are "chronically short of money—shorter, that is, than most governments usually are." Brinton notes that R. B. Merriman, in a study of six 17th century revolutions—in England, France, the Netherlands, Spain, Portugal and Naples—finds that "they all had in common a financial origin, all began as protests against taxation." The old, failed governments were "chronically short of money" for a good reason. They were afraid to ask their people for taxes. They knew they would be thrown out as soon as they did—they had too tenuous a hold on their people's affections to ask them for any sacrifices.

TABLE 2.17

Consumer Debt 1980-1990

	September 30, 1980	September 30, 1990
Credit Cards	$ 54.9 billion	$215.8 billion[6]
Car Loans	$111.9 billion	$285.2 billion
Home Equity	0.0	$100.0 billion
	$166.8 billion	$601.0 billion[7]

New York Times

[6]Credit card interest is a major siphon from the American middle class to the banks. Since interest rates are close to 20 percent, the cards bring the banks about $40 billion a year. Congress has added to the middle-class burden by (1) deregulating interest rates on cards; and (2) making the interest payments non-deductible as part of the so-called Tax Reform Act of 1986. Congress, at the time, said the purpose of making interest non-deductible was to encourage saving and reduce borrowing which it hoped would make us more like the Japanese. The cards are fantastically profitable because the banks are paying less than 6% on their money market accounts — borrowing at 6% and loaning at 19% — is what the bankers call a very positive spread.

[7]Probably it will cost the taxpayer about this much, $600 billion, to bail out the S&L's. This gives some idea of what an incredible amount of money that is — you could, for the same amount, wipe out all the credit card, car loan, and home equity debt in the country.

TABLE 2.18

Decrease in Worker's Earnings Between Age 40 and Age 50
1953-1983

	40 Yr.-Old		50 Yr.-Old	Increase
(1953)	100%	(1963)	154%	+54%
(1963)	100	(1973)	128	+28
(1973)	100	(1983)	86	-14
(1983)	100	(1993)	?	?

Bureau of Census

TABLE 2.19

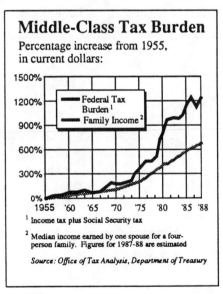

Middle-Class Tax Burden

Percentage increase from 1955, in current dollars:

Federal Tax Burden [1]
Family Income [2]

[1] Income tax plus Social Security tax

[2] Median income earned by one spouse for a four-person family. Figures for 1987-88 are estimated

Source: Office of Tax Analysis, Department of Treasury

Wall Street Journal, January 26, 1990

TABLE 2.20

*Take Home Pay for Working Couple Compared
to Couple Where Wife Stays Home*

He Works/She Stays Home		*He and She Both Work*	
Husband	$70,000	Husband	$ 70,000
		Wife	$ 50,000
Total Income	$70,000	Total Income	$120,000
Taxable Income	$57,928	Taxable Income	$102,159
Total Federal Tax	12,002	Total Federal Tax	25,094
State & Local Tax	5,922	State & Local Tax	11,691
Social Security	3,924	Social Security	7,749
Total Taxes	$21,848	Total Taxes	$ 44,534

ADDITIONAL EXPENSES

Child Care	$ 15,600
Social Security for Child Care	1,627
Work Clothing	1,500
Commuting	598
Lunches	2,080
Total Additional Expenses	$ 21,405

Total Expenses	$21,848	Total Expenses	$ 65,939
They Have Left	$48,150	They Have Left	$ 54,061

New York Times

CHAPTER THREE

The Oil Gouge And Third World Debt, Or How The U.S. Gave Its Wealth Away

In 1950, the U.S. had two-thirds of the world's assets. Nine of the ten largest banks in the world were U.S. banks. By 1988, the U.S. had one-third of the world's assets. The largest U.S. bank, Citibank, ranked 27th among the world's big banks. The economy, of course, needs a strong banking system which will lend business money for sound projects.

How did the foreigners get all the money? The obvious place to look is our trade deficits with each country. Our trade deficits with each country explain some of it: we ran trade surpluses with Germany until 1966. The total deficit with Germany, since 1966, is $84 billion. We ran trade surpluses with Japan until 1965. The total deficit with Japan, since 1965, is $355 billion. The total German and Japanese deficits, $439 billion, are less than we expect to pay for the S&L fiasco and only about one-third of the annual U.S. budget. Our combined trade deficits with Germany and Japan are therefore not that much—certainly they do not come close to explaining why the U.S. is sinking like a rock.

The major causes of the U.S. decline are the Oil Gouge (1973 and 1978) and the Dollar Devaluations (the first was in 1971 when Nixon took us off the international gold standard and the second was the 1985 Reagan Plaza Hotel Accord). The impact of the Dollar Devaluations is shown in Table 3.1.

The Oil Gouge, since 1973, has cost the country at least $3 trillion. The government allowed the Arabs and other overseas producers of oil to siphon off a huge amount of middle-class American wealth. The American wage level and standard of living started downhill in 1973.

TABLE 3.1

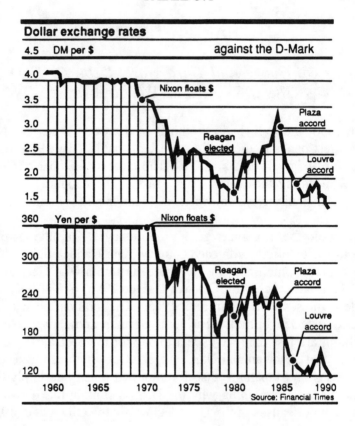

The Attack

> *"Now we are the masters and our former masters are our slaves."*

The Shah of Iran, 1973

In retrospect, the Oil Gouge, was about as unlikely an event as can be imagined. In 1970, oil was selling for $1.20 a barrel (with production cost of 10 cents) and the big worry of the oil countries and companies was whether that price could possibly be *maintained* in view of the world's vast oil reserves and producing capacity. In 1970, 3 percent of U.S. oil supplies came from Arab countries. The U.S.—with the British gone—provided security to the ruling Middle Eastern families, protecting them from external enemies and from their own people. We protected the families allowing them to draw great wealth from the Saudi and Kuwaiti oil while spending their time far from the burning sands of Araby—in Paris and the Riviera. By 1973, the price of a barrel of oil was up to $2.50 with a lifting cost of 15 cents.

At this point the Shah, who was supposed to be a U.S. puppet, quadrupled the price—up to about $12.00 a barrel—and then stepped back to see what would happen. The implications were obvious enough—intelligent people looked at the figures, projected what a huge tax this increase would be on the productive capacity of the West, and thought it ridiculous. They can't get away with it, they said. It was a declaration of economic war. The analysts said the burden was not sustainable. It would slowly grind us down. Each year the U.S. economy had to pay a huge extraterritorial tax to the oil states. They predicted that there was no way the U.S. could stand for it, it would bankrupt us. They were looking at the world in pre-abandonment terms.

The U.S. government, however, was accommodative. It said the matter, which was clearly a tax imposed by foreign governments, was a question of "supply and demand." They owned the oil and they could set the price, it was "the free market."

In a real free market, prices bear some relation to the cost of producing something.   Someone making a huge profit will attract competitors. Competition will drive the price down pretty close to cost. But oil does not follow free market theory. In 1980, J.B. Kelly, the British oil expert, wrote in *Arabia, the Gulf and the West*:

> The marginal cost of production of Saudi Arabian oil is roughly 15 cents a barrel, that of Kuwaiti oil about 10 cents a barrel. A posted price of $18.00 a barrel, such as obtained in the case of Saudi Arabia from 1 June 1979, is equivalent to 12,000 per cent of the cost of production; while a posted price of $19.50, such as Kuwait imposed from 1 July 1979, is equivalent to 19,500 per cent. It is hard to think off-hand of any Western manufacture which is priced comparably.

On December 17, 1973, a few days after Iran sold a barrel of oil for $17.40, the *New York Times* editorialized:

> There was nothing particularly unexpected about the rapid increase in crude oil prices. Whatever individual profiteering may be under way, in a general way the laws of supply and demand are at work.

In a "general way"?

This was the origin of the Great Oil Scarcity (1973-1982) during which we were told that the world would run out of oil in 2007. Jimmy Carter was a great believer in the scarcity theory because it coincided with his basic belief that all Americans were the cause of their own problems because they were conceived in sin.

The Shah could raise the price to whatever he liked, but what made him think anyone would pay? Clearly, the Third World could not pay. As Federal Reserve Chairman Volcker put it in his February 2, 1983, testimony to House Banking Committee:

> At the time oil prices first rose sharply, great concern had been expressed that industrialized and developing countries alike might be unable to finance the increased cost of oil imports.

But why was there "great concern" about this? Suppose we were "unable to finance" it? Why should we worry about "financing" an economic war aimed at us? Only one of two things could happen, either (1) the Arabs could keep their oil or (2) the price would drop back to where it came from. What was wrong with that? Here was a situation where the free market *would* have worked to the advantage of the middle class if given a chance.

But the free market was not allowed to work. It was at this point that the "scarcity" story and the artificially inflated price of oil turned into an opportunity for profit. The bankers intervened with what was called "recycling." The Arabs deposited their revenues in the banks and the banks loaned the money to the poor countries so they could pay their oil bills. Then the cycle could begin again. The money went from the poor countries who couldn't afford their oil to the Arabs who didn't need the money, to the international bankers who took brokers' fees every step of the way. And it kept on going till they had several trillion dollars that used to belong to us.

OPEC, in 1970, received $7 billion in oil revenues. In 1974, with this strange financing mechanism in place, oil revenues were $74 billion, and in 1980 they were $300 billion. If you kept your eye on the money and ignored labels, what happened was that the money started out in the Western industrial countries, the rich countries. It then went to the Arabs. From the Arabs, it went to the international banks. From the banks, it went to the poor countries. From the poor countries, it went to the Arabs. From the Arabs, it went to the international banks.

The bankers' game was to confuse analysis by putting familiar legal labels on them. Some things were called "payments for oil"; some were called "deposits" and some "loans." But the oil payments were not oil payments and the loans were not loans. They were, in fact, transfers of wealth.

Were there any risks in the bankers' game? Not from the Third Worlders; they had to have the oil, and if you offered them the money so they could buy it, they had to take it. What about from the strong countries who would pay? Would they just let you drain their wealth? Would they sit still for an annual $300 billion tax on them? Would they accept a confiscatory tax which, if allowed to stand, had to cripple their economies? You were not talking about Zaire and Malawi, you were talking about the most powerful country on earth and its allies. Could Iran tax the American middle class? Yes, that was a major abandonment.

In classical economic terms what the bankers had created was a distortion. The price of one commodity was allowed to rise, which would ordinarily mean that the price of all other goods and services must fall. Arthur Burn's Fed, and later, William Miller's, however, created new money to prevent this from happening. The resultant OPEC-induced inflation was the second abandonment of the middle class.

The government was able to create new money because Richard Nixon, in August 1971, had cut the country's last tie to the gold standard—he closed the gold window at which foreigners could exchange their dollars for gold. Government, under a gold standard, can only expand the money supply by getting more gold. Under a paper money system, on the other hand, government can just order the mint to print more. The Nixon decision to desert gold was the final victory of William Jennings Bryan's free silver movement. Theodore Roosevelt, on August 19, 1896, wrote to Henry Cabot Lodge:

> Down at the bottom the cry for free silver is nothing whatever but a variant of the cry for fiat money or a debased and inflated currency. Brooks Adams' theories are beautiful, but in practice they mean a simple dishonesty, and a dishonest nation does not stand much higher than a dishonest man.

The "recycling" process also reflected the banks' convictions about their own political strength and influence. The banks stood to profit enormously in the brokerage of national wealth to foreigners. The banks lent to entities which were patently not creditworthy. They failed to carry out even minimal supervision over the use of the money borrowed, so as to make an informed judgment on the ability to repay, or on the advisability of lending more money.

The bankers were aware of their unique position. Theirs was a critical industry which would give them a claim to the public treasury to insulate them from loss. The mentality driving the initial loans and the interminable subsequent "rescheduled" loans necessary to preserve the appearance that the loans were solid was not the traditional banker's mentality. Rather, it was a conviction that the middle-class taxpayer was there to shoulder any economic loss.

The Bankers

> *"[T]he universal church of Money [transcends] national, political and cultural lines."*
>
>> Bill Moyers - PBS Program on David Rockefeller's trip to 1979 IMF Meeting.

The U.S. bankers, in 1970, bestrode the world like a colossus. Seven of the eleven largest banks were U.S. The country had run trade surpluses since 1914. Our per capita income and standard of living were by far the world's highest. The bankers, as fiduciaries for their depositors, held the accumulated wealth of the country. Their traditional role was a secondary, but critical one—to accommodate the country's productive economy. George Champion, a pre-Abandonment banker who was chairman of the Chase Manhattan Bank from 1961 to 1969, has explained that the banker's historical role is to "lend to the individual endowed with character, energy and ability to compete or develop new products, which is the basis for economic progress."

During the 1970s, the bankers abandoned the American middle class in favor of a glamorous new international class they had just joined. To join the new class, the bankers had to reject the pre-Abandonment concept of a banker—a fiduciary to whom funds are entrusted to be judiciously handled through prudent loans and investments. The greatest trust was involved when you were handling funds that were not your own. As members of the new supranational class, the post-Abandonment bankers now adopted some very new concepts and some very large illusions as to their role in the world.

In 1979, Bill Moyers produced an excellent documentary for PBS on David Rockefeller's trip to the 1979 IMF meeting in Belgrade, Yugoslavia. Moyers took off from Westchester Airport in Rockefeller's Gulfstream II. On the way, the plane stopped in Newfoundland, Ireland, and Strasbourg, France (where the group had lunch). In Belgrade, the Chase gave a cocktail party for a thousand friends and clients from all over the world. As the cocktails flowed, Moyers asked freelance writer John Dizard what was going on. Its simple, said Dizard, these people had gathered to "reaffirm, well, a feeling that they're part of the real global elite, which is after all, what they are." These people, he continued, "place the limits, in effect, on what any sovereign nation can do."

On the way home, the Chase group stopped over in Rome to visit some clients at the Vatican. As he stood in St. Peter's Square, Moyers reflected:

> Men like David Rockefeller move beyond religious, political, cultural, national boundaries with great ease. And here in St. Peter's Square, the heart of the Roman Catholic faith, there's something very symbolic to me about that. The Church has always transcended national, political, and cultural lines, and so, in its own way, does the universal church of Money. It goes where it will, and the laws of no single country can regulate it.

These were very heady illusions, indeed. And as the bankers lived by them in the 1970s and 1980s, more and more of the country's wealth eroded. By the time the illusion burst, the bankers had given away the accumulated wealth of the country. The German and Japanese bankers were giving the cocktail party, and the U.S. bankers were lucky if they received an invitation.

"Recycling" was the centerpiece of the bankers give-away. The bankers went to history for their bizarre model. After World War I, the English and French had imposed reparations upon Germany that the Germans couldn't pay. The English and French owed war debts to the U.S. that they said they couldn't pay. The U.S. had plenty of money. American bankers, with stunning ingenuity, came up with a scheme to get the American public to pay the German reparations. The bankers sold German bonds to the American public; the proceeds, minus fees, went to Germany, which paid England and France, which paid the U.S. Treasury. One hundred and fourteen German bond issues were sold here; the new loans paid the interest on the old, and the reparations, too. The German game was going so well the bankers peddled to the American public the bonds of other foreign countries, including Argentina, Bolivia, Brazil, Bulgaria, Chile, Costa Rica, Ecuador, Mexico, Peru, and Romania. However, by 1933, $25 billion of foreign bonds were in default. The bonds the bankers sold to U.S. investors turned out to be gifts from U.S. investors to foreign countries.

The bankers made no apologies for selling the bad bonds to the public. They explained to the Senate Finance Committee in 1931 that they were just doing their job. Charles E. Mitchell, chairman of the First National City Bank, testified: "With respect to the bonds generally, we are merchants." Thomas W. Lamont of J. P. Morgan & Co. supported Mitchell: "We are merchants. That is what we are, just like any merchant, in the grain business, in the cotton business, or anything else." As one witness told the Senate Committee on Manufactures, "I do not think you would be justified in holding the bankers responsible for the wide speculative craze that worked through the country. I think we were trying to supply what the customer wanted . . . I think the banker is like the grocer. He supplies what his customer wants." After the bond fiasco, Congress imposed new laws to direct the bankers back into their traditional custodial and fiduciary role.

Memories, even the most bitter, fade. By 1973, the bankers were ready to try the same game again. Again, the U.S. had most of the money. This time the money was pumped from the U.S. to poor countries who passed it to the Arabs who passed it back to the banks. The money transfer was tremendous. In 1972, the Arabs received $24 billion from the rest of the world. In 1980 they received $300 billion. Since all oil prices followed OPEC's lead, in the U.S. the cost of oil went from $20.3 billion in 1972 to $225 billion in 1981. The extra cost came to $820 per person, or $3,300 for a family of four. The Arabs, with the banks brokering the deal, had made a major withdrawal from the West. The public was told that OPEC had control of the world's energy and could charge what it liked.

Beginning in 1973-1974 the Arabs, with the bankers' cooperation, became international tax collectors. They sought simply to employ their corner on oil to capture all of the West's capital and real wealth. The West, its economic sovereignty rapidly eroding, made no response at all. Poor countries, of course, could not pay the new tax. The banks loaned the money to Zaire so it could pay its tax to the Arabs who then deposited the tax collections back in the banks. The parties thought the debt merry-go-round could go on forever. In year one the banks loaned Zaire enough to pay its oil tax, say $1 billion. In year two the banks rolled over that billion and had to loan enough new money to cover year two's oil tax, say another billion, plus the interest on the outstanding debt, say $200 million. The geometric progression of compound interest worked heavily against the poor countries. The borrowing had to increase, and increase at an accelerating rate. Within a few years, the figures were outlandish. Mexico, for example—when it collapsed in 1982—owed, in interest alone, $250 million *a week*. Brazil was about the same. The bankers had disregarded the fatal weakness of a debt merry-go-round—that you can't get off.

Because of the basic principle of the merry-go-round, the debt balloons in proportion to the certainty that it cannot be repaid. Borrowing is needed increasingly just to pay interest rather than to finance imports. Mexico's debt jumped from $40 billion in 1980 to $80 billion in 1982; Argentina's shot from $13.7 billion in 1978 to over $40 billion when it decided to invade the Falklands; Poland, before Solidarity, ran its debt from $10 billion in 1976 to $27 billion in 1981.

In June 1982, according to then Treasury Secretary Donald Regan, the poor countries owed $265 billion to private Western banks. Latin America alone owed $168 billion to the banks. Including loans from Western governments and international agencies, the poor countries owed $500 billion. Counting the loans to companies in poor countries, the total was $700 billion, of which $400 billion was owed to the banks. Even for a grocer, that's a lot of lettuce.

In the foreign bond scam of the 1920s, the bankers were pure middlemen or brokers. The foreign governments paid them a fee for selling the bonds to the U.S. public. The foreign governments got the proceeds, the bankers got their commission and fees, and the U.S. public got the ultimate loss. The current recycling variation couldn't use bonds—the U.S. investors did remember that much. You couldn't sell them the bonds of Argentina, Bolivia, Brazil, and Bulgaria, to say nothing of Zaire, Zambia, and Poland. And it was unthinkable to try to sell Russian or East German bonds to Americans. The impossibility of bond sales forced bankers to become "committed middlemen." So they took in Arab deposits and made loans to poor countries. They were then vulnerable from both directions.

By the time one of the authors wrote a piece for *The New Republic* called "The Bankers Dilemma" on January 27, 1979, the recycling fiasco was totally out of control. The author wrote that the banks had become committed middlemen. They are "captive to both Arab creditors and LDC debtors. They are vulnerable both ways." The banks reasoned: "can the government stand aside while the U.S. banking system goes bankrupt?" The author concluded that the "banks remain supremely confident that the government will come to their rescue [and the] loss will be socialized by getting the American taxpayer to bear it." Did the bankers know sooner than 1979? Did they know when they could have still survived the hit? It seems clear they must have known by late 1974. On September 23, 1974, Rimmer DeVries, Vice President of Morgan Guaranty Trust Company and a highly respected banker, wrote in *World Financial Markets:*

> Looking ahead, it should be made clear that the international commercial banking systems cannot be counted on to contrive to increase its international intermediary role at the pace experienced so far this year . . . [the] limits to the ability of existing mechanisms to cope with the problem are being approached.

DeVries was viewing the situation as a pre-Abandonment banker. It didn't make sense, it couldn't make sense; his colleagues knew it didn't make sense; and yet it went on and on.

You had to be a new banker—a banker of Abandonment—to understand what was going on. For example, Citibank Chairman Walter Wriston was a model of the new banker. Wriston's background is intellectual and academic. He was born in Middletown, Connecticut on August 3, 1919. His father was Henry Merritt Wriston, a history professor at Wesleyan University who later became president of Brown University. Wriston graduated from Wesleyan University in 1941 and received a masters degree from the Fletcher School of International Law and Diplomacy. He did post graduate work at the Ecole Francaise of Middleburg College in Vermont. He worked in the State Department during the war and, in 1946, joined First National City Bank where he spent his entire career. He was chairman during the critical years 1970-1984.

In 1968, two years after the death of his wife, he married Kathryn Ann Dineen, a lawyer with Shearman & Sterling, Citibank's lawyers, who was then 28. The Wristons have an apartment in United Nations Plaza and a farm near Sherman, Connecticut for weekends.

Citibank reflected Wriston's personality—brilliant and arrogant. Traditionally, a banker was not supposed to be that clever. As Walter Bagehot pointed out in his book *Lombard Street*, published in 1873, banking "ought to be simple; if it is hard, it is *wrong*."

Under Wriston, however, Citibank fostered a reputation for brilliant complexity. Its managers are acclaimed as geniuses. The 1960s were smashing. In 1961 Wriston invented the Certificate of Deposit, a deposit with a time limit; in 1968 came Citicorp, the first-ever bank holding company, which permitted diversification and added more borrowing power. Both of these innovations would later cause trouble, but at the time seemed brilliant. Citibank staffed its branches abroad with, as Martin Mayer writes, the "same hard-driving, bright, vain people" who ran the bank at home. But the 1970s brought hard times: the foreign loans became a bad joke. The bank's foreign operations contributed two-thirds of total earnings, but it was becoming increasingly clear that the principal of the loans would never be paid.

Wriston was nonetheless constantly reassuring about the foreign loans. At an 1982 IMF meeting in Lusanne, Switzerland he said:

> It is no secret that over the years a lot of intellectual capital has been invested in the proposition that massive defaults by the Third World will cause a world financial crisis. Those who have taken the view since 1973/74 have been proved wrong, and those of us who believed the market would work proved correct.

Much of Wriston's charm comes from the fact that he is a plain talker. Normally bankers use euphemisms as reflexively as preachers use analogies. A poor country is a "less developed country" and that gets abbreviated to "LDC"; a default is a "rescheduling"; a second default is a "re-rescheduling"; and "fund availability risk" is the possibility that tomorrow you won't have any money because the Arabs have pulled out their deposits. A sour loan is a "nonperforming loan."

During 1982, chairman Wriston shifted his basic position from his original They Always Pay theory to a new They Never Pay theory. He was asked on "Face the Nation" on January 24, 1982, how Poland could possibly pay any interest—much less principal—due in the future. He replied: "As far as paying off debt is concerned, there are very few instances in history when any government has ever paid off debt . . . What we are talking about is access to a marketplace." "Market access," of course, is a euphemism for more borrowing.

It was at this time that Wriston began to clearly reveal himself as a post-Abandonment banker. He made debt the centerpiece of his fiscal and economic analysis. Debt was the solution to the nation's worsening economic outlook. Wriston identified financial soundness with debt. Under his theory, how much you are worth is determined by how much you can borrow. Wriston's theory allowed consumption to replace production and accumulation as a measure of economic worth. The theory was tailor-made for the new age: it had a seductive intellectual ring and it averted consideration of difficult real-life problems. The financial opportunities revealed by the New York City crisis were picked up by Wriston and the bankers who began to employ the new improved theory of debt on a global scale.

On September 14, 1982, Wriston wrote an *New York Times* op-ed article entitled "Banking Against Disaster" that fully developed his "They Never Pay" theory. Wriston's article became one of the most famous documents of the debt crisis. It upset club members. It led England's Lord Lever to call Wriston the "Peter Pan" of the international banking world. Robert V. Roosa, a partner in Brown Brothers Harriman and former under secretary of the treasury called it "just plain cotton candy." The Christian Broadcasting Network asked Wriston if he would do a reading of the piece for a TV film; their request was refused. Wriston himself later said of the article: "I knew I'd take a lot of flak but I wanted to throw it out in the marketplace of ideas."

Wriston wrote that if the U.S. government followed a truth-in-government act comparable to the truth-in-advertising law, "every note issued by the Treasury would have to be captioned, 'This note will be redeemed with the proceeds from an identical note which will be sold to the public when this one comes due. We carry out this activity weekly and call it a Treasury bill auction.'" Wriston was 100 percent right on his basic premise. (See discussion of short-term nature of the national debt on p. 51.) "But when basically the same process is conducted abroad in a foreign language, our news media usually speak of a country's 'rolling over its debts' with the implication that the world is about to go bankrupt and take the banking system with it." The doom-sayers who took that view in 1973-74 "have been proved wrong, and those of us who believed that the market would absorb the shock of skyrocketing oil prices proved correct."

Yet the perception of disaster persists. The doom-sayers are wrong again, wrote Wriston. To see why, "it is only necessary to understand the basic facts of government borrowing." First, "there are few recorded instances in history of government—any government—actually getting out of debt." Anyone lending to our Government expects to be paid, not out of taxes, but by a new borrowing:

> These obvious facts suggest two corollaries: first the holder of the bill has justifiable confidence that the Government will acknowledge the debt; second, the Government will have ready access to a market ready and willing to buy a new piece of paper. These facts suggest that the availability of financing, from commercial banks, or official agencies, is the crucial element in assessing a country's situation. When problems arise, they are problems of liquidity, not insolvency.

That was the new banker's credo—there could be no default because there was no due date. Solvency, up to this point, meant meeting obligations as they became due. Solvency, to Wriston, meant you were able to borrow to meet them. Thus, Wriston's new "debt-as-wealth" concept revolutionized the theory of debt.

Debt had previously been understood to mean something which must actually be repaid. The concept was as ancient as civilization itself. The word "debt" comes from the Latin "debitum," or the past participle of *debère*, which literally means "to owe." The *Oxford English Dictionary* lists the Middle English applications of the term to money, stating that a debt is "anything which one person is under obligation to pay or render to another." All the etymological applications of the term debt contain the idea of repayment. A debt is also defined as a "legal liability," and is considered an obligation rather than an asset. The genius of the new bankers' view is that debt became totally conceptual. Rolled-over debt, to Wriston, is just a part of some infinite process in which the original debt naturally grows and multiplies. It also is detached from any of its traditional negative features: for example, that it represents a liability. As such, the debt process is to be viewed not as a source of worry, but a source of strength.

Wriston considers himself a strict free market man; indeed, he views consideration of national or moral factors as "mercantilism." At a party in New York City in October 1983, Wriston was asked: "Don't you think its unwise from a national standpoint to participate in loan bailouts to Nigeria, Venezuela, and Mexico who are part of the OPEC market corner of oil which resulted in huge transfers of U.S. wealth to OPEC—hundreds of billions?" The chairman replied:

> *"You're asking me to make moral judgments.* Don't forget we recycled OPEC surpluses during the seventies which fostered much growth in South America and overseas."

The questioner followed up: "It seems to me these OPEC surpluses shouldn't have been recycled. It would have been better for the world if the oil price had been lower and the money kept within our shores for domestic investment." The chairman answered:

> "Then there wouldn't have been as much money for overseas loans."

The "You're asking me to make moral judgments" theme is an important one to Wriston. OPEC, U. S. farmers, and Indians all seem the same under Wriston's intellectual relativism. Asked whether we "should subsidize OPEC who is out to transfer our wealth from us to them?" Wriston shot back:

> "Doesn't the U. S. Government subsidize the farmers?"

Later, by way of clarification, he added:

> "Maybe I shouldn't loan money to the railroads because they stole the land from the Indians."

In late 1983, Stanley Schienanbaum, a member of the California Board of Regents, approached Walter Wriston in the Concorde Lounge in Paris Airport. He asked: "Why have the banks extended so many shaky loans to the Third World?" Without hesitation, Wriston replied: "Because the government wanted us to." This was a new theory—"They Made Me Do It." But Wriston never said "Who?" Or "When?" Or Where? He never said when he had told his depositors and stockholders the government was muscling the bank to make a lot of stupid loans.

Only Congress has the authority to bind the American people. Wriston knew that much civics. But, supposedly, if pressure was applied along with winks and encouragements, the taxpayer would pay if they ran into trouble. Academics supported the Wriston theory. They were quick to shift the responsibility onto the American taxpayer. By this time academics had completely abandoned the middle-class American. His basic function now is to take the blame and provide the funding for any failed project. For example, in April 1983, Professor Benjamin Cohen of the Fletcher School of International Law and Diplomacy testified to the House Banking Committee: "May I suggest that our government and other governments of the industrial world encouraged banks to do this . . . I think that our elected representatives, over the last decade, played a role in encouraging the banks to do this and the residue of that is that the taxpayers now are faced with having to bear some of the burden." The taxpayer was the guilty party all along.

It didn't, of course, follow that taxpayer liability was the inevitable "residue"—if Walter Wriston wanted to risk his depositors' money based on winks from Richard Nixon and Henry Kissinger, that was his affair, and their affair. And it is certainly true that the myth never surfaced as long as the bankers thought they were going to make money on the foreign loans. For example, George Costanzo, vice chairman of Citibank, told the House Banking Committee in 1977:

"First of all, let me say that I would not propose and we never have, granting aid to any countries for the purpose of bailing out the banks. I think it is a fundamental principle with us that as a private institution dealing in the private marketplace, we take risks and we are man enough to take our losses when they arise . . . We have never taken into consideration any bailout possibilities.   As far as we are concerned, that is a zero factor."

In his 1986 book, *Risk and Other Four Letter Words*, Wriston doesn't repeat his Concorde Lounge, or "They Made Me Do It" theory; he seems to be back to his original, or "Everything is OK" theory. Wriston's reputation rolls on.   Charles Keating, who put together The Keating Five, thinks that a "financial genius" like Wriston should be put in charge of the savings and loan clean up.

The Banks have never disclosed the extent of their bad loans to particular countries.   But, in August 1990, the Central Bank of Brazil revealed that Brazil owed Wriston's Citibank $3.4 billion and David Rockefeller's Chase Manhattan $2.3 billion.

In September 1982, Dennis Healey, former British Chancellor of the Exchequer, called the Toronto meeting of the IMF the "last chance to save the world from a catastrophe even greater than the slump of the 1930's."   *The Economist*, in an article entitled "Not With a Bang But a Fonda," described "two theories of how the banking world could end: the big bang theory and the gradual-disappearance-down-a-black-hole theory."   As in Jane Fonda's movie, *Rollover*, the big bang theorists postulate a major default, say of Argentina, which sets off a chain reaction of defaults in the highly interdependent banking system, collapsing it within twenty-four hours.

The black-hole theorists see a more gradual process driven by the poor performance of bank stock and commercial paper and increasing "tiering." "Tiering" means simply that lenders distinguish among banks based on credit quality.   The banks themselves are beginning to discriminate in the critical interbank market—where Bank A, with extra funds, will loan to Bank B, which has found itself short, perhaps because it just failed to receive $100 million from Argentina. Bank B, if it can't get an acceptable rate from Bank A, will slide gradually into a downward spiral of high rates for funds, lost deposits, and disappearing profits. Since the banks are all tied together by past interbank loans, each one slipping in will pull some others in behind it. The bankers, however, do not consider themselves at risk. They are confident that the U.S. taxpayer, like the bondholders of the 1920s game, will take the loss.

Where was the money that the banks had sent to the Third World? The bankers had no idea. Could anyone find $27 billion in Poland? Or $40 billion in Argentina? Very little of the money could be traced to productive projects. Most went up in smoke, covering balance-of-payments deficits.

Did the West, and particularly the U.S., need the capital the bankers were giving away? Well, the 1982 study, *The Deindustrialization of America,* by Barry Bluestone and Bennett Harrison, estimated that 30 to 50 million jobs were lost during the 1970s as a result of plant relocations, closings, and contractions. The U.S., at an extraordinarily fast rate, underwent "deindustrialization," a process that was fatal to the future strength of the country. The authors estimate that 70 percent of private-sector jobs existing in 1970 were gone by 1980. They were replaced by jobs in the growing "service" economy—i.e., non-manufacturing jobs. The term "service" economy is a euphemism for an economy that can't make anything. The term implies that a country can survive when all it can do is sell foreign goods to its citizens. The bankers turned down meritorious domestic borrowers with the simple, unanswerable question: "Why should I lend money to you when I can make so much more lending to Mexico?"

Realistically, the foreign loans don't exist anymore: they continue, however, to have a spiritual presence. The bankers will not write them off: loans to Poland, Zaire, Mexico, and Argentina are still counted as assets of the banks at face value. Although they have not the weight of a wisp, they continue to balance the books. The bankers have created a fictional world where the loans are still good. No country, according to the bankers' new definition, is bankrupt unless it can't borrow to pay the interest anymore. The bankers and poor countries have had a mutual interest in maintaining the fiction. The poor countries, if they told the truth, wouldn't get any more money. The bankers, if they told the truth, would have to write off almost $400 billion of bad loans. But reality is breaking through; now the interests seem to be diverging as the poor countries look ahead to fifty years of IMF servitude to pay off foreign bankers.

In the second half of 1982, Treasury Secretary Don Regan testified that U.S. regional banks (all of those except the largest) "have sought to limit or reduce exposure." To the extent they are successful, the Secretary added, "they place a greater and disproportionate strain on the resources of the larger banks and official lenders that are committed to the international financial system." The big banks also criticized the regionals. The regionals, they said, were eager enough for high returns while things were good, but now, at the first hint of trouble, they had run for cover. Jacques de Larosiere, managing director of the IMF (which is itself almost out of money), lectured the regionals that they should evaluate each loan "flexibly and pragmatically, keeping in mind that a cooperative international effort will best serve the interests of all the parties involved and, ultimately, the financial system itself." What had the regional banks done to reap such a bitter and threatening harvest? It was simple. They had begun to act like bankers again. They were attempting to reassert discipline and sense in a world that could live only on fiction.

The losses, the banks say, should be shifted to the taxpayer. The whole deal had been set up to evade democratic procedures, but now that it has gone bad the taxpayer should pay for it. Indeed, say the banks, the taxpayer has no choice. He can pay now or pay later, but he has to pay. If he wants, he can pay through the IMF or the Federal Reserve, but he has to get dollars to Mexico so Mexico can pay Chase.

Both the official Republican government and the shadow Democratic government agree with the bankers that the taxpayer must pay. For the shadow government, Felix Rohatyn, recommends a new Reconstruction Finance Corporation to take over the bad loans—in essence, the federal government would bail them out. He wrote in 1982 that the "mere existence" of his new RFC "would help remove the widespread concern about the soundness of our banks, which is clearly detrimental to an economic recovery."

The official government takes a similar tack. In a November 1982 speech in Boston, Federal Reserve Board Chairman Paul Volcker told bankers to keep on lending: "New credits should not be subject to supervisory criticism." George Champion, chairman of the Chase

Manhattan Bank from 1961 to 1969, wrote for the *New York Times* in 1984 that "a conflict of interest and responsibility is apparent as never before at the Federal Reserve Bank.   The Fed is responsible for administering monetary policies so vital to our financial and economic health; while at the same time responsible for the examination of all member banks that are not in the national system."

In December 1982, the administration asked Congress to appropriate $8 billion for the IMF Treasury Secretary Regan, in testimony to the House Banking Committee, denied that the idea was to bail out the big banks. Far from it, he said: "Our efforts are primarily in defense of the average American and his own economic interests." How will the average American benefit from keeping the merry-go-round going? The secretary described the bleak result if the U.S. and major Western governments "follow a 'hands-off' approach to the debt problems." He believed that the banker would not supply new money unless the taxpayer chipped in, and, consequently, the "hands-off" approach "would most likely result in a cessation of new private lending to LDCs [less developed countries] in general."   Since these countries had received $45 billion of new bank loans in 1981, a drop to zero would deprive them of $45 billion of purchasing power. Without a new $45 billion of loans, they could not buy $45 billion worth of goods from the industrial West. The secretary testified: "This would represent a direct loss of 0.3 to 0.5 percent of GNP in the industrial countries; secondary effects could double that loss." In the U.S., "growth would be about 1 percent less than we're expecting, and our trade deficit would grow very rapidly." That's what the "hands-off" approach would get you.

Many people who voted for Ronald Reagan thought they had voted for the "hands-off" approach, which during the election campaign was known as "getting government off the backs of the people." Times change, and the administration adopted a particularly perverse Keynesianism, under which we had to give poor countries money so they could buy goods from us. (Poor American people, of course, do not qualify.) Giving huge sums to Arabs and Third World countries and to the Soviets creates demand. These welfare recipients will buy U.S. goods, creating jobs, and so on. Of course, this is exactly what the bankers have been doing since 1973. And if that makes sense to you, as the song goes, I've got some oceanfront property in Arizona you might be interested in.

The second bad result of the "hands-off" approach, the secretary testified, is that the banks will have to recognize the losses. What happens, he asked, "if foreign borrowers do not receive sufficient assistance to adjust in an orderly way?" What if they can't pay the banks? American workers in "Providence, Pascoag, or Woonsocket" are then, he said, in real trouble. He posed, hypothetically, a sound, well-run U.S. bank of $10 billion in assets (loans) with $600 million of capital. Regulators require the bank to maintain at least $6 in capital for every $100 in assets. "What happens if 10 percent, or $60 million, of its capital is eroded through foreign loan losses? It must contract its lending by $1 billion." The net result is that $1 billion in loans can't be made in that community—20,000 home mortgages at $50,000 each that can't be financed, or 10,000 lines of credit to local businesses at $100,000 each that can't be extended.

Republican perversity was now building up. A loss plainly exists, but if we don't cover it up, if we recognize it, the insolvent bank will have to cut back its lending. Families will not get housing and business will not get needed credit. They will get houses and credit if the taxpayer gives money to the IMF, which gives it to Mexico, which gives it to Chase.

The secretary's hypothetical example demonstrates how pathetically thin the capitalization of the U.S. banks is. The regulators only require capital equal to 6 percent of loans, which leaves very little room for error. In 1930-1933, when 7,000 banks failed, capital requirements were much higher. Today, the exposure of the twelve major banks in Mexico and Argentina alone exceeds 100 percent of their capital.

The IMF works closely with governments in order to "help identify the causes of their economic problems and to identify the appropriate economic policy adjustments." Together, they develop a stringent program to restore domestic and external health. Usually the program includes higher taxes, less spending, lower subsidies for food, lower subsidies for industry, and currency devaluation—all designed to increase exports and reduce imports. In a word, austerity. A Mexican peasant may think things are pretty austere already. He may think the IMF program is designed to secure funds for foreign bankers. The problem is that the IMF programs do what they are intended to do. They increase unemployment, reduce growth, and lower a standard of living that is marginal to begin with. Third Worlders say, "An application to the IMF is a recipe for a coup d'etat."

All this might go down if the Mexicans or Brazilians or Argentinians thought the debt was fairly incurred to begin with. But it's very clear that they don't think so. Not unreasonably, they think they are victims of a lot of horsing around beyond their control. They couldn't stand up to the Arabs, but the U.S. could and didn't. They think at least half the debt is not real debt, but unconscionable interest that has piled up because of a U.S. experiment with the theories of Milton Friedman. Much of the borrowing was by corrupt regimes for their own purposes, which included oppressing the people now asked to pay. The debt was run up by military dictators during the 1970s and early 1980s. When civilians took back control in the mid-1980s they inherited this unsustainable mountain of debt. Almost all the loans were made by bankers who must have known they were far beyond the capacity of the country to repay.

The last argument on behalf of the merry-go-round is that if it stops, a lot of players will get scrambled. Without question, many governments will be shown the door by their people. But failed governments should be replaced. The U.S. has no interest in stabilizing communists, military dictators, and other rulers whose people don't want them. Propping up repressive regimes on the chance they may cooperate with the bankers is not a middle-class American aspiration. Nor is the use of U.S. government muscle to collect bad loans for bankers.

During the 1980's the administration followed one feckless plan after another. First there was the Baker Plan; that did nothing. Then there was the Brady Plan; that did nothing. The administration could not break away from the bankers' story that the Third World loans had some continuing legitimacy.

In the Fall of 1990, the Bush administration told Brazil that renegotiation of Brazil's $115 billion foreign debt is, as the *New York Times* put it, "a private affair between Brazil and the banks." Since the Mexican default in 1982, the Latin American countries have paid out a lot more in interest on the debt then they have received in new loans. The interest pay out depressed domestic growth to the point that Latin

American economists refer to the 1980s as the "lost decade." And, after all this sacrifice, they are exactly where they started—staring at unsustainable mountain of debt. Obviously these countries cannot stay in a contorted economic position forever.

The debt issue, many Latin Americans believe, controls the future of democracy. Brazil's President Fernando Collor de Mello told President Bush we "are not talking of a banking problem." Brazil has a foreign debt of $115 billion. President de Mello spoke, on December 4, 1990, at a dinner in honor of President Bush who was beginning a 5-nation tour:

> We are not talking of a banking problem, but a question that involves 150 million people and one of the largest and most important countries in the world. My government cannot demand more sacrifices if it is not convinced that these efforts will be the price for a consistent, balanced and feasible solution.

The first oil shock was called by Henry Kissinger: "One of the most pivotal events in the history of this century." Between October 1973 and January 1974, the Arabs pushed the price of a barrel of oil from $3 to $13. *The Economist* points out this brought to an end the "rapid economic growth that the world had enjoyed since the 1950s." The Big Seven Industrial countries had to pay an extra $80 billion (2 of GNP) a year to pay their oil bills. Business slashed investment while consumers spent less. Output fell by 0.5 in the second half of 1974 and at the rate of 3.0 percent in the first half of 1975. The average inflation rate rose from 7.9 percent in 1973 to 14 percent in 1974.

The second oil shock drove the price of a barrel of oil from $13 a barrel at the end of 1978 to $39 a year later. The industrialized nation's oil bill again rose by 2 percent of GDP, average inflation ran from 7.8 percent at the end of 1978 to 13.6 percent in the first half of 1980. Output, which had grown by 4.6 percent in 1978 stagnated towards the end of 1979 and did not recover until 1983.

The third oil shock came in August-October 1990, when Sadaam Hussein invaded Kuwait and the Bush Administration sent 300,000 troops to the Gulf. The price of a barrel of oil ran from $20 on August 1 to $40 on October 15. The administration said it sent the troops to the Gulf to prevent Sadaam from gaining control of the world's oil supply.

The danger was, the administration said, that Sadaam would hold the world hostage and charge outrageous prices—say $40 a barrel—for oil. It was a "threat to the American way of life." The price run-up was embarrassing to the administration and the President blamed "speculators." In fact, of course, the market was simply reacting to the uncertainty of any future supply created by having 300,000 U.S. troops sitting in the oil fields.

What was hard to understand was the government's stated concern for the consumer. The government itself, as part of the budget deal of 1990, wanted to increase the tax on a gallon of gasoline by 12 cents. In the 1970 the government had watched calmly as the price of oil ran from $3 a barrel in 1973 to $39 a barrel in 1979. At no time during the oil gouge did the government threaten, or lift, a military muscle against the Saudis, Iran, Iraq or Kuwait. What was different now?

The biggest losers from the bankers' recycling game, aside from the U.S., were the developing countries. By 1980 their debts came to 30 percent of their collective GNP. The banks then cut the money off. The 27 Latin American countries, at the end of 1989, had a combined foreign debt of $434.6 billion. Since 1982, the Latin American countries have paid creditors, mostly U.S. banks, more than $250 billion. During that time they received about $50 billion in new loans. The oil shocks of the 1970s became, said *The Economist*, "the debt shambles of the 1980s."

The bankers say it is not their mistakes that have caused the trouble. In their view, the world has been inundated by a series of great waves. Impersonal forces, beyond anyone's control, produced inflation, recession, high interest rates, high oil prices, and low commodity prices. In fact, actual, identifiable people took specific actions that had predictable results.

The banks, by any honest accounting, were bust by 1980. Once they were bust, the *New York Times* reports, they had nothing more to lose by betting the depositors' money on ever more risky projects such as highly leveraged stock buy-outs and commercial real estate. During the 1980s, the banks placed a lot of bets. The banks, along with the S&L's and insurance companies, put more than $1 trillion into commercial property development—office space, malls and multi-family projects. What, you might ask, would we have done without that stuff?

The *Times* reports: "Almost 45 percent of the office space ever built in America was constructed during the 1980's." Further, "Fees from new loans would allow them to pay salaries and dividends while they waited for really big payoffs to restore their institutions' solvency." By 1990, it was clear the bets were not going to pay off.

In the late 1980s, the banks pumped $50 billion into stock buy-out loans for highly leveraged transactions—what they called HLTs. Citibank alone carried $7.8 billion of the stuff on its books as of September 30, 1990. The loans paid very large fees and very high interest rates. For example, in 1986, a $535 million loan to buy-out Revco Drugs brought in $20 million in fees. In December 1990 the Revco loans were selling at 60 cents on the dollar. Federated Department Store loans were selling at 45 cents on the dollar.

In summary, the collapse of the big banks is simple enough—they made a lot of loans that could not be collected. Karin Lissakers, in *Banks, Borrowers and the Establishment* (1991), writes: "The dry rot in bank balance sheets began in the LDC loan portfolio that had generated the bulk of big bank profits in the 1970's, then spread to the domestic side as banks tried to compensate by plunging into activities that turned sour even more quickly . . . In 1989, one third of all U.S. money-center bank loans were for real estate."

In 1929-31, a lot of banks collapsed because they had invested heavily in corporate stocks which lost their value. Congress said "Never again," and passed the Glass-Steagall Act of 1933, which barred banks from buying or underwriting corporate stocks and bonds. In 1991, the bankers explained they were bust, not through any fault of their own, but *because of* the Glass-Steagall Act. Why, you may ask, was Glass-Steagall responsible? Well, they had to do something with their money and Glass-Steagall kept them out of stocks and bonds. It had really forced them to make the stupid Third World loans, risky loans on commercial real estate and loans to highly leveraged corporations and people (including millions in unsecured loans to Donald Trump). What choice, the bankers say, did they have?

Treasury Secretary Nicholas Brady, on November 30, 1990, told the Securities Industry Association in Boca Raton, Florida that he agreed with the bankers and that the administration would work for the repeal

of Glass-Steagall. Brady's solution—expanding the investment powers
of busted banks—is exactly what led to the $500 billion S&L loss.

The new internationalist-class bankers insouciantly rolled over
their depositors, pre-Abandonment bankers and the American middle-
class taxpayer.   George Champion, who was chairman of Chase
Manhattan Bank from 1961 to 1969, is a pre-Abandonment banker. He
has a clear sense of the banker's overriding fiduciary duty to his
depositor. In July 1986, he wrote a friend of one of the authors:

> Walter Wriston is a fine man but he and I have never seen eye to eye
> on the handling of funds that are not your own. It seems to me that,
> if you are planning for the future with any degree of wisdom, you must
> study the past if you are going to have the right yardsticks in measuring
> your future program. In lending to these foreign countries, as you well
> know, a large majority of the loans were made to the governments in
> the developing countries or their own entities guaranteed by the govern-
> ment. One of the primary yardsticks for lending is to have reasonable
> assurance that the individual, company or country agrees to limit their
> total borrowings. Insofar as the developing countries are concerned,
> there was obviously no check on the total amounts the countries and
> their companies within the countries were committing themselves to
> repay in the future.
> In the second place, as you well know, there is no way to get a
> bankable commitment that future heads of government will honor past
> commitments. Commercial banking involves a great trust when you
> are lending somebody else's money. Walter has said in the past that
> after all the United States was started by bank loans from Europe but,
> at that time, there were no commercial banks in Europe. These were
> the private bankers that loaned their own funds here on a long term
> basis with an equity position that proved very profitable to them. We
> had, in the 1960s, some economists that said there would never be any
> ups and downs any more and that we didn't have to worry about
> recessions. Unfortunately, too many in the financial world agreed with
> them.

Too many had agreed with them. That's what had happened, and
by the time the bankers were done, the accumulated wealth of the
country—that was needed to run the economy—was gone.

CHAPTER FOUR

The Tax Abandonment

If you ask the common man today what he thinks about taxes he will say they are very high and he doesn't believe he gets anything for them. He is exactly right. The problem is abandonment—the government is pursuing one set of goals and the people another. One result of a government alienating itself from its people is that the people stop believing they are responsible for it. That is what we went through with George III. Taxes, without representation, are exactions. The future of taxation in the U.S. therefor, until the democracy is restored, will be grim. The people will be increasingly unwilling to pay and the government will be increasingly arbitrary and coercive. Also, of course, when a government is bankrupt—i.e. its liabilities are unlimited—the appetite of its taxing system is similarly unlimited—it will try to get all the money the citizen has. When a government's liabilities are infinite no tax system makes any particular sense. No matter how much money it collects, it's not enough.

The history of taxes is the history of a major tool of abandonment working out. The idea behind the original 1913 Income Tax Act was simple and direct—to raise money. It was called "An Act . . . to Provide Revenue for the Government." During the Senate debate, one of the bill's draftsmen said, "the object of this bill is to tax a man's net income . . . it is not to reform men's moral characters, that is not the object at all." The original act was 15 pages long, written in simple English, and taxed income up to $20,000 at 1 percent, income between $20,000 and $50,000 at 2 percent, and topped out at 6 percent on income over $500,000.

The agrarian Populists in the late nineteenth century first originated the idea of an income tax. William Jennings Bryan and his followers did not think of it as a revenue raiser; they thought the income tax was the perfect way to redistribute wealth. Such a tax would allow government to take the profits of the railroads and trusts and let the workers and farmers who produced the wealth end up with some of it.

But Theodore Roosevelt, whose support of the income tax brought the idea into the American mainstream, was not interested in redistribution. What he saw was the fantastic potential of the income tax for raising the revenue the United States needed to take its rightful place on the world stage. Roosevelt needed a powerful revenue base; Great White Fleets could not be financed out of tariffs.

As the years went by, rates went up during war and down in peace time. The money kept rolling in. Our system was the most efficient revenue-raising machine in world history. The public, except for a few tax evaders, voluntarily accepted the system on a simple commonly held theory—we have to pay for the soldiers and the ships and the bombers, this is a fair way of doing it. After paying their taxes, citizens could do what they wanted with what was left. Commerce prospered as capital moved in a free market.

Today, revenue raising is running a distant second to the social engineering and special interest give-aways that have become the main purpose of the Internal Revenue Code. Revenue raising still takes about 15 pages of the code; the remaining 4,000 pages are devoted to influencing personal and economic behavior, and to special-interest handouts. There are no longer any general principles which apply to all citizens equally. Instead, we have a series of treaties between the government and discrete interest groups. The code is a living archeological record of purchased favors. Ring after ring after ring.

The policy which Congress pursues in the revenue code can be capricious, depending, as it does, on Congress' perception of what faults in the people need correction at the moment. In 1981, government decided that our problem was that we didn't save as much as the Japanese, so it increased the return on savings by giving it a tax break—the popular Individual Retirement Account (IRA). In 1986, it decided that saving was not so important after all, and all but eliminated the IRA deduction. The same 1986 act repealed the interest deduction on consumer debt on the theory that repeal would encourage saving which was critically important. Of course, anytime Congress seriously wanted to encourage savings it could follow the Japanese lead and allow individuals to put up to $85,900 into tax-free savings accounts.

The code's capriciousness is matched by its disparate impact on taxpayers. Certain industries, for example, are effectively exempted from taxation by Congress. The House-Senate Joint Tax Committee reported in 1983 that the chemical industry had an effective tax rate of *minus* 1 percent meaning that they ended up with a credit towards future tax years. The construction industry at that time paid 0.7 percent tax on its earnings. As of 1985, General Electric had not paid a dollar in federal corporate income tax for three years, despite earnings of 5 billion dollars during that period. Where did all the money go that G.E. saved by not paying taxes? In November 1989, John W. Welch, Jr., chairman of G.E., announced that G.E. would buy up to $10 billion of its own stock over the next 5 years. Buying its own stock, Welch said, was a better way to generate value for the shareholders than taking a "wild swing" on investing in research for a new technology.

Some recipients of congressional generosity don't seem in need of a handout. For example, taxpayers over 65 years of age are a much favored group. In 1976, the median income for an over 65 married couple was $5,358. By 1986, thanks to drastically increased Social Security benefits, the median income for the same couple was $20,520. As we will see in a moment, the tax system's inverted values have transferred money from the middle class to the rich in the 1986 Tax Reform Act.

From a simple revenue-raising mechanism the tax code has evolved to a system that decides what citizens spend their money on or, in the current phrase, how resources are allocated. The tax code—with no accountability—decides who will be wealthy and who will not. Those who are not to be wealthy will pay most of the taxes. The favored class, on the other hand, can accumulate wealth because they pay less taxes. The people who do pay provide the protection for them and their wealth.

During the 1970s, as social engineering and purchased favors mushroomed, the public became aware of the new ways Congress was using the tax system. The public attitude towards tax cheats changed in a shocking way. Tax evasion, while illegal, became morally acceptable. The unlucky few cheats who are caught and prosecuted are viewed with some sympathy. Maybe not Leona Helmsley, but she was carrying a lot of baggage, and she was very indiscrete when she told her maid: "We don't pay taxes. Only the little people pay taxes."

Taxes are viewed, not as a common obligation, but as a taking by the government. This is an old attitude in Europe, but new in this country. The problem is that the governmental money machine, burdened with so many extraneous functions, is faltering. People today, according to IRS studies, think the tax system is so unfair that 19% of the taxpayers surveyed anonymously admit they are cheating on their tax returns. The underground economy in the U.S. is probably as large as the combined gross national product of France, Italy, and Britain.

In late Mayan society, the taxpaying citizens, when they had had enough, stopped paying their taxes and simply walked off into the jungle. No democracy, however, can stand if its people stop believing in its ideals, or if people don't believe the government faithfully expresses those ideals. To decide not to pay taxes is to opt out of society. As a growing legion of lobbyists go to Congress to get their clients excused from contributions to the common goals of the country, the ordinary people, in large numbers, have just excused themselves. Like the Mayans, they have voted with their feet. Government has lost the working loyalty of too many people, and now the serious question is whether this loyalty can be restored.

Congress, since World War II, has directed the tax system more and more against the middle class. Under traditional income tax theory, an individual is not supposed to be taxed at all until he has earned enough money to provide for the essentials of life—food, shelter, etc. A family of four making the median income is not able to, and should not pay, any income tax. This is known as a "tax threshold." This was the idea behind the personal exemption which was $1,000 in 1939. At $600 in 1948 it was probably fairly accurate. Today, just to adjust for inflation, the personal exemption should be $6,000-$8,000, not the $2,050 it is. The effect is dramatic. As Steve Schlosstein in *End of the American Century*, (1989) points out, in 1948, the median income for a family of four was $3,468. However, because of the personal exemption and standard deduction, only $801—or 23 percent of income—was subject to any tax. Today, the same family had an income of $29,184 of which $20,421—or 70 percent—is subject to tax. As shown in Table 4.1 the 1948 family paid only 6 percent of their income in taxes and social security—today's family pays 19 percent.

It is, of course, preposterous for Congress to claim that a family of 4 earning $29,000 in America today can afford to pay $5,484 in taxes. If you are taking that kind of money from the average American family it raises one question: who are you giving the money *to*?

By 1985, the public was totally cynical and bored as the Administration floated out its tax reform proposals—the first draft was called the "Hindenburg of Tax Reform." The polls showed the public disliked the existing law, but apparently perversely, equally strongly, did not want the law changed. This seemed strange since if you don't like something normally you want it changed. But the polls kept coming back the same way: we really don't like it and we really don't want it changed. The explanation for this puzzling position is simple enough—the public didn't trust the people in charge of changing the law. The public knew it would be worse off when Congress got done. This curious phenomenon posed a political problem: How do you get something passed that the public doesn't want?

President Reagan had a very clear theory on what was wrong with the tax code. As an actor in Hollywood in the 1940s and 1950s, he had seen talented people stop working when they reached the 91 percent top bracket (on incomes over $200,000). When he reached that point, the worker only got to keep 9 cents of a dollar earned, which is not much of an incentive to work. So you would make a couple of pictures and then go to the seashore. Table 4.2 shows the trend of the top bracket since World War II.

Reagan accomplished his goal—he dropped the top rate from 70 percent to 28 percent. That is what he meant by "tax reform." For the middle class, however, there was nothing so dramatic. Rates came down a little but (1) inflation pushed them back into higher brackets; (2) they lost a lot of good middle-class deductions (interest and medical); and (3) they were hit with huge increases in social security taxes. Reagan was definitely right—the high top brackets were wrong. He failed to see that you can have a low top bracket and a miserable code. Which we do.

The Tax Reform Act's supporters, of course, knew exactly what it was going to do from the beginning. The data before the Senate Finance committee projected that the much maligned "Princes of Privilege," a class comprised of 359,000 American taxpayers earning over $200,000 per year, would receive an *average* tax cut of $52,535. It was clear that the proposed bill would raise taxes on 1,797,000 low-income taxpayers (earning between $0 and $10,000) an average of $186. (Many taxpayers who paid at an 11 percent rate would pay 15 percent under the new bill.) It was clear that *one-third* of all Americans earning between $30,000 and $40,000 would get an average *tax increase* of $525, and that *forty percent* of those earning $20,000 to $30,000 would have an average *increase* of $339.

Proponents of the bill, to divert attention from the facts, took a very high moral tone. Senators called it "pure," "sweeping" or "fundamental" reform. One called it a "miracle." Senator Packwood, when he was introducing the bill on the Senate floor, said, "The moment has now arrived." The tax bill was about to be discussed. Senator Packwood said he had a coalition which was only four weeks old. It was a great movement, a crusade that cut across the spectrum, everyone from business to labor. He had the National Association of Manufacturers, the AFL-CIO, Women and Taxes, and Bread for the World. His coalition was growing by the moment, he himself couldn't keep track, they were "coming on daily," they were coming down the aisle now. "All taxpayers will be winners" except for what he called the "Princes of Privilege." He said he had cracked down hard on them.

The media was caught up in the mood of reform and instead of analyzing the bill, raised the moral level even higher. The *New York Times* said, "There's a distant roar when something monumental is about to happen in Washington . . . A roar is rising now; tax reform is thundering down the tracks, unstoppable." If anyone got on the track, say one of those Princes of Privilege, he could look forward to getting squashed. The *Times* went on: "A revolutionary idea had taken hold with such strength that all who would resist it are finally powerless." The nation, the *Times* assured, "will get the benefit." *The New Republic*, led by Michael Kinsley, was another cheerleader.

TABLE 4.1

Comparison - 1948 and 1990
Percentage of Family Income Going to
Federal Taxes and Social Security

	Median Income, Family of 4	Deductions for Personal Exemptions and Standard Deductions	Percentage of Income Subject to Tax	Fed. Tax and Soc. Sec. Paid	Fed. Tax and Soc. Sec. Paid as a % of Income
1948	$ 3,468	$2,667	23%	$ 197	6%
1990	29,184	8,763	70%	$5,484	19%

Schlosstein, *End of the American Century*

TABLE 4.2

Top Income Tax Rate
On Incomes Over $200,000

1941 - 1964	-	91% Bracket
1964 - 1981	-	70%
1981 - 1986	-	50%
1986 - 1991	-	28%
1991 -	-	31-35%

Internal Revenue Acts - 1941 to date

Strangely, tax reform had not become a deeply moral issue till May 1986. Before that, it was anything but. In 1985, in the House, Chairman Rostenkowski, with the ease of a Chicago alderman, made deal after deal to patch together a narrow majority for the bill. The chairman didn't claim that his bill had a particularly high moral tone. His job was to get it passed, and he did, but once you said that you'd said it all.

Over in Senator Packwood's Finance Committee things quickly went from bad to worse. By April 25, 1986, tax reform had collapsed in a frenzy of special interest lobbying. Fairness and simplicity lay all over the floor of the Senate committee. The proposed bill had been transformed into a mess of special interest handouts. Everyone agreed the bill was dead. It was, in fact, a national embarrassment.

But, by May 6, when the same Senate Finance Committee voted out (20-0) a revised proposal, tax reform was on its way to the greatest comeback since Shoeless Joe Hardy joined the Washington Senators in *Damn Yankees*. Senator Packwood said he had taken reform "from immovable to unstoppable in 24 hours." The rush to pass the bill was astounding. The Senate, which didn't see the 1,500 page bill until May 31, passed it by a 97-3 vote on June 24.

When the bill passed the Senate, the president pronounced, "The score is Taxpayers 1, Special Interests 0." The bill was described countless times in the nation's press as "lowering taxes" or "lowering tax rates." The impression intended by the public statements about the new bill was that people would now pay less taxes. The *New York Times* reported that the bill was a "sharp shift in tax policy," and that "the tax system would play less of a role in shaping society and its economic foundations" by "letting most taxpayers retain—and spend—more of their income." The incessant theme was less tax, less government, less influence for the special interests, and more fairness.

The odd thing was that, at the time, the public didn't believe any of it. Not the promised cuts, and not the claimed fairness. Not Senator Packwood, not his coalition of special interests, not the president and not the media. A *New York Times*/CBS poll—taken around the time the bill steamrolled through the Senate—could not find a single demographic group which thought the legislation would produce a fairer tax system. Despite two months of heavy news coverage reporting that the new law would cut all taxpayers' bills, the poll found only *11 percent* of the people believed they would pay lower taxes. *Thirty-six percent* thought it would *increase* their taxes and 33 percent said it would make no difference, it would be a wash. The bill did even worse among those who said they had read a lot about it—*50 percent* of those thought it would *increase* their taxes.

The public, clearly, could care less about the revolutionary winds sweeping out of Washington. That was not surprising. The public had never asked for tax reform. The president tried very hard to stir up some interest. He called tax reform his number one domestic priority, but his swing through the country was cut short by overwhelming public indifference. The middle class was, and is, deeply cynical about tax reform. They know, after all the moral rhetoric, they will end up with the bill. They always do. *Any tax bill is going to soak the middle class because that's where the money is.* The only way to help the middle class is to cut the need for taxes by cutting government spending.

The most recent figures provided by the Internal Revenue Service are based on 1984 returns and are set out in Table 4.3. The figures show:

(1)   The lower middle class ($19,000-40,000) pays one-third of all tax collections.

(2)   Adding in the middle middle class ($40,000-75,000) the group pays 63 percent of all collections.

(3)   Adding in the upper middle class ($75,000-150,000) the group pays 75 percent of all collections.

Would the new bill change that in any substantial way? The middle class didn't think so.

The reason they didn't think so ran back a long time. In 1939 only 1 American in 33 paid *any* federal income tax. Those who did pay didn't pay much. A doctor earning $4,229 a year—which was what the average doctor earned—with a wife and 2 children, paid $25 in federal income tax. A highly successful businessman earning $16,000 paid less than $1,000. Overall, individual income tax payments were about 1.5

percent of total personal income, i.e., on average, taxpayers paid $1.50 tax on $100 of income.

In 1939, as noted, the income tax really only reached pretty well-off people—only 1 in 33 Americans. A "tax and spend" policy in that kind of society means you are taxing the wealthy to give benefits to the many. Today, about 1 in 2 Americans pay income tax. The 1987 figures show 128 million taxpayers out of a population of 244 million. So half the people you see walking around the streets, including little toddlers, are paying some income tax. In this kind of society, the "tax and spend" rules are reversed. Now you are taxing the general population for the benefit of the few, those special interests which can control government spigots. Obviously, the benefits do not go back to the taxpayers who fund them. It would be a waste of everyone's time to tax the working middle class and then return the money to them. So that does not happen, the money returns above them and below them.

In the early 1940s, taxes were sharply increased to support the war. By 1944 income tax payments were up to 10 percent of personal income. After 1944, taxes never really go up or down. All during the postwar years, despite endless talk of tax cuts and tax hikes, the figure runs along pretty close to 10 percent. In 1989, it was 10.6 percent. Using taxable income, rather than personal income as the measure, the figure runs along pretty close to 20 percent. In 1948, income taxes were 20.6 percent of taxable income; in 1985 they were 21.0 percent. Obviously, the endless talk about taxes, and their "fairness," is intended to shift the tax burden from a favored group to an unfavored one. It has practically nothing to do with the overall burden the income tax imposes on Americans. Tax reform is a non-starter with the people because the citizen understands two facts: (1) every tax law is going to soak the middle class and (2) income tax payments, when the dust settles, will be 10 percent of personal income and 20 percent of taxable income.

Senator Bill Bradley of New Jersey originally thought the trouble was that the public just didn't understand the 1986 law. Once they understood it, they'd like it. But the more you knew, the more fantastic it became. The Senate, to dredge up some money to pay for the $52,535 tax cuts for those earning over $200,000, passed the so-called "Kiddy Tax." This peculiar proposal denied the legal existence of children under 14 years old. It taxed income from assets given by a

parent to a child under 14 at the parents' rate. Senator Long of
Louisiana explained that America's parents are not doing a good job of
raising their children: "These young people who come into possession
of this money when they are teenagers often are the worst spoiled brats
on God's green earth. The less we encourage that the better off they are
and the country, too."

TABLE 4.3
1984

*Taxes Collected
By Income Level*

Income Reported On Return	Percent Of Tax Collections
Under $19,000	10%
$19,000 - $40,000	33%
$40,000 - $75,000	30%
$75,000 - $150,000	12%
Above $150,000	15%
	100%

Internal Revenue Service, Statistics of Income

The children were also the target of another Senate provision. The
bill required every child aged 5 or over to obtain a Social Security
number if the parent claimed the child as a dependent. The Senators
claimed this would prevent divorced parents from each claiming a child
as a dependent, but this seemed to most to be too trivial a problem to
bring on such a massive Big Brother solution. More likely, requiring

the little children to sign up for Social Security is part of Senator Long's campaign to instill some responsibility in them.[8]

The "reform bill" was the first in history to use *reverse progressivity*. That is, the more money an individual makes, the lower the rate he pays. Because of complicated provisions "phasing out" the personal exemption and the benefits of the 15 percent rate, the tax rate was 15 percent to $30,950, 28 percent up to $74,850, 33 percent between $74,850 and $155,320, and back down to 28 percent for everything above $155,320 (see Table 4.4 below). When the Social Security tax is considered, the system's regressivity became vicious. (See discussion below under the Social Security Sting.)

The Senate's insouciance in throwing out the progressive system was stunning. Progressivity, of course, has been characteristic of the system from its beginning in 1913. In 1906, Theodore Roosevelt advocated the graduated income tax explaining: "The man of great wealth owes a peculiar obligation to the state, because he derives special advantages" from its existence. He should "recognize this obligation in the way he leads his daily life and in the way he earns and spends his money, but it should also be recognized in the way in which he pays for the protection the State gives him." In this, Roosevelt was restating what John Locke had said in 1690. Locke pointed out the link between taxes and the "consent of the people." In his essay *Concerning The True Original, Extent and End of Civil Government*, he wrote:

> 'Tis true, governments cannot be supported without great charge, and 'tis fit everyone who enjoys his share of the protection should pay out of his estate his proportion for the maintenance of it. But still it must be with his own consent, i.e., the consent of the majority, giving it either by themselves or their representatives chosen by them; for if anyone shall claim a power to lay and levy taxes on the people by his own authority, and without such consent of the people, he thereby invades the fundamental law of property, and subverts the end of

---

[8]Forcing parents to get I.D. numbers for babies is now a favorite idea of Congress. In 1988 the age was dropped from 5 to 2. The Budget Deal of 1990 (see below) dropped the age from 2 to 1. Does Congress think their constituents like getting I.D. numbers for tiny babies? Do they think their constituents believe it is necessary or in the national interest?

government. For what property have I in that which another may by right take when he pleases himself?

But under the 1986 act, the "man of great wealth" paid a lower rate than those who earned less. The upper middle class paid at a higher rate of tax than Michael Milken on his 1987 income of $550 million. Americans had been told the act had a top rate of 28 percent. But many upper middle class Americans were surprised to find out when they went to fill out their returns that they were paying at 33 percent while Milken was enjoying the 28 percent rate. They were the "Bubble People." The Bubble People, according to Kevin Phillips, make up 20 percent of American households. Under the 1986 act, the "Bubble" for a married couple started at $74,850 and ended at $155,320, as shown in Table 4.4.

For a single person the "Bubble" started at $47,650 and ended at $97,620. Once you got "through the Bubble" you went back to paying 28 percent. Congress had singled out the upper middle class, our most productive citizens, to pay the highest rate of tax. The Bubble People were also heavily hit by the Social Security tax.

Congress, to get at the hated Bubble People, had accomplished a historic first it had reversed the system's progressivity so that a higher income person paid a 28% rate while a lower income person paid at 33%. The Bubble People, as they gradually found out what Congress had done to them, began to feel abandoned.

At times the misrepresentations used to promote the bill ran into one another. One of the very biggest was "the Rich Don't Pay Anything Anyway." Senator Packwood explained that the existing system's high rates on high income were an *illusion* because the wealthy all hide in tax shelters. In fact, the Senator said, his bill was really *more* progressive than the existing system.

However, there was no question the Packwood bill was generous to the rich—those earning more than $200,000, one-half of one percent of taxpayers (1984 figures), would receive 16 percent of the bill's benefits. Why should we be so generous to people who already aren't paying anything? When Senator Mitchell of Maine tried to raise the top rate on the rich Packwood said that would be unfair. Senator Packwood, momentarily forgetful of the earlier "Rich Don't Pay Anything Anyway" theory, said the rich are heavily burdened now, in fact, the "Rich Pay

Too Much." "What percent of the tax do they pay now? . . . I did not want to leave the impression that somehow, they were not paying income taxes." The truth, of course, does not support either of Packwood's propositions—some of whom he would call rich get away with murder but most contribute substantially. Taxpayers earning over $100,000, 1.8 percent of taxpayers (1984 figures), pay about 20 percent of total tax collections.

TABLE 4.4

Tax Rates

TAXABLE INCOME			TAX RATE
$0	-	$30,950	15%
$30,950	-	$74,850	28%
$74,850	-	$155,320	33%
Above	-	$155,320	28%

1986 Code

Since the act was supposed to be "revenue neutral," Senator Packwood had to increase taxes by as much as he cut them making the bill a zero sum game for taxpayers. The Senator said he got the money to cut the rates by increasing taxes by $150 billion over the next 5 years. He said he got $100 billion from increasing taxes on corporations. (The middle-class consumer can expect to pay that since business will surely pass along the higher operating costs if it possibly can). Then he got another $50 billion from what he called "tightening loopholes" on individuals. The $150 billion was raised mostly from corporations for a specific political reason. The administration knew that every poll ever taken shows the public does not support tax reform. There is simply no constituency for it; the public has been burned too often. The administration thought it could sell tax reform if it could tell people the major cost was going to be borne by someone else—the corporations.

This clever idea fooled no one; the polls still showed the same disapproval, the people did not want tax reform for free.

The 1986 act took dead aim on the middle class. The promised across-the-board tax reduction was in fact a tax increase for them. Consider a family of four with $30,000 in wage income, $200 in interest income and $500 in dividends. They formerly took deductions of $2,250 for an Individual Retirement Account, $6,000 in mortgage interest, $3,000 in interest on a car loan, $1,700 in state and local income and property taxes and $300 in sales tax, and paid tax of $1,843. Their tax bill jumped to $2,220 under the 1986 law, a startling 21 percent tax increase.

A typical urban couple with no children and a combined income of $60,000 in salary and $1,000 in interest income paid 39 percent more than under previous law. Assume they had deductions of $4,000 on an IRA, $13,000 in mortgage interest, $5,000 in interest on cars and credit cards, $4,109 in state and local income and property tax, $426 in sales tax and $1,000 in charitable contributions. Their tax bill of $5,127 jumped to $7,141 under the 1986 law.

Under the 1986 act, basic middle-class deductions—including interest on car loans, credit cards and education loans—were abolished or weakened. A wealthy person could deduct all the interest on two $500,000 homes, but a middle-class person could not deduct the interest on a loan to put his children through college. Also abolished was the "two-earner marital deduction," most IRAs, the state and local sales tax deduction and the lower rate for capital gains. The lower capital gains tax, to some extent, reduced the impact of inflation on taxpayers. A fair tax system, of course, would not tax inflationary gains at all. Assume a taxpayer buys land in 1970 for $10,000 and sells it in 1991 for $40,000. The Code now taxes him on a $30,000 "gain" which is attributable solely to inflation. This is obviously improper because a rise in price due to inflation is not a gain to the taxpayer; he is just holding even. For the government to profit from the fact that it did not keep the money honest is an abandonment.

Other deductions, such as home interest and state and local taxes, were retained but became far less valuable. For example, a family in the 50 percent bracket under prior law paying $20,000 in mortgage interest saved $10,000 in taxes and was only out of pocket $10,000.

Under the 1986 law, the family will save $5,400 in taxes and be out of pocket $14,600—an increase in out-of-pocket cost of 46 percent. The value of homes declined to reflect the increase in after-tax cost. The home, of course, is the basic middle-class asset.

Middle-class families earning $30,000 to $60,000 were surprised to learn that Congress considers them "high income." The act subjects them to its highest tax rate. "High income," according to the 1986 act, starts at $30,950 for married taxpayers and $18,550 for singles. The Joint Committee on Taxation says: "Over 80 percent of all taxpayers will have a tax rate no higher than 15 percent." Assuming that's true the 1986 law benefits the taxpayer at the very bottom, and a thin upper crust of the super rich at the top. In between is the squeezed middle, once more.

What Congress is calling high income is, of course, bedrock middle-class America. Because of inflation, a person making $12,000 in 1972 in 1986 made $30,000; a person making $15,000 in 1972 in 1986 made $37,300 and a person making $22,000 in 1972 in 1986 made $54,758. The Internal Revenue Services reports that tax returns showing more than $25,000 of income grew from 3.5 million in 1972 to 27 million in 1982—a stunning increase of 771 percent.

As the 1986 law was put into operation, new victims kept floating up to the surface: the disabled, the unemployed. Some are members of small groups like professional entertainers. Only about 15 percent of entertainers are successful enough to make their living from performing. The other 85 percent work at part time jobs to earn money to pay for acting and voice lessons, photographs and resumes. They must also pay union dues and, when they get a job, pay a 10 percent commission to an agent. These professional expenses had always been deductible since the tax is supposed to be on *net* income not *gross* income. The act disallowed all these deductions.

Senator Packwood had been politically clever in buying support for his bill. He said he and his coalition had cracked down on the special interests, the "Princes of Privilege." In fact, the Princes did not slink off to their posh clubs after the 1986 tax act took effect. The steel companies were very well taken care of—they received $500 million in checks from the Treasury in 1987 for part of their "unused investment tax credits." "I want," Senator Packwood said, "to get the money to these distressed companies as soon as possible because they need it now." Oil and gas tax shelters were not touched. A lot of other Princes were hiding out in a complex set of "transitional" rules attached to the bill.

These transitional rules were the core of the Reagan tax policy in practice. These rules created 174 special exceptions for corporations including Unocal, Phillips Petroleum, Texaco, Pennzoil, General Motors, Chrysler, Goldman Sachs, Manville, General Mills, Walt Disney, Pan Am, Northwest Airlines, Delta, Control Data, Multimedia and Metromedia. A few foreign Princes rolled up to the trough and got their own transitional rules, including Mitsubishi and Toyota. In 1988, Don Barlett and Jim Steele of the *Philadelphia Inquirer* won a Pulitzer Prize for their brilliant, deeply detailed, study reporting exactly who benefited from these specially tailored private tax laws and how they came to get their favors.

The transitional rules, of course, were the way Senator Packwood paid for support. His coalition included 31 senators who agreed before the bill was introduced to oppose any amendment to it. It is easy to match the 31 Senators with the 174 transitional rules to see what each received, an average of 5.6 rules per senator. One senator, Pete Wilson of California, signed on with the group to get a transitional rule for Unocal, a California company. Then he wandered off to vote in favor of a pro-IRA amendment. The coalition quickly disciplined him. The next day, when the Unocal rule was stricken from the bill, Wilson called it "retaliation." Senator Packwood said it was not retaliation, but that after he had thought about it, the Unocal rule was not a good transitional rule after all. A Packwood aide told the *Washington Post*: "We didn't get any help from the Senator from California. Why should the coalition work for him?"

After that show of power, Senator Packwood just had to threaten. When Senator Sarbanes of Maryland forgot he was a member of the group and started asking embarrassing questions, Senator Packwood issued a cold warning: "You make me feel very bad now because at your request we put in the Owings Mill Town Center, Harbor Place and the Baltimore Stadium in the transition rules." For a morally uplifting movement, it could, at times, get kind of sordid.

Similarly, over in the House, Chairman Rostenkowski was also buying support with transitional rules. The 36 members of the Ways and Means Committee were heavily lobbied by applicants and they made their requests to Chairman Rostenkowski. Each request was put on its own 3 x 5 card. Requests, of course, vastly exceeded the available give-away. Near the end, Chairman Rostenkowski and Senator Packwood held a last private meeting to decide who was going to get what. The Ways and Means members hung around in the hall outside. After awhile, the meeting broke up and Chairman Rostenkowski came out with a stack of 3 x 5 cards in his hand. These were the winners, the transitional rules that were going to be law. The chairman, as the members crowded around, handed out the winning cards to the member who had requested it: Joe, you get 2, Harry 1 and so on. One Ways and Means member, recalling the 3 x 5 card in the hallway scene, said: "I had never realized, till that moment, the real nature of power."

The biggest obstacle to the passage of the bill was, of course, the possibility that someone would look at the numbers and figure out that the middle-class taxpayer was in for it. Someone could take random, typical examples of a middle-class family, and compute exactly what the new reform act would do to it. The coalition always talked in "averages" and "percentages." Senator Packwood said his bill would cut taxes of the "average" American earning $20,000 to $40,000 by 6.6 percent. The coalition resisted and overcame any senator who wanted to talk about facts and individual cases. Packwood brushed off individual cases saying they were "atypical" and you couldn't design a system to take care of "atypical" cases.

Senator Levin, Democrat of Michigan, one of the only members of the Senate to be inquisitive and outspoken about the bill, requested figures to get behind the averages. *How many* taxpayers would have their taxes increased, *how many* decreased, and by *how much*? Packwood replied: "The Joint Committee does not think they have valid and sufficient data to tell you within an income class, $10,000 to $20,000, $20,000 to $30,000, even on average, how many people will have their taxes go up or go down." If that was true how were the cited averages figured? How could anyone know what was "atypical"?

Senator Levin had good reason to be suspicious, as the examples of typical taxpayers discussed above show. Senator Levin persisted, and asked the U.S. Treasury what they had determined the bill would do. Senator Levin received the Treasury's reluctant response on June 10. Then, for the first time, he learned about the 359,000 taxpayers earning over $200,000 who were going to get an average tax cut of $52,535. He discovered the very large numbers of middle-class taxpayers, almost 40 percent of those earning $20,000 to $40,000, who were not getting the promised cut, but were getting a large tax increase. The Treasury's figures showed the bill would *raise taxes for 25 million taxpayers*, and would leave the taxes of *33 million more unchanged*. The bill, in short, had no legitimacy; it was based on illusory and false statements. Senator Levin had found out the Emperor had no clothes.

About this time one of the authors ran into a draftsman of the bill in the Charlotte Airport:

AUTHOR: People are being told this bill will cut their taxes but when they make out their tax returns in April we know there won't be a cut. Aren't you afraid of a backlash?

DRAFTSMAN: No, we'll say a lot of the provisions are transitional and you have to let them settle down before you see the impact.

AUTHOR: Well it will only get worse as it settles down.

DRAFTSMAN: Yes, but time is passing, other things come up.

AUTHOR: What about the upper middle-income Bubble People who have been told the top rate is 28 percent but will find, when they make out their returns, that their top rate is 33 percent?

DRAFTSMAN: There are so many variables from tax year to tax year, why should they blame us if their taxes go up a little?

AUTHOR: Because you told them their taxes were going to go *down* and it's not that hard to figure out.

DRAFTSMAN: Then we'll go to Plan B.

AUTHOR: What's Plan B?

DRAFTSMAN: Whatever we think up next.

For **Plan B**, see Budget Deal of 1990 below.

The bill rolled on. It was a joke and no reasonable person could possibly support it but it rolled on. In the frenzy for quick passage, the bill's supporters couldn't even count right. Very late in the day, on July 24, Senator Packwood discovered his bill was short $21 billion. He had, of course, promised the public over and over that the bill was "revenue neutral" but it wasn't. The next day he "found" $25 billion by making some changes in retirement plans and the deductibility of home mortgage interest, but it was like the 13th chime of the clock. It was not only discordant in itself, but it made you wonder about the other 12.

What was behind it? That was the mystery of this strange bill, this unstoppable bill, which whizzed through the Senate. The bill was unread, it had no intellectual coherence, and it had no measurable public support, but it barrelled along. And, of course, with the economy dead in the water, it was a crazy time to begin a basic reconstruction of the tax system. Washington insiders said they had never seen a bill of such complexity, touching every transaction in the country, passed in such a frenzy.

What could explain the now or never rush? The bill took away deductions from taxpayers to pay for high income benefits. Taxpayers were not eager for that. There might have been some popular support for the anti-tax shelter provisions, but there definitely was no popular demand for removal or reduction of the medical deduction, consumer interest, the IRA, the two-earner deduction, the charitable contribution deduction, the sales tax deduction or changing the rate on capital gains. Experts can argue the desirability of these provisions but there was no public clamor for their elimination. Quite the opposite.

You had to figure out the real intent of the bill and the reason behind the frenzy. Notice who benefits and how much they benefit. For most of those earning more than $200,000 the tax cuts are beyond the dreams of greed. Senator Packwood, and the other friends of the bill, knew it had to be passed before the public found out what was in it. The truth, if it had a chance, would come out. Senator Long said "We'll be talking behind closed doors and by the time the lobbyists find out what it is we're trying to do, it'll be too late." It wasn't the "lobbyists" he was worried about—they were all hanging around the hallways anyway.

The act was designed simply to increase the percentage of national income received by the highest income group. The top one-half of one percent (.5)—those earning more than $200,000—got 16 percent of the bill's benefits. The 1986 law aggravated what was already a disastrous trend in the country—the rich are getting richer, the poor poorer, and the middle class is sinking.

The act was also designed to reinforce the new dominance of the "service" economy—fast food, retail, trading and media—over the country's traditional manufacturing economy. The code, until 1986, had always provided incentives to manufacturing and investment in productive assets; for example, accelerated depreciation (1954) and the investment tax credit (1962). Also, since 1913, the code has taxed capital gains at a lower rate than other earnings. The capital gain preference encouraged investment rather than consumption. The 1986 act swept away the traditional manufacturing incentives. The act was premised on a theory known as tax neutrality, which said all the incentives are unfair and that every dollar earned, no matter how it is earned, should be taxed at the same rate. If government is neutral, the theory goes, money will flow to the activity with the highest return. That's true but not very helpful—a dollar invested in a productive asset is more important to the country than a dollar invested to finance the takeover of RJR-Nabisco. Manufacturing investment leads to new jobs and new income.

The act's complexity quickly became a public joke. The Reagan administration tripled not only the national debt but also the number of pages in the Internal Revenue Code. *Money* magazine, in 1988, sent 50 professional tax preparers a hypothetical case of a family (3 children) making $100,000 with fairly normal deductions. What tax, *Money* asked, should the family pay? *Money*, as you have probably guessed, received 50 different answers. Worse, the answers were wildly different ranging from $7,202 to $11,881. *Money* repeated the test each year for the next three years to see if the problem was that the experts were initially unfamiliar with the 1986 law. But, instead of improving as the years passed, the answers became more divergent. Results of the Fourth Annual test, reported in March 1991, showed that only one expert got the correct answer—$16,786 in taxes due on an income of $200,000.

The other 48 contestants reported a tax due ranging from $6,807 to $73,247.

In June 1991, the IRS reported that tax compliance by small business dropped sharply in the 1980s. IRS Commissioner Fred Goldberg told Congress that most of the noncompliance was unintentional: "Much of it is due to the complexity of the tax laws." The inordinate complexity of the Code is, of course, a terrible burden on economic activity in the country. The 1986 act, coming along during the country's experiment with non-democratic government had pushed the system over the cliff.

In the fall of 1990, Bill Bradley, whom the *New York Times* described as the "architect of the Tax Reform Act of 1986," was seeking re-election to a third term. His opponent was a previously unknown former member of the State Public Utility Commission. The national Republican party, thinking Bradley would win easily, gave very little support to their candidate.

During the campaign, Bradley was, the *Times* reports, "strangely silent" about the very issue that brought him fame. Bradley hoped his "low profile" and "muted voice" on taxes would help the people forget his part in passing the 1986 Act. He explained to the *Times* that "he had chosen not to include tax reform in his television commercials because the topic was too complex to explain quickly." To prove his point about how complex things are he wrote an article for the *Wall Street Journal* defending the Bubble. It really wasn't unfair, he wrote, once you understood it. Back in May, Bradley had written a "Dear Colleague" letter enclosing a "Don't Pop the Bubble" article from the *Wall Street Journal*. Bradley explained:

> Unfortunately, many people believe—incorrectly—that taxpayers subject to the 33% rate are being treated unfairly compared to higher income taxpayers whose top marginal rate is 28%.

The enclosed article, Bradley said, would explain this "complex" subject. Unfortunately the issue was only complex to Bradley. The Bubble people—20 percent of American households—all believed that 33 percent was a higher rate than 28 percent, and they thought that was unfair.

"Bill is in a delicate position," said Michael McCurry, a former officer of the Democratic National Committee: "Emotionally and intellectually, he has invested himself in tax reform and tax simplification. But most people are saying: 'My taxes didn't get reformed. My taxes didn't get simpler.'" The New Jersey situation was aggravated by Governor Florio's $2.8 billion tax increase tied to a new socially-engineered school refinancing law.

Bradley was reelected by a margin of 55,180 votes out of 1.9 million cast. The next day, Bradley said he had detected the voter fury over taxes about a week before the election but it was too late to do anything about it. Bradley said, "I got the message; I got the message."

The current Income Tax Code is an embarrassment. An income tax can be a fair tax but because of the inherent complexity of determining net income, the code is vulnerable to special interest manipulation. It is easy to hide the handout. The country's 25-year experiment with non-democratic government turned the code into a maze of special interest handouts and arbitrary rules.

The tax policy of a nation reflects what a nation is about. The tax system reflects the society, and a society with an idea of what it is trying to do will have a pretty fair tax system. A society, like the late Mayan civilization, that has lost its way, should just get used to watching the remaining taxpayers walk off into the jungle.

CHAPTER FIVE

Social Security - The Sting

Quick history of maximum annual payroll tax paid by employee:

1960	-	144.00
1975	-	824.00
1987	-	3,131.00
1988	-	3,379.00
1989	-	3,604.00
1990	-	3,924.00
1991	-	5,123.00

In 1991 a worker earning $20,000 paid $3,060 in Social Security taxes counting both his and his employer's share. That is a very big tax and certainly more than the worker pays in income taxes. The Social Security tax is abandonment government's favorite since it is the closest thing we have to a Stealth tax. Its advantages are (1) it reaches all the way down to first dollar of wages paid—there are no exemptions; (2) there are no refunds because the tax is on gross wages and (3) there is no annual accounting, like an income tax return, which will recall the painful matter to the taxpayer's mind. People have a much clearer idea of what they pay in income tax than in social security tax. A government which has lost the people's trust has to rely on the most automatic and hidden tax.

Since 1944, as discussed above, income tax payments have consistently run around 10 percent of total personal income for all taxpayers combined. In 1989 the figure was 10.6 percent. Social Security taxes, by contrast, have shot through the roof. From 1950 to 1955 Social Security taxes averaged 2.9 percent of personal income; in 1985-1990 Social Security taxes averaged 9.4 percent of personal income. For the middle class, the Social Security tax went from being a minor irritant to a major hit.

It is also increasingly clear that the "Social Security" tax is mislabeled; there is no earmarking, no trust fund; the tax is simply a payroll tax for the general purposes of the government. Calling it a "Social Security" tax, as if it were earmarked for a trust fund, is a fraud on the public. In fact, the money taken from the worker's paycheck under the heading "FICA" is just part of government's general revenues which is used to pay interest on the national debt, increased salaries to congressman and so on. Since World War II, as shown in Table 5.1, government has reduced individual and corporate income taxes and greatly increased the "Social Security" payroll tax.

Between 1948 and 1990, open and visible taxes (income and excise) dropped from 94 percent of revenues to 64 percent while the hidden mislabeled payroll tax ran from 5.9 percent to 36.8 percent. At 1991 rates, a working couple, each earning $53,400, will pay, counting both the employee and employer share, a stunning $16,340 in "Social Security" tax. For 1992 the maximum earnings subject to tax increases from $53,400 to $55,500. Each year the wage base increases automatically by a cost of living adjustment. No congressional action is needed.

The centerpiece of the Reagan administration abandonment of the middle class was the Social Security "reform" of 1983. The evening news told the public the changes were proposed by a blue-ribbon commission headed by Dr. Alan Greenspan to insure the fiscal integrity of the system.

Until then the system was pay-as-you-go. In 1940, five years after the system was started, there were 159 workers paying in for every beneficiary; in 1950 the ratio was 16 to 1—a ratio which was probably financially sustainable. However, by 1988, the ratio had fallen to 3.2 workers paying in for each beneficiary, and the projected figure for 2010 is 2 to 1. The drastically changed ratio of retirees to taxpaying workers is a built in time bomb for the system.

In the 1970s and 1980s, congress greatly increased the problem by voting large benefit increases far outstripping the cost of living. Since 1975, Congress has pushed benefits up over 300%. In 1975 total pay-outs by the system were $58.5 billion, in 1987 they were $186.6

billion. The number of beneficiaries, on the other hand only increased about 20 percent (1975—32.1 million to 38.6 million in 1988). The maximum annual contribution paid by an employee roared from $824.85 in 1975 to $3,924.45 in 1990—almost a 500% increase. Inflation, as measured by the Consumer Price Index, about doubled during that time.

TABLE 5.1

Government Revenues

	Individual & Corporate Income Tax	"Social Security" Payroll Tax	Estate & Gift & Excise Tax	Total
1948	73.4%	5.9%	20.6%	100%
1965	68.5%	15.6%	15.9%	100%
1975	64.2%	27.5%	8.3%	100%
1984	59.7%	33.1%	7.3%	100%
1990	56.7%	36.8%	6.6%	100%

The 1983 problem, the Greenspan Commmission said, was that the baby boomers (Americans born between 1946 and 1964) were moving through the country's population like a pig through a python. There was not much ahead of the pig and not much behind: The not much behind—(post-1964 births) meant that, in 2010, when the baby boomers start hitting retirement, there will not be much of a base to support them, about 2 workers to every beneficiary. That, so the story went, would mean an outlandish tax on the workers. The workers would refuse to pay, outvote the retirees, and the system would collapse. That, of course, might not be so terrible. In a democracy, when people are taxed for something that has become too expensive, they are supposed to be able to vote to cut it out.

So, the fear of democracy aside, there was no need for the Great Rescue of 1983. The real point of Senator Moynihan's recent proposal is that there never was a 1983 problem. Also there was something familiar about this. Not that long ago we had heard that the Social Security system was in a "crisis" and needed to be "saved" by a huge tax increase. It was President Carter who in 1977 told us he had rescued the collapsing system and that a tax increase he had just signed "would guarantee that from 1980 to 2030 Social Security funds will be sound." How many times were we supposed to save this thing?

President Reagan, in 1981, to save a little bit of money for the recently "guaranteed" system, struck benefits for the children of dead workers who were attending college. The children had previously been eligible for the Social Security "student benefit"—a small survivors benefit until they were 22 if they were attending college. While the benefit was small it might have been enough, together with the widow's contribution and the child's earnings, to keep the child in college. After the Reagan cost-saving law, all benefits were cut off at 19. This was a particularly nasty shot at an unrepresented and defenseless group—the children of dead workers who were aspiring to the middle class.

Congress gave five reasons for abandoning the fatherless children. (S. Rep. No. 97-139, 97th Cong. 1st Sess. (1981)). Said the Report: (1) the student is "not required to show" that he was pursuing a degree; (2) the student is "not required to show" that "his academic performance has been satisfactory"; and (3) the student got the benefit in the summer when he might be working instead of going to school. How any of the three got to be the government's business is lost on the authors but let's say we comply with all three, then can we have the benefit? Absolutely not. The benefit does not (4) "take into account the amount of income which may be available to the student." The child might have a trust fund and not need the money. Finally the benefit does not (5) "reflect the actual expenses incurred by the student." The child might be living on air and pocketing a lot of extra money. Congress, in short, applied a standard to the students that applied to no one else in the system. David Rockefeller gets his Social Security check even if he has some outside income. Congress added that someone else might help the students—"State, local and private resources would also be available to assist these students." That is possible, someone else might help them, or they might win the lottery. Or someone else might not help them. What Congress did to the children was shameful but it was only a prelude.

There were limits to how much you could save off of the children, so President Reagan, in December 1981, appointed the National Commission on Social Security Reforms directing it to "identify problems that may threaten the long-term solvency" of the Social Security fund. Dr. Alan Greenspan, the president of the economic consulting firm Townsend-Greenspan & Co., Inc., was appointed chairman. The commission had 15 members, including 4 Senators and 3 Representatives. The point of appointing a commission, of course, was that everyone knew a huge tax increase was coming and both the president and Congress wanted to be able to lay blame on the commission.

The commission reported to the President and Congress on January 20, 1983. The commission's final report noted it had been unable to hold any public hearings "because of the brevity of the time in which [it had] to complete its work." Chairman Greenspan reported that things had not gone well since President Carter and the Congress "guaranteed" the solvency of the system in 1977. In fact, it was short $1.6 trillion (the 1983 discounted value of the 75-year deficit). Chairman Greenspan testified to the Senate Finance Committee:

> The 75-year deficit to be addressed and eliminated is judged by the Commission to be 1.8 percent of taxable payroll. [$1.6 trillion] We recognized, as a commission, that making judgments about the size of the deficit over such an extended period of time is subject to a rather substantial margin of error. Nonetheless, I suspect that most, if not all, of us concur that the probability that the deficit could in fact be zero and, hence, need not be addressed is exceptionally small.
> Hence, the commission agreed to a set of recommendations which would eliminate a deficit amounting to 1.8 percent of taxable payrolls through 2056.

A bill based on the Greenspan Commission's recommendations breezed through the Congress. On April 20, 1983, congressional leaders met with the president on the South Lawn of the White House for the signing of the bill into law. The president spoke first. The bill was "landmark legislation." It demonstrated our "ironclad commitment to social security." It also showed "that our system can still work." Just a few months ago, there was "legitimate alarm that Social Security would soon run out of money." In "the eleventh hour, a distinguished bipartisan commission—began to find a solution." Political leaders of "both parties set aside their passions and joined in that search." Now, before us, ready to be signed into law, was this "monument to the spirit of compassion and commitment that unites us as a people."

Americans of middle age, the president concluded "need no longer worry whether their career long investment will pay off. *These amendments guarantee it.*" (emphasis added) Maybe, if the president had left it at "ironclad commitment", someone would have believed it, but by bringing out the old Carter "guarantee" he had pushed credibility over the edge. Current polls consistently find that about *60 percent* of the people don't think Social Security will pay them *anything* when they reach retirement.

The congressional leaders joined the president in praise of the bill. Speaker O'Neill thought "this is indeed a happy day." He agreed it showed "as the president said, the system does work." Senate Leader Howard Baker was in a more philosophical mood; it was a little noticed but most important part of the "civility of American government that on occasion we rise above politics." We address "on a bipartisan basis" the great challenges facing the Republic. Sometimes its been an issue of war and peace, sometimes on the "rights and opportunities of minorities" and "once on the salvation of the Union itself." Senator Baker seems to think the Civil War was ironed out, "on a bipartisan basis," in a conference committee. Anyway, Senator Baker commended all involved,

> on a successful conclusion of another chapter in the real greatness of the American political system; that is, the subordination of our own particular ambition in favor of the greater good.

The one thing the leaders said that was true was that it was a bipartisan job. That was the pure 100 percent truth. The sting to get $250 billion more in taxes each year out of the middle class cut across party lines.

Greenspan's "rescue" scheme, called for monumental increases in Social Security taxes. Table 5.2 shows the increase in Social Security taxes collected by the "rescue." So the real purpose of the Social Security "rescue" gradually became clear—we were now going to take $250 billion more each year—comparing 1983 with 1993—out of the middle class. That was the point. Calling it a "Social Security" tax was simply a cover for a general tax increase.

But, said Greenspan, what was not needed currently (and we didn't need *any* increase currently) will go into a trust which will accrue interest. When the baby boomers reach retirement, that trust fund will have built up enormously, and will take care of them. Workers, in 2010, will not have to be upset by a sharp increase in taxes. The system will come through the crisis, the waters will be smooth again and it will sail on forever.

The whole scheme sounds as if it is fiscally conservative. In fact, it will destroy the middle class. The middle-class taxpayer, under the Greenspan plan, is so heavily taxed during his working life that he or she cannot save anything. There will be nothing to pass on to children.

Suppose you were offered your choice of two financial plans, Plan A and Plan B. Under Plan A, each year during your working life the government will tax you $7,848,90 (counting both employee and employer share and assuming the 1990 rate is not increased over the next 40 years). Over your 40-year working life, the government will take $313,956.00 from you which, if it was invested at 8 percent interest, would produce a fund of $2,195,973. If you die at 64, your children will get $255. If you live past 65, you will get a maximum of $16,000 each year. When you die your children will get zero. That is Financial Plan A—the existing Social Security system.

Under Financial Plan B you can put your $7,848.90 per year into a private plan or your own plan. At age 65, you will have a fund of $2,195,973 which should produce an income between $150,000 and $200,000 per year. You will be able to pass all your $2,195,973 to your children.

TABLE 5.2

Social Security Taxes Collected
1960 - 1993

1960	-	14.7 billion
1970	-	44.4 billion
1975	-	84.5 billion
1980	-	157.8 billion
1983	-	209 billion
1985	-	265.2 billion
1990	-	382.5 billion
1993	-	460.2 billion (estimate)

Historical Tables, Budget of the United States - 1989

Now, the easy question for the day is, coercion aside, would anyone agree to Plan A over Plan B? Senator Moynihan calls Plan A "thievery" and "embezzlement," and it obviously is. Government increased the tax take from $44 billion in 1970 to $382 billion in 1990—almost all of it out of the middle class.

A few days before New Year's Day 1990, Senator Moynihan started shredding the deceptions holding up Social Security. Trust funds were not in trust, a surplus was not a surplus, a reserve was not a reserve. Nothing, under Social Security, was what it appeared to be. Some trickery had been originally built into the system, it referred to "contributions" and "insurance" when all it ever was was a tax. But the deceits built into the Great Greenspan Rescue of 1983 make all others pale by comparison.

Since we have to provide, said Greenspan, for large expenditures from 2010 to 2030, we have to put aside money now—in a trust—which, with the interest it will earn, will enable us to meet the obligation. That is basic middle-class reasoning, and was readily accepted. The Greenspan Plan was, however, so tricky that it took years before people figured it out. His plan provided for a lot of *extra* (not needed for current payout) money—$50 billion in 1990 running to $150 billion in 1997. What did we do with that? Greenspan said that's where the trust comes in. We buy Treasury bonds and notes and put them in my trust. That sounded OK, until you thought about it. Who was going to pay off the Treasury bonds and notes in 2010 to 2030? The same taxpayers who, if we had done nothing, would pay the Social Security obligation in 2010 to 2030. Under Greenspan's plan, the right hand pocket owed the left hand pocket, obviously not a transaction that creates wealth. The taxpayers had swapped the obligation to pay Social Security benefits, which they could have gotten out of, for the obligation to pay interest and principal on Treasury notes, which they could get out of only by default.

The plan did something else; it raised huge amounts of money for the government to spend. The money came out of the worker's checks and went to the Social Security system. The system took the money and bought Treasury notes from the Treasury. Then the Treasury spent this money as it did any other.

That was the plan that Senator Moynihan uncovered. He said that it is totally crazy. It is a horrible and unfair burden on the middle class. Let's cut out the extra collections and go back to pay-as-you-go, he said. If we did that, we would enjoy a $50 billion cut, and, he says, we would not get back to the current very high rate of tax till 2020.

The Social Security tax is an economically depressing tax because it is imposed on an employer for hiring someone. He must pay a tax of 7.65 percent of the employee's gross wages, whether the business makes money or not. It imposes an extraneous cost on employing people which, of course, discourages employment. It is an excise tax on labor. Moynihan believes his proposed cut in the Social Security tax would create between 500,000 and 1 million new jobs per year.

"The hope was," said Cornell Professor Olivia Mitchell, "that Social Security for the baby-boom generation would be more of a supplement to retirement income and less of the mainstay that it is today." "Now," adds the professor, "that hope is fading." Private pension plans expanded greatly in the years following World War II—from covering about 25 percent of workers in 1950 to about 50 percent in 1979. The expansion reversed at that point and is currently down to 46 percent. Moreover, of those over 65—22 million—only 25 percent receive any company pension and of those that do *only 7 percent* receive more than half their income from that source.

The erosion of the private pension system is attributable to (1) the replacement of high paying union manufacturing jobs with low paying hamburger turning jobs; and (2) a series of burdensome laws passed by Congress beginning with the 1974 Employee Retirement Income Security Act (ERISA). Many companies terminated their plans, on the advice of counsel, rather than incurring the risk of legal liability by trying to conform to the complicated requirements of the new law. For those companies that did not terminate their plans, Congress has required that each plan in the country be completely rewritten several times.

The Moynihan proposal created a firestorm, since he called the system a "fraud," and it obviously is. But the Democrats wouldn't support him because the idea of any tax cut went against their grain. A few conservative Republicans went with him, but most stayed with President Bush, who called him "irresponsible" and said the "last thing" that we need is someone "messing around" with Social Security.

Indeed, the President and Congress are so fond of the payroll tax that it is a centerpiece of the Budget Deal of 1990 which increased earnings subject to the Medicare tax from $53,400 to $125,000. Until next year, Americans earning more than $53,400 have enjoyed some end of the year paychecks with no Social Security takeout. No more. The 7.65 percent Social Security takeout has two parts—6.2 percent is labeled for retirement and 1.45 percent for Medicare. The retirement part will shut off at $53,400 but, under the Budget Deal, the 1.45 percent medicare takeout will continue up to $125,000. For example, a taxpayer earning $85,000 will pay an additional $449.50 and a taxpayer earning $100,000 will pay an additional $663.00. A taxpayer earning $125,000 will pay a total payroll tax of $5,123.30. Congress, in the Catastrophic Health Care Act of 1989, had put the cost of elderly benefits on the elderly. The elderly reacted so violently that Congress decided, for the future, to put the cost of new elderly benefits on the non-elderly, non-represented, unorganized middle-class taxpayer.

Senator Moynihan, as noted above, proposed cutting the Social Security taxes so as to restore some honesty to the system. Senator Ernest Hollings of South Carolina introduced a proposal before the Senate Budget Committee to accomplish Senator Moynihan's objective. Senator Hollings stated that it was time for some "truth in budgeting," and argued that the current perversion of the Social Security system was masking the full magnitude of the federal deficit. On April 26, 1990, his proposal was rejected by the committee by a vote of 17 to 6.

Greenspan, now advanced to chairman of the Federal Reserve for his good work, came over to the Senate Finance Committee on February 27, 1990, to explain why Moynihan was wrong. His explanation was very complicated, but it seemed that his idea was that the extra tax money was a forced national saving. If you let the people keep their money, they might spend it. They might, but that had previously been thought to be their right. It was also unclear how national saving was advanced by the government (1) taxing the people; (2) using the tax to buy Government debt; and (3) spending the money. Step 2 doesn't do anything but cover the trail. How steps 1 and 3 accomplished national saving is way over the heads of the authors. Bob Strauss appeared right after Chairman Greenspan, and claimed that he understood it.

The basic fact was that Government wanted, needed and intended to have the extra $250 billion a year. Senator Moynihan was the little boy in the crowd who said the Emperor was not wearing anything. Hans Christian Anderson doesn't finish the story but it looks as if the little boy ends his days getting called "irresponsible" and being ignored. The Social Security deceptions, however, are starting to wear very thin with the people.

In April 1991, the Moynihan proposal reached the Senate floor for a vote. It would cut every worker's Social Security tax by up to $300 per year; every paycheck would be a little fatter. The total tax cut was about $195 billion over 5 years. How could it lose? Who was against a tax cut? It would return the system to its pre-1977 pay-as-you-go basis, which meant money could just go to benefits. The money could not be diverted to other purposes like paying interest on the national debt. What was wrong with that?

The previous October, 1990, Moynihan also thought he had a majority of the Senate on his side. The Senate had voted 54-44 to waive the Budget Act so it could consider his proposal then. He needed 60 votes to get this waiver so he failed, but he thought the 54 who voted with him on the procedural point were on his side. This time he only needed a majority. And since October he had persuaded some high-profile, politically diverse senators to join him—Senators Mitchell, Kennedy, Hatch, Wallop, and Symms.

On the other side, there was one good reason to expect Moynihan to lose—the life or death opposition of the powerful American Association of Retired People (AARP), which claims to have 33 million members. There are an awful lot of social security beneficiaries; for example, in New York there are 15,564 beneficiaries out of every 100,000 people. Moynihan's proposal was no immediate threat to the AARP, but they correctly saw a long term danger—democracy. If you go back to pay-as-you-go, the people have full control again over the Social Security program. They can terminate the program if it becomes too burdensome. At some point, the AARP fears, the voters are going to say the burden is too heavy, let's put a means test on Social Security to determine who really needs it. At that point, the rich and most of the middle class leave the program. The AARP correctly sees that Social Security will rapidly lose its constituency. If it turns into a welfare program, it will have a constituency like a welfare program. The immediate political issue for Moynihan was whether a powerful special interest group like the AARP would outweigh the interests of unorganized workers benefitted by his bill.

On April 23, Senator Moynihan opened debate noting that Social Security was bringing in about $1 billion a week more than it needed for benefits. Within 5 years it would be taking in $2.5 billion a week more than it needed. These extra funds were not held in any trust, and were spent as any other general revenue of the government. This, said Senator Moynihan, was "thievery," "embezzlement" and "abuse of trust."

Senator Domenici (R.,N.M.) was offended by Moynihan's tone. It "disturbs [me] greatly," said Domenici, "when the Senator from New York speaks of "embezzlement, thievery, and abuse of a trust fund." It was Moynihan, said Domenici, who was trying to "raid the Social

Security Trust Fund." Moynihan's opponents always spoke of the Trust fund as if it were a real thing. The opponents, of course, knew perfectly well that the only thing in the trust was some Treasury notes, a promise by the Government to raise taxes on the people so the Government could pay the holder, what we have called an obligation on the part of the left hand pocket to pay the right hand pocket. Debt, as the reader knows, is not an asset to the debtor; it is a liability.

"The truth of the matter," said Senator Symms (R., Idaho), "is there is nothing in the trust fund. It is IOUT's that is what it is: IOUT's: I owe you taxes. That is all it is." The opponents, led by Senators Domenici, Sasser, Bentsen and Dole, never questioned the truth of what Symms said. But they kept referring to the trust as if it held something of value. That was why they were morally outraged that Moynihan was trying to raid it. If all it contained was some old shoes, who cares if Moynihan raids it?

The next day, April 24, 1991, the moral level rose pretty high. Senator Bentsen, chairman of the Finance Committee, opened saying Moynihan was out to "undermine the faith of the American public in the Social Security system and the strength of the national economy that supports that system." It was wrong, said Bentsen, to say the Treasury notes in the trust fund had no value. They had the full faith and credit of the United States behind them. The Germans and Japanese would not buy them if they were not valuable. Bentsen must have been smiling when he said that. The chairman of the Finance Committee obviously understands that Treasury notes are valuable to the Germans and Japanese because they collect their face value at maturity, whereas we have to tax ourselves to pay them off.

Senator Dole agreed with Bentsen that if we cut this tax "we are only cutting the safety net for future generations of Americans." The trust fund is "a sacred trust between our Government and our senior citizens." President Bush wrote a letter dated April 23 to Senator Dole. The president said the Moynihan proposal would "drain" away funds belonging to Social Security, drive it to the "brink of insolvency," and "threaten to bankrupt" the system:

Senator Moynihan's proposal, for example, would return Social
Security to the same financing scheme that drove the system to
the brink of insolvency in 1982. His proposal would drain
roughly $23 billion from Social Security trust fund reserves in
1992 and $170 billion by the end of 1996. Under pessimistic
economic assumptions, adoption of this legislation could again
threaten to bankrupt the Social Security system.

We rescued the Social Security system eight years ago on a
bipartisan basis. When we did, we made a promise to every
American who receives Social Security benefits, to those who
support the system today, and to those who will rely on it when
they retire. We have worked together to assure that today's
benefits are protected and that the system will be strong enough
to continue providing benefits to future retirees. I intend to
assure that we keep our promise.

Sincerely,
George Bush

That is, of course, a fairly high moral tone to take for an Administration
that collects money from workers' paychecks under the label "FICA"
and uses it to pay interest on the national debt.

    Friends of Social Security, like the president, always talked of the
"brink of insolvency" and threats to "bankrupt" the system. As we have
seen, there is no trust fund so there is nothing to become insolvent or go
bankrupt. Social Security is just another government program funded by
taxes. The people may decide they don't want their taxes going up, and
discontinue the program but that's democracy, not bankruptcy.

    The friends of Social Security did tend to convert English words
to mean their opposite—what George Orwell called "Newspeak."
Senator Moynihan chastised them noting that if "ever we learned
anything from George Orwell and his generation, it is that corrupting the
language of politics is a profoundly serious thing." Senator Hollings
agreed:

It is an embarrassment, I have expressed my pride in being a professional politician, but in 40 years this is the worst display of the worst kind of politics I have ever seen. When up is down and black is white. When you try to stop a raid, they call it a raid. When you try to defuse a time bomb, they say you are creating a time bomb. How, after all this lying, are we going to make ourselves honest?

The friends of Social Security assume, as Senator Moynihan charged, "that the American people do not understand this system, [and] will not take the trouble to learn," and that generations of mislabelling have confused the people past understanding.

The Moynihan proposal was voted down 60-38, a dramatic drop from the October 1990 vote, which had been 54-44 in his favor. Twenty-three senators who were with Moynihan in October 1990 (when they knew he could not win) switched sides in April 1991, when the AARP told them it was time to get serious. The Hall of Shame includes: Senators Baucus, Gramm, Breaux, Grassley, Bumpers, Heflin, Burdick, Lautenberg, Cohen, Levin, Conrad, McConnell, Damato, Mikulski, Daschle, Packwood, DeConcini, Shelby, Dixon, Simon, Ford, and Specter.

The antidemocratic mechanism of debt—debt payable by future unrepresented generations—had eaten up the Social Security system. The novel twist here was that the taxpayers first provided the money to buy the debt, then provided the money to pay the interest on it, and then, in 2010, were supposed to provide the money to pay the debt off. It was another first. Once again, debt showed itself the best barometer of the health of democracy. As each governmental endeavor became debt-reliant, the mileposts of abandonment loomed clearer and clearer. However, the worst was yet to come.

CHAPTER SIX

The Savings and Loan Fiasco

In June 1982, one of the authors wrote an article for *Fortune* magazine (June 14, 1982) called "The Baleful Bailout Bandwagon." He wrote that the U.S. government was about to "sign on to the biggest bailout in history." You did not have to be a great genius to figure that out. All you had to do was spend a couple of weeks talking to people in the industry. Most of them were very depressed but wanted to talk about it. Politicians, however, were strangely bashful. Two of the architects of disaster, Representative Fernand St. Germain (D.R.I.) (House Banking) and Senator Jake Garn (R., Utah) (Senate Banking) broke appointments made by *Fortune* to talk with the author.

What the industry people said was that they were, at that time, sitting on $200 billion of "unrealized" losses. That is, they had loaned out $523 billion in mortgages which, because interest rates had risen, were worth no more than $315 billion. For example, a 7 percent, 30-year, $100,000 mortgage was worth only $50,000 when interest rates rose to 14 percent. That meant the industry, as a whole, was insolvent. Its assets (loans), if marked down to their market value, did not equal its liabilities (deposits)—it was about $200 billion short. Put another way, if all their depositors wanted their money back they would be short, after selling the mortgages, by $200 billion.

The 1982 *Fortune* article said the existing losses were not going to go away because Congress didn't want to recognize them. The time had come to allocate the losses, absorb what had to be absorbed, and get on with business:

> The traditional savings and loan industry no longer exists and so cannot be saved. The practical question is how to manage and pay for the failures the industry is trying to put behind it.

But Congress, when the cost was manageable, would not recognize the losses. The losses, if recognized, would limit other spending programs the Congress and executive branch wanted to do.

Now it is clear the savings and loans have swallowed up at least $500 billion, money that's not coming back. The real cost, as we said before, is infinite; it is whatever the middle class has now or will have in the future.

How did such a simple idea as the saving and loan institution get so fouled up? The answer is the Executive, the Congress, the courts, the lawyers, the Keating Five (Jake Garn also has a Keating connection), Fernand St. Germain, Tony Coehlo and Jim Wright. To see how it was done, we have to look at the traditional savings and loan, and then at the 1980-1982 congressional conversion of the savings and loan into a major source of speculative money supported by what are usually thought to be taxpayer guaranteed deposits. The new savings and loan was a major buyer of Michael Milken's junk bonds.

How could this take place? Charles Keating, in mid-April 1989, held a press conference where he said:

> One question, among the many raised in recent weeks, had to do with whether my financial support in any way influenced political figures to talk up my cause. I want to say in the most *forceful* way I can: I certainly hope so.

The Traditional S&L
1831-1982

> *No partner, this isn't where I work. It's where my money works*
> *for me. I know my savings are safe here because wherever you*
> *see that insurance emblem displayed you know your savings are*
> *protected by an agency of the U.S. government.*

> Gary Cooper, in an old S&L advertisement (circa
> 1950), talking to a 12-year-old boy while leaning
> against an S&L.

The names of the thrift institutions conjure up an earlier and more
frugal America: the Union Dime Savings Bank, the Emigrant Savings
Bank. Many have a nautical theme: the Seamans Bank for Savings, the
Dry Dock Savings Bank, the Anchor Savings Bank. The names evoke
clipper ships, lamplighters, Christmas caroling, hardworking seamen and
mechanics, and solid moral values like thrift.

The savings and loan system derives from two modest ideas that
implanted themselves in American soil early in the last century. The
first was borrowed from the English building societies. In 1831, in
Frankford, Pennsylvania, thirty-seven people organized the Oxford
Provident Building Association. Each member paid five dollars down
for a share and three dollars a month thereafter. There were no
depositors and the association paid no interest. When the association had
enough money for a loan of $500, a meeting was called and the loan was
auctioned off to the member paying the highest premium. The fellow
most eager to build his home would bid the highest premium. The first
winning premium was ten dollars. The loan could only be used to build
or buy a house approved by the association. The process continued until
each member had a house loan. Since the association's only investments
were loans to members, it wound up its affairs once every member had
a house. The first Oxford Association lasted ten years.

The second root of today's thrift industry is exemplified by New
York's first savings bank, which was chartered in 1819. The charter
was granted on the petition of the Society for the Prevention of
Pauperism. Unlike a building society, a savings bank had depositors.

It took such "small sums of money as may be saved from earnings of tradesmen, mechanics, laborers, minors, servants and others." The commercial banks, citadels of Hamiltonian aristocracy, would not let this crowd in the front door. The savings bank gathered up its small deposits and invested in government bonds. This afforded, wrote the draftsman, "the twofold advantage of security and interest." Government bonds were the only investment permitted, even though return on the bonds was low, to assure that the depositors' "small sums" would be conserved. The savings bank paid its depositors the interest it received on the bonds, less management expenses. The bank was legally nonprofitmaking.

The legislature granted the first savings bank charter because, as the draftsman put it, they considered it "their duty to cherish all laudable attempts to ameliorate the condition of the poor and laboring class of the community." Consistent with this theme, the trustees and officers agreed to serve for no pay. The motive was not totally charitable. The trustees were businessmen who had found that even though they had no legal liability, they could not realistically avoid paying some employee welfare costs, particularly burial expenses. The savings bank was intended to encourage employees to self-insure against life's rude shocks.

The two streams, building societies and savings banks, flowed together into the thrift industry, or "savings and loans," across the country, and "savings banks," mostly in New York, both taking money from small depositors and lending it to home buyers. While commercial banking became more sophisticated and more national in scope, the thrifts stayed with this one simple, profitable, local transaction. Their folksy, benevolent image earned them favored status with the government, and with the public.

In Frank Capra's 1947 movie *It's a Wonderful Life*, Jimmy Stewart plays an officer of a building and loan association in the Depression who spends most of his time preventing a greedy commercial banker (played by Lionel Barrymore in a wheelchair) from swallowing up his institution. At one point Stewart must beat off a panic by depositors. He tells the clamoring townspeople:

You're thinking of this place all wrong. As if I were keeping your money in a safe back here. Your money isn't here. It's in Joe's house . . . right next to yours. And in Kennedy's house and the Macklins' . . . and a hundred others. You lent them the money to build and they're paying you back as best they can. What do you want me to do? Foreclose on them?

The speech, together with $2,000 of personal savings that Donna Reed slips to him, holds off the run. As for that commercial banker, Stewart warns:

He's out to get us. Why? Because we're cutting into his business . . . Nick, you lived in one of his houses. Have you forgotten it? Have you forgotten what you used to pay for that broken down shack . . . If Potter gets hold of this Building and Loan there'll never be another decent house built in this town.

Potter's theory was that people should save their money until they could pay for a house in full. Jimmy Stewart disagrees:

Just remember, Mr. Potter, this rabble, as you call them, do most of the working, most of the paying, most of the living and most of the dying in this community. Is it too much for them to work and pay and live and die in a couple of clean rooms and a bath?

By 1930, the S&Ls had acquired assets worth $9 billion. The traditional mortgage issued in 1925 required the principal to be paid in one balloon payment due in five years unless the borrower renewed. At that point the S&Ls were pretty well matching their liabilities, short with short. The risk of rising interest was on the homeowner, since he would have to renew at the higher rate if he wanted to keep the mortgage. But as the Depression struck, the balloon mortgage led to massive foreclosures, and to the loss of buyers' homes when the five years were up. They could neither pay nor qualify for renewal.

To take care of immediate problems, the government set up a bail-out device called the Home Owners Loan Corporation, which bought up $3 billion worth of sour mortgages. To get the building industry going again, the Roosevelt administration invented a new financial instrument: the long-term mortgage, featuring a low down payment and level monthly payments of combined principal and interest for twenty to thirty years. The new instrument was central to a new national policy of encouraging home ownership and decent housing. The Roosevelt policy, after World War II, turned into a brilliant success. The suburbs began to grow, financed by the S&Ls. Owner-occupied housing grew from 14 million units in 1930 to 23.6 million in 1950 and 32.8 in 1960.

The savings and loans were restructured during the Depression: they were tax-exempt; they had federal government charters and federal agency guarantees for their depositors; they were guaranteed a low ceiling on the interest they paid but a competitive edge over the commercial banks.   Finally, there was the interest payment tax deduction, amounting to a subsidy of the S&Ls' only product, the home mortgage.

Under the new rules, S&L assets grew from $9 billion in 1930 to $658 billion in 1982. The thrifts were protected from all possible contingencies short of nuclear war, except one: rising interest rates. The new long-term mortgage shifted the risk of rising interest from the borrower to the lender.

The trouble was that the S&L system funded long-term fixed-interest assets (mortgages) with short-term liabilities (deposits), which could stay forever or could leave tomorrow. (Commercial banks, by contrast, mostly lend short.) A typical transaction in the good old days was a thirty-year, 7 percent mortgage funded with money from passbook savings accounts paying 5 percent. The bank's 2 percent spread was quite enough to take care of management perks and provide a reasonable net worth. The system worked because long-term rates were always higher than short-term. The simple theory for this was that money was at less risk if it was to be paid back sooner rather than later. It was a good theory, but it turned out not to be an immutable law. The S&Ls assumed that short and long term interest rates in general would hold their two-point spread. As long as rates were relatively stable, the outstanding mortgages retained their value. If an S&L had any need for cash, it could sell old mortgages for 100 cents on the dollar.

Cracks in this structure showed as early as the mid-1960s. In the last half of the 1970s, two things went seriously wrong. First, interest rates became volatile, and in 1979-81 took off for the sky as the Federal Reserve pushed interest rates up to 20 percent as it tried to stamp out the Oil Gouge-induced inflation. This destroyed the value of the outstanding mortgages which had low yields. They could be sold, on the average, for only sixty cents on the dollar. Meanwhile, the backbone of the S&Ls, the passbook saver, began fleeing for higher interest. Passbook savings made up 91 percent of all deposits in 1966; 59 percent in 1967; 43 percent in 1975; and 21 percent in 1980.

When these passbook savers started asking for their money back, the S&Ls were in the Jimmy Stewart fix. The money had been invested in mortgages, which could only be sold at an enormous loss. The only way to replace the lost depositors with new ones was to offer higher rates. But if you had to pay 12 percent to get deposits to balance mortgages that were paying you 9 percent you had, what they called, a "negative spread."

The second thing that went wrong in the late 1970s was that short-term interest rates went higher than long-term rates, creating what the experts call an "inverted yield curve." That was as bad as it sounds, because it meant that the S&Ls would earn less even on their *new* mortgages than they had to pay for new deposits. That is like buying apples at 11 cents and selling them for 8 cents. The S&Ls stopped making mortgages. The S&Ls lost their economic function.

On October 28, 1785, Thomas Jefferson wrote to James Madison: "[I]t is not too soon to provide by every possible means that as few as possible shall be without a little portion of land. The small landholders are the most precious part of the state." The yeoman farmers, to Jefferson, are the heart of the democracy. They are, in the last analysis, the only ones who care what happens to the country. The rich are always ready to pull up stakes at a moment's notice and run to Monte Carlo. The underclass could hope for profit in turmoil; they might think the overthrow of the constitution would improve their situation. The rich and the underclass are not really part of the country, the middle class is.

Through the 1960s, the traditional savings and loans accomplished
Jefferson's goal in a simple, but brilliant, way. The depositor was
satisfied with a 3 or 4 percent return and the borrower could afford a 6
percent mortgage to help him buy a $20,000 home. As long as the
government kept the money honest that could go on forever. In fact, of
course, as the reader well knows, government gave us the inflation of
the 1970s. The value of existing long term obligations, including the
mortgages the savings and loans held, was sharply impaired. Interest
rates started for double digits to reflect the fact the lender would be
repaid in less valuable dollars than he had loaned.

The Financial Abandonment of the 1970s killed the savings and
loans. They could no longer accomplish their mission. The savings and
loans customers could not afford to borrow a lot of money at high
interest rates. The savings and loans needed two things the Financial
Abandonment destroyed: (1) low interest rates (say 6-8 percent) and
(2) reasonably predictable rules.

By 1982, the people in the business were very depressed. Each
S&L projected its "negative spread" to determine the exact date its
capital would be used up. The executives morbidly spoke of the months
remaining till insolvency. The time they would become, as they put it,
a "zombie" thrift.

That was the traditional S&L and the problem it ran into. The
S&L certainly had a problem. The $200 billion of unrealized losses
were real. The industry was insolvent. But the basic value was there,
the mortgages were solid, the money was eventually coming back. The
losses were caused by rising interest rates and would disappear as
interest rates went down.

In 1982, the options for the S&Ls really turned on what the
government was going to do about general interest rates. If rates were
going down to a basic 6 percent rate again, the S&Ls were going to
right themselves with no problem. Then they could go back to what
they were doing. If government wasn't going to get interest rates down,
the S&L was dead as the dodo bird and had to be liquidated at the least
cost.

The cost to the taxpayer, upon liquidation, should not have been
much, if anything. It was interest rates, not bad investments, that had
created the $200 billion unrealized loss. Volcker, to control inflation,

had pushed the prime rate to 20 percent. That, of course, meant the value of debt already outstanding at lower rates fell like a rock. But interest rates were not going to stay at 20 percent and, as interest rates came down, the value of the mortgages came back. Table 6.1 shows how the unrealized loss melts like a snowman as the interest rate comes down. So the original 1982 problem was not that serious, and was going to right itself if you left it alone. The worst that could happen was that every S&L depositor would demand his money back. If that happened, the system was $200 billion short. But, while it had to be covered, it was just a short term financing problem. Even if the government had to buy all the outstanding mortgages at face to provide funds for depositors there would be little or no ultimate loss because the value of the mortgages would get back to face as interest rates fell.

All the bad trouble came from the 1980-1982 congressional solution. Congress took the one thing that was okay, the quality of S&L investments, and turned it into an awful joke. Jimmy Stewart and Gary Cooper's favorite institution would end its days as Michael Milken's favorite pigeon.

TABLE 6.1

Unrealized Loss on Outstanding Mortgages

	Mortgages Outstanding	Average Interest Rate on Outstanding Mortgages	When Prime Rate is	Value of Outstanding Mortgages is	Unrealized Loss is
1982	$523 Billion	10%	17%	$315 Billion	$208
1983	$523 Billion	10%	14%	$380 Billion	$143
1984	$523 Billion	10%	12%	$435 Billion	$ 88
1985	$523 Billion	10%	10%	$523 Billion	-0-

Prepared by Authors

The Congressional S&L
1980 - End

Voters were more important than contributors in Congress as late as the 1970's, though by then it was becoming a close call.

Martin Mayer, *The Greatest-Ever Bank Robbery*

By 1980, as Martin Mayer reports, it was pretty clear that contributors had become more important to Congress than voters. Accountability, of course, in a political system running on money, flows to the contributor not the voter. Congress devotes itself to bills the voters have no interest in but which the contributors do (see Tax Reform Act of 1986). At times, Congress stirs the pot by taking up bills with no serious intent of passing them but because they bitterly divide the business community. The *Wall Street Journal* calls these "cash cow" bills and gives the example of "reform" of the civil racketeering law, known as RICO, which has been introduced each year for the last six years to induce contributions from both sides of a divided business community. (See also California legislature's handling of unitary tax issue from 1980-1990.) By 1980, Congress fit Churchill's description of the French Parliament in the 1930s—one-third was corrupt; one-third was confused; and one-third was too cynical to care.

Another example is Congress' sudden fascination, starting around 1980, with banking bills. Since the Depression, the Senate and House banking committees have had jurisdiction over both housing and banking. Before 1980, when the voters were more important than contributors, the committees worked mostly on housing which was of some interest to constituents. Banking, on the other hand, was only of interest to bank and S&L lobbyists. Further, the commercial banks and S&Ls were usually at odds with each other since they had distinct missions and were different socially and culturally. The bankers thought the S&L officers were very middle American. After 1980, when the contributors became more important than the voter, the Congressional committees dropped housing like a bad habit and turned their hand to what they always called banking "reform"—reform after reform after reform. They gave us the congressional S&L, which was not like anything which had ever been seen before.

The basic franchise of the traditional S&L was safety; that is what Gary Cooper talked to the little boy about. In 1980 and 1982, Congress deregulated a busted industry. They induced tremendous new deposits (thought to be guaranteed by the taxpayer) when they were sure to be gambled away. They encouraged sleazy new people to come into the industry. Regulatory oversight was short circuited by Congress (see discussion of the "Keating Five" below) but most of the insanity was legal. After Congress changed the rules in 1982, it was legal for an S&L to invest in junk bonds, mortgage backed securities, collateralized mortgage obligations, futures, puts and calls, and repurchase agreements. Gary Cooper didn't talk to the little boy about that stuff. Is anyone surprised they lost all that money?

"Saturday Night Live," in April 1990 did a spoof of the famous Jimmy Stewart lines: "You're thinking of this place all wrong, your money's not here it's in Joe's house and Kennedy's house." In the "Saturday Night Live" version, the Stewart character says, "Your money isn't here"—so far, so good—"it's in condos, and Van Goghs, and yachts and fancy women and junk bonds and Swiss bank accounts."

In 1980 and 1982, Congress passed new laws which authorized the S&Ls to (1) pay market rates for deposits; and (2) invest in anything they liked—they could forget that single family home stuff. Overnight, the S&Ls were put into direct competition with the commercial banks who had been operating like that for years and had all the good customers. This kind of deregulation is like releasing the family cat in the middle of the jungle and hoping everything will come out alright. The Wall Street tigers could not believe what a tasty morsel they were getting.

Many of the S&Ls, as discussed above, were already on a death watch. Now they thought there might be a way out; if they could grow rapidly they might be able to generate new capital. They offered very high interest rates on deposits so they could grow rapidly. A new business grew up: broker originated deposits. The new industry might involve a pension fund, for example, hiring a broker to place money at the highest rate possible wherever he could find it. The broker split the money into $100,000 accounts to get what he thought was the taxpayers' guarantee. The S&L was now definitely a national financial institution.

The brokers were only taking advantage of what Congress gave them. In the early 1930s bank failures wiped out the life savings of many citizens. The insured deposit was intended to prevent that happening again. Congress had run the insured amount from $10,000 to $15,000 in 1966; from $15,000 to $20,000 in 1969; from $20,000 to $40,000 in 1974. In 1980, Fernand St. Germain pushed it from $40,000 to $100,000. The public never asked for the run-up in insurance. How many readers have more than $10,000 in the bank? Together, the authors don't. Congress, by running up the insurance, basically changed the old nest egg protection theory. The nest egg theory was designed to protect the depositor; the run up in insurance was demanded by the S&L industry and designed to help the industry.

The blame for the $500 billion of S&L losses is very easy to assign. If Congress had stuck to the nest egg theory it could not have happened. If Congress had left the insurance at the 1969 level—$15,000—there would be no losses today. S&L deposits exploded as Congress raised the insurance first to $20,000, then to $40,000 and finally to $100,000. Table 6.2 shows how total deposits at FSLIC insured institutions rose.

TABLE 6.2

FSLIC Insured Deposits

1970 -	141.6 Billion
1981 -	512.3 Billion
1988 -	971.7 Billion

Congress used deposit insurance to create a new investment instrument. An investment which paid high interest and which was thought to have no risk to the investor. Nothing like it had ever been seen before. Congress, consistent with its new bank-account-as-investment theory, allowed an investor to buy as many $100,000 accounts as he wanted. Traditionally, the system had allowed depositors to split funds into different accounts and banks. But what was allowable when the insured amount was $10,000 was a recipe for disaster when the insured amount had been run up to $100,000.

As Jim Adams writes in *The Big Fix:*

> With the increased guarantee, *thrift owners soon realized that no matter what they did, they had access to almost unlimited deposits.* Buyers of jumbo CDs [$100,000] cared only about the interest rate, which was almost always highest at the weakest thrifts. "Hot money" flowed into the hands of the worst managers at a phenomenal rate. Their thrifts grew a thousandfold and more in just four years and kept growing as their losses mounted. [Emphasis added]

The problem, as the reader already sees, is that the S&Ls rapid growth gamble was a gamble with someone else's money. If it went well, fine, but if not, it was the taxpayers' loss. Congress had provided irresistible inducements to fiscal irresponsibility. That policy decision is what is costing the taxpayers $500 billion.

At this point, many of the traditional S&L officers left the industry and were replaced by a bunch of crooks. Almost all of the large S&L failures show a change of ownership in 1982 or 1983 as the crooks came in.

The immediate cause of the $500 billion S&L loss is the decision of Congress in 1980 to raise deposit insurance from $40,000 to $100,000 at the same time it deregulated the interest rate an S&L was allowed to pay for deposits. Further, in 1980 the S&L regulator, the Federal Home Loan Bank Board, which had prohibited S&L's from getting more than 5 percent of their deposits from deposit brokers, removed that prohibition. These changes created the money broker industry which collected large blocks of money, broke them down into insurable $100,000 pieces and placed them in the S&L paying the highest interest. Don Regan, Merrill Lynch and Drexel Burnham were very active money brokers. Public Citizen, a Ralph Nader group, reports Regan was known around Merrill as the "father of brokered deposits." *(Who Robbed America* (Random House, 1990), p. 30.) The point was that Congress, by providing big dollar insurance and removing interest rate controls, converted the traditional bank account into a high interest bond, a unique bond that was thought to have no risk of loss to the investor. The S&Ls across the country then went into the business of selling high interest bonds through the money brokers.

Congress had divided very neatly the upside from the downside or, as Martin Mayer puts it, the reward from the risk. All gain went to (1) the depositor, who got very high rates at no risk; and (2) the S&Ls which got the money to play with. All the risk of loss went to (3) the taxpayer. Congress said to the S&Ls, "Here's $100,000, you go to Atlantic City; if you win keep your profits, if you lose, come back and we'll give you another $100,000." If you raised children that way, would you be surprised if they didn't turn out to be wonderful?

Martin Mayer, in *The Greatest-Ever Bank Robbery* (Scribners, 1990) writes that "the essence of the Pratt deregulation and the Garn-St. Germain Act had been the promotion of growth to get out of the trap of low-yielding assets." Michael Lewis, in *Liar's Poker* (Norton, 1989), writes that when the S&Ls began to flounder "the U.S. Congress decided to let the savings and loans try to speculate their way out of trouble and though it meant, effectively, gambling with the government's money, they were allowed to buy junk bonds." The 1982 congressional solution was certainly a new one, taking a bankrupt and telling him to grow, or speculate, his way out of trouble. The Atlantic City solution. Actually, telling him wouldn't have been so bad, it was bankrolling him that hurt.

The administration is ready to do it again. On November 30, 1990, it proposed the Atlantic City solution for the commercial banks. Between 1929 and 1931 many banks collapsed because they had invested heavily in stocks which dropped out of sight. Since the 1930s, the Banks have been prohibited by the Glass-Steagall Act from selling and investing in corporate stocks and bonds. Now that the Banks are bust they blame, not their own abandonment of principle, but, if you can believe it, the Glass-Steagall law. The law forced them, they say, to make risky commercial real estate loans and loans for highly leveraged stock buy-outs. Treasury Secretary Nicholas Brady, in a speech to the Securities Industry Association in Boca Raton, Florida, said he agreed with the bankers and would support repeal of Glass-Steagall. Might as well.

Did Congress know what it was doing when it set up the taxpayer-lose game? Does anyone remember a lot of public clamor in 1980 demanding the insurance be raised from $40,000 to $100,000? The correct answers are Yes and No. Very few Americans needed $100,000 insurance to cover their savings; or $40,000 for that matter. The public didn't demand the increase, the public didn't know it was being done. The $100,000 made its first public appearance on March 24, 1980. There were no hearings in the Senate or House. There was no explanation in any Senate or House report. There was no floor debate in the Senate or House. In the Senate, there was not even any record of which Senators had voted for or against it. On March 31, one week after its first public appearance, President Carter signed it into law.

How did it come about? The authors of *Inside Job* (McGraw Hill 1989) report: "While legislators were hammering out the details of the Depository Institutions Deregulation and Monetary Control Act in a late-night session on Capitol Hill, Glen Troop, chief Washington lobbyist for the powerful U.S. League of Savings Institutions, and an associate convinced congressmen to make the increase. 'It was almost an afterthought,' a House staffer later told a reporter."

Jim Adams, in *The Big Fix*, adds detail. The push, Adams writes, came from one man, Fernand St. Germain, the "slick and not overly scrupulous" chairman of the House Banking Committee.[9] One night in

---

[9]Calling Fernand St. Germain "not overly scrupulous" is a real understatement. St. Germain was poor when he went to Congress in 1960. He was worth millions in 1988 when the people of Rhode Island's First District kicked him out of office. Beginning in 1985, Brooks Jackson in the *Wall Street Journal* wrote a series of articles explaining how St. Germain became rich on dealings with people under the jurisdiction of his House Banking Committee. There were deals with a subsidized housing developer, there was 100 percent financing from federally regulated banks to buy International House of Pancakes restaurants, and there were real estate partnerships with the head of Florida Savings and Loan. St. Germain explained: "It's like anything else. You sit down with your buddies and say 'Do you want in?' And you either say yea or nay."

In 1983 St. Germain's office made numerous phone calls to the Federal Bank Board in Washington and Atlanta on behalf of the Florida S&L to clear its conversion from a mutual association to a stock corporation. The

the high-ceilinged conference room in the United States Capitol, "St. Germain pulled off a fateful coup." He proposed the $100,000 limit: "It was a United States League [of Savings Institutions] special," says one thrift regulator. "But they were surprised they got it." Tim McNamar, then deputy secretary of the Treasury, adds "We were lucky they didn't get a million."

Martin Mayer, in *The Greatest-Ever Bank Robbery*, agrees it was a dark of the night deal. In March 1980, The Depository Institution Deregulation and Monetary Control Act, a Carter administration initiative was moving through Congress. The bill was going to phase out all interest rate ceilings over 6 years. The "S&Ls were losing one thing they cared about enormously—the interest-rate ceilings of the Fed's Reg. Q, with the differential that let them pay a little more than the banks." Mayer reports that the House and Senate bills were quite different and the conference contentious. A similar bill had failed to emerge from conference a year earlier and it seemed "at least possible" this conference, too, would fail. At this cliff-hanging point, Mayer writes:

---

regulators gave the clearance, and in May 1983, St. Germain bought $30,000 worth of the S&L's stock.

Jackson reports that St. Germain was seen night after night in Washington eating and drinking in the company of James "Snake" Freeman, lobbyist for the U.S. League of Savings Institutions. The U.S. League picked up large tabs for St. Germain at the Prime Rib restaurant and Pisces, a disco club. Jackson notes that often the "bills listed St. Germain and female companions as 'staff.'"

In April 1987 the House Ethics Committee reported that it could not find much wrong and recommended that no disciplinary action be taken against St. Germain. In May 1988, the Justice Department announced it would not indict St. Germain with respect to illegal gratuities or bribery. They sent it back to House Ethics.

The Keating Five, who suffered through two months of televised Senate Ethics Committee hearings on C-SPAN, compared to Fred St. Germain or Jim Wright, are pretty thin beer, but timing, as they say, is everything.

Finally, the big California S&Ls agreed to withdraw their objections to the bill on one condition. The limit on insured deposits had to be raised from $40,000 to at least $100,000 per account. Sen. Alan Cranston carried their water to the table. Although an increase in the maximum savings account that could qualify for insurance was not in the draft bills that had gone to conference and no words of instruction on the subject were in the briefings by the staffs to the negotiators, the deal was cut late at night, and the bill passed.

One participant, Senator Jake Garn (R. Utah) tells a different story. In July 1990 Bill Buckley wrote a column about the decision to raise the insurance from $40,000 to $100,000. In Buckley's view, the difference between $40,000 and $100,000, in terms of ultimate taxpayer loss "may mean something like, oh, $200 billion." The decision, he wrote, was made in a back room in the dark of night. Jake Garn, in some dudgeon, wrote Buckley to deny the back room stuff:

> Let me state clearly and for the record: No such meeting took place. The increase in deposit insurance was suggested and debated during a public session of the House-Senate conference committee in 1980. The views of the then FDIC (Federal Deposit Insurance Corp.) Chairman Irvine Sprague were solicited through his representative at this public meeting, and his official response was that he did not object to the increase to $100,000. Based on this information, the conference committee members voted to accept the proposal.

The record, which Senator Garn wants to state for, shows that the $100,000 provision first appeared in the world on Monday, March 24, 1980 and that it became law one week later. Senator Garn may view that as the orderly working of democratic procedures. Everyone else, however, may think it smells a lot like a back room dark of the night deal would smell. Let's look at the record.

Diary of the $100,000 Deal (1980)

During the week of March 24, 1980 the prime rate was 19.5 percent; 6-month Treasury bills paid 14.6 percent; phone company bonds paid 13.45 percent; and tax exempt municipals paid 9.7 percent. Commercial banks, limited by Federal Reserve Regulation Q, paid only 5 1/4 percent on savings deposits. The S&Ls, by Regulation Q, were allowed a 1/4 point differential, which permitted them to pay 5 1/2 percent on deposits.

The 1980 legislation, to which the $100,000 provision got attached, was designed to get rid of Regulation Q. This was what President Carter called deregulating interest rates. Which he thought would put the small saver on a parity with those who could afford to buy $5,000 money-market certificates or Treasury bills. In the process, however, the S&Ls were going to lose their protected environment and their 1/4 point differential.

The simple fact is that the S&L has no economic or social mission in a high interest world. The S&L's great achievement was to put lower-middle and middle middle-class people into their own homes. The S&Ls put Jimmy Stewart's friends, who had always rented from Lionel Barrymore, into a house they owned. But you were not going to be able to do that with mortgages of 10 percent or 12 percent and up. The traditional S&L customer could not afford it. He would be paying so much interest to the bank he might as well be paying rent. He could not build up any equity. For example, the owner with a $100,000 mortgage at 10 percent, will pay, in just 7.2 years, $100,000 in interest alone, an amount equal to what he borrowed in the first place. The owner has paid for the house once and still owes the whole principal. This is obviously no way to get rich. If government could not restore a low interest world, it had to put the S&Ls through an orderly liquidation.

Congress, instead, took the S&Ls out of their quiet little corner of the financial world and put them into a brand new national money business. This, as we said above, is like throwing the family cat into the jungle deregulation. The cat, in this case, was a little hesitant; it said, "I don't know what will become of me with all the rules changed. This may not work out." "Don't worry," said Congress, "we will guarantee you a flow of deposits by giving you $100,000 per account insurance."

The $100,000 insurance did guarantee a flood of money. How you were going to make a profit with those deposits was, of course, something else. The cat said, "I'll try." End of cat. End of taxpayer.

March 24, Monday: "The following provisions of the Federal Deposit Insurance Act are amended by striking out $40,000 each place it appears therein and inserting in lieu thereof $100,000." (Section 308 of the *Depository Deregulation Act of 1980* (conference bill)). This was the first public appearance of the $100,000 provision. The conference Report was submitted by the chairmen of the respective banking committees, William Proxmire (D., Wis.) in the Senate and Henry Reuss (D., Wis.) in the House. The explanatory section of the conference report made no mention of the $100,000 provision.

March 25, Tuesday: The conference bill did not comply with House rules since it contained matter which appeared in neither the House or Senate bills it was supposed to be compromising. On Tuesday, the House adopted H. Res. 620 "waiving certain points of order against the conference report on H.R. 4986."

March 26, Wednesday: No action.

March 27, Thursday: The conference bill, after a few hours of boring discussion, swept through the House by a 380 to 13 vote. Chairman Reuss introduced the bill saying, "Unprecedented interest rates have made it imperative that we act now to modernize our financial system in the interest both of the stability of financial institutions and the needs of their customers." Reuss was followed by John LaFalce (D.,N.Y.) who also supported the bill because he found it in "keeping with the President's recommendation for an orderly transition to a banking system" which gave the consumer a fair return while allowing "the thrift industry time to adapt and continue in their role as housing lenders."

The only thoughtful comments came from Robert McClory (R., Ill.) who said he believed the commercial banks and the S&Ls should "strive to retain their specialized identity, their particular characteristics." Instead "we are confusing the identity of these individual institutions." McClory added: "I question the wisdom of savings and loan institutions being ambitious to get into the commercial banking business." The S&Ls, at some point, are "going to regret this kind of legislation."

The only mention of the $100,000 was by Jim Leach (R., Iowa) who said the jump from $40,000 to 100,000 was "an important part of this legislation [that] relates directly to the safety and soundness" of the commercial banks and S&Ls. He didn't explain, and no one thought to ask, how increasing the insurance was going to help the "safety and soundness" of the banking system. It assured a flood of money, but it didn't assure you could make a profit on it. As far as the House was concerned, the deal had been made and that was it. The deal, broadly, was that the S&Ls were being put into the banking business, where few thought they could survive, and they were given the $100,000 insurance to induce them to go along.

Thursday morning over in the Senate, Senator Robert Byrd (D., West Va.) proposed a unanimous consent agreement that H.R. 4986 be debated Thursday afternoon and Friday at 12:30 p.m. and "that there be no roll call on final passage." The agreement was accepted by the Senate as no objection was made. Senators, of course, know that recorded votes on disastrous laws can be campaign nightmares. A voice vote, on the other hand, leaves no footprints in the sand. The Senators chose, in the case of the banking bill, to have a no record vote. They agreed unanimously that was the right way to do it.

Senator Proxmire opened discussion Thursday afternoon saying H.R. 4986 was the "most significant banking legislation" since the passage of the Federal Reserve Act of 1913. A major theme was that the new law would put the S&Ls into the banking business. Proxmire said it "provides new lending powers to thrift institutions in order to enhance their competitive viability." Proxmire made one small mention of the $100,000 provision, it would (1) "meet inflationary needs" and (2) stabilize "deposit flows among depository institutions and noninsured intermediaries." The Keating Five hearings in November and December 1990 before the Senate Ethics Committee turned up some new facts about Proxmire. An aide to Senator Cranston testified that when he was chairman of the Senate Banking Committee, Proxmire had cut off all public funds for staff travel. The staff thereafter routinely traveled at the invitation and cost of lobbyists for the banks and S&Ls.

That Friday afternoon, the time the Senate had agreed to end debate, things got more exciting. Senator Jim Exon (D., Neb.) said he appreciated "that the votes are well marshalled and in line to pass the conference report." Still, he said, he had to note the attack on states rights which the bill made by allowing the Federal Reserve to override state usury laws. Senator Bill Armstrong (R., Colo.) had an even deeper problem. No one had told him about the unanimous consent agreement to evade a record vote. "[I]magine my surprise," he said, while reading the Congressional Record this morning, to learn that at the request of the majority leader, Senator Byrd, the Senate had agreed to hide the vote. Byrd, miffed, asked if Armstrong had "discussed this matter with his own leader?" [Senator Howard Baker (R., Tenn.)] Armstrong said he had not had that opportunity. Byrd suggested that in the future he do that before chastising the majority leader. At this interesting point, Senator Baker arrived and started pouring oil all around. He said he was very sorry he didn't know Armstrong had a problem with the no record vote procedure. He had asked the ranking Republican on the committee, Senator Garn, and Garn had agreed to it. He just didn't know, and it wouldn't happen again. Armstrong was not pacified: "The reason we have record votes is not for Senators. It is for the public, so they may know how we conduct our business." Senator Byrd shot back, saying he could tell Armstrong how to get a roll call if it was so important to him; after the bill is passed he should move to reconsider and demand the yeas and nays on the motion to reconsider that would give him, "in essence," a vote on the bill. Senator Baker said that sounded a little contrived. Byrd said it was just a suggestion if this little issue would otherwise "keep [Armstrong] awake at night, and cause him to lose his good humor, and his equanimity and possibly impair his health."

All that sarcasm and ridicule was visited upon Armstrong because he wanted a record vote. Chairman Proxmire now entered the discussion to say a record vote was out of the question; it would delay passage of the bill till Tuesday which would be "disastrous":

> I cite that for two reasons. In the first place, Tuesday is April 1, and that is the beginning of the next quarter. The end of the quarter is a rollover. At that point, it could be crucial for savings and loans, and banks, which many are in difficulty because of the very high interest rates, and the extremely difficult position homebuilders, and others, are in.

For that reason, the $100,000 insurance provided in this bill goes from $40,000 to $100,000, by far the biggest increase the government provided.

It is very important that come on track promptly and that we act for that purpose, so the President can sign the bill on Monday.

It was, said Proxmire, now or never. A few minutes later, the bill, by voice vote, passed the U.S. Senate.

March 31, Monday: The signing ceremony was held in the East Room of the White House at 11:33 a.m. President Carter said the new law was going to control inflation and strengthen our financial system which, the president said, "is the envy of the entire world." The new law had been a hard fight, passage, the president said at one point, seemed "doubtful." The president singled out for special thanks, among the assembled congressional luminaries, Fred St. Germain, Jake Garn and Bill Proxmire. The president made no mention of the $100,000 insurance provision which had first appeared in the world last Monday and that he was now going to sign into law. The new law was, he said, part of his deregulatory movement. As he put it, it was an "extremely important move toward deregulation by the federal government of the private enterprise system." Already we had had, in his view, "remarkable success" in deregulating the airlines. We were now going to repeat this remarkable success, he thought, in the "rail industry, trucking industry, and the communication [phone] industry." Somehow, President Carter thought his deregulation theories were consistent with $100,000 government deposit insurance.

The president, in closing, repeated his thanks to the members of Congress who had made this day possible. "Theirs is the gratitude that we owe, and I want to let them know how much we appreciate this remarkable achievement." Can we count the ways?

The Keating Five

The congressional manipulation fueled an explosive growth in S&L assets—from $658 billion in 1982 to $1.1 trillion in 1986 and $1.39 trillion in 1988 when the system collapsed. That is, in just 6 years, about $700 billion of new money rushed into the S&Ls. But, the S&L industry, as we all remember, was insolvent—that was the reason for the 1980 and 1982 Congressional solutions. An insolvent industry was gathering in billions of new brokered deposits daily. Did that concern the congressional watchdogs? Jim Wright and Jake Garn were undisturbed. They thought the new deposits proved the good job they had done in 1980 and 1982. What were the S&Ls going to do with all those new billions? Michael Milken, among others, was soon going to tell them. An awful lot of that new $700 billion, maybe half of it, was headed right down the drain.

One California S&L, Columbia Savings and Loan Association, closely associated with Michael Milken, owned, at one point $4.5 billion in junk bonds. It got the money to buy this junk from deposits thought to be guaranteed by the taxpayers. Columbia's assets rocketed from $373 million in December 31, 1981, to $10 billion in December 1986 roughly a 3,000 percent increase. Milken and Drexel Burnham owned 20 percent of Columbia. Columbia, in 1990, admitted it was insolvent because of huge losses in its junk bond portfolio. But federal regulators did not shut it down until January 25, 1991. It will cost the taxpayer $1.5 billion to pay for Columbia's losses.

What did it mean when you said an S&L could pay market rates for deposits? It meant that an S&L, because of the $100,000 insurance, could get all the deposits it wanted. It also meant to get a positive spread they had to invest in things that paid *more* than the market. This pushed the S&Ls away from the traditional single family mortgage and toward speculative real estate development loans, futures, options and junk bonds. As one S&L executive told Martin Mayer: "We had to follow a strategy of desperation to carry the bad assets."

The junk bond story is truly lunatic. The S&Ls, playing with what was thought to be taxpayer-guaranteed money, bought a large chunk of the most speculative junk in the country. Michael Milken's big buyers were the S&Ls, insurance companies, and pensions, all entities with some kind of government guarantee. People playing with other people's money. Without these guarantees, the junk bond market might have existed, but it would not have amounted to much, certainly not $200 billion. "The trouble with Wall Street," as Michael Lewis told a New York audience on October 24, 1991, "isn't what's illegal, its what's legal."

What about the $200 billion in unrealized losses that started the trouble? What was Congress going to do about the basic insolvency of the industry? Absolutely nothing. That was treated as an accounting problem. The S&Ls were insolvent measured by generally accepted accounting principles (GAAP). Congress let the Bank Board change the accounting rules so they'd be solvent. The rules were called RAP or regulatory accounting principles. They were very imaginative. Anything that came close to an S&L could be booked as income. The most metaphysical things, such as "goodwill", could be counted as assets. The S&Ls, in other words, were allowed to cook the books.

What about the basic insolvency of FSLIC, the corporation which was supposedly guaranteeing the deposits? It was no secret that FSLIC was bust. One of the authors wrote that it was in the June 1982 *Fortune* article. No one denied it. What was Congress going to do about that? Again, absolutely nothing. Maybe it would go away. The fact that FSLIC was bust meant it could not close busted S&Ls because it had no money to pay off the depositors. It means the busted S&Ls had to drift on. The losses rolled on, keeping the honest S&Ls behind the eight-ball and encouraging the crooked S&Ls to gamble with taxpayer-guaranteed funds.

By now, the reader knows that Felix Rohatyn is a favorite of the authors; what does he say about the congressional handiwork?

> The colossal amounts of money wasted by the savings and loan industry in investments in worthless real estate, in junk bonds, in speculation and corruption of all kinds, could have been invested in new, productive investments. Instead, half a trillion dollars were diverted from productive investment to the most blatant kind of fraud. The enormous capital drain caused by the S&Ls is one reason for our high cost of capital.

New York Review of Books, April 12, 1990.

That's a very good statement, but to speak of colossal amounts of money wasted by the "savings and loan industry" points the gun the wrong way. It wasn't really the "industry." It was the government, not a couple of crooks, that did it. The official Bush administration line was that some crooks had made off with $500 billion. Where would they hide it? President Bush, on June 22, 1990, announced a plan to send "teams of razor-sharp prosecutors and auditors" to pursue and speed fraud investigations. Bush spoke after the Marine Band played "Hail to the Chief" and "God Bless America" to 93 U.S. attorneys brought to Washington from around the nation who gathered for the photo opportunity in the flag-draped Great Hall of the Justice Department. The president said, "These cheats have cost us billions and they will pay us back with years of their lives." Indeed, said the president: "We will not rest until the cheats and the chiselers and the charlatans spend a large chunk of their lives behind the bars of a federal prison." This kind of vindictive rhetoric had previously been reserved for the hate crime crowd that the president wanted to track down.

Two problems with the president's plan are (1) it points to the wrong culprits, the money was lost not so much by criminal stealing as by the actions of the Congress and president in creating irresistible inducements to speculate; and (2) the president's reliance on the U.S. criminal justice system is misplaced since it has not been able to enforce any law for the past 20 years.

In late 1988, insiders stirred up a witches brew of three ingredients: (1) FSLIC was still bust; (2) hundreds of S&Ls were similarly bust, and everyone knew it; and (3) a fat S&L tax give-away, passed in 1981, was going to expire on December 31, 1988. The touchstone of the tax give-away was what they called "covered losses" which meant the S&L could take a tax loss on the sale of property even when the government guaranteed it against loss and paid it cash so it didn't have a loss. For example, if an S&L sold an asset with a book value of $100 for $40 it could take a tax loss of $60 even though FSLIC paid it $60 to cover the loss. The Bank Board, since FSLIC had no money to pay depositors, wanted new buyers to come in and keep the failed S&Ls open. Otherwise, the FSLIC bankruptcy had to become public. The Board, in 1988, sold 199 seized S&Ls to private entrepreneurs. The new buyers, as the tax break deadline approached, saw they had a tremendous bargaining advantage and made a last minute dash for the trough. The sweetheart deals, closed in the last week of 1988, will cost taxpayers an estimated $70 billion.

For example, Ron Perelman (a pal of Michael Milken) took over First Gibraltar and Vernon Savings for $315 million cash and in return got tax deductions valued at $897.3 million. Martin Mayer reports that Perelman "got $12.2 billion list price in assets supported by a $5 billion FSLIC assistance package for his $315 million investment." In 1989, Perelman's First Gibraltar reported payments from the government of $461 million and net profit to Perelman (tax-free) of $129 million. FSLIC, although it was flat as a pancake, was happily giving guarantees and issuing notes. Equally happily, the Congress continues to appropriate money to pay off the phony FSLIC notes.

By 1989, it was clear the 1980 and 1982 solutions were a disaster. The president and Congress looked for a new solution to cure the earlier solutions. They quickly agreed the new solution was to add $500 billion to the national debt—let the middle-class taxpayer pay for it. Congress also agreed with the president that the borrowing be off-Budget which was more expensive but didn't show up in the deficit. Ralph Nader writes: "Congress went along with President Bush's demand (under threat of vetoing his own bill) to remove the bailout from the federal budget so as to minimize the impact on the deficit. The bipartisan effort to hide the cost of this calamity continues apace."

The use of taxes to pay for this generation's mistake was not even discussed—everyone agreed debt was the thing. They set up an extraordinarily complex bureaucracy to pay out the $500 billion. The centerpiece of the new bureaucracy, the Resolution Trust Corporation budgeted $500 million for 1990 to be paid to outside lawyers.[10]

---

[10]Does any reader have a doubt the lawyers will soak up the $500 million? The lawyers have created a new publication to keep abreast of the latest developments, a biweekly newsletter called the *Bank Bailout Litigation News* (cost - $595 a year). A letter soliciting subscriptions to the *Bailout News* reports that in the "wake of massive failures of banks and thrifts" the government "predicts well over 80,000 lawsuits will flood the courts, with 85 percent of the government's legal work going to outside counsel." Charles Keating, according to Martin Mayer, estimates he spent $70 million in legal

They also were disingenuous in saying how much the bailout would cost the taxpayer, but no one believed them anyway. The public had already heard the 14 estimates of Bank Board Chairman Danny Wall (former aide to Senator Jake Garn). (These are fully set out in H. R. Rep. No. 101-54(I) pp. 305-06, accompanying the *Financial Institutions, Reform, Recovery and Enforcement Act of 1989*, also known as the Bailout Law). As late as the summer of 1987, Martin Mayer reports, Wall told Comptroller General Charles Bowsher that "you only have a $2 billion problem here." They had already heard Federal Reserve Chairman Greenspan tell the House Banking Committee, on March 22, 1989, that "in our judgment, all things considered, the $50 billion should be adequate." The public knew they were all liars and lies. They were going to have to pay, "all things considered," for a huge party they hadn't been invited to.

Congress and the president, when they got together in early 1989 to draft the Bailout Law, had 3 options available:

---

fees fighting delaying actions with the Bank Board. During the 1980s, on the way in, the great law firms of New York and Washington caused a large part of the public loss by throwing sand into the wheels of the regulatory machinery. Now, on the way out, they intend to carve off another nice piece.

If the future resembles the past, and it usually does, the Resolution Trust Corporation (RTC) will be lucky to show a profit from collections after the lawyers are finished. In 1990, the FDIC, using outside lawyers, reported that it spent $1.00 to collect $1.50.

In April 1991, it was announced that the FDIC had agreed to pay as much as $600 an hour to Cravath Swaine & Moore, the New York City law firm. The fee agreement gave Cravath a minimum fee plus a contingency and, according to the *New York Times* is "potentially the most lucrative ever between the Government and a law firm." The *Times* also reports that, since the bailout began, the FDIC is the nation's largest employer of lawyers.

OPTION	*COST TO TAXPAYER*
(1) Do Nothing.	$0.00
(2) Assume the S&L losses and pay for them with immediate taxes.	$130 Billion*
(3) Assume the S&L losses and pay for them with 20-30 year bonds	$500 Billion*

*These figures are subject to being doubled or tripled at anytime.

Option 1, the Do Nothing option, is based on the fact that government has no legal liability with respect to the S&L losses. That sentence probably comes as a surprise to the reader. Most Americans think the little plaque on the counter by the teller means that their S&L deposits are insured by the Federal Government up to $100,000. In fact, federal liability was limited to the assets of the Federal Savings and Loan Insurance Corporation (FSLIC) and now to its successor, the FDIC. The S&L insurance system was designed to deal with particular problems banks, not with the collapse of the industry. FSLIC was bust in 1982; the FDIC is bust now. The taxpayer, in short, is not liable for anything. If the taxpayer is not liable, why is he paying $500 billion?

Under Options 2 and 3, the Government *voluntarily* assumes the S&L losses—whatever they may be—and imposes the cost on the taxpayer. Money will move from the pockets of taxpayers to the pockets of bank depositors. Under Option 2, the losses are paid for by immediate taxes. Felix Rohatyn, for example, has suggested a 5 percent income tax surcharge for 3 or 4 years which he estimated would produce between $25 and $35 billion per year. Mr. Rohatyn told the National Press Club on June 14, 1990, "We should not compound the felony of what happened by dealing with it irresponsibly." He continued:

> Borrowing the money will turn a $130 billion problem into a $500 billion drain—or much more—over the next 20 to 30 years, leaving it to our children to pay off our own stupidity.

Congress and the president, as the reader knows, selected Option 3, which was the most expensive and dishonest choice. The only debate centered on whether the new borrowing should be on- or off-budget. Bush and the Congress agreed: (1) the taxpayer should pay and (2) Borrowing was the way to keep him from getting angry.

On March 22, 1989, Chairman Greenspan came over to the House Banking Committee to explain why the taxpayer should voluntarily pay what he did not owe:

> The reason for public expenditure to support deposit insurance is the basic benefits to the economy as a whole that we derive from deposit insurance. The certainty and stability provided by deposit insurance benefits the nation as a whole, while it protects the individual from catastrophic loss. By giving the public confidence in the safety of its funds we avoid the deposit withdrawal and losses that disrupted the payments system and the savings and investment process in the 1930s. Losses of the kind that we face today should not happen, but with the gains to society as a whole that come with deposit insurance we must accept both the possibility and the reality that there will be losses to be borne by society as a whole.

That was all okay, but maybe, at a $500 billion cost, the "certainty and stability" provided by deposit insurance was a little pricey. *The democratic failure is that the taxpayer has never been told he has the option. The President, Congress, and the media all tell the taxpayer he is legally obligated. But it's not true.* The taxpayer accepted the Bush-Congress solution because he thought he had no honorable choice. He thought it was his obligation and he wouldn't renege on it. He would never have gone along if he thought it was a big welfare handout for bank depositors who should have been more careful.

Who was being bailed out? Who was receiving the voluntary payment? Was it the small depositor with his life savings at risk? Not really. The bailout law made no effort to target the small individual depositor. Just paying, for example, up to $10,000 on a deposit would not be that expensive. And special provision for more in the case of hardship would not add that much more. The bank depositor was really asking the taxpayer for a welfare handout so it would be reasonable to require some special showing.

As noted above, between the 1982 Garn-St. Germain Act and 1988, about $700 billion of new deposits flooded into the S&Ls. Where did this tremendous amount of new money come from? Who were these people who, like a bunch of starlings, suddenly decided it was smart to move their money into S&Ls? Were they Wall Street sharpies after a high return on what they thought was a government guaranteed investment? A desperate S&L might pay 12 or 13 percent while a Treasury Bill paid 7 or 8 percent. Did they evaluate the quality of the investment or did they rely on the supposed government guarantee? Did they know that FSLIC, their legal guarantor, was bust at all times between 1982 and 1988? Why were they so confident Congress would bail them out even though there was no legal liability? Why were they right? Why is there so little official curiosity about who, exactly, is being bailed out?

The Keating Five, as they became known, were bipartisan. There were 4 Democrats, including one super-liberal, and one republican. The honor list reads: Senators Alan Cranston of California, John Glenn of Ohio, Don Riegle of Michigan, and Dennis DeConcini and John McCain, both of Arizona. Riegle was chairman of the Senate Banking, Housing and Urban Affairs Committee; Cranston was the second-ranking Democrat on the committee. In England the Keating Five were also known as the "Lincoln Brigade" after Keating's bank, Lincoln Savings. The Lincoln collapse will cost the taxpayers $2.6 billion, more than any other busted S&L. Keating, on September 17, 1990, was indicted by California for state securities fraud in the sale of junk bonds out of Lincoln branches. In December, 1991, the jury found Keating guilty. One week later, the federal government charged Keating with criminal racketeering and fraud in a 77 count indictment.

The Keating Five said they were just trying to make sure a constituent (Keating was everyone's constituent) got a fair shake from the banking regulators. But there was no question that political pull had reined in the regulators for a $2 billion taxpayer tab. Keating was a client of Alan Greenspan who, among other duties, testified on behalf of Lincoln against some Ed Gray regulations in congressional hearings in February 1985. On behalf of Lincoln, Greenspan also wrote, on February 13, 1985, to Tom Sharkey, Principal Supervisory Agent of the Federal Home Loan Bank in San Francisco, requesting exemption from the 10 percent limit on direct investment, i.e., non-loan investment. Greenspan said he had reviewed Lincoln's application for exemption and its audited financial statements. Keating had bought Lincoln a year earlier and Greenspan extravagantly praised the new management. Lincoln's new management, he wrote, is "seasoned and expert" in selecting investments; it "has a long and continuous record of outstanding success in making sound and profitable" investments, it has restored the association to a "vibrant and healthy state"; and it has "developed a series of carefully planned, highly promising, and widely diversified projects. Greenspan concluded:

> Finally, I believe the denial of the permission Lincoln seeks would work a serious and unfair hardship on an association that has, through its skill and expertise, transformed itself into a financially strong institution that presents no foreseeable risk to the Federal Savings and Loan Corporation.

Keating paid Greenspan $40,000, Martin Mayer reports, for his 1985 testimony and letter.

Was there any reason for Greenspan and the Keating Five to wonder about throwing in with Charles Keating? Well, it was known Keating was a lawyer for Cincinnati billionaire Carl Lindner. It was known that Keating, in 1979, had signed an SEC consent decree to a complaint charging that he arranged fraudulent loans to himself and his associates from a bank owned by Carl Lindner. (SEC Docket 1149 (1979).) Senator Dennis DeConcini told the Senate Ethics Committee that he thought Keating was okay because Mother Theresa had told him Keating was a friend. Probably Mother Theresa didn't know about SEC Docket 1149.

Keating estimates, according to Martin Mayer, that he has spent $70 million in legal fees; Mayer writes:

> More than eighty firms, for example, represented Charles Keating and American Continental Corporation (the parent of Lincoln Savings) in his five years of tussles with the Bank Board. Among them were Akin, Gump, Strauss, Hauer & Feld of Dallas; Arnold and Porter of Washington, D.C.; Baker & Botts of Houston; Hogan & Hartson of Washington, D.C.; Jones, Day, Reavis & Pogue of Cleveland; Kaye

Scholer Fierman Hays of New York; Sidley & Austin of Chicago; Stroock Stroock & Lavan of New York; Vinson & Elkins of Houston; Weil, Gotshal & Manges of New York. All these firms have more than two hundred lawyers to feed; and Keating has estimated his legal fees as high as $70 million.

The great law firms of Washington, New York, Chicago, Dallas and Los Angeles are "in large part" responsible, Mayer writes, for the failure of the Bank Board to control the "egregious crookedness" of many S&Ls. Mayer lumps the lawyers in with S&L owners, trade associations, senators, congressmen, lawyers, accountants, Wall Street prestidigitators [conjurers], professors, and consultants, "*all of the scoundrels* who had found ways to make money out of the government's mistakes and were willing to fight to the death to prevent the government from correcting them." [emphasis added]

During Charles Keating's ownership of Lincoln Savings, it had grown 4,000 percent on brokered deposits. Residential loans, at the same time, plummeted from 32.5 percent of Lincoln's assets in 1983 down to 1.7 percent of assets in 1988. As the regulators closed in, two meetings were held—"the four senator meeting" and "the five senator meeting." Ed Gray, chairman of the Federal Home Loan Bank, was told to come alone to a meeting at Senator DeConcini's office in the Hart Office Building at 6:00 p.m. on April 2, 1987. Gray later said that he had been told to come with no staff to give the Senators "deniability." They later availed themselves of this privilege by saying Gray's account of the meeting was all lies. The four senator meeting (DeConcini, Glenn, McCain and Cranston) told Gray to withdraw a regulation Keating didn't like. The five senator meeting (adding Riegle) was held a week later with the regulators from the San Francisco office who were directly dealing with Lincoln. The regulators stood firm against the Keating Five. Couldn't Lincoln be saved?, the Keating Five wanted to know. One regulator replied:

> It's like these guys put it all on 16 black in roulette. Maybe they'll win, but I can guarantee you that if an institution continues such behavior it will eventually go bankrupt.

Keating's friends thought, "The San Francisco regulators are a real pain, how can we get them off the case?" On July 1, 1987, Ed Gray was replaced as chairman by Danny Wall, former Garn aide. Wall, over cries of anguish from the West Coast, called the case back to Washington where, he said, his staff would handle it. Years passed. Lincoln was only declared insolvent after Keating had been forced to put its parent, American Continental Corporation, into a Chapter 11 bankruptcy. The Bank Board did not declare Lincoln insolvent until April 13, 1989—2 years after "the four senator meeting."

Keating's contributions to the Keating Five are (as reported by the *Detroit News* in early 1988):

SENATOR	DIRECT	INDIRECT
Cranston	41,000	935,000 (get-out-the-vote committees)
DeConcini	43,000	---
McCain	112,000	---
Glenn	34,000	200,000
Riegle	66,130	---

On June 22, 1990, Keating told the editors of the *New York Times* "that he had made the payments to the Senators only after being asked by them or their staffs for contributions." Common Cause, on June 28, 1990, reported that the S&L industry contributed $11.7 million to members of Congress during the 1980s. Ed Gray told CNN that Congress "had been bought lock, stock, and barrel by the savings and loan industry."

Senator Alan Cranston, in April 1990, disclosed to the Senate Ethics Committee that he had encouraged Keating to ask Michael Milken to give more money to Cranston's voter registration committees. Milken, in November 1990, was sentenced to 10 years in jail for securities law violations. Cranston said that Keating asked him who else was contributing to the voter registration groups. Cranston told Keating the Rockefeller family had, and Drexel Burnham, where Milken worked, so to speak, had given $25,000. Cranston testified that Keating was "outraged":

> He was outraged, that he was giving me large sums and Milken, who has earned a lot more and is worth a lot more, had only given $25,000, and he said, "I'm going to call him up and tell him he ought to give you a half million dollars or something like that." And I thought that would be great.

Milken, however, never came through with any more money.

On February 27, 1991, the Senate Ethics Committee (Senators Heflin (D., Ala.), Pryor (D., Ark.), Sanford (D. N.C.), Rudman (R., N.H.), Lott (R., Miss.) and Helms (R., N.C.), after more than a year of investigation, including two months of C-SPAN televised hearings, announced that there was "substantial credible evidence" that Cranston had violated Senate ethics. He had, the committee found, engaged in a "pattern of conduct in which fund-raising and official activities were substantially linked." The committee recommended the case against the other four Senators be closed. The conduct of DeConcini and Riegle gave the "appearance of impropriety" and was marked by "insensitivity and poor judgment." But the committee found they had not broken any specific Senate rules. The committee rejected the argument of committee counsel Bob Bennett that it wasn't a question of specific rules, DeConcini and Riegle had violated the purpose and spirit of Senate ethics. The committee found McCain and Glenn had "exercised poor judgment."

Critics were very harsh to the committee report: Common Cause called it a "cop-out and a damning indictment of the committee." *Public Citizen* said it was a "whitewash." Michael Kinsley, in *The New Republic* pointed out we didn't need the committee to tell us the Senators were guilty of "appearance of impropriety" we knew that before the committee started. The committee was supposed to tell us if there was impropriety or not. The *New York Times* found the whole thing a "farce": "The Keating Five is now the Keating Eleven—five Senators who got caught and six committee members who let most of them go." The *Economist* said the committee seemed to have adopted the standard that Bob Bennett warned them against: "Anything short of bribery is permissible."

The S&L stain ran broad and deep into the Democratic and Republican leadership. In April 1989, the House Ethics Committee investigating Jim Wright cleared him on charges related to his interference with federal regulators on behalf of Wright's S&L friends. Speaker Wright, in 1986 and 1987, held a $15 billion bailout of FSLIC hostage while he squeezed regulators on behalf of Don Dixon's Vernon Savings (see below). Wright had figured out that his S&L friends could not be closed down if FSLIC didn't have any money. The committee found, as reported by the *Washington Post* on April 5, 1989, that Wright had done was "proper and consistent conduct" for a congressman. The truth, though, as John Dean used to say, always comes out. Martin Mayer details the facts about Wright in *The Greatest-Ever Bank Robbery*. Speaker Wright made his resignation speech to the House on May 31, 1989.

Tony Coehlo, House Majority Whip, announced his resignation on May 26, 1989. Coehlo had created the highly successful Democratic Congressional Campaign Committee. Coehlo built his power on the money raised and dispensed by the committee. Coehlo, in 1986, in exchange for a promise to publish only after the November elections, gave *Wall Street Journal* reporter Brooks Jackson close access to the committee's workings. Said Coehlo "I'm going to treat you like staff. You'll see everything we do." Jackson's book, *Honest Graft* (Knopf, 1988) published 2 years later, reports that the only patronage system close to Coehlo's committee was old Tammany Hall as described by George Washington Plunkitt: "The old system used municipal jobs and contractors; Coehlo's patronage was the federal government's array of subsidies, entitlements, tax breaks and commercial regulation."

In 1986, Coehlo, after receiving a tip, asked to be cut in on some Beatrice Foods junk bonds sold by his friend Michael Milken. The bond issue was oversubscribed and looked like it would make money but Coehlo had no available funds. Tom Spiegel, CEO of Milken's Columbia Savings Bank (Spiegel's 1986 salary was $10 million making him the country's most highly paid thrift manager), bought $100,000 of the bonds which, he said, belonged to Coehlo when he could come up with the money. Coehlo came up with the money after it was

established the deal was profitable. The *New York Times* reported
Coehlo made $6,806. Half the money Coehlo needed to pay Spiegel's
"loan" came in a $50,000 low interest "loan" from Columbia. Coehlo,
in 1989, admitted that he did not report the "loans" on his 1986
Financial Disclosure Statement. Coehlo has never identified the person
who gave him the tip on the Beatrice Foods bonds.

In 1985 and 1986 Coehlo's campaign committee held 11 fund-
raising parties aboard the *High Spirits*, a 112-foot yacht, moored on the
Potomac River. *High Spirits* was owned by a Texas S&L, Vernon
Savings, which Don Dixon bought in 1982 and which failed in 1987,
holding $1.7 billion of assets. *High Spirits* was built in 1928 as the
sister ship to the presidential yacht, *Sequoia*. Dixon picked her up in
Boca Raton for $2.6 million and moved her up the coast to the Potomac.
Jim Wright was also a friend of Dixon's and used the *High Spirits*.
Coehlo's committee paid Vernon Savings $48,450 for use of the yacht
after Federal bank examiners questioned whether or not the free use of
the yacht was an illegal political contribution.

On June 13, 1990, a Dallas grand jury indicted Don Dixon for
using Vernon to make illegal political contributions and other payments.
The contributions were made to, among others, Speaker Wright and
Tony Coehlo in the House, and to Jake Garn and Alan Simpson in the
Senate. Dixon, according to the indictment, also used Vernon to pay
$10,500 to an unspecified number of women for one evening. The
women, said the *Times*, "accompanied Vernon executives and guests at
a party for Vernon's directors in June 1985 at [Dixon's] house in Solana
Beach, which was followed by a yacht cruise in San Diego harbor."
The jury found Dixon guilty and, on April 3, 1991, he was sentenced to
five years in prison.

Bob Strauss, who has appeared often in these pages, represented
Speaker Wright in 1988 after *Banker's Monthly* published a two part
series detailing Wright's intervention with Ed Gray on behalf of Don
Dixon which included, as noted above, holding reform legislation
hostage. Strauss persuaded the magazine to run an article by Wright
rebutting the charges.

By 1988, Strauss was already deeply involved in the S&L mess.
In 1963 John Connally, governor of Texas, appointed Bob Strauss to the
Texas Banking Commission. Strauss served as a banking commissioner

until 1976. He was chairman of the Democratic National Committee from 1972 to 1976. As we reached the early 1980s, Strauss began diving for profits in the river of opportunity created by the S&L fiasco. Strauss and his son Richard and his colleague, Livingston Kosberg, a former nursing home operator, were major shareholders in the ironically named Texas S&L, Gibraltar Savings, which they acquired in 1983.

In 1984 Martin Mayer was in Bob Strauss's office, interviewing him about the upcoming election, when they received news that the Federal Home Loan Bank Board had approved Kosberg's First Texas (a $2.8 billion S&L) to acquire First Gibraltar (a $4 billion S&L). Charlie McCoy, a reporter for the *Wall Street Journal*, then 23-years old, called to verify some facts which Strauss did not want the public to know. Strauss, with Martin Mayer sitting there, told the young reporter that, if those facts appeared, Strauss was close to Warren Phillips, McCoy's boss, and he "would have his ass." Mayer writes:

> In my presence, he chewed McCoy out on the telephone for a quarter of an hour, informing him that he (Strauss) was close to Warren Phillips, CEO of Dow Jones, and thus McCoy's employer, and Strauss would have his ass if there was stuff in the story of which Strauss disapproved.

Gibraltar, in late 1988, was seized by federal regulators and sold off to Ron Perelman, who, in 1985, acquired Revlon with Drexel junk bonds. As part of the Gibraltar sale, Perelman was given $897 million in tax benefits. Gibraltar, beginning in 1984, put $330 million into Stonebridge Ranch, a 6,250-acre residential and office park development 30 miles north of Dallas. Stonebridge included million dollar homes, scenic golf courses, 13 man-made lakes and an equestrian center. Stonebridge, at the demise of Gibraltar, was transferred to FSLIC rather than Perelman.

With astonishing persistence, Strauss returned to seek one more profit from the collapsing industry. In 1989, he opened up negotiations with the federal regulators to buy Stonebridge. According to the *New York Times*, Danny Wall "reached a tentative deal for the government to sell the property to Mr. Strauss." Publicity upset the deal and, in June 1989, the regulators decided to sell Stonebridge by competitive auction. The winning bid, $61 million, was from an Osaka industrialist, Yukio

Kitano. He also has large real estate holdings in Hawaii. The $270 million loss (Gibraltar loans $330 minus $61 million sale) will be paid by American taxpayers. In January 1991, Mr. Kitano edged away citing financing difficulties. Insiders said Stonebridge is probably worth $20 million. Maybe there is still a chance for Bob Strauss.

Chairman Greenspan, as we've said before, often develops concepts that are way over the heads of the authors. His S&L cost theory probably sails the highest. The S&L costs, he told the *Financial Times*, are "illusory," just a transfer of money from one pocket to another. That says the chairman, does not affect our productive resources. Our capacity to produce is undiminished. The money moves from the taxpayer's pocket to the pocket of the people who lost it in the first place. It is just, according to the chairman, a question of the ownership of money. You could look at it that way, of course. But, if that's the case, why move the money from the taxpayer to the bank depositor in the first place?

The Resolution Trust Corporation has taken over a lot of assets from the failed S&Ls—marinas, golf courses, etc.—but are they worth *anything*? Can you sell any of them for cash? On May 15, 1991, Resolution Trust conceded its past efforts to sell the assets had failed; it announced a new plan to sell $100 billion of properties in bulk sales to big buyers. Chairman Seidman said it was the only way left: "We'll never make it by selling these things piece by piece. The only way to do it is by making large sales to large buyers." But what the chairman called "sales" were not really sales. The "buyer," under the new program, pays a small down payment and agrees to pay part of future profits, *if any*, toward the rest of the purchase price. During the Depression, banks made similar no liability deals on foreclosed buildings to induce "buyers" to take on the responsibility of running them. If things went well the buyer paid off the bank out of profits and kept the building—if not, it went back to bank. In 1991, the Resolution Trust Corporation, following this old model, had divided the future upside (profit)—which went to what Seidman called the "large buyers"—from the downside (loss)—which stayed with the taxpayer. Why did that sound so familiar?

Congress, by Thanksgiving 1991, had voted $180 billion of taxpayer funds for the continuing bank bailout. Congress refused to limit the $100,000 deposit insurance which caused all the trouble. It is still possible to get unlimited federal insurance by holding any number of deposits at less than $100,000. Congress may say that, at this point, it would not help much to repeal the $100,000 provision but a farmer shuts the barn door, even though the horse is gone, because he wants to reestablish some order.

CHAPTER SEVEN

Filing for Bankruptcy - The Budget Deal of 1990

On August 18, 1988, George Bush said, "The Congress will push me to raise taxes, and I'll say no, and they'll push, and I'll say no, and they'll push again, and I'll say to them, 'Read My Lips: No New Taxes.'" In May 1990, it was George Bush who approached Congress to discuss a tax increase. The next 5 months were such a circus that even a jaded public could not believe it.

Abe Beame always said that what he had was a "budget gap" or "cash flow" problem. The City's finances were fundamentally sound, he said, but there were some timing problems which had to be solved. New York City, by constitution, had to have a balanced budget for each fiscal year. But since no one involved intended that the budget really be balanced, they engaged in an elaborate ritual dance. Each year from 1970 to 1975, about a month before the start of the fiscal year, the mayor would announce a new "budget crisis." There was a revenue "shortfall" of a few hundred million. What was to be done? The mayor, the governor, and the power brokers went into desperate round the clock meetings. They always produced a last minute "solution." The solution was always a combination of spending cuts, which never took place, and new nuisance taxes (sales tax, hotel occupancy tax, etc.), which always did take place and never went away. Part of the solution was usually some innovative accounting gimmicks which could make income and expense appear and disappear at will. The *New York Times*, next day, always carried a picture of the weary heroes whose all night meetings had "saved" the City. The people, after a couple of "savings," believed nothing.

In the late 1980s, the New York City show took to the road down in Washington, D.C. The national audience did not like the show any better than the City audience had. The *Times*-CBS poll asked the public, in September 1990, if they thought government was *serious* about trying to reduce the deficits. The poll found that *59 percent of the public thought the Congress and the president were not serious.* In other words, the audience hated the 1990 show before it started.

In 1985 Congress passed the first Gramm-Rudman Act, officially known as the *Balanced Budget and Emergency Deficit Control Act of 1985.* It was passed to quiet public fears about the fact that deficits, since 1981, had been running around $200 billion each year. Gramm-Rudman promised that austerity and fiscal discipline would annually cut the deficit resulting, for the year beginning October 1, 1990, in a zero deficit. Nonetheless, from 1985 to 1990, the deficits ran consistently around $200 billion each year. For the year beginning October 1, 1990, after five years of austerity and fiscal discipline, the deficit will be around $400 billion.

How you state an issue usually determines how you will answer it. The solution to a "Budget Gap" may well be a bunch of "anti-Bubba" taxes (gas, beer and cigarettes). The solution to a national bankruptcy is something else. Bankruptcy is the inability to meet obligations as they come due. Borrowing to meet them doesn't count. The original Budget Deal, announced October 1, raised taxes on gas, alcohol, and tobacco. One working paper, Table 7.1, which was leaked to the *New York Times* on October 2, showed the leaders knew exactly who was going to be hit by these taxes. The reason, of course, is that the average car uses 500 gallons of gas a year whether it is driven by a person making $20,000 or $200,000. Same for the alcohol and tobacco—excise taxes are always regressive.

Suppose we did everything the leaders proposed, what would we get? They said savings of $40 billion this year and $500 over the next 5 years. Somewhere we'd heard that before. It was also a little rosy—it projected 5 years of wonderful economic growth. It was also a little incomplete; it left out the cost of the S&L bailout and Desert Storm.

For fiscal 1990-91 the most they promised, if we did everything they wanted, was that a $294 billion deficit would be reduced to $254 billion. It did not stir the imagination. *The Economist* said it left you with one big fact—this year you were going to have to borrow at least another $250 billion.

TABLE 7.1

Tax Increase by Income Level

INCOME	TAX INCREASE BY ORIGINAL BUDGET DEAL
$ 20,000 - 50,000	3.0%
$ 50,000 - 100,000	2.0%
$100,000 - 200,000	1.5%
Over $200,000	.3%

New York Times, October 2, 1990

President Bush, the night of October 2, addressed the nation to gain support for the Budget Deal. He said the $500 billion of savings were real: "No smoke, no mirrors, no magic act, but real and lasting spending cuts." The Budget Deal promised $64.8 billion in savings over the next 5 years by *reduced interest payments on the national debt.* No smoke, no mirrors. He threatened: "If we fail to enact this agreement our economy will falter, markets may tumble and recession will follow." He asked listeners to call their congressman and tell him to get behind the Budget Deal.

While this budget crisis was going on, how were austerity and fiscal discipline doing? On October 4, Attorney General Thornburgh started passing out $20,000 checks as reparations to Japanese interned during World War II. Congress, on October 10, voted $36 million for the National Endowment for the Arts. On October 23, the *New York Times* reported that House and Senate negotiators had agreed to spend $22.6 billion for a wide range of social welfare programs including $998,000 for a performing arts and cultural center in North Miami Beach. Additional billions in foreign aid poured out to unlikely "allies" like Jordan. The IMF was giving Iran a $300 million loan with the approval of the Bush administration. A specific provision in the budget package appropriates $500,000 to restore Lawrence Welk's childhood home in Strasburg, North Dakota. Sure, why not?

The people were furious, and some democracy came through. All those people Bush asked to call their congressmen did call but they told them to vote the Deal down. Late at night, on October 5, the House rejected the Budget Deal by a 254-179 vote.

Two weeks after the budget was defeated Congress and the president were still trying to put together a majority for some kind of bill. On October 22, the *New York Times* reported that the pork-barrelling necessary to get the "deficit reduction" bill through would not only eat up the announced cuts but could well *increase* the deficit over the originally projected $294 billion. A "little noticed" provision in the House bill, the paper reported, would raise the statutory limit on the national debt to $5 trillion. The thought was to avoid the "annual ritual" of increasing the debt ceiling which many lawmakers found "politically embarrassing." As finally passed the statutory limit was raised to only $4.1 trillion.

Following the October 5 vote-down, the Democrats decided the deal their leaders had agreed to was "unfair." What was "unfair" about it? It was soft on the rich. "Soak-the-rich," they said. The Democrats were trying to relive the glory days of their youth. But, as the Democrats well knew, there is no real revenue to be gained in soaking the rich. To get revenue you have to soak-the-middle-class. On October 14, *Washington Post* writers Tom Edsall and E. J. Dionne pointed out that the working and middle class shifted to the Republican Party as they became the target of Democratic taxes to fund programs the middle class didn't believe in. They are now anti-tax as Reagan showed very clearly. Edsall and Dionne write: "Gone were the New Deal days when Democrats taxed Republicans to pay for programs for Democrats. Now, it seemed, traditional Democrats were being taxed to help other Democrats." The days of youth were gone.

Kevin Phillips, in *The Politics of Rich and Poor*, is surely right in seeing a major political shift coming. Disposable income has been falling for 15 years in this country. In 1991, the top 1 percent of families, with an average income of $617,214, received more income than the bottom 40 percent of families. The "Reagan Republicans" know the party has sold them out at every turn—to Big Money, to the

Japanese, to whoever. They need a more comfortable home, but there is no reason in the world to think they are going back to the Democrats who want to tax them and redistribute their money to the minorities. They are caught between one party which is currently selling them out and another party which wants the opportunity.

How did the Democrats define "rich"? There was the rub. The Democrats and President Bush agreed to burst the Bubble with a new top rate of 31 percent. The new top rate applies to single people earning $47,050 and to married couples earning $78,400. These are people who think they are middle class, not rich. Flattening the Bubble at 31 percent slightly lowered taxes for the Bubble People—who were paying 33 percent—and raised taxes for the 700,000 households who had gotten through the Bubble—and who were paying 28 percent. The net revenue increase projected for the new 31 percent bracket was a pitiful $1 billion per year or 1 percent of the total deficit reduction the Deal was supposed to provide.

The old Bubble People—whose top rate is cut from 33 percent to 31 percent—may think they have a tax cut coming but it's not so. They will save the 2 percent cut on taxable income within the old Bubble. But that will be more than made up by the Budget Deal's biggest soak-the-middle-class tax. A new 1.45 percent payroll tax on gross wages and salary from $51,300 to $125,000. The new tax is taken out of the paycheck like Social Security and is supposed to be for Medicare. It will cost a taxpayer earning $100,000 an additional $663 and one earning $125,000 an additional $1,069. A two-income professional family will be very hard hit—say a husband and wife are partners in a medical practice and earn $125,000 each. Since they are self-employed they will have to pay both the employee's and the employer's share which will add up to a truly impressive total payroll tax of $20,493.20. Which is a lot to pay for nothing. The Medicare hike is the biggest money raiser in the Budget Deal costing taxpayers $26.9 billion over the next 5 years. The whole $26.9 billion will come from the upper middle class—those earning between $51,300 and $125,000.

The country's upper middle class, the old Bubble people, are a favorite tax target because they are not organized. Not like the elderly and the other special interests. The special interests put together a new set of transitional rules and specific give-aways including (1) developers of low income housing; (2) oil and gas producers (Senators Dole and Bentsen); (3) all property and casualty insurance companies; (4) selected wineries (Senator Packwood); and (5) charitable deduction for full fair market value of painting given to museum. (Senator Moynihan). The Joint Committee on Taxation reported, on October 26, that the Budget Deal revenue *losing* provisions would cost taxpayers $27.4 billion over the next 5 years.

The Budget Deal also creates—can you believe it—a new Bubble. The new Bubble, according to the *New York Times*, is a compromise between the Democrats desire to have a 33 percent top rate and the president's insistence that the new top rate could not be more than 31 percent. The compromise is to accomplish what the Democrats wanted but by indirection. Two hidden rate hikes are put in for families earning $150,000: (1) phasing out the benefit of personal exemptions; and (2) limiting itemized deductions—for each $10,000 of income above the $150,000 the family loses $300 of deductions. For these taxpayers, the new Bubble People, the top rate is somewhere between 31 and 35 percent, but it is impossible to tell except by individual calculation. Could it get much worse?

The bigger mystery is why the Democrats believed George Bush when he said no 33 percent tax rate. They had just rolled through 4 major Bush fortifications: (1) No new taxes, read my lips; (2) no new income taxes; (3) no new income taxes without a 15 percent capital gain; and (4) no raising of income tax rates.

The House passed the modified Budget Deal, by a 228-206 vote at 7 o'clock in the morning, Saturday, October 27. The Senate passed it that afternoon by a 54-45 vote. The last minute hard sell was fierce: "I know this is a bad budget bill, the taxes are terrible and the cuts are conjectural. But it is the *only* budget bill we have and there will be chaos if we pass nothing."

The Budget Deal's five year costs and benefits, as the *Times* reported on October 28, are a "grand statement of social policy and political priorities" favoring the elderly and the poor. Almost all the cost—$165 billion in new taxes over the next 5 years—will be paid by the middle class. The benefits go to the elderly and poor—the poor get $18.2 billion in new tax credits. Student loans, which *might* help the middle class, are cut by $1.7 billion. After the October 27 vote,

Congress quickly left town to find out just how mad the voters were. On November 5, without any ceremony, the president signed the bill. There was no demand for pens. President Bush then campaigned saying (1) the Democrats had forced him to agree to the tax increases; but (2) the Budget Deal was an excellent law which could save the country. The President maintained the $490 billion of deficit reductions over the next 5 years were real. No smoke, no mirrors, no hopeless confusion.

There is not a single person in the country who believes that. There is not one American who thinks the Budget Deal of 1990 will reduce the deficit by a dollar. The people had moved beyond cynicism.

On January 8, 1991, Robert Reischauer of the Congressional Budget Office announced that the 1991 operating deficit was not going to be $250 billion, as the Budget Deal promised, but at least $400 billion. That meant that $1 of every $3 the Government was spending was borrowed. You can't run a country on borrowed money. Reischauer said: "It is going to face Congress with a very difficult situation with the American people, who will be shaken in their faith in Congress. Congress just enacted the largest deficit reduction package in the nation's history and now we will be treated to the largest deficit in the nation's history."

Well, how were the American people enjoying all this? Not too much. A Kettering Foundation Report, issued in June 1991, reports that Americans believe they are victims of a "hostile takeover" by a professional political class. The people think it is like the old Kevin McCarthy movie, *The Invasion of the Body Snatchers*. The courthouse in the town square looks as it always had. So did the Congress and the Executive. But they aren't the same. The people believe "they have been squeezed out [by] politicians, powerful lobbyists and the media" who communicate with each other in a unique new language. The "takeover group" is "out of touch with citizens and their concerns." The monied interests and politicians are so close that, "[i]n the end, citizens believe that they do not—cannot—have a say in the system." The report concludes: "The legitimacy of our political institutions is more at issue than our leaders imagine."

The people's protest against the legitimacy of government has taken the form of what Pat Buchanan calls the permanent tax revolt. The tax revolt has suceeded: the national, state and local governments are all—simultaneously—broke. A tax revolt is the predictable response by people to 25 years of debt financing. Jefferson said debt was anti-democratic for two reasons: (1) it allowed government to go ahead with expensive unpopular programs without having to ask the people to pay for them and (2) it casts the burden on future unrepresented taxpayers without their consent. The only reason the debt exists is that the government was trying to circumvent the democracy, it wanted to go ahead with programs that it knew the people didn't believe in and were not willing to pay for. So, it shouldn't be a surprise that when you ask taxpayers to pay a $283 billion interest bill, what you get is a tax revolt.

What was the money spent for? Over the past 25 years, according to HUD Secretary Jack Kemp, the country has spent $2 trillion for programs to uplift the poor. Lyndon Johnson said he would reduce poverty and crime and make our cities into "Model Cities." Pretty quickly, though, it became clear the programs weren't working. The government responded to failure by spending more money. It was operating without the consent of the governed. Did it work? Charles Murray, in *Losing Ground* (1984), reports that family life, poverty, and crime, by every objective index, are much worse than they were in 1965.

Our experiment with non-democratic government has destroyed American's Economic Constitution. Paul Weaver analyzes the change in American business in *The Suicidal Corporation* (1988). Well into the 1960s, Weaver writes, business exercised a "formidable capacity for saying no" to inflationary schemes and other governmental violations of the Economic Constitution. By the 1970s, however, business had retreated from leadership and responsibility. The Business Roundtable, made up of the chief executives of about 200 large corporations, came into prominence, and was a great favorite around the Carter White House. The Roundtable was the "most accommodationist and least confrontational" of business groups. The Roundtable divided very large corporate America from medium and small business. Very large business got the idea it did not need the protection of the Economic Constitution anymore—it thought it could make a private treaty with government. Led by the Roundtable, business would go-with-the-flow of government proposals, as Weaver puts it, "almost regardless of how bad they might be, in exchange for subsidies, loopholes, or other benefits, real or imagined, that businessmen hoped would compensate them for the harm done. "

Corporations in the nineteenth century had influenced government. No question of that, they sought tariffs and land give-aways (the railroads). But, in the end, business aimed at producing and selling some quality product. Businessmen produced the industrial giant which ruled the world in the 1950s. But, as time passed, big business abandoned its mission; it let the Economic Constitution go. Business took what the failing government could give: (1) subsidies; (2) special entitlements; (3) tax deals; (4) regulatory preferences; and (5) taxpayer bailouts. The new partnership with government supplanted the quality, utility, and affordability of the product as the key to business success. Government gave its new partners monopolies and special tax deals, in effect, sharing the sovereign taxing power with them. The antitrust laws were forgotten. It was a lot easier, business found, to collect taxes in the form of monopoly prices than to make competitive products. The American economy drifted away from production and manufacturing. It gave us paper entrepreneurs, who are much more richly rewarded than Henry Ford, Alexander Bell, or Thomas Edison ever were or wanted to be.

In the late 1970s and 1980s, the government deregulated the airline, trucking, and banking industries which, until then, were largely decentralized. Deregulation, it was argued, would improve competition by removing legal restraints on entering and operating a business. Medium and small business favored deregulation but asked, "What is going to stop the big fish from eating the little fish?" The Justice Department replied that it would strictly enforce the antitrust laws. Of course, as the reader knows, deregulation led to the destruction of medium and small business and tremendous concentration of market power. The new cartels outrageously exploit the consumer.

A corporate state is one in which the state and big business are very close. The new cartels resulting from the deregulation experiment are, of course, natural allies of the existing cartels and the government.

The Money Abandonment undermined the legal and economic constitutions that had provided the American citizen control of his material and political condition. The citizen, because of Abandonment, has lost his economic sovereignty. With that gone, he can expect to lose his political sovereignty. Ultimately, political power depends on economic means.

PART II

The Political Abandonment

Watch what we do, not what we say.

> Attorney General-Designate John N. Mitchell explaining prospective Nixon Administration civil rights policies to thirty southern black leaders, 1968.

Nowadays its hard just to get someone to drop their bag of Doritos long enough to cross the street to vote.

> Connecticut Governor Lowell P. Weicker, Jr. explaining his view of the American democracy, October 25, 1991

CHAPTER EIGHT

The Homeless Majority

What would America look like today if the Democrats had won every election since 1968? Maybe taxes would be a little higher, but almost everything else would look the same: debt, affirmative action, the federal takeover of education and law enforcement. That's the first great political mystery of the past 25 years—the people consistently vote strongly for the most conservative presidential candidate. But nothing happens. The country continues to roll along in the opposite direction. There is a reason why the people's vote has made so little difference but it takes a little explaining.

We have to start with what we call the "Political Constitution" as it existed in 1965 when most of what was important to a middle-class family was decided locally. The main features of the 1965 Political Constitution were:

1. Education was governed by local school boards subject to statewide plans or guidelines.

2. The state power to tax was subject to state or local electoral control and state constitutional limits.

3. The spending power also was subject to state or local electoral control and state constitutional limits.

4. The power to create debt, similarly, was subject to state or local electoral control and state constitutional limits.

5. Criminal laws were largely the subject of state legislation and the state and local police were primarily responsible for their enforcement.

6. Political subdivisions, from cities and towns to school boards, were created by state law and controlled by the communities they served.

7. The boundaries of state assembly and senate districts were drawn by the state legislature.

8. The public health and welfare was controlled by state law; whether abortion was legal, whether young people could drink at 18, or whether a car could turn right on a red light, were up to the state.

9. Business hiring practices and the employment contract were basically matters of state law. Judges and other government officials with whom the citizen had to deal were not selected on the basis of racial preferences.

10. State budgets were funded with state money.

11.   State law, and the federal Constitution, assured the legal
       equality of every citizen. Government could not decree that one
       individual had greater rights than another. Nor could it decree
       that one group had greater rights than another.

12.   Most things were left to the control of private groups. Business
       arrangements and social relations were matters of personal
       choice. Admission to private universities, and admission to
       clubs were governed by private decisions.

The 1965 Political Constitution operated efficiently because the
local government was responsive to the voters who elected it. If elected
officials weren't responsive they were kicked out. Congress and the
federal judiciary had the power to interfere with state and local
government, but did so only when it was necessary to prevent
unconstitutional discrimination. The middle-class family, by use of the
vote, had political control over most of the things that mattered to
everyday life.

Twenty-five years later, all that is gone. The federal government
funds about 25 percent of state budgets. Federal controls, of course,
follow federal money; also, federal controls can come without money.
Congress and the federal courts mandate that the states pay huge sums
for Medicaid and prison construction. The federal judiciary and
administrative agencies now intervene in every facet of state and local
government: how a town educates, how the police go about their jobs,
how a town collects its taxes, how much it collects and what the taxes
are spent for. We end up with a state and local government that can't
tax, educate, house, arrest criminals, or make traffic ordinances except
pursuant to federal guidelines and as monitored by the federal
government. A town can't even put a crèche under its Christmas tree
unless it also puts a blue smurf along with it. The federal judiciary
reaches down into the most routine local police functions. Morristown,
New Jersey, in November 1991, paid $150,000 to a homeless man for
his promise to stop suing the town and harassing its police. In a
previous lawsuit the homeless man had forced Morristown to let him in
the town library despite the fact that the court conceded he was
olfactorily offensive. The federal district court approved the $150,000
payment.

The citizen's continuing right to vote for local and state officials is largely futile since these officials have so little power and what power they have is subject to pervasive federal regulation and oversight. Fewer quality people, of course, are now attracted to state and local governmental office because they are required to act as federal functionaries. The old 1965 democracy worked from the bottom up—the citizen controlled his life by voting for lots of local and state officials who, at the time, had the power to determine the important things in the citizen's life.

Well, you might ask, if democracy at the state and local level is dead, what about the citizen's continuing power to vote for a congressman every two years, a president every four years, and two senators every six years? Can the citizen control the national government with those four votes? Can the citizen control his destiny from the top down.? To answer the question fully, we must look separately at Congressional and presidential elections. But the short answer, before too much tension builds up, is not very well.

"America is the only country where we can clearly see the point of departure of a great nation," said Alexis de Tocqueville. We are the only country created by an open and orderly political debate, where the ideals and principles of government were adopted and written down at a Constitutional Convention. The United States Constitution, embodied five ideals: (i) a written compact setting up (ii) a governmental structure of separated powers based on (iii) majority rule, whose ends were to promote (iv) justice and (v) equality.

The framers intended that Americans would never again be subjected to a strong centralized power, like the British king. They developed two ideas to assure that governmental power over the citizen would always be fragmented. First, there was the separation of legislative, executive and judicial powers, which was designed so that each branch of the federal government would restrain the other two. Second, there was the idea of concurrent sovereignty which meant that the federal and state governments shared power in the same geographical area. The essential national powers—war, peace, treaties, the power to regulate commerce between the states—belonged to the federal government. All the rest—the powers to provide for the security and welfare of the citizen—belonged to the state. Separation of powers and federalism were both designed to prevent the growth of highly centralized government. Since 1965, however, the Supreme Court-led Revolution has greatly expanded Washington's power. Federalism, at this point, was twisted from a benign principle to a malignant one. Congress, according to the principles of federalism, is accountable to the people regionally rather than nationally. Consequently, the Supreme Court-expanded congressional power is not accountable to, and cannot be controlled by, the national voting majority; only the president is accountable nationally.

Lyndon Johnson's Great Society extended national power to housing, race relations, crime, education, and many other issues which had previously been the primary responsibility of state government. Essentially, Johnson—and the Revolution that followed him—acted to replace equality of opportunity—in which the majority believed—with equality of result—in which the revolution believed. The expansion of national power, begun by the Great Society, was bipartisan; it continued apace under Republicans and Democrats. Federal power and money took over one traditional state and local area after another. As E.J. Dionne reports in *Why Americans Hate Politics* (1991):

> [N]ixon might have tried to cut this or that liberal program, but he had already decisively shifted the government's spending priorities in a liberal direction....
>
> Thus, between the 1968-69 budget, the last budget fully crafted by Johnson, and Nixon's 1971-72 budget, social security spending was up 55 percent, nondefense spending was up 44 percent—and defense spending was down by 3 percent.

President Reagan restored defense spending but also allowed social spending to increase giving us the deficits of the 1980's.

The government, under Democrats and Republicans, used federal power to enforce equality of result. The majority, however, never stopped believing that the proper function of government was to be a fair umpire, to protect equality of opportunity. The people understood that there was no real distinction between affirmative action and racial preferences and quotas. When politicians said they supported affirmative action it meant they supported preferences and quotas. The majority, however, was, and is, unable to change the government's direction. The

NBC News/*Wall Street Journal* poll for October 25-29, 1991 reports that 62 percent of Americans disapprove of the job Congress is doing while only 26 percent approve. Nonetheless, 96 percent of all congressmen are reelected every two years. What explains the coexistence of the high disapproval rate with a 96 percent incumbency rate? How do we have a group whose collective action meets with our disapproval, and yet one to which we usually return our own representative?

The incumbency win rate is always high because a congressman has name recognition, access to the press, and easy fund raising. A congressman, absent some national or local disaster, should get re-elected. Our opinion on the performance of the Congress, as a whole, however, turns on an entirely different proposition—whether we think Congress is doing a good job of regulating the details of our daily lives.

As long as Congress viewed itself as holding defined and limited powers, and the other branches checked any expansion of those powers, that question did not come up. Congress did not try to run our lives. Congress, under the Constitution, was supposed to take care of war, peace, tariffs, taxes, and regulate interstate and foreign commerce. Congress didn't think it had the power to tell people how to educate children, monitor local police, and control the daily life of the citizen. Congress now thinks it does and the majority of people think Congress has undertaken a job it is not designed to do and, predictably enough, fouled it up.

The Supreme Court authorized Congress to undertake its new duties. The Court's action, starting around 1960, was part of a very broad "agenda-setting role [undertaken by] the federal government," according to Thomas and Mary Edsall in *Chain Reaction* (1991). The Court, in a series of decisions, found "criminal defendants, many of them poor and black—and some clearly guilty—entitled to a new range of fundamental constitutional protections and rights." In case after case the Court created new rights for "criminal defendants, atheists, prisoners, homosexuals, the mentally ill, illegal aliens, publishers of pornography and others." In each case the Court overruled the actions of the local police or board of education, or the state laws under which the local officials acted. The Court routinely denied the majority will.

The Court, as the Edsalls point out, barred prayer from public schools (*Engel v. Vitale*, 1962); made local prosecution for obscenity difficult (*Jacobellis v. Ohio*, 1964); barred state laws limiting the sale of contraceptive devices (*Griswold v. Connecticut*, 1965); barred state prohibition of abortion (*Roe v. Wade*, 1973); immunized the media from liability for untrue statements about local officials unless the officials could show "actual malice" (*New York Times v. Sullivan*, 1964); and, finally, took over from the state legislatures the power to draw the lines of their own election districts. (*Baker v. Carr*, 1962).

The Court-led Revolution against the majority's values and interests was assisted by the executive branch. The president directed his agencies and departments to issue regulations, and exercise their contracting powers, in aid of the Revolution. The guidelines for federal contracts practically mandated racial quotas. Initially, the legislative branch played no active role in the Revolution. However, around 1980, as Martin Mayer points out in *The Greatest-Ever Bank Robbery*, (1990), a congressman's contributors became more important than his constituents. Congress was then, and is now, ready to join in the Revolution; its actions have become increasingly separate from—and opposite to—the wishes of the majority. It, for example, passed the Civil Rights Act of 1991 although every poll reported that 80 percent of the voters hated quotas. Similarly, it passed the Tax Reform Act of 1986 although every poll showed that 80 percent of the people did not want *any* tax bill. At Thanksgiving time, 1991, Congress added $100 billion to the Bank bailout although all the voters favoring the bailout would fit in a small meeting hall.

Americans, following World War II, believed that the allied victory had assured the survival of fairness, equality of opportunity, and judgment based on individual merit. The majority believed in full legal rights for all citizens. The Gallup poll, in November, 1955 asked white citizens: "The Supreme Court has ruled that racial segregation in the public schools is illegal. This means that all children, no matter what their race, must be allowed to go to the same schools. Do you approve or disapprove of this decision?" 71 Percent of whites, outside of the South, approved of the decision while 24 percent disapproved. By contrast, Southern blacks, in November, 1955, approved the decision by the much narrower margin of 53 percent approval to 36 percent disapproval. Gallup, in May, 1964, asked whites: "If two candidates of your own party were alike in all respects except that one candidate took a strong stand in favor of civil rights and the other a strong stand against civil rights, which man would you be more likely to prefer?" 65 percent of whites, outside of the South, preferred the candidate taking a strong stand in favor of civil rights while 19 percent preferred the anti-civil rights candidate. The Edsalls report that, as late as April, 1965, 71 percent of the people believed the Johnson Administration was "pushing racial integration" either "about right" or "not fast enough"—only 28 percent thought it was "too fast." The essential premise of the Court-led Revolution is that it had to take power from the majority because the majority has bad values; it is, for example, racist. The Revolution's premise, however, as the polling makes clear, never had a factual basis. The majority believes in fairness, not racism.

The majority's opinion, in 1965, was about to start reacting against the Court-led Revolution. By September, 1966, the majority of people, 52 percent, thought the Johnson Administration was pushing too fast. What caused the majority to change its mind? "The costs and burdens of Democratic-endorsed policies," the Edsalls write, "fell primarily on working and lower middle-class whites who frequently competed with blacks for jobs and status, who lived in neighborhoods adjoining black ghettos, and whose children attended schools most likely to fall under busing orders." The Edsalls continue:

> In time, the national consensus behind the drive for black equality began to fray. The federal judiciary and the federal regulatory apparatus adopted remedies that sharply increased the political, economic, and social costs of the civil rights movement, including busing, affirmative action, strict legislative redistricting requirements, and a widening system of racial preferences. Traditionally Democratic whites—whites who felt themselves to be increasingly pressed economically, who felt that they bore the largest share of the burden of the civil rights revolution [left the Democratic Party.]

The Court-led Revolution, what the Edsalls call a revolution from the top-down, imposed the revolutionary values upon the majority. It was almost immediately clear that equal opportunity and the use of merit and objectively-measured performance in setting educational and occupational standards would not produce the revolutionary goal of equality of result, so the Revolution let merit go along with majority control.

The citizen, it is true, still has some power over Congress; he can vote for his one representative and two senators. Does that allow the citizen any real ability to control Congress? Obviously it is a little thin, and particularly so since the election of his representative is likely to turn on local issues and the vote for his senator will probably also be at least partly local.

Now there's nothing new about that—the citizen never could control Congress as a whole and he wasn't supposed to. In the federal system the citizen was supposed to have regional representation. The Framers gave the central government power only with respect to matters of national necessity. The original system worked fine until the central government broke out of the corral; until it determined it had the power to decide if a car in Rapid City could turn right on a red light. Since then, the pieces don't fit together. The Court-led Revolution so altered the balance between central and local powers that the federal principle began to work against effective democracy. The Court, with some assistance from Congress and the Executive, reversed the effect of federalism envisioned by the Constitution.

Do Congressmen from California vote on whether someone from South Carolina pays more income tax, or whether he should assume liability for the S&Ls, or on any other matter affecting his fortunes? Of course, they do. Do the citizens of South Carolina vote on the senators and representatives from California? Of course they don't. It is impossible to control the *collective* behavior of a body of 100 people when you can only vote for two, or the *collective* action of 435 when you can only vote for one. But—when the central power becomes unlimited—the result is that we have nationalized authority, but require only regional accountability. A national legislature has to be accountable to a national electorate. Because of this lack of accountability, nobody in Congress pays a political price for even the most massive foul-up. The S&L fiasco and the congressional salary grab make the people very angry, but no one has lost his seat because of them. Congress is practically immune from popular anger. With the Courts and Congress both beyond democracy, did the citizen have anywhere else to turn?

How about the citizen's vote for president? During the past 25 years, our political parties have drifted toward their natural constituencies at opposite ends of the socio-economic spectrum. The Republicans renewed their historic attachment to the upper end—the plutocrats Theodore Roosevelt had fought against. The Democrats drifted to the lower end. The Democrats *actually* represent the people who were most visible at their 1988 Convention—a "rainbow coalition" of minority interests and, to a small extent, some remnants of organized labor. In other words, they *actually* represent perhaps 15 percent of the total population. The Republicans *actually* represent a small percentage at the upper reaches of the socio-economic spectrum—the top five percent at most. This leaves 80 percent of the population without a political party. Neither the Republicans nor the Democrats serve the 80 percent majority which lies between the top 5 percent and the lower 15 percent. But how, can both parties ignore 80 percent of the population?

That is the second great political mystery of the last 25 years. How can political parties, which need to get elected, disdain the 80 percent? The explanation goes back to the 1964 election. In 1964, race, for the first time since the Civil War, became a partisan issue. The public, in 1962 polls, saw no difference between the political parties on race. By late 1964, however, the Edsalls report that when asked which party was more likely to support blacks and whites going to the same school, 56 percent said the Democrats, 7 percent said the Republicans and 37 percent said it would make no difference. In the 1964 election the racial issue benefited the Democratic Party. Lyndon Johnson, after his overwhelming victory in 1964, based his Great Society on the use of national power to impose his theories of social justice. The voters in 1968 said "Never again." The 1968 returns were:

Richard Nixon	31,785,480 (43.4%)
Hubert Humphrey	31,275,166 (42.7%)
George Wallace	9,906,473 (13.5%)

The vote for Nixon was very close, just about 500,000 votes, but the vote along anti-Democratic lines was not close at all. The Nixon vote combined with the Wallace vote was around 57 percent, a landslide.

But to Nixon, his victory was very narrow. Nixon also thought the 1960 election had been lost, or stolen, in the big northern cities where the minority vote was very important. When Nixon and Mitchell sat down in 1969 to plan strategy for 1972 they had one big, critical advantage. The Democrats had decided that their heart was with the counterculture, the crowd in the Chicago streets. You couldn't be sure they would nominate McGovern in 1972, but it was clear they were starting down the road to oblivion.

That gave Nixon and Mitchell a wide open field to work with. They agreed that the 13.5 percent Wallace vote could never find a home with the counterculture. The Wallace supporters, unless they wanted to continue casting wasted protest votes, would have to start voting Republican. Nixon and Mitchell agreed to direct some rhetoric their way. They said "Law and Order" and "No Forced Busing." The Southern Strategy included trying to get a southerner on the Supreme Court. The conservatives got the rhetoric and a few high-profile appointments, but that was it.

The real policy was moving in the opposite direction. The real policy was pro-quota, and carried the social agenda of the Johnson Revolution even farther than Johnson had. That's why John Mitchell said "Watch what we do, not what we say." The 1969 Philadelphia Plan was the first mandated racial quota program—Lyndon Johnson had not dared to do it. John Mitchell, on September 22, 1969, wrote his opinion, as attorney general, to the secretary of labor, supporting the legality of the Philadelphia Plan. The plan was followed by Secretary of Labor Order 4, 35 Fed. Reg. 2586 (1970), which mandated quotas for all federal contracts and federally assisted jobs. Any company doing business with the government had the choice of being cut off or going along. All major corporations, at this point, went to quotas to avoid trouble. They decided they preferred a close and friendly—as opposed to an adversarial—relationship with government. For a generation, hiring and promoting in large corporations has been done on a racial basis. Higher education followed suit. Yale Law School, beginning in 1971, reserved 10 percent of its entering class for black students. Nixon and Mitchell fastened quotas on American society.

Nixon and Mitchell had devised a political strategy that would disorient American politics for the next 25 years. It developed naturally from Mitchell's 1960 invention—the "moral obligation" bond. Nelson Rockefeller wanted to build housing projects but the constitution required a referendum before the state could issue debt and the people voted his projects down. Rockefeller asked Mitchell to figure out a way to get it done without asking the people. The legislature, Rockefeller said, would pass any statutes that Mitchell wanted. Mitchell cooked up the "moral obligation" bond. The bond was based on deceit; Mitchell said we didn't need the constitutionally required people's vote because there was no legal liability, but he had the legislature enact statutes and told investors the state was "morally" obligated. So there was no referendum because the state wasn't liable; but the state was bound. Rockefeller and Mitchell issued a bond that was intentionally calculated to circumvent the public will.

In 1969, the "moral obligation" bond, applied to national politics, became the Nixon-Mitchell "last vote" theory. The conservatives had no place to go, they had to vote for you. So give them some rhetoric to keep them happy. Push your real policies for the last vote. Where is the last vote? It is right next to the Democratic position on any issue. So you adopt *actual* policies which get as close to the Democrats as you possibly can. Just like the "moral obligation" bond, you say one thing and do something else; your words mean the opposite of what you say. People have to watch what you do, not what you say.

Obviously, this could only work if the Democrats were going to stay in a pitiful huddle around the 20-yard line and never make a serious move to the middle of the field. The Democrats seemed happy to do just that. With that piece in place, Mitchell's plan made a horrible kind of sense. Since 1965 virtually all governmental power has become national, but only the Republican party can win the presidency. In a one-party system, the "last vote" theory is the logical political technique, since it maximizes the pool of possible favorable votes. For example, President Bush, by moving left of center on civil rights, the environment and the handicapped, gives the Democrats no running room toward the center. They have to move further and further to the left.

From 1968 to 1972 Nixon and Mitchell applied the "last vote" theory diligently. Also, by 1972, as the Edsalls report, the public was increasingly aware of an unelected liberal elite that was pushing racial preferences, not through the Congress, but through the courts and the regulatory system. The 1972 election results showed:

Richard Nixon	47,165,234 (60.7%)
George McGovern	29,170,774 (37.5%)

Nixon increased his popular vote over 1968 by more than 15 million votes. He took every state but Massachusetts. Nixon biographer Stephen Ambrose, in *Nixon - The Triumph of a Politician 1962-1972* (1989), is a little puzzled by Nixon's great victory:

> It was all the more remarkable considering that he had been unable to deliver on many of the promises he had made in 1968, including an end to busing, getting tougher with criminals, prayer in the schools, welfare reform, an end to the war in Vietnam, and a halt in the growth of government. It was *ironic* that his great achievements, the ones he was proudest of, including the opening to China, dètente, and the beginning of arms control, had more appeal to his opponents than to his friends. (emphasis added)

It is easy to add to the list of things with "more appeal to his opponents than to his friends," for example, wage and price controls, large deficits, indexing of social security benefits, and the creation of the Environmental Protection Agency (EPA) and the Occupational Safety and Health Administration (OSHA). But there is nothing "ironic" about this—it is just the "last vote" theory working out.

"If affirmative action was interpreted properly," according to Democratic National chairman Ron Brown, "there would be much greater support from people." Peter Brown, in his *Minority Party* (1991), writes that it is the "almost unanimous sense in the upper echelons of the Democratic party" that it is "perfectly just for whites to suffer to help blacks because blacks at one time had been victims of legal discrimination." Americans who had never discriminated against blacks, or profited from past discrimination, did not, however, agree that they should pay for it. Mr. Brown quotes Stanley Greenberg,

Democratic pollster: "It's almost a nonissue in that it comes out
regularly in focus groups we do with middle-class voters. There is no
debate on affirmative action. Everybody's against it. There is a very
small share of the [white] electorate—zero—that believes they have
personal responsibility for this. That they ought to be paying for the
injustice. They will acknowledge there was injustice. But people do not
feel they are personally responsible and that they ought to be paying for
it. They can't even begin to understand the logic of it. *It does not even
reach the level of common sense for the majority of Americans.* They
think they are being asked to pay a bill that is not theirs." [emphasis
added]

In 1980, 1984, and 1988, Brown reports, "whites were 85 percent
or more of the electorate" according to network exit polls. America, it
is increasingly clear, is a one-party state as far as the presidency is
concerned. The Democrats, absent financial catastrophe, cannot win.
Most Americans don't think the Democrats are capable of being fair to
all the people. The Republicans win even though the people don't
believe in their philosophy. John Judis reports in *The New Republic* that
throughout the 1980s opinion polls showed Americans did not believe in
Ronald Reagan's free market economics or his apocalyptic
anticommunism. Why did they vote for him? In *Chain Reaction*, the
Edsalls document how race became the critical issue in American
national politics after 1965. Other issues, such as taxes, crime and
government spending, have become encoded with a racial element so
that many voters are not aware their vote is racially motivated. Judis,
reviewing *Chain Reaction* for *The New Republic*, writes that traditional
Republican positions—anti-tax, anti-spend, anti-government—became
racially coded as white voters "associated higher taxes with useless
expenditures on the black underclass, which appeared to be expanding
despite (or because of) government aid." *U.S. News and World Report*
(October 28, 1991) finds that "programs designed to benefit
minorities...today cost $150 billion annually—and have cost more than
$1 trillion over the past 25 years."

What are the implications of a one-party system? First, by
definition, a one-party government will not present meaningful options
on important issues for the citizens to decide. It will seek to avoid
controversy. A one-party administration governs diplomatically—by

granting enough concessions to every identifiable group to keep things, in its mind, on an even keel. The national interest—the wishes of the unorganized majority—is not represented. A one-party administration will use "last vote" theory as its political technique. "Last vote" theory, of course, is based on disorienting, rather than leading, the country. Financially, a one-party system leads to ruin. The government has no serious beliefs or mission beyond staying in office. The people, of course, have no affection, loyalty or sense of responsibility for the government. Consequently, it can't support itself with taxes. It will, therefore, borrow all the money it can and spend it like a sailor on leave in order to buy votes. The one-party administration is unrestrained until the system collapses.

Since the Republicans have followed the "last vote" theory, the conservatives get rhetoric on emotional issues: pledge of allegiance (old), flag burning (new), abortion (old), forced busing (old), law and order (old), Willie Horton (reprise). The actual policies, on the other hand, seek out the "last vote." Take, for example, the Civil Rights Act of 1991 that President Bush, for 20 months, called a "quota" bill. The citizen, hearing rhetoric like that, might think there was a philosophical gulf between the Bush bill and the Democratic bill. The citizen might think the country was finally having the debate it should have had 25 years ago. But if he went to listen he would have heard the most arcane, the most inscrutable, debate in history.

In the early days of the Court-led Revolution, in 1971, the Court ruled on Duke Power Company's requirement that all job applicants have a high school diploma and pass a general intelligence test. Duke had adopted the requirement, the district court found, with "no intention to discriminate against Negro employees." That should have been the end of the case, since as a matter of normal English usage, discrimination has to be intentional; you can't discriminate against someone unintentionally or accidentally. However, despite Duke's lack of discriminatory intent, the Court, in *Griggs*, found Duke had violated the Civil Rights Act of 1964 which prohibits discrimination because of race, color, religion, sex, or national origin because the test had a "disparate impact" on blacks, i.e., 58 percent of whites passed the intelligence test as compared with only 6 percent of the blacks. The "disparate impact" theory invented by the Court means, as a practical

matter, that the racial makeup of the company's workers had to mirror
the racial makeup of the area. The company, the Court said, could
escape liability only if it could show the test was related to job
performance as a matter of "business necessity." The company had to
show the test had "a manifest relationship to the employment in
question."

Now, no one knew what that meant. What reasonable person
could? How could an employer tell if he had violated a standard he
could not understand? The drift of the Court-led Revolution was,
however, clear enough. The employer knew he was going to lose. In
response, every large and medium corporation adopted some form of
quota system just to avoid lawsuits. The only way to avoid legal
expense, as a practical matter, was, and is, to hire by the numbers.
Supporters of *Griggs*, such as Professor Paul Gerwitz of the Yale Law
School, in *The New Republic* (August 12, 1991), believe that the case
"had tremendous practical consequences." Through litigation, "fear of
litigation, or acceptance of its basic principles, it deserves more credit
for integrating America's workplaces than any other case law." The
Court-led Revolution successfully imposed basic social and economic
policy on the country. Congress was silent as a tomb.

In 1989, the Court, in *Wards Cove*, slightly cut back on its *Griggs*
holding. It left intact the basic source of the trouble, the "disparate
impact" theory, but adopted a different standard—one of business
"justification" not "necessity." Also, the burden was moved to the
employee—to show the absence of that justification. It is hard to believe
that this slight modification of *Griggs* would have had much practical
effect. However, civil rights groups, writes Elizabeth Drew in *The New
Yorker* (June 17, 1991), organized to overturn it because they
"concluded that the Supreme Court had to be deterred from cutting back
on minority rights."

The Democrats, because of their rainbow constituencies, had no
choice; they had to go along with the civil rights groups and try to
overrule *Wards Cove*. They had to do so even though they knew it was
a political disaster for them in that (1) they knew it would be called a
"quota" bill because it was; (2) the American people hate quotas; and (3)
it didn't make any difference because almost everything in the country
is already running on quotas—every university, law school, government,

and large and medium corporation. The Democrats in Congress would have preferred to let the dog sleep.

But what about Bush? He had a choice. Why did he agree with the Democrats that *Wards Cove* should be overruled? Why not make a principled defense of the decision? For 25 years the Republicans have promised us a conservative Supreme Court; it seems inconsistent to ask Congress to reverse the Court when it makes a conservative decision. Bush, however, applying "last vote" principles, positioned his bill right next to the Democratic bill. Both bills reversed *Wards Cove* and shifted the burden of proof to the employer. The difference in language was negligible. Michael Kinsley, in *The New Republic* (June 24, 1991), reports the Bush bill required the employer to prove that his employment standard "serves in a significant way . . . legitimate employment goals." The Democratic bill required the employer to prove the standard has a "significant and manifest relationship to . . . job performance." President Bush, for 20 months, said that this gossamer distinction was the difference between a good civil rights bill and a bad quota bill. The president, on October 25, 1991, announced that he had come to an agreement with the Democrats on the bill. The agreed upon language required the employer to prove the standard is "job-related for the position in question and consistent with business necessity." The president said it "does not resort to quotas and it strengthens the cause of equality in the workplace." He promised: "it is very technical and all I know is I can simply certify that it is not a quota bill." Despite President Bush's certification, section 105 of the Act codifies the central quota concept—"disparate impact."

On November 20, 1991, the day before the president was scheduled to sign the Civil Rights Act, word drifted around Washington that Bush was going to order the end of race-based hiring by the Federal Government and by federal contractors. At the same time he signed the Civil Rights Act he was expected to revoke earlier Executive Orders, dating back to 1965, which provided for racial preferences. A presidential aide told the *New York Times*: "The President wanted to make clear tha he was really sincere when he said he would not sign a quota bill." The Executive Order, which the president was supposed to sign the next morning, directed that "any regulation, rule, enforcement practice or other aspect of these programs that mandates, encourages, or otherwise involves the use of quotas, preferences, set-asides" or other devices on the basis of race, sex, religion or national orgin are "to be terminated as soon as is legally feasible." That is exactly what the great majority of Americans believe is the only fair way to do things. Civil rights groups, however, learned of the draft proposal and called on the president to revoke his revokation. Early the next morning, November 21, the president assured the civil rights groups that the proposed Order would not be issued and that it had been drafted by the White House Counsel without his knowledge. The president said as he signed the new quota bill: "I say again today that I support affirmative action. Nothing in this bill overturns the Government's affirmative action programs."

The "last vote" theory is built on two propositions: (1) that the Democratic party is not competitive; (2) that your friends have no place to go. As long as those propositions are true the theory works. It subdues both the liberals and the conservatives. Why didn't the Democrats, for example, trump Bush's civil rights tactic by saying, "Okay, we'll accept your bill"? They can't, they are captives of Bush's rhetoric. Their constituents would say they are selling out. Why didn't the conservatives say,"The Supreme Court has done a good thing, so let's get behind the court"?, "Let's attack Bush's bill as a quota bill, which it is"? The conservatives can't do that; they are loyal, they voted for Bush and don't want to walk out on him. All of which means the theory works. The theory has some odd side effects—it is only because of the "last vote" theory that the black vote, a negligible influence in recent national elections, is consistently courted by Republicans. After the 1988 election, the late Lee Atwater, then chairman of the Republican National Committee, said it was reasonable to believe the Republicans could make deep inroads into the black vote. This is the logical extreme of the "last vote" theory; he thought he could take away the Democrat's black voters. He thought he could leave them with no voters at all.

In summary, the Court-led Revolution pivoted on three major shifts in power: (1) it cut the heart out of state and local authority; (2) it expanded the power of judges to create new rights, in effect, to legislate; and (3) it expanded the power of the national government. These three changes, together with bipartisan abandonment and the limited accountability inherent in federalism, allowed the Revolution to dismantle the democracy and the economic foundation it rested on. The

Revolution destroyed the middle-class individual's sense that he can participate meaningfully in government, or has any responsibility for it.

How have the people enjoyed the past 25 years? During the presidency of Dwight Eisenhower, in 1958, 75 percent of Americans said they trusted the "government in Washington to do what is right" most of the time; the figure rose slightly to 78 percent during John Kennedy's presidency. From 1964 forward—as the Court-led Revolution got going—the figure started a steep decline till it reached a low point of 26 percent under Jimmy Carter in 1980. It recovered about 10 percent during Ronald Reagan's term and, in October 1991, reached 36 percent. So, today, about one-third of Americans trust Washington to do the right thing most of the time. A Washington Post-ABC News poll taken in October 1991 reports that 61 percent of the people have *little or no* confidence in Washington's ability to solve a problem; 65 percent believe Washington is "not really interested in solving" problems; it only wants to *appear* to solve them.

Thomas Jefferson, in his first inaugural address, argued that good government required "absolute acquiescence in the decisions of the majority," which he believed was "the vital principle of republics." Jefferson felt that majority rule would be reasonable, and would protect the interests of the minority. He believed that the power of the central government should be carefully limited. For Jefferson, the real strength of government came from "the steady character of our countrymen," who would support the ends of good government because they believed in it, and not because they were forced to do so. Jefferson responded to the argument that a limited central government would be unequal to the challenges of a troubled complex world:

> I believe this, on the contrary, the strongest government on earth. I believe it is the only one where every man, at the call of the law, would fly to the standard of the law.

In contrast to Jefferson, Alexander Hamilton advocated a centralized and powerful government. Hamilton had little confidence in the virtues of his average countryman, or the power of a democracy to govern well. Hamilton attended the Constitutional Convention of 1787 as a delegate from New York. Madison reports that Hamilton had been "silent on the business before the Convention" until June 18, 1787, when he took the floor to argue against the form of government which was taking shape. Hamilton proposed what amounted to a monarchy without a king. Hamilton advocated having a president who served for life and had an absolute veto power over all legislation. He also argued against a federal system, since it would enable the general population represented through their state governments to resist the power of the central government. For Hamilton, the issue of central versus state authority was all or nothing. He argued,

> The general power, whatever be its form if it preserves itself, must swallow up the State powers. Otherwise it will be swallowed up by them.

He proposed that the central government appoint all state governors, and that these governors be given absolute veto power over all state legislation. Hamilton's proposals were based upon his view of human nature. Hamilton proclaimed:

> Take mankind in general, they are vicious . . . There may be in every government a few choice spirits, who may act from worthy motives. One great error is that we suppose mankind more honest than they are.

Where Jefferson saw the strength of the nation in the character of his fellow citizens, Hamilton believed in a government run by the select few. He proposed a governmental structure which reduced the power of the people to interfere with a government run by "a few choice spirits."

The country understood, in 1787, the critical difference between a Jeffersonian federal system and a Hamiltonian central government—that the political theories are based on opposing opinions of human nature. Since 1965, the Hamiltonian vision of human nature and government has supplanted the Jeffersonian one. The 25-year Court-led Revolution to establish equality of result has given us, instead, an ugly landscape and a bitterly divided and bankrupt country.

Liberals today, now that it has all gone wrong, say that it is not their fault. Whose fault is it? It is the common man's fault, they say. On October 25, 1991, Governor Lowell P. Weicker, Jr. of Connecticut expressed his view of the 40,000 citizens protesting his income tax who had marched on Hartford: "Nowadays it's hard just to get someone to drop their bag of Doritos long enough to cross the street to vote. Ours is a democracy. If people are upset with the daily results, it is because they have become absentee owners." We have deficits and bankruptcy, according to the liberals, because the people want more services than they're willing to pay for. The liberals thought they had uncovered a major flaw in democracy: the people are no good. Said Weicker, "The 1980s brought selfishness to new heights. They preached that you can get something for nothing. Today, we're picking up the refuse of that philosophy." The liberals have declared open season on the common man, the one innocent party in the whole deal. The liberal position is: We took away all his power because he is a racist but now that the experiment has gone wrong, it's all his fault. The problem, of course, has not been too much democracy, it's been too little.

Can the modern political parties produce capable leadership? It doesn't seem likely. The Democrats abandoned the common man on behalf of their real constituency and in order to pick up some crumbs from the national feast by virtue of their control of Congress. The Republicans abandoned the common man on behalf of their real constitutents who wanted to control the wealth of the country. Bipartisan abandonment has occurred before. Theodor Mommsen, in his *History of Rome*, writes of the declining Republic, during which both parties "were equally worthless." Mommsen writes:

> Throughout the republic's last century the annual public election, especially to the consulship and censorship, was the real focus of political activity; but only in rare and isolated instances did the opposing candidates represent different political principles. Ordinarily the contests were purely between personalities, and it was a matter of practical indifference whether the majority of votes fell to a Caecilian or a Cornelian. The Romans thus lacked the great compensation for the evils of party politics—the spontaneous choice by the masses of the goals which they preferred—and yet endured all those evils solely for the benefit of the paltry game played by the ruling clique. Both parties

> contended alike for shadows, and numbered in their ranks none but
> zealots or hypocrites. Both were equally tainted by political corruption,
> both were equally worthless. Both were necessarily tied to the status
> quo, for neither had a single political idea (not to mention a political
> plan) reaching beyond the existing state of affairs. Accordingly, the
> two parties were in such entire agreement that their ends and means
> dovetailed at every step, and a change of party was a change of
> political tactics rather than of political sentiments.

The Roman Republic, at this point, was exhausted and the empire about
to take over. Similarly, both parties today are equally tainted by
corruption, both are equally worthless, and both necessarily tied to the
status quo.

The American democracy, so far, has shown a lot of resilience.
From the end of the Civil War to 1900, the great aggregations of capital
had pretty much their own way; they ran the government and the courts.
Brooks Adams, in *The Theory of Social Revolutions,* writes:

> The great aggregations of capital . . . [had accumulated] to a point
> where they began to grasp many important perogatives of sovereignty,
> and to impose what was tantamount to arbitrary taxation on a large
> scale.

The Republican Machine, as William Roscoe Thayer calls it, won all the
presidential elections except for Grover Cleveland's two terms. In his
biography, *Theodore Roosevelt,* Thayer writes that the Machine "was a
special organ of Capital, by which Capital made and administered the
laws of the States and of the Nation." The antagonism between capital
and labor had become chronic. "Capital was arrogant. Its advances
since the Civil War had been unmatched in history." The wealth poured
in and the men who created the wealth "lost the sense of their proper
relations with the rest of the community and the Nation." A great gulf,
Thayer continues, had opened between labor and capital, which was
further aggravated because American labor was largely foreign born:
"Now a community can thrive only when all its classes feel that they
have common interests." The United States had "ceased to be the Land
of Promise, where any hardworking and thrifty man could better himself
and even become rich. The gates of Opportunity were closing."

Theodore Roosevelt, upon succeeding to the presidency in 1901, intended to reopen the gates. Capital had to give ground so the American promise could be restored. Roosevelt had written six books before he was 30. He was friendly with Progressive reformers like Jacob Riis and Carl Schurz. He believed in patriotism, courage, and the sacrifice of self to country and to the cause of right. America loved Theodore Roosevelt.

The Republican policy of "Let Alone," Roosevelt wrote, "is thoroughly vicious"—the immigrant is not "an industrial asset to be allowed to drift or to be put at the mercy of the exploiter." We cannot afford the low wage rates "which mean the sacrifice of both individual and family life and morals to the industrial machinery."

The solution was what Roosevelt called "an American standard of living." Capitalism had to be regulated—by enforcing antitrust laws, outlawing child labor, improving working conditions and limiting hours, enacting health and inspection laws, and preserving the country's natural resources. Roosevelt achieved a compromise between democracy and capital which operated efficiently until the 1960s.

Roosevelt had his own version of America's Constitution. There were, he said, "three principal essentials":

(1)   The need of a common language, English, with a minimum amount of illiteracy;

(2)   the need of a common civil standard, similar ideals, beliefs and customs symbolized by the oath of allegiance to America;

(3)   the need of a high standard of living, of reasonable equality of opportunity and of social and industrial justice.

Above all, Roosevelt wrote, the "one essential for success" is that "our citizens should act as Americans; not as Americans with a prefix and a qualification—not as Irish-Americans, German-Americans, Native-Americans—but as Americans, pure and simple."

Americans, Roosevelt thought, can solve whatever problems they face: "[T]hough there is every reason why we should realize the gravity of the perils ahead of us, there is none why we should not face them with confident and resolute hope, if only each of us, according to the measure of his capacity, will with manly honesty and good faith do his duties incident to American citizenship."

The majority may, at times, be wrong. The idea of democracy is that it will correct itself and the society can then move forward again. But the majority, leaving aside constitutionally protected areas, has to be free to be wrong. Governments, Jefferson wrote, derive "their just powers from the consent of the governed." The American majority is now disenfranchised. We are, as de Tocqueville said, a great nation recently born as a democracy. Yet our official culture today rejects the concept of majority rule. How did the custodians of the constitutional system—the judges and professors—let that happen? Or, is it possible, they are the ones who did it? That's the next story.

PART III

The Legal Abandonment: Trustees of the Temple

For it is the solecism of power, to think to command the end, and yet not endure the means.

Francis Bacon, "Of Empire," 1605

For over two centuries, Americans have maintained an extraordinary amount of faith in their Constitution to solve often bitter national disputes. Even after a bloody civil war, the Constitution became the accepted common ground for rebuilding the country. Other countries with similar written constitutions, such as several of those in Latin America, have flown apart time after time. Nations with a much more powerful and coercive central government, such as the Soviet Union, have not maintained constitutional continuity even half as long as the United States. Why?

The main thing which has given strength and durability to the United States Constitution is the popular, public understanding of what it means. Despite the documented fact that few Americans have any real command of the actual provisions of the Constitution, it has come to symbolize certain shared values and mutual interests. This identification in the public mind with certain rather simple propositions has caused the vast majority to stick by their constitution as few other modern people do.

This is not an original observation. In 1889, A. Lawrence Lowell of Harvard commented on the importance of the popular or public understanding of the United States Constitution, which permitted it to serve as "a symbol and pledge of our national existence, and the only object on which the people could expend their new-born loyalty". Michael Kammen, the constitutional historian, has brilliantly surveyed our popular understanding of the Constitution in *A Machine That Would Go Of Itself: The Constitution in American Culture.* Throughout our history, public opinion on the general meaning of the Constitution has revealed what Kammen describes as "the well-established pattern of conflict within consensus." General allegiance to the Constitution held us together through occasional conflict.

In a similar vein, Edmund Burke ascribed the durability of England's unwritten constitution to the fact that it had slowly been shaped by the customs of the people it governed, and was based on "the peculiar circumstances, occasions, tempers, dispositions, and moral, civil and social habitudes of the people, which disclose themselves only in a long space of time." In other words, the English populace came to identify their constitution with certain widely-accepted and highly-regarded principles, thus allowing the resolution of serious conflict while preserving the constitution itself—"conflict within consensus."

Yet despite similarities with England, America became something unique in all of modern constitutional history: Until the 1960s, America was a large nation in which the vast majority of the population, the judicial bench, and the legal profession were in agreement about what the most important principle identified with the constitution really was. This common understanding embraced by the majority is what we refer to here as our "Legal Constitution." For the majority, the central principle of the Legal Constitution was simple: that all Americans should enjoy a constitutionally guaranteed common citizenship of equal dignity.

This proposition had been repeated countless times and in countless ways. Writing for the Supreme Court in 1938, Chief Justice Hughes ruled that the refusal of a state to furnish legal education facilities for blacks and whites alike violated the constitutional guarantee of equal protection, despite the argument of the state that negroes as a group had not exhibited much demand for such education. Treating citizens according to their racial group was not proper, said Hughes, because the Constitution's guarantee of equal protection was "a personal one."

Great strides were made throughout the 1950s toward achieving a just and equal treatment for every individual. What Alan Bloom called "the unbroken, ineluctable progress of freedom and equality" had been the story of America, and that story appeared to be continuing into the 1960s. By the time of the Civil Rights Act of 1964, the idea of a common and equal citizenship seemed to be triumphant. Under this ideal, the law would not tolerate the use of race, creed, color, ethnic origin, or any other factor to vary the benefits or burdens of common and equal citizenship.

Belief in Constitutional rights shared on an equal basis by every individual citizen has proven to be the single most powerful and irresistible force in our national history. The vast majority lent their support and allegiance to this belief. It represented the majority's personal view of how individuals should be treated. It was the idea most frequently identified with the Revolution that produced the United States.

This nearly universal conviction distinguished the United States from almost every other country in the world, past or present. Many countries are composed of what archaeologists and historians call "kin group forms of allegiance." Many modern countries, such as Syria or Lebanon, lack the commonly shared convictions necessary to peacefully unite a nation. As Thomas Friedman says of such countries in his classic study of the Middle East, *From Beirut to Jerusalem:*

> The warring tribes, clans, sects, neighborhoods, cities and hinterlands could not find a way to balance the intimacy and cohesion of their tribe-like groups with the demands of a nation-state that would be run by certain neutral rules and values to which everyone agreed. Most peoples in the area simply could not achieve the level of consensus needed for such a polity.

The result, says Friedman, is the inability of Middle Eastern countries to form stable nation-states. These countries lack the one thing necessary to give them a national identity:

> [N]eutral spaces where men can come as equal citizens, check their tribal memories at the door, and enter into a politics governed by mutually agreed-upon laws.

When such a common consensus defines the national identity of Middle Eastern nations, they will become successful, independent self-governing countries. Says Friedman:

> Only then will the words 'parliament,' 'constitution,' and 'political parties' have any real meaning to these countries and their peoples.

As a result of our unique history, America became a country "run by certain neutral principles to which everyone agreed." Our consensus gave us unrivalled strength because it gave our government a legitimacy unattainable in other nations. Time and time again, it moved the majority of Americans to turn their hand to a common purpose. As Thomas Jefferson correctly predicted, it made us the strongest country on earth. We were not only the strongest, but also we held the greatest promise of carrying the "ineluctable progress of freedom and equality" to its logical conclusion.

However, after 1965, the president and Congress directly challenged the common consensus that formed America's Legal Constitution. They attacked the central precept which the majority identified with the Constitution itself—the legally equal individual. Rather than resisting this challenge, the Supreme Court employed a revolutionized concept of judicial power, and dethroned the individual as the centerpiece of constitutional government. Until well into the twentieth century, the Supreme Court had been restrained from directly challenging the majority's view of its Legal Constitution by a limited theory of judicial authority. In other words, the courts and the legal profession adhered to a theory of judicial power which prevented them from overthrowing what the majority believed to be their Legal Constitution. This older view of the judicial role was a cornerstone upon which the constitutional order rested. After examining this traditional view of judicial power, we will look at the new theory which has replaced it, and examine the Legal Constitution of today, under which the equal individual has been abandoned.

CHAPTER NINE

Cornerstone

[C]ommon sense, in its application to the every-day transactions of human life, speaks the same language, and is regulated by the same motives of convenience, and policy, and justice, in all civilized countries, however wide their distance or remote their ages from each other.

Joseph Story, 1835

In the fall of 1842, the nine members of the United States Supreme Court returned to Washington, D.C. from their respective circuits around the United States. For several months out of the year, these justices sat in their home circuits or districts and heard local cases. They then made the difficult trip to Washington, all complaining of the ardors of the journey, and resumed the hearing of appeals from the lower federal courts or from the highest state courts of any cases involving the United States Constitution or some principle of federal law. They often stayed together at the same hotel, and frequently spent evenings after supper discussing the things that mattered to them. They came to the gathering fresh from their districts, in which most of them were born and raised, and so brought together knowledge and insights on widely differing local political and legal issues. In many ways, it was a confederation of emissaries from a variety of regional cultures periodically united to expound and apply a common constitution, rather than a central court headquartered in Washington.

In that year, 1842, a seemingly ordinary case came before the Court. For all but the enthusiastic specialist or the litigants in the case, the facts were about as prosaic as could be imagined. However, as sometimes happens with the solution of very ordinary problems, this case required the examination and analysis of one of the most basic and important issues in the entire constitutional and legal system. As the atom or molecule represents a very small entity whose behavior controls enormously powerful processes, this case involved a fundamental component around which large legal and constitutional issues revolved.

Instrumental in resolving the unique case was, as fate would have it, a unique member of the Supreme Court. Joseph Story, the youngest man ever appointed to the Supreme Court, was born in Marblehead, Massachusetts, on September 18, 1779. Marblehead, a fishing village on a rocky peninsula with a fine harbor, had drawn immigrants from Cornwall and the Channel Islands who came to make a living by fishing. In the seventeenth century, one Marblehead fisherman became famous by ending an argument with a preacher by saying, "Our ancestors came not here for religion. Their main purpose was to catch fish!" When Story was born, the village had five thousand inhabitants and an annual catch of fish valued at over £35,000 Sterling. This tradition of success and independence made its citizens prominent in the Revolution. Joseph Story's father, Elisha, the village physician, helped throw tea from three British ships into Boston Harbor on December 16, 1773, while disguised as an Indian. Elisha's children heard the story many times growing up in his large family; Story's father had seven children from his first marriage, and Joseph was the eldest of eleven by his father's second wife.

Story was red-headed, left-handed and had a readiness to fight when offended or challenged. When he was disciplined for "chastising" a classmate who had insulted him at Marblehead Academy, he quit the academy and gained early admission to Harvard College by tutoring himself to meet the entrance requirements. He graduated second in his class in 1798, right behind his friend, William Ellery Channing.

In his early days, Story was a romantic at heart. In 1798, he wrote the class poem "Power of Solitude," though he decided to study law as a career. He apprenticed to a Salem lawyer, Samuel Putnam, and set about to master the deep lore and forbidding technicalities of the English legal tradition. He approached the monuments of the law, Matthew Hale's treatises and the ponderous volumes of Sir Edward Coke, with solitary dedication. Legend has it that he retained a copy of one of Coke's Institutes, a formidable book by any standards, because its pages showed the stains of tears shed during one long night of frustrating study which had finally exhausted him.

He finished his apprenticeship and began practicing law in Salem in 1801. In 1805 he married Mary Oliver and published his "Power of Solitude" poem and a small treatise called *A Selection of Pleadings in Civil Actions*.

Then, suddenly, both Mary and his father died. He was reduced to terrible depression, bought all the copies of "Power of Solitude" he could find, and on a cold Salem evening, threw them into a lonely bonfire where he commemorated the tragedies of life and thought on the future.

Because of his growing reputation, he was retained by the Massachusetts legislature to represent the claims of local citizens arising out of the Yazoo land scandal, in which the State of Georgia had tried to rescind the property rights acquired by the claimants under a previous Georgia grant. Story successfully vindicated the property rights of his clients against state power, culminating in the famous opinion of the Supreme Court in *Fletcher v. Peck*. Story had won his case and his fame.

In 1808, Story was elected to the United States House of Representatives, where he groped his way through the evolving issues of Federalism versus Republicanism. He served out the unexpired term of the former incumbent, until 1809, when he did his best to grapple with the impact of Jefferson's trade embargo on the economy of his home state and village. He came back to law practice in 1810. Over retired President Jefferson's objections, Madison nominated him for a vacancy on the Supreme Court. He was confirmed in 1811 at the age of 32. His fame as a master of the law had so spread that he quickly came to be regarded as one of the great jurists of America, and his opinions soon found an acceptance and following both here and in England.

By 1829, he had also become a professor at Harvard Law School and began producing a series of legal and constitutional treatises which his biographer describes as "unrivalled in the history of legal writings." He was retained by the governor of Massachusetts to render a report on the nature of the common law system and feasibility of reducing the state's jurisprudence to a code. Published in 1836, his report is a

masterpiece in the history and tradition of Anglo-American jurisprudence. By 1845, he had written nine major books, which have since
undergone countless editions and translations.

Story was still a romantic, whose bonfire in Salem had affirmed
rather than purged his sense of romance and tragedy. He cherished the
memories of his youth: his father's stories, snow, and the blue
afternoon light of a clear May day on the water of Marblehead Harbor.
He told his son William, an artist, of his own affection for the first great
Federalist, George Washington; William sculpted the statue of
Washington that was placed on the Capitol grounds in 1884 (today it is
displayed on the lower level of the Supreme Court building). Late in
Story's career, out of a seemingly ordinary case, one of the truly great
constitutional principles of nineteenth century jurisprudence arose in a
case before the court, one which in its long-term consequences
transcended all the others in his unique career. The historic happen-
stance of Story's presence on the court and the occurrence of a case
raising this particular issue were to generate great repercussions in our
constitutional history.

The facts of the case were routine. A Mr. Swift had some time
earlier loaned money to two land developers, Nathaniel Norton and
Jarius Keith. Apparently, Norton and Keith were putting their money
into real estate ventures, and they offered to sell some land they had
acquired in Maine to a Mr. Tyson of New York City. For the land,
Tyson gave them an instrument known as a "bill of exchange," which
was in effect a documentary transfer of the right to claim a stated sum
of money from Tyson on a date six months after the bill was made.
Norton and Keith, or anyone to whom they transferred the bill, could
call on Tyson to pay it at the end of six months. Being able to transfer
the right enabled Norton and Keith to exchange the bill for something
valuable to them. When their loan from Swift came due, they gave him
the bill in payment, which he accepted even though he never actually
met Tyson. Unfortunately, when he presented the bill, Tyson refused
to pay, since Norton and Keith had not given Tyson clear title to the
land. Tyson said he had been defrauded by Norton and Keith. Swift
sued Tyson, claiming he should pay despite the fraud, since Swift had
nothing to do with the fraud.

Swift brought his claim in the federal circuit court in New York, under a federal law allowing federal jurisdiction over claims between litigants of "diverse citizenship," that is between parties from different states. Tyson was from New York, Swift from Maine, so the federal court was open to them. The problem with Swift's suit turned out to be that he had taken his bill of exchange in payment of the existing debt owed to him by Norton and Keith. It was a commonly understood requirement of commercial law that Swift had to have taken the bill in "due course." This meant he must not have known of the original fraud on the maker of the bill of exchange, Tyson, and that he must have acquired the bill in the due course of business by giving something valuable—"consideration"—for it. Here was the rub: there were several judicial opinions from New York courts which suggested that relinquishing an existing debt (an "antecedent debt") was not good consideration. Though this contradicted the accepted law of every other state, and most of the Western commercial world, that was what the New York cases purported to say. The original Judiciary Act of 1789 contained a command to the federal courts to follow the state legal rules unless they were displaced by some federal law. The pertinent section reads:

> [T]he laws of the several states, except where the Constitution, treaties, or statutes of the United States shall otherwise require or provide, shall be regarded as rules of decision, in trials at Common Law, in the Courts of the United States in cases where they apply.

Thus the Supreme Court was squarely faced with an enormously important question: the command of the Judiciary Act required the federal courts to follow state "laws." Were the New York judicial opinions "laws"?

Tyson's lawyer argued strenuously that they were, since the application of the New York cases would relieve his client of the obligation to pay the bill. Justice Joseph Story rendered the final opinion. On this inescapable and significant question, Story ruled that state judicial opinions were not in fact "laws" at all:

> In order to maintain the argument, it is essential, therefore, to hold, that the word "laws," in this section, includes within the scope of its meaning, the decisions of the local tribunals. In the ordinary use of language, it will hardly be contended, that the decisions of courts constitute laws. They are, at most, only evidence of what the laws are, and are not, of themselves laws. They are often re-examined, reversed and qualified by the courts themselves, whenever they are found to be either defective, or ill-founded, or otherwise incorrect. The laws of a state are more usually understood to mean the rules and enactments promulgated by the legislative authority thereof, or long-established local customs having the force of laws.

This opinion portrays a totally different orientation to judicial power from that prevailing today. The judge's "common law" function was adjudication—the resolution of a dispute—and simply did not as a matter of accepted theory include any legislative function, i.e., to "make" laws. The decision of a court was not a "law"; it was not legislation.

Where did governing "laws" come from? In common business transactions, autonomous from the edict of any sovereign, private parties pursuing their personal business had universally adopted convenient practices or customs. These private practices had been referred to in the adjudication of prior cases and came to be reflected in a body of judicial precedent common to both the state and federal courts. Each such case was not a sovereign command to do this or that, but was rather a recognition and partial recording of common custom which had evolved from the immense latitude the older common law system permitted for unregulated individual action. These customs were the controlling laws. Story's opinion did not involve any sovereign federal pronouncement or command which preempted and displaced any local state rule. The aberrant New York cases had simply attempted to invoke a common pool of precedential information about the content of the particular custom involved, and they had gotten it wrong.

There was nothing revolutionary or novel about Story's approach; it epitomized the prevailing American view of legal power and judicial review. It was widely acknowledged that the autonomous behavior of private parties was, by and large, where "private" (i.e., non-constitutional) law came from.

Much private "law" was, in its beginning, really the same as a "fact." Adjudication thus was an increasingly reliable record of the evolving standards of private behavior. "Law" depended upon the regular practice and the general and repeated acceptance of certain standards of conduct by private individuals.

As Justice Redfield of the Vermont Supreme Court remarked in 1854,

> The more important question growing out of the case is, perhaps, what is the true commercial rule established upon this subject? And it is of vital importance in regard to commercial usages, that they should, as far as practicable, be uniform throughout the world. And such is necessarily the ultimate consideration and will inevitably be the final result. It is, therefore, always a question of time as to uniformity in such usages. The basis of such uniformity is convenience and justice combined, and until such rules become measurably settled by practice, they have to be treated as matters of fact, to be passed upon by juries; and when the rule acquires the quality of uniformity and the character of general acceptance, it is then regarded as a matter of law. It is thus that the commercial law has from time to time grown up.

This inherited view of adjudication provided a convincing defense against charges about the dangers of "judicial legislation." Under the early medieval English view, a judge was the emissary of the king himself, and could enforce the king's sovereign will as law. The judge could also disregard a statute at will. This view had been transcended by half a millennium of political history. The result was common law adjudication of a modern sort, which functioned primarily to promote and preserve the conditions which made individual freedom of action, commercial and otherwise, possible.

This concept of adjudication exemplified by Story in *Swift* suited a society which placed its faith in growth and development in the ordering process of individual action, rather than the dictates of sovereignty. At any given time, any recorded "black letter" rule of law was an imperfectly articulated representation of but a small part of an on-going process of individual private action. By the time of William Blackstone in mid-eighteenth century, he could say with accuracy that the general private law of England rested "upon general reception and usage." For the common law judge, "[T]he study of the judicial decisions of their predecessors . . . [was] the principal and most authoritative evidence, that can be given, of the existence of such a custom as shall form a part of the common law."

Story's opinion in *Swift* excited no comment or adverse reaction. Essentially it repeated what had been announced in his federal judicial opinions thirty years earlier. It simply articulated the received view as a part of constitutional jurisprudence. It was well grounded in early modern legal writing of the seventeenth century as well as in eighteenth century summaries of English jurisprudence, such as Blackstone's book. It was yet another adumbration of very old ideas of popular sovereignty which had never been realized in any practical way until the political revolutions of the seventeenth and eighteenth centuries. Under these ideas, consent was the cornerstone of the law.

Consent as a legitimizing principle for law was, of course, not new. In a strikingly modern passage, St. Thomas Aquinas observes in his *Summa Theologica* of 1273-1276: "[T]he consent of the whole people expressed by a custom counts far more in favor of a particular observance, than does the authority of the sovereign, who has not the power to frame laws, except as representing the people." But until approximately five hundred years later, the demographics were not right for realizing in practice the consequences of such a radical notion. For twelve centuries, from the sixth century until 1800, the entire population of Europe did not exceed 180 million people. From 1800 to 1914, slightly over a century, the population mounted to 460 million. With these increases came inescapable pressure in favor of popular government and constitutional reform. The late eighteenth and the entire nineteenth century represented the practical culmination of many old ideas, among them various constitutional doctrines relating to popular sovereignty. One of the greatest contributions of the common law system which Story described in the *Swift* case was harmonizing judicial action with consent as a legitimizing principle.

The common law process as it developed during the later epoch demonstrates one of the best of these historical maturations. For example, all of the generally useful legal codifications of recent years, such as the Uniform Commercial Code, owe their strength to derivation from principles produced during this period in the common law's development.   Nothing comparable has come from other creative sources, such as the genius of state managers or government officials. The nourishing fruit of the common law sprang and grew from old fields, and supplied a need for freedom of action, common sense, utility and predictability that the legal system has been completely unable to produce from any other source.

The orientation of this judicial approach is, as we shall see, an inversion of what is practiced today.   In 1842, a private "law" became "common," i.e., became "common law," by representing common practice in fact.   The significance of the older theory of adjudication lies in its impact on the individual and his relation to society.   The traditional common law process was democratic in a natural sense.   The individual *was* sovereign, and the least democratic of all modern governmental branches, the judiciary, had evolved a decisional system in theory and practice which could coexist with popular sovereignty.   Individuals under the old common law system were collectively capable of the sovereign act of creating law, even outside the legislative branch.   Ours was a legal system bound by traditional theory to follow the individual, rather than the other way around.

Leaving aside the intricate history of the operation of such a system, it is clear that this initial orientation, this single precept of judicial action, produced results far different from those in our more recent past.   Significantly, the rules governing common law adjudication were highly detailed, and concerned proof and recognition of private custom where no statute was concerned.   By definition, this custom was established through the consent of the parties who created it.   Recognizing provable custom had the same virtue as the ancient common law evidentiary presumption that every individual is presumed as a general matter to intend the natural and probable consequences of his acts.   By entering into a stereotyped and familiar transaction, using familiar terms and following familiar arrangements, the parties were bound to assume the responsibilities commonly associated with such transactions.   They were presumed to intend to be bound by the well-known consequences of their acts.   Thus customary private law had this in common with legislation: it originated in the consent of those subject to the rules it contained.   Consent as a general basis for the legitimacy of binding legal rules stood as the cardinal principle of American constitutionalism.   In

later discarding the decisional techniques based on the common law
tradition, the Supreme Court began a process by which judicial
commands could eventually go far, far beyond consent.

The doctrinal heritage of the *Swift* case prevailed throughout the
nineteenth century. There was naturally very little of the modern-
sounding discussion about the "enforcement" of the private law, since
enforcement as such was infrequently needed and not difficult. As an
American lawyer said in 1841, judicial reference to customary law "to
which individuals are familiarized by habit . . . has the great advantage
of deriving its force from the evidence of the justice and reciprocity
which have suggested it. . . . It convinces and persuades without
appealing to command; and conviction secures to it a willing obedience
which mere authority with difficulty obtains."

This tradition, and the consequences and importance of its
perpetuation, was keenly understood by leaders of the legal profession
well into the twentieth century. Story's decision represented common
law process at its most basic level of application. It represented an
approach to judicial action which made the greater constitutional
generalities about limited government actually work in practice.

So powerful was the democratic view of the common law process
and its identity separate from the command of the sovereign state that a
prominent member of the New York bar, James Coolidge Carter, could
say in 1905 that the source of law under such a system of adjudication
was grounded in human conduct and not sovereign will. Speaking to the
bar, he said,

> The final conclusion of the inquiry, what rule or rules in point of fact
> governed human conduct, was that, so far as social conduct is con-
> cerned, custom is not simply one of the sources of law from which
> selections may be made and converted into law by the independent
> arbitrary fiat of a legislature or a court, but that law, with the narrow
> exception of legislation, is custom, and, like custom, self-existing and
> irrepealable.

What, precisely, was the contribution of a theory and practice of
adjudication built on such a view of the source of private civil law?
Clearly the contribution was *not* in the ability of the judicial process to
meet all the needs of a growing, changing country for new and useful

substantive rules of law. The Sherman Antitrust Act of 1895, for example, could hardly have evolved by custom, though there were some common law analogies. None of the other legislative reforms aimed at preserving and reducing the excesses caused by unequal economic forces fell within the reach of private custom. But the point is that such reforms were viewed under our constitutional system as legislative matters. Thus the greatest contribution the traditional common law process made to our constitutional system was this: It had produced the view that sovereignty resided *elsewhere* than in the judiciary. This view embodied specific and elaborate principles of judicial action designed to conserve the authority of a non-judicial sovereign. In the United States, that sovereignty was supposedly exercised by the people through elected representatives, since we had assumed the form of a modern democracy, as England had done. The older common law process had allowed the judiciary to assist the evolution of the substantive private civil law in areas defined by custom, and the legislature was to do the same for areas which custom did not reach. Traditional common law process conserved the valuable substantive and constitutional creations of Anglo-American jurisprudence, rather than generating general law reform.

As Carter spoke to the New York Bar in 1905, this system was being abandoned by the United States Supreme Court. Their decisions set the jurisprudential stage for the eventual revolution and abandonment of the older constitutional theory about the source of legal rules. In the space of one sentence, the old concept of non-judicial sovereignty upon which judicial action had been based was swept aside. It was replaced by a new "science" of the law.

CHAPTER TEN

Renovation

In his continued affiliation with a law school while sitting on the court, Justice Joseph Story in many ways represented the shape that legal education would take. The patchwork array of apprenticeship, formal training, complete deregulation common in his day was heading toward standardization in which the formal law school would become enormously influential. Harvard Law School, begun in 1817, had adopted a standard curriculum in 1852. This curriculum proved to be a durable model, and served as an example for formal legal education at other schools. Yet the bar continued to perpetuate its own internal standards for admission, including educational prerequisites for admission. It seemed that very little could be done to impose regulations on the legal profession from the outside, or from the law schools. As Robert Stevens puts it in his study of the development of American legal education, it appeared that "the legal profession was virtually indestructible."

Out of a smattering of law courses offered at universities in various states, the concept of a separate "law school" grew, so that by 1870 there were twenty-one law schools in the country. As the number of law schools grew, their direction came to be set largely by the example of a few brilliant and creative men. In 1870, Christopher Columbus Langdell, a graduate of both Harvard College and Harvard Law School, was appointed dean at Harvard Law School. He was appointed by President Charles William Eliot, a former professor of mathematics and chemistry at Harvard and M.I.T., who had been chosen as president of Harvard in 1869. With Eliot's collaboration, Langdell set out to reform the law curriculum. By 1878, the law course took three years. In 1896, he announced that a college degree would be required for law school admission, a requirement fully implemented by 1909. Most importantly, he introduced a teaching method which radically departed from the older tradition (Joseph Story's tradition) of reading treatises. Langdell's new "case method" required students to study and reason through actual law cases, extracting legal principles from them.

During this same time the country's state universities grew. As the land grant colleges spread after the Civil War, university presidents and the legal profession had Langdell's model for legal education, along with other older and less successful ones, to evaluate and emulate as they wished. Langdell's experiments with both the structure and content of legal education triumphed. The curriculum itself was based on that of 1852, with progressive revisions. By 1920, the pattern of accepting the Langdell model—a college degree, three years of law study based on a standardized curriculum, the case method, and final examinations—was established, with most older and newer law schools striving to achieve it. As Robert Stevens remarks,

> Legal education had failed, in an earlier period, to produce an aristocracy. Now, at least, it could be recognized as the cradle of "technique."

Thus the "technique" and the doctrines of the earlier national period, represented so vividly by Story's view of adjudication, were perpetuated by the growing legal education industry. There was nothing in Langdell's approach which was revolutionary as far as accepted legal and constitutional doctrine was concerned. His was a technique of analysis without any intent to revolutionize the content of the law. But the conversion of legal training to academic training came more and more to mean that what students absorbed under this technique formed the foundation of their views about the legal profession, law practice, about the law itself. The law schools were gaining a monopoly over the minds of future lawyers, and in the renovation of their techniques, they were drawn more and more to the analogies and models of scientific investigation.

For Langdell, his approach was in fact scientific, as he was fond of saying:

If law be not a science, a university will best consult its own dignity in declining to teach it. If it be not a science, it is a species of handicraft, and may best be learned by serving an apprenticeship to one who practices.

However, this adoption of a scientific orientation by legal education could not really abolish the irrevocable difference between the physical sciences and law study. This difference came from the fact that scientific inquiry itself is directed toward an independent, external, physical reality, which the different methods of experimentation and of organizing and expressing data reflect. Chemistry, microbiology, physics and all the rest have some common aim. The scientific method means using all available tools, specialties, and any available and useful method of expression to capture reality as nearly as may be done. This evolutionary process depends upon effective symbols and an open mind. Yet it is always directed at external nature, at physical reality. The object of Langdell's "science" was, to the contrary, whatever principles of law the books and cases contained. In point of historical fact, it was directed to the perpetuation of evolving principles which had been part of what Roscoe Pound called the "taught legal tradition." Langdell's "science" was merely an analytical technique for understanding and perpetuating whatever that tradition contained. In a sense, it was a technique directed toward and linked to a reality external to itself. But its object was not the extant natural reality of the physical sciences; it was simply whatever the cases and law books said the law was.

Most importantly, Langdell's great achievements prepared the way for a later revolution not envisioned by him. Langdell established the theoretical and doctrinal fashions of the law schools as the most influential and powerful determinants of how law students looked at the law. It made current judicial opinions the main source of the substantive rules which the students learned. To be sure, this perspective was tied to the view the courts took on any given issue, particularly the nation's highest court. Langdell's reforms placed the law schools in control of what growing generations of law students and lawyers would believe about law itself, including constitutional law and theory. It resulted in the establishment of an efficient network for translating, via "scientific" inquiry, the theories of law into action. But under the case method of study, the courts were the main source of these theories. It was a network of informational distribution unparalleled in the history of the law. As Harvard Model came to represent the trend of the future, the growing influence of the legal education which it promoted would be rededicated to totally new constitutional theorem. This happened when the courts changed their views on the nature of judicial action. When this happened, the new judicial theories flowed smoothly into the students' primary legal education. The traditional scholarship of learned treatises took a back seat to current judicial opinion.

The demise and replacement of the old cornerstone conception of the nature of judicial action began in the 1920s. The glory and glamour of the coming revolution belonged mainly to the law schools at Columbia and Yale. With the understated approval of the dean of Columbia Law School (Harlan Fiske Stone), Professors Herman Oliphant, Walter Wheeler Cook and Underhill Moore began to remake the curriculum of Columbia Law School, and the direction they took was heavily influenced by Langdell's science metaphor. In fact, Dean Stone had toyed with the idea that law could somehow be synthesized with the "soft sciences," and in 1923 he wrote that "law is nothing more than a form of social control," equating law with popular theory in the new discipline of sociology. From this suggestive speculation came the term "sociological jurisprudence." It represented, consciously or unconsciously, a diversion from the historically rooted common law tradition, which had been coming increasingly under attack as the century progressed. The diversion to a soft scientific approach eventually led to an academic reevaluation of what Columbia law professor Thomas Reed Powell termed the "social and economic conditions which create the need for the law." Academic pursuit of "legal science" displaced concern for private customs as a source of governing law. Driven by Langdell's science metaphor, legal academics used the newly evolving social sciences, such as psychology and sociology, to prescribe ideal "scientific" legal rules, detaching legal inquiry and analysis from the world outside the law schools.

By 1926, Dean Stone was convinced of the need for revolutionary curricular reform and set in motion a process familiar to any modern faculty member. Ten task forces launched a self-study project and in 1928 produced the outline for the brave new world of legal education. Even the nomenclature of law was revised to "reflect the connections between law and modern life." Social science taxonomy provided the organizing principles for newly defined fields of legal society—"familial relations," "political relations," and so on. "Political relations" was infused with jargon familiar to psychology and sociology ("intergroup relations and the individual versus the group"). Even so, the new plan in large part also directed itself toward practical training for the solution of business and commercial legal problems.

Yet the formulation of the new Columbia approach did not revolutionize the Columbia faculty or law school itself, as some had hoped it would. The idea that law could *only* be viewed as an expression of the social sciences, and that the familiar and traditional legal classifications were irrelevant or useless, was held by only a small minority of the Columbia teaching community. Additionally, many members of the profession saw the immediate effects of experimental training as hindering the training of effective practicing lawyers, however interesting and entertaining the new subjects might be. As law faculties became more accustomed to viewing the law schools as laboratories, the ability of the legal academic to understand and solve the practical problems of the outside world predictably diminished. To the ordinary citizen or businessman, law as an academic subject seemed less useful and less relevant than law as a problem-solving profession.

Young B. Smith succeeded to the deanship at Columbia in 1928, after Calvin Coolidge appointed Harlan Stone to the United States Supreme Court in 1925. Smith had determined that the speculative and academic direction represented by Oliphant and the others should not be allowed to cause Columbia to "relinquish its hold upon prospective members of the Bar." A profession whose purpose is to solve the problems of real people would suffer by becoming a totally academic and scholastic exercise.

Smith's determination brought the matter to a head. Four bright young professors who were sold on the soft science revolution resigned. Among the four was a young professor from Maine, Minnesota, William O. Douglas, who would be appointed to the Supreme Court by FDR in 1939. Along with Underhill Moore, Douglas headed off to Yale, where Robert M. Hutchins was dean. At Yale Law School, the innovators found a more hospitable environment for their pursuit of interdisciplinary studies. Meanwhile, a formal evaluation of the real-world results of attempting to integrate law and social science had been begun by Dean Smith at Columbia, who in 1930 pronounced the whole undertaking somewhat disappointing. He remarked:

> It has not been an uncommon experience for the dissatisfied legal scholar, who had made excursions into the realm of economics, or philosophy, or of psychology, to return with a feeling of relief to the more settled and orderly domain of the law.

Hutchins was sympathetic to the new undertaking at Yale. However, after he left to become dean at Chicago in 1929, he also assessed the practical achievements of the new approach in about the same way as Smith. Remarking on an attempt at Yale Law School to teach the law of evidence as just another branch of psychology, he allowed,

> What we actually discovered was that psychology had dealt with very few of the points raised by the law of evidence; and that the basic psychological problem of the law of evidence, what will affect juries, and in what way, was one psychology had never touched at all.

So much for two years of effort at a project which seemed like such a good idea at the time. This willingness to launch interesting and expensive experiments based on the exciting and novel generalities of the new soft sciences was symptomatic of the growing view of legal training as a primarily scholastic and academic undertaking, a sort of jurisprudential science with the law school as the laboratory. Langdell's innovations had propelled the "scientific" metaphor into the forefront of academic legal analysis and training. The process was aided by an eager and receptive academic community in the nation's rapidly multiplying law schools. The impact was profound.

Older judicial decisions setting forth slowly evolved customs and practices were re-evaluated under a crude version of the scientific method, and the rules of law these decisions reflected were increasingly challenged. The scientific method as understood in the hard sciences entails experiments conducted under carefully limited and controlled conditions. Experiments are found to produce invariable and predictable results. A fixed amount of ingredient A added to a fixed amount of ingredient B under rigidly controlled conditions C yields results D in all cases. A cause and affect are recorded which enables the scientist to predict future events, but only under very limited circumstances. Under the limits of a controlled experiment, this permits a prevision of future events arising out of current conditions. However, when this previsionist approach is applied to circumstances containing infinite and unknown variables, the ability to predict the future results of the experiments fails. Where the subject of the experiment is not a set of carefully controlled laboratory conditions, but society at large—the case with legal experiments—the ability to accurately assess the future consequences of experimental action vanishes.

Scientists themselves have been mindful of the limitations inherent in applying the scientific method outside of the restrictions of the scientific laboratory. Judges and lawyers, however, were not. Lawrence Brown, (an engineer) in his compendious study of Western science and social history, *The Might of the West*, commented on the effect of misappropriating true scientific concepts to the study of history:

> [T]his very school of scientific thought, the positivism of *J.S. Mill* and *Compte*, which is the philosophical atmosphere of our time, asserts that the true nature and possibly even the definition of science is the ability to predict the consequences of known causes.
> The illusion of having accounted for the past by a causal analysis permits the extension of plausibility to a desired future.
> What is lost track of the awareness that scientific foresight is never vague but only conditioned, while mechanistic political foresight is never conditioned but always vague.

The result of misapplication of the "scientific method", says Brown, is that our conviction that all things are governed by mechanistic causality is confirmed, "so that we feel entitled to extend the certainty we have attained under controlled conditions to the universe at large where conditions can neither be controlled nor even identified."

Among legal academics and the growing number of judges attuned to the new" scientific jurisprudence" of the early twentieth century, very little thought was given to the inherent limitations of the scientific method, which had proven its remarkable ability to unlock the workings of the natural world.

The puny results of the first wave of law-as-science programs were not inspiring. Many of the innovators drawn in the mid-1920s to the excitement of a new approach at Columbia had scattered about in disappointment, ready to try something else. However, the real flame of innovation and newfound fashion continued to burn brightly at Yale, where it has smoldered ever since. Yale, in the words of one professor, became the center for "the nonprofessional study of law," dedicated to making the law "more nearly in step with the complex developments of modern life." The results have somehow remained disappointing at Yale just as they had elsewhere. Underhill Moore culminated one laborious project described by an observer as a series of "faintly unrealistic studies of parking offenses in New Haven." For this project, Moore spent many hours standing on the streets of New Haven watching how people parked their cars. Yet the newfound mission of Yale gathered steam, and as it did, the collective enthusiasm of the new-age legal education was matched only by their visceral detestation of the old legal system. As Robert Stevens summarizes in his brilliant study of the growth of American law schools,

> The work of Charles Clark, William O. Douglas, Abe Fortas, Walton Hamilton, Wesley Sturges, Edward Robinson, and others during these years poured scorn on centuries of scholarship.

Despite the evidence of practical failure which began almost immediately to mount against their attempts to remake "centuries of scholarship" and legal tradition, the force of the Yale movement gained strength akin to a religious movement. This community of innovators became known as the "realists." Thus an enormously powerful but basically unconstructive skeptical movement assigned the apparatus of the common law to the scrap heap almost overnight. There appeared a body of literature capturing the new approach, giving it a concreteness and plausibility, including the influential *Law and the Modern Mind* by Jerome Frank. The realists gave the impulse to scientific inquiry a new twist by sending the direction of inquiry inward, into deep internal psychological and emotional processes. They denied the independent existence of rules of law, since all legal action was viewed as merely another value-laden manifestation of phenomena only the soft sciences could illuminate. Where the judicial approach of Joseph Story and a host of similar judges viewed legal rules as emerging from a painstakingly-kept record of past custom and practice, evidenced by common law decisions, the modern judge was increasingly drawn to the "scientific" notion that intellectually constructed innovative decrees would produce predictable and desirable results in the society to which they applied. The principles of the social sciences, such as psychology and sociology, could be "scientifically" used to shape the future.

Scientific Jurisprudence threw a large spanner into the clockwork machinery of Justice Story's legal and constitutional theories. This was the modern way, and more than anything else it killed any reasonable in-depth analysis of how the pre-1920 legal system actually had worked. Though the curricular structure of Yale Law School was imitated by few others, the habits of mind stimulated by the realist movement and its superficial plausibility and attractiveness have had an impact far beyond New Haven, Connecticut. They reached ultimately to the Supreme Court itself.

CHAPTER ELEVEN

The New Legal Science

Only when it is wrongly assumed that all rules of just conduct have deliberately been made by somebody do such sophisms become plausible as that all power of making laws must be arbitrary, or that there must always exist an ultimate 'sovereign' source of power from which all law derives.

Friedrich A. von Hayek, 1980

Louis Dembetz Brandeis was born in Louisville, Kentucky, on November 13, 1856. His father, an immigrant who fled the political revolutions in Europe in 1848, became a prosperous merchant in Louisville. When Louis was sixteen, he was sent to the *Annenrealschule* in Dresden, Germany, where he was subjected to two years of the most rigid and formalistic academic discipline in the world.

He entered Harvard Law School at age eighteen, with no college training, completing the law course in two years and scoring the highest marks in the school's history. When he arrived at Harvard, Langdell's scientific case method was just getting underway, and it made the law as it then stood accessible to Brandeis's scientific mind. In deducing the essence of the law out of the current cases and producing hard, concise summaries of legal principles, Brandeis had no equal. He was one of the first of many generations not trained in the grand old style or immersed in the memorabilia and tradition of the common law. His reductionist skills, more characteristic of a European civil lawyer than a common law jurist, made him a wizard within the new system.

After a year of graduate study and eight months in St. Louis, Missouri, he came back to Boston and entered a partnership with a law school classmate, Samuel D. Warren, Jr. In the course of developing a growing corporate law practice, he read deeply into sociology and economics.   His career began in the heyday of the Progressive Movement, with big capital and organized labor much in the public mind.   Brandeis developed a deep, unquenchable, burning intellectual urge for reform.   He said he could not imagine "anyone being really able who was not a reformer." He was a strange professional paradox, earning large fees representing big corporations while developing the reputation of a "people's attorney." He plunged into every activity in his life with zeal and discipline, whether it was representing business, representing the small man, or Zionism.   The progressive image stuck and, to the shock of Wall Street, President Wilson appointed him to the United States Supreme Court on January 28, 1916.   Former President Taft, who would eventually become Chief Justice, said Brandeis was "not a fit person" to be an associate justice, and he was widely regarded as radical and unpredictable.

His knowledge and intellect ran deep, and in displays of what one of his law clerks described as "absolute convictions on the nature of truth," he would quote Goethe, in German, during arguments.   He was unafraid to enter the field of constitutional jurisprudence as an analyst, with a probing scientific and creative mind.   He could delve into the most unruly data, absorb and collate it, and produce summations and deductions of great brilliance and high literary quality.   In his association of science with the study of law, he was a modern.   He was attracted to the Yale realists and their plausible scientific clues to the secrets of jurisprudence.   He was referred to by a contemporary acquaintance as the "Scientist of the Law," and he loved facts, statistics, and the final triumph of scientific conclusion over seemingly uncollatable detail.

The realists found a sympathetic ally in Brandeis, and he turned his disciplined methodology to the task of analyzing the Constitution of the United States.   In one of his 528 legal opinions, he chanced across the very same issue which Joseph Story found lurking in the background of the dispute between Messrs. Swift and Tyson in 1842: were judicial opinions "laws"?   The results of applying his scientific views to this same issue initiated a revolution in judicial power.   Though Louis Brandeis was ostensibly a spokesman for judicial restraint, his actual practice and philosophical bent were to move American constitutional jurisprudence away from limitation and restraint.

The chance for Justice Brandeis to elaborate on his views of judicial action and common law process came in a case involving an accident. While Harry James Tompkins was walking along an Erie Railroad right-of-way near his home in Hughestown, Pennsylvania, he was struck by what appeared to be a door projecting from the side of a passing Erie railroad train, and lost an arm. He sued the Erie Railroad Company in New York, where the company was incorporated, in federal court. If any state rule of law were to be applied to Tompkins's case, it would be the law of Pennsylvania, the place of the accident. Under Pennsylvania decisions, someone on a railroad right-of-way was considered a trespasser and thus was considered not to be owed the normal duty of reasonable care usually required by law. Yet the trial judge refused to follow these opinions, and permitted the jury to award Tompkins $30,000. The court of appeals affirmed, holding that the Pennsylvania decisions would not be governing authority in any case. The federal courts could, they reasoned, exercise an independent judgment on the content of the law as they had done in *Swift v. Tyson*. Clearly this was an abuse of the *Swift* doctrine, as were a number of earlier federal opinions permitting deviation from state law. This was abusive because no provable customary standard existed on the subject of duty owed to those on a railroad right-of-way, nor was this a subject on which custom could be expected to evolve.

There is no question that Brandeis was a person of great integrity and the very highest intellect. And he correctly recognized that an uncritical and improper reading of *Swift* had somehow permitted departure from local law in the past. Yet it is also clear that he had no understanding of the actual judicial process or system which *Swift* represented.

Nevertheless, the same issue raised by *Swift* again faced the Court: Were the decisions of the Pennsylvania courts binding in the sense that they were "laws"? However, the issue was viewed in terms of twentieth century scientific positivism, rather than the historical tradition of the common law. At the heart of Brandeis's treatment of this case lay a new definition of sovereignty and its relation to judicial action. It was, more-over, a new definition that which would later produce astounding and far reaching changes. Brandeis relied heavily on Oliver Wendell Holmes's theories set forth in his classic, *The Common Law*. Brandeis wrote,

The fallacy underlying the rule declared in *Swift v. Tyson* is made clear by Mr. Justice Holmes. The doctrine rests upon the assumption that there is "a transcendental body of law outside of any particular State but obligatory within it unless and until changed by statute," that federal courts have the power to use their judgment as to what the rules of common law are; and that in the federal courts the parties are entitled to an independent judgment on matters of general law... But law in the sense in which courts speak of it today does not exist without some definite authority behind it. The common law so far as it is enforced in a State, whether called common law or not, is not the common law generally but the law of that State existing by the authority of that State without regard to what it may have been in England or anywhere else. . . .

[T]he authority and only authority is the State, and if that be so, the voice adopted by the State as its own [whether it be of its Legislature or of its Supreme Court] should utter the last word.

The strange irony of this decision was that it was calculated to serve federalism by deferring to the sovereign authority of the states as expressed by their own courts, who were now regarded as speaking for the sovereign itself. This jurisprudential principle would, however, eventually transform the theory of judicial action itself and ultimately work against the original goal of federalism. Private customary behavior was to be rejected as a fictitious "invisible hand," incompatible with governmental sovereignty.

It was precisely this idea of an "invisible hand," a sovereign voice outside of the state, which aggravated the utilitarians like Jeremy Bentham and the legal positivists like John Austin, Oliver Wendell Holmes, and finally Louis Brandeis. Earlier, Holmes had himself endorsed legal positivism, the view that law is exactly what the sovereign wills it to be, in American constitutional law. In 1922, he wrote an opinion in *Western Maid*, in which he disposed of the argument that a person could actually possess rights against the United States government but be unable to enforce them because of the sovereign immunity doctrine. In Holmes's view, the rights simply did not exist:

There is no mystic over-law to which even the United States must bow. When a case is said to be governed by foreign law or by general maritime law that is only a short way of saying that for this purpose the sovereign power takes up a rule suggested from without and makes it part of its own rules.

Brandeis took this jurisprudential generality and applied it to the judicial process itself. Relying heavily on Justice Holmes's sympathetic rendition of the legal positivism made fashionable by the writings of John Austin, Brandeis rejected the notion of law as anything other than the command of the sovereign. Henceforth, judicial opinions expressed the command of the sovereign. *Judicial opinions were laws.*

In this way, the view that law is nothing more than scientifically determined social policy joined the principle that law is nothing more than the command of the sovereign. The new theories of the Yale realists were blended with a version of legal positivism, and were given a scientific twist. One could easily view a rule of law as an intellectual proposition detached from the consent of those to whom it applied. Intellectualism had become wed to the inward sovereign that now resided in every common law judge.

The effects of this combination have reverberated to this day. The result has converted the entire field of American constitutional law into a free-wheeling intellectual policy debate among the academics and the bench, and has disconnected the debate from any reference to the consent of those governed by the Constitution or laws passed in accord with it. The structure of the Constitution which was designed to promote consent as the basis for the legitimacy of legal rules was overwhelmed by the intellectual judicial sovereign and an energetic cortège of academics.

The 1938 gospel of inward sovereignty has since passed to a legion of lesser reformers on the bench and in the law schools. But the new disciples are unlike its creator—Louis D. Brandeis. They have neither the brilliance of mind nor disciplined learning of Brandeis.

By the time Earl Warren was appointed to the Court in 1953, this sovereign realism was well established as the theoretical foundation of judicial action. The statistical profile of judicial action in the Warren years gives a clue to the significance of the new sovereign realism, which had, under Brandeis's guidance, come to replace the common law

cornerstone of an earlier day. At the date of Warren's swearing in, the
United States Supreme Court had overruled its own prior decisions a
total of twenty-seven times during its 163-year history. During the
sixteen terms of Warren's Chief Justiceship, it did so thirty-one times.
Even in the hands of a moderate Republican, the new tool of judicial
sovereignty proved easy to use.

The conversion of the first principle of judicial action, the
cornerstone, which Brandeis's new theory accomplished, was to have far
reaching effects. It meant that the object of judicial inquiry, the
theoretical source of law itself, was converted from something external
to the individual judge, that is from custom, to something internal.
Rather than inquiring without, the judge was to ponder in his own heart.
The primary judicial objectives began to be described increasingly in
personal, inward-looking terms as judges came to rationalize their role
as that of "the national conscience." The older principles were, it is
true, admonitory. They were only principles, and judicial discretion was
then, as now, a part of life. But the basic precept under which
inevitable human discretion operates is, as events were to prove, a
powerful force. When the fruits of the new view adopted by Brandeis
matured, the rule of law declined. The sovereign was found to be
within the judge himself.

The saga of the new inner judicial sovereignty shows that the first
principles and precepts held inwardly by men and women profoundly
influence the history of their outward actions. Once again it was
reaffirmed that "Ideas rule the world" and that the individual matters
immensely. Without the German scholasticism and the writings of early
precursors of realism (works by Oliver Wendell Holmes and Roscoe
Pound) and the rational and scientific view of the law as sovereign
command foreshadowed by John Austin, there would have been no Louis
D. Brandeis. Without Louis D. Brandeis, there would have been no
Earl Warren or the more modern examples of sovereign judicial
creativity.

In 1938, the Supreme Court finally located the very sovereignty
of the government in the judiciary, which became the equal of the
legislature as a law-giver. The singular and fundamental idea which was
so hard-won by the Revolution—that the elected legislative branch of
government was the exclusive apparatus for expressing governmental

sovereignty—now had been dethroned. From then on, the judicial power would be a sovereign competitor. Unlike the ponderous and cumbersome legislature, the judiciary was at work every day. It worked on every human affair that gave rise to a lawsuit. This single revision of basic constitutional theory began a slow-growing revolution which has only now fully unfolded.

What have these changes produced? How has the world been made a different place because of them?

To begin with, the serious discussion of the structure of the federal government, of the constitutional law of separation of powers, has virtually disappeared from the professional world in the last twenty-five years. Professional and academic circles now think there is simply no theoretical justification or practical reason for ever discussing such a theory.

The current status of legal academics is instructive. Significantly, only two major books in the past fifteen years has put forth serious argument for the traditional separation of powers theories associated with pre-World War II constitutional scholarship. The first was by Raoul Berger, published in 1977 and entitled *Government by Judiciary: The Transformation of the Fourteenth Amendment*. The second was by Robert Bork, published in 1990 and entitled *The Tempting of America: The Political Seduction of the Law*.

It was Berger's 1977 book that set off an academic firestorm that brought the predominant trends in legal and constitutional scholarship to light. Reaction to Berger's book revealed how far the academic legal "scientific" view of the law and the Constitution had diverged from popular conceptions (the Legal Constitution) by 1977. Berger's book focuses upon the records of the 39th Congress, which formulated the Fourteenth Amendment. The arguments Berger makes and the reaction of the academic community to them is revealing.

Berger's basic thesis is that the records of the 39th Congress demonstrate a vital link between both statutory and constitutional measures for the benefit of freedmen and the "privileges and immunities" clause in Article IV of the United States Constitution. This clause says, "The citizens of each State shall be entitled to all privileges and immunities of citizens in the several States." As revealed in the case of *Corfield v. Coryell*, this privileges and immunities clause protects residents of any state from statutory discriminations related to specified "fundamental rights." These rights consist of "(1) personal security; (2) freedom of locomotion; and (3) ownership and disposition of property." Linking the 1866 Civil Rights Act to these enumerated rights by virtue of the frequent references in its legislative history to both *Coryell* and Article IV, Berger construes this 1866 Act to outlaw discrimination against these fundamental rights.

The privileges and immunities clause of the later-adopted Fourteenth Amendment extended the protection that Article IV of the Constitution afforded transient citizens to the newly created citizens of each state; this protected those new citizens from discrimination in matters covered by the same trinity of basic rights. Further, in formulating the basic clauses of the Fourteenth Amendment—the privileges and immunities clause, the equal protection clause, and the due process clause, the Framers intended to exclude both suffrage and segregation from its coverage. As to these three clauses, "one revealed the scope and nature of the rights protected, the next established an equality of enjoyment as to these particular rights, and the latter guaranteed the judicial protection of these rights on an equal basis for all residents."

Therefore, says Berger, these constitutional provisions not only fail to justify the creation of *additional* substantive constitutional rights, but they actually exclude such creation from their scope. As Berger has stated, "It is . . . as if the Amendment expressly stated that 'control of suffrage shall be left with the States.'" Therefore, argues Berger, the landmark opinions of the United States Supreme Court in *Baker v. Carr*, *Oregon v. Mitchell*, and *Reynolds v. Sims*, which brought the Supreme Court into the field of reapportionment, were unconstitutional. Likewise, there was no constitutional warrant for Chief Justice Warren's desegregation opinion in *Brown v. Board of Education*.

Many of the details of Berger's reconstruction of the legislative history of the Fourteenth Amendment were challenged. But the reaction to his book revealed something which went beyond mere scholastic detail. Berger's arguments forced his critics to reject his fundamental assumption that the clearly expressed intent of the framers of *any* given constitutional provision is relevant, even if it can be demonstrated. That is, Berger's critics accepted the idea that the judicial function includes revising or ignoring clear constitutional provisions on policy grounds. Thus, if one gets past the thorny question of interpretation and arrives at a clear meaning in a constitutional provision, Berger raises what is in fact the most important and basic question of constitutional law. The interpretation of the Constitution is really a lesser issue included in the greater issue of judicial authority. Berger poses this fundamental question straightforwardly: "On traditional cannons of interpretation, the intention of the framers being unmistakably expressed, that intention is as good as written into the text." Therefore, we confront the issue: "[G]iven a clearly discernible intention, may the Court construe the Amendment in undeniable contradiction of that intention?" This was the same question raised by the New York City crisis. It is a question which goes to the heart of popular convictions about consent as the basis for governing law, surely the cornerstone of the Legal Constitution as it is generally understood.

Surely Berger's thesis is sufficiently fundamental and important to call for an answer. And the answer from the legal academy to Berger's basic question (can the Court contradict clearly expressed intent?) has been a mysteriously convoluted "yes." The significance of this question is quite obvious and stems, as Berger says, from the "almost universally accepted importance of consent as a prerequisite of valid and binding rules of constitutional (or other) laws—because of the primacy of democratic theory in our constitutional scheme." If it is possible to have judicial decrees supersede the most fundamental expression of consent in our system, it is vital to know precisely how this authority came about, why the judiciary is believed to possess it, and what conditions there are, if any, to its exercise. Moreover, it is just as important now as it was in 1775 or 1842 to understand just what theories and practices are observed as guides to judicial conduct. It is not only a matter of academic speculation but a matter of vital concern to every citizen.

The events following the publication of Berger's book provide a glimpse into just what the new academic theories about judicial conduct contain. Two years after its publication, *Government By Judiciary* drew a storm of criticism gathered in one notable symposium published in the *Hastings Constitutional Law Quarterly* in 1979. Strikingly, *all* the contributors to the symposium were opposed to Berger's views in one way or another, and to his thesis about the binding effect of clearly expressed constitutional intent. Virtually all commentators from every corner of academia were arrayed against Berger in the years that followed.

Professor Louis Lusky of Columbia Law School made a contribution to the Hastings symposium, suggestively entitled "What Price Legitimacy," typical of the "yes" answers to our seminal question. In fact, Professor Lusky's attempt to justify judicial action that transcends consent and intent provides an almost comprehensive litany of the rationale of pro-activist scholarship; thus, the basic features of his essay deserve notice. Professor Lusky's "yes" answer is constructed against the background of certain a priori assertions about the patently "inadequate" nature of a more limited form of judicial authority, and identifies the acceptance of older, "inadequate" theories with a now outmoded form of legal training. Some homage is paid to democratic theory with yet another assertion that a limited view of judicial authority resting on precise constitutional content is no longer "acceptable to the American people." He asserts as a matter of historical fact that his new theory of judicial power is what people have come to want. In this way, Lusky further asserts that the new constitutional revisory power enjoyed by the judiciary has been somehow harmonized with democracy since "the people at large have accepted the legitimacy of the basic decisions claiming enlarged judicial power." In short, if the people are not revolting, they are consenting.

These observations are clearly peripheral to Lusky's basic thesis that seeks to legitimize the extensive judicial power addressed in our basic question: Can the Court override clearly expressed constitutional intent? His primary justification has two prongs. First, he asserts that the new judicial authority is an accomplished fact, arising from a recent "seismic" change in the Court's impression of its own powers to revise the Constitution and to repudiate the older limits on judicial review. The Court thus adopted a "new and grander conception of its own place in the governmental scheme." In other words, the Court's claim to the power is a fait accompli; therefore, it is unrealistic to presume it reversible. Second, he claims that the correctness of the results reached by the newly claimed judicial power demonstrate its legitimacy. This is probably the most common feature of all modern constitutional scholarship. Lusky underscores the "practical effect" of a more restrictive view and emphasizes "the value of the Court's work over the last four decades" in an attempt to demonstrate "the immensity of the stakes" involved in the choice between limited and unlimited judicial power. A "moral authority" thus enables the Court to exercise the power, and the thrust of this essentially pure result orientation rests upon certain *a priori* assumptions about the correctness of particular "national commitments."

For all his equation of the "seismic" change in self-proclaimed judicial authority with pure physical science, calculated to drive home its inevitability, Professor Lusky's "limiting" principles are purely admonitory directions to the Court to exercise "self-restraint" and to give "reasons for claiming to be the final word on constitutional questions." Those directions fail to provide any meaningful or intelligible guide to either limiting judicial authority or to answering the fundamental questions for political democracy which such authority raises.

What Professor Lusky actually articulates as a test for judicial authority is nothing more than a ratification of a unilateral judicial claim to power. It accepts unlimited judicial power as a real-world inevitability as inexorable as the laws of physics, coupled with a commendation of the results of judicial action. Reduced to a fundamental axiom of constitutional law, the test he actually employs identifies what the Court *has* done with what it *can* constitutionally do; he then declares, in an amazingly simple and straightforward manner, that "what is" is correct and accords with his impression of the historically inevitable, and therefore should be supported.

Regardless of this facile historiography (what fait accompli cannot be asserted to be, by definition, a product of the pressure of inexorable historical forces?), this approach fails to address the basic constitutional question of majority rule. Like all the other leaders of new-age constitutional scholarship, Lusky thinks that anyone who disagrees with the new orthodoxy just doesn't know what's good. One of the basic flaws in Berger's work, according to Lusky, is that he does not really appreciate the "value of the Court's work over the last four decades," that is, the results the Court has produced. Even here, he pays some homage to the framers by asserting that they would really have wanted things to be the way they turned out "had they been living and acting in the middle of the 20th century." What would these same people have wanted with respect to the protections offered by the Fourth Amendment? One wonders. Would conjecture about this question be an adequate basis for allowing warrantless ex parte searches of a home to fight unprecedented crime? This conjectural time-transportation theory has many possibilities. Lusky seems to envision that transmutation of the Fourth Amendment is possible too, and this causes him much anguish:

> [A]t the risk of seeming needlessly alarmist I say that though they lack the numbers and military strength to mount an armed revolt, nonwhites are fully capable of creating such civil disorder that wholesale searches, arrests without probable cause, official censorship, and other police state trappings would be thought essential for societal survival here, as they were in Italy during the spring of 1978 when Aldo Moro was kidnaped and killed.

There you have it all; what has happened must be accepted because it happened, what has happened must be accepted because it is good, and it is good because those who created the Constitution would be, as reasonable men, bound to agree were they alive today. If you don't accept it, you just don't know what's good for you.

These standards, more than anything, involve a basic apology for judicial action based on the acceptability of results. The new scholarship assumes that if judicial authority claimed and exercised is accompanied by laudable results, it is legitimate. Thus, under the new scholarship, a narrative or purely descriptive account of the Court's self-perception and altered claims to authority de facto, and the evaluation of results, are the keystones of legitimacy. A clearer invitation to judicial revision of the Constitution, hedged by admonition to be shrewd, restrained and guided by the educated consensus of academe, could not be found.

The remaining essays in the symposium mainly present variations on this theme, both in the direction of somewhat greater restraint than the Lusky approach and in the direction of an even more fervent commitment to result orientation and unlimited judicial authority. Another contributor, Professor Henry Abraham of the University of Virginia, proposes a test for judicial authority calling upon the "spirit" of any particular constitutional provision. He suggests that invocation of this spirit can, in fact, justify judicial contradiction of express intent.

This contradiction is, he says, defensible in connection with the Fourteenth Amendment basically because, true to the fundamental credo of result-orientation, to have done otherwise would "have perpetuated injustice."

The theories of all the contributors make only theoretical protestations and gestures toward democratic government by suggesting some limits on judicial authority, but as a practical matter justify judicial action by resort to some consensus about injustice which they perceive as shared by the enlightened among the legal intellectual community. This stance is incompatible with majority rule, past or present.

This attempt to equate results with legitimacy in particular instances but to preserve generally the appearance of majority rule as an option (presumably as insurance against a Court disposed to "injustice"), can at best be considered a gamble resting on pragmatism rather than intellectually definable principle.   It is a gamble that only those dissatisfied with majority rule, with democracy, ever decide to take.

Professor Arthur Miller of George Washington University also represents the modern academic view in his rebuttal of Berger. The Court, says Miller, can clearly determine "what overriding values" there are or should be, and he does not attempt to hide his conviction that "the Constitution does not require that cases be decided 'in accordance with the specific intentions of the framers even when those intentions are ascertainable.'" Simplistically reducing judicial decision making to an election between discernible but conflicting policies, he engages in the typical apologist's antipathy to judicial history, which offers a rich and complex intellectual structure by which to analyze and distinguish different degrees of judicial discretion and authority. Since judging is simply a "creative act," the Supreme Court—not to be confused with an "ordinary court of law"—is free to be completely result-oriented, rather than confined to "a formula or a dogma [which] is intellectual death." Miller comes as close as anyone to embracing an undiluted, perfectly nondemocratic evaluation of judicial power according to the result it promotes. He states explicitly the anti-majoritarian premise that what really limits judicial power is what judges can get away with: "Their discretion is in fact limited to that which the public will accept." Ironically (but also typically), Miller in the same breath identifies the Court's primary mission as promoting "the democratic ideal," though in practice "judicial thought should ultimately be in terms of consequences, of results and of alternative decisions." Although we have the usual exhortation to judges "not to roam at will," Professor Miller's constituted theory, functionally and practically analyzed, espouses a judicially self-determined authority to overrule even clearly expressed popular will whenever the "authoritative faculty of social ethics," which our Supreme Court has become, so decides.

Concluding with the inevitable jargon, Professor Miller tells us that "[t]he Constitution is a politico-legal palimpsest," leaving us with the insight that nothing is ever really unconstitutional, some things are merely unpopular.

Other contributors to this volume espouse the "vacuum theory" that excuses judicial action whenever "politically accountable legislators . . . abdicate their proper policy roles." That apparently excuses judicial action, even if contrary to popular will, when doing so would "respond to injustice." Thus, the newly articulated tests to measure the limits of judicial authority are clearly incompatible with a previously viable constitutional first principle, i.e., the commitment to consent as a basis for government and to popular or majority will as the ultimate basis for law. This essential abandonment of majority rule, the indulgence in the luxury of "elective" or "sometime" democracy, depending on the issue, raises the most basic political and constitutional problems.

Academic writers have carried forward this revolutionary view of adjudication and provided nearly universal acclaim for the actions of the Supreme Court. Aside from Professor Alexander Bickel, one of the last men of letters to teach American Constitutional law, there has been very little official academic criticism of the Court. The monopolistic and introverted "scientific" approach of American law schools meant that a whole new wave of young lawyers could be nurtured on this new jurisprudential theory, and would provide growing professional approval for the judicial actions it permitted. The law schools had come to represent an institutional arrangement which could turn on a dime, which it did in the 1960s.

The scholarly expositions discussed above are merely extensions of the predominant academic fashion espoused earlier by Professor Archibald Cox of Harvard Law School (who later became famous for his role in the Watergate investigation). Cox wrote *The Warren Court:*

Constitutional Decision as an Instrument of Reform in 1968. This book seized the fashionable high ground by providing the literary but non-analytical apology for the new judicial age which the Warren Court had inaugurated.   Cox's view is that the Supreme Court should act vigorously when needed reforms have not emerged from the legislative branch of government.   This view is, of course, fraught with serious constitutional implications. It removes the very decision about what the national agenda should be from representative branches of government and places control entirely in the non-representative branch—the courts. Commentators were quick to pick up on the new functional role Cox had assigned to the judiciary, without bothering to acknowledge that it had by definition implied a purely legislative and policy-making role for the court.

These developments underscore the risk in ratifying judicial over popular will. What happens if the Court decides in effect to eliminate the Fourteenth Amendment or to ratify "separate but equal" education? What can be said at that future date but that the Court has undergone another "seismic change," another shift in self-perception, and has achieved "a new and grander conception of its own place in the governmental scheme."

We are told this new judicial power is necessary to allow us "to escape the dead hand of the past." May we now escape the dead hand of Earl Warren, if so minded? Will we finally reach the point where adjudication to vindicate the spirit of a provision precludes resurrection of what was in fact the original intent? Will some academic counselor tell us that the spirit comprehends everything but what was intended? The answer to these amazing questions is a definite "yes," as we shall see momentarily when we examine the work of the current Supreme Court. The point is, however, that we now have a standard for judicial authority which is merely a calculation of the perceived social utility of judicial action. This is coupled with the belief that a judicial opinion is a sovereign command which is not subject to popular will or consent. This is really what is meant by "constitutional law" today.   Raoul Berger openly discussed an unappealing intellectual basis for pro-activists.   Thus, we see why reaction to him is so universal and splenetic.

It is safe to say that some analytical structure tying judicial action to ascertainable intent or constitutional meaning is needed to make sense out of a democratic constitution. The overt declaration that judicial power stands above *known* intent is an assertion difficult to comprehend from the perspective of a democratic law-making process. One may argue that intent cannot be perfectly known. How, then, do we extract this useful core of intent from the various provisions of our Constitution? For example, when Congress proposes certain words that the states ratify, might the variations in intent among the drafters and among the states be so great that the search for intent is fictional and without purpose? Its purpose is to provide an analytical apparatus to impose upon the judiciary limits and principles formulated in the constitution-making or amendment process. Although those limits and principles are plagued by occasional ambiguities, without them the democratic process certainly fails. Rather than moving within the universe of an intellectual and analytical dialogue, we would simply be awaiting the final decree of the judge. Under the jurisprudence of the legal scholars discussed above, any effort to formulate a constitution or law would be pointless. Moreover, we would never progress toward more effectual and useful constitutional declarations of majority will. What difference would this effort make if the fundamental law of the land can be ignored?

Of course, one of the most attractive features of the modern constitutional scholarship is its ease. The rhetorical generalities it employs are so much easier than the laborious pursuit of intent or meaning, which calls on powers of analysis and painstaking historical construction of context. Thus, in the late 1960s and thereafter, law schools were increasingly peopled by those who had distinguished themselves by their fervor for the new fashion overtaking scholarly analysis, rather than by their analytical skills. In this, they resembled the new wave of academics coming into collegiate education in the 1960s. Unfortunately, today's law schools all contain a healthy number of these "legal scientists." They genuinely fear the disputation and open dialogue that a high-quality mind and broad education might bring their way, thus disturbing their complacent adherence to the easy fashion of modern "scholarship."

In a very real sense, Alexander Bickel's work represented the last manifestation of the open-minded liberalism and broad views which were well represented in education before 1960. In 1970, he published *The Supreme Court and the Idea of Progress*, which broke with the emergent fashion of judicial sovereignty and called into question the tenets of the new-age school. Bickel dealt openly with the implications for democracy of the new school, and he outraged rank and file academe to no end. His death, in 1974 at age forty-nine, marked the passing of literate constitutional scholarship, and the future fell to Cox, Miller, and the others previously discussed. American constitutional law scholarship became by 1975 a nearly universal apology for the new view.

Unfortunately, the essays discussed above give an accurate picture of the current condition of constitutional "scholarship" in today's law schools. This new orthodoxy has all the characteristics of a new-found religion: the excitable rhetorical tone, the constant and predictable appeal to the implicit rightness of particular dogma, the obsession with certain inspired goals, the complete lack of humor, the fanatical sense of mission, the measurement of all things, all people and all actions by their service to the cause.

What are the basic characteristics of the new academic legal orthodoxy? First, the new scholarship is largely apologetic. It justifies the Court's newly asserted, extensive revisory powers by describing them as accomplished fact, a result of claims the Court has already made, as irreversible as they are inevitable. Being essentially apologetic, this view analytically confuses a narrative explanation of a controversial judicial development with a justification for it. Mere identification of a trend is thought to validate it. The new popular scholarly consensus largely identifies approved results with legitimate judicial authority, a sort of "what you see is what you get" scholarship.

Secondly, academic analysis of judicial power is typically dishonest. It makes gestures toward principles which would limit judicial power, but avoids them all. It is thus cocooned in qualifying expressions which its authors know are devoid of functional value or importance. These expressions preserve the impression of theoretical limits on judicial authority but are always, in fact, purely personal and admonitory—for example, the admonition directed to the judiciary to be restrained or "sensitive," to "respond to injustice," but only "so long as society tolerates." These statements do not consist of independent intelligible principles and are virtually always accompanied by an opinion that judicial will is superior to majority will. The limits on proper authority are, like the legal rules such authority advocates, personal and dependent upon the expectation that the wielders of self-defined power will be shrewdly tuned to popular opinion, as well as restrained.

At the ratification convention for the Virginia Constitution in 1776, Patrick Henry commented on the risks of authorizing extensive authority on the theory that only "good people" would be appointed or elected:

> Where are your checks in this government? Your strongholds will be in the hands of your enemies. It is on a supposition that your American governors shall be honest, that all the good qualities of this government are founded; but its defective and imperfect construction puts it in their powers to perpetuate the worst of mischiefs, should they be bad men; and, sir, would not all the world, from the eastern to the western hemisphere, blame our distracted folly in resting our rights upon the contingency of our rulers being good or bad? Show me that age and country where the rights and liberties of the people were placed on the sole chance of their rulers being good men, without a consequent loss of liberty! I say that the loss of that dearest privilege has ever followed, with absolute certainty, every such mad attempt.

Indeed, such fears prompted the creation of the first ten amendments to the Constitution, to ensure against such governmental abuse. Others, too, echoed the emphasis on principle, rather than on confidence in people, as essential to the constitutional scheme. As Jefferson observed,

> Confidence is everywhere the parent of despotism—free government is founded in jealousy, and not in confidence; it is jealousy and not confidence which prescribes limited constitutions, to bind down those whom we are obliged to trust with power; that our Constitution has accordingly fixed the limits to which, and no further, our confidence may go.

Debate about judicial action, conducted entirely in terms of results and supportive of judicial authority that endorses the contradiction of intent expressed in the Constitution, marks a radical departure from our traditional constitutionalism. It represents the takeover of constitutional law by the new "scientific" legal intellectual.

In fact, of all the qualities of American constitutional scholarship, dishonesty stands out as the most prominent. The scholarship reflects a certain selective and intentional blindness to the solid traditions and core principles of constitutionalism. It employs a cynical appropriation of the terminology and trappings of a majoritarian constitution, but only so far as it supports the purest form of *realpolitik*. The new scholarship attempts to soften popular antipathy to judicial action by averting blunt questions about power and authority and obfuscating them with fatuous jargon. The practitioners of the new school have become literary masters of palatable misdescription. They persistently refuse to extrapolate basic principles inherent in the particular positions that new school proponents find so attractive. Further, they always refuse to apply any principles generally or hypothetically.

We are seriously expected to believe, as an asserted historical fact, that the Framers, who declared their opposition to unrestrained judicial modification of the Constitution, actually "intended . . . to empower the Court to serve as the Founders' surrogate for the indefinite future." The framers' intent here is contorted in such a way as to legitimize a sweeping power that they condemned. Are we to believe that the public demands rule by judiciary and clamors for the results it brings? There is, in fact, no such popular clamor for the revolutionary judicial powers exercised by the federal courts today, despite occasional fatuous allusion to "the people" or to "forces" driving the judiciary "beyond the straightforward, orthodox conception of judicial review."

The common understanding essential to the maintenance of a representatively democratic system is, like the representations of a political candidate, a trust that all silently and implicitly assume will be honored. The intellectual structure of principles represented by a bewildering array of concepts—common law, majority rule, limited authority, and the like—rests mainly upon the straightforward intellectual honesty of its custodians, whether in the courts, the bar, or the university. Over the history of the world, the willing acceptance by individuals of this intellectual trust has enabled them to perpetuate some of society's most valuable ideals and hold them, however feebly, above the temptations of the moment, and occasionally above the transient benefit of attractive results that abandonment of the ideals might facilitate. These ideals are autonomous and are useful only within this intellectual trust. Thus, they are inheritable principles capable of being passed on over time, as opposed to results, which are not.

No one who browses through modern scholarship on American constitutional law can doubt what academia has done with its trust. For in no area of legal scholarship have the techniques of the committed polemicist and the rhetoric of result-oriented journalism come to so dominate as in the area of American constitutional law. If we feel at all moved by Trevelyan's dictum that "[d]isinterested curiosity is the life-blood of real civilization," we may benefit by asking ourselves whether our satisfaction with results has been so great as to cause our scholarly standards to atrophy and thus allow us to lose an invaluable tool in the preservation of consensual, democratic government.

This scientific and prescriptive view of constitutional rules is everywhere mirrored in the attitudes of the scholarly community we discussed earlier. For example, a little-known but highly lucrative cottage industry among United States law professors who teach constitutional law is the writing of constitutions for "emerging" nations. They have played a large part in the proliferation of written constitutions worldwide in recent years: three-fourths of all the world's constitutions have been written since 1965. Prominent in the process are Professors Laurence H. Tribe of Harvard and Albert P. Blaustein of Rutgers Law School. What is the significance of a constitution to many of these consultants, and how do they go about their job? Professor Blaustein says,

> I ask them what they want, what values and heritage they want to see reflected in the document, and then I make suggestions, drawing on my knowledge of different constitutions from all over the world.

It seems a little like ordering a pizza. And who exactly are "they" who specify "what values and heritage" consultants use to top off the final product?

Another involved professor affirms that it is nonetheless a good idea to get a constitution:

There is a perception among new regimes that they should have a constitution because it is good public relations.

Thus, cultures, like knowledge, need not evolve. They can be prescribed. The historical obtuseness of these craftsmen inspires wonder. After thirty years of judicial abandonment of clear constitutional language and doctrine, Professor Blaustein can say with the attitude of a confident chef,

Our document is too general, so we've had to fill in the blanks over the years with case law. We can save others the trouble of all that by making explicit choices at the beginning and putting those choices in the constitutions.

All these years, we thought we had made at least a few explicit choices ourselves.

What accounts for the success of this post-democratic theorizing? For anyone who has spent much time around American law schools over the last two decades, the answer is fairly obvious. As the "case method" of learning the law worked naturally to augment the concept of judicial sovereignty and an academic "scientific" concept of legal studies, the law faculties were transformed. The intellectual drift carried them far away from practical concerns, including the practical concerns of constitutional government. As the population of law teachers nurtured on breezy scientific jurisprudence multiplied, they became more and more hostile to the traditional craft of the lawyer or the traditional concerns of the constitutionalist of years past. Their rallying cry became, "diversity," as it did in other realms of academia (See Part IV, following). But in fact, they were dedicated to a scorched-earth strategy which all but destroyed the jurisprudential and constitutional conventions over which the law schools had assumed trusteeship in the past. The number of people who had found polemic exercise more agreeable than rigorous training reached a critical mass in the early 1980s. A majority or a sizeable minority of just about every law faculty in the country became dedicated to converting law school into an academic and intellectual preserve from which its members could devote their energies to dictating to society, rather than studying or conserving it. Since most faculties require a two-thirds majority to hire new members, the new-age faculty could obstruct any restoration of quality by blocking a vote for an unorthodox traditionalist. They could also count on an increasing supply of new candidates trained in the "non-professional" way, who could be hired at junior levels and intimidated into an alliance with the new post-democracy law professors. Though they intoned "fairness" and "diversity," their credo became rule or ruin.

Thus, it has come about that no evaluation of our overall constitutional performance is ever undertaken. Legal academics do produce a torrent of written material supposedly about the Constitution; annually some 800-plus law reviews and dozens of treatises and textbooks published or reissued in new editions. But, virtually all this work constitutes a battle over esoteric trivia, and it is virtually always designed to publicize the writer's orientation on some point of professional orthodoxy—feminism, affirmative action, desegregation, etc. It is almost never an analysis of any of these governmental measures according to any standard other than results. Essentially, this writing forms a moral roll call for the orthodox academic, supported almost completely by vast mutual-citations to other orthodox declarants (what else would they cite as authority?) This is not the sort of information real people want or need. In short, it is worthless.

Moreover, the message of the new-age legal academic reproduces for the most part merely a jargonized version of what the Supreme Court of the United States *actually* believes and practices. These are not scholarly voices urging a resistant judiciary to grasp the reins of power in the service of noble ends, but rather are the voices of support and encouragement for theories which the Court has already embraced and put into practice. By itself, this fact illustrates the abandonment of the independent role which alone makes the academy useful. It is highly unlikely that we have somehow entered a halcyon epoch of twenty-plus years in which the Court has achieved jurisprudential perfection, and thus earned the respect and fervent support of the academy in the process. Rather, the nearly universal collaboration between the bench and academia, both protected by lifetime tenure, has created the rationale for a nondemocratic form of sovereign authority. And so the public, which by and large does not read law reviews and scholarly books on constitutional law, has had a hard time realizing that the new judicial authority is *known* to be and *intended* to be nondemocratic. Nor do they realize that the perpetrators of the new nondemocratic experiment consciously decided that the results they sought to achieve would be worth the costs of departing from the democratic model.

This conversion explains why the subjects of civil rights and civil liberties literally take up two-thirds of any constitutional law casebook used in today's law schools. Structural issues, that is those addressed to the basic form of government which the Constitution is supposed to support, such as federalism and separation of powers, take up no space at all. The policy objectives of constitutional law scholarship and adjudication have subsumed considerations about our form of government. The triumph of the scientific case method approach to the study of law has concentrated the minds of fledgling law students on the most recent judicial pronouncements contained in these lopsided books. They learn practically nothing of the common law system or the political science and history upon which the Constitution is based.

In 1990, the publication of Robert Bork's *The Tempting of America* revived literate interest in the workings of the constitution and the Court. Bork's book was a lucid exposition of the philosophy and method of the democratic theory of constitutional law, which assumes that the intent of those who made and approved the document is central to its interpretation and enforcement. This "originalist" theory is the same as that espoused in Berger's *Government by Judiciary*, published thirteen years earlier. Bork best expresses the vital link between his theory of judicial action and democracy in his own words:

> The Constitution preserves our liberties by providing that all of those given authority to make policy are directly accountable to the people through regular elections. Federal judges, alone among our public officials, are given life tenure precisely so that they will not be accountable to the people. . . . But if judges are, as they must be to perform their vital role, unelected, unaccountable, and unrepresentative, who is to protect us from the power of judges? How are we to be guarded from our guardians? The answer can only be that judges must consider themselves bound by law that is independent of their own views of the desirable. They must not make or apply any policy not

fairly to be found in the Constitution or a statute. It is of course true that judges to some extent must make law every time they decide a case, but it is minor, interstitial lawmaking. The ratifiers of the Constitution put in place the walls, roofs, and beams; judges preserve the major architectural features, adding only filigree.... The person who understands these issues and nevertheless continues to judge constitutional philosophy by sympathy with its results must, if he is candid, also admit that he is prepared to sacrifice democracy in order that his moral values may prevail. He calls for civil disobedience by judges and claims for the Supreme Court an institutionalized role as a perpetrator of limited coups d'état. He believes in the triumph of the will. . . . The man who prefers results to processes has no reason to say that the Court is more legitimate than any other institution capable of wielding power. If the Court will not agree with him, why not argue his case to some other group, say the Joint Chiefs of Staff, a body with rather better means for enforcing its decisions? No answer exists.

By now everyone knows that these particular beliefs caused the United States Senate to reject Bork's nomination to the Supreme Court. Indeed, what Bork said about abandoning democracy was not only true of legal academics. It was revealed in the Senate, where many explicit remarks made by the Senators during the confirmation hearings revealed the democratic abandonment with stunning clarity. The closing remarks of Senator Joseph Biden to the committee on the judiciary leave nothing to doubt. Said Biden:

I think the Constitution is more expansive than I think you to read it, and I think judges have more latitude and should have more latitude than you think they should. I believe that the Constitution—well, from Magna Carta to the Constitution, 800 years of English jurisprudential history, 900 years, have produced an abiding, consistent notion that I am who I am because I am, not because any constitution tells me.

The Senatorial rejection of Bork's plea for a democratic constitution marked the end of the story. The post-democratic constitution was fully entrenched in academia and the Senate. It remains fully entrenched on the court, as we shall see.

CHAPTER TWELVE

The Modern Court

The academic fashion described by Bork accurately reflects what the Supreme Court does and thinks. The Court has displayed the same intellectual detachment common to academia, a detachment which consistently permits it to pursue theoretical goals of no practical value to ordinary people. Justices are also masters of trivia, delving unrestrainedly into the minutiae of American life, producing an ever-diversifying torrent of philosophical commentary about any subject that takes their fancy. They have reached a point where consensus on constitutional doctrine has so eroded that hardly any justice agrees with another on anything—except a system of the unrestrained result orientation that has *become* constitutional law. Their decisions reveal the inner feelings of each of the Court's nine members on any given issue. The decisions, consequently, hardly ever contribute to any doctrinal development, but rather represent hairsplitting controversy conceived out of personal conviction.

Additionally, the members of the Supreme Court themselves leave no doubt that they agree with the new-age scholarly view. In an October 1985 speech at Georgetown, entitled "The United States Constitution: Contemporary Ratification," then sitting Justice William Brennan explained that the original intent of the drafters of the Constitution is not binding on the Court. The Constitution is not like a law, but rather is "a sublime oration on the dignity of man," and as a result, "the demands of human dignity will never cease to evolve." The Constitution acts merely as a starting point, an original license, for the Court's mission in updating the "sublime oration." Brennan went on to state that the courts are the best and most natural organ of government to do this updating because they are not accountable to the people. This, he said, will let the evolution of the continuing judicial update, the "contemporary ratification" of new rules that the Court provides, occur without interference with "self-absorbed and excited majoritarianism."

Brennan did allow that there was one "ideal of human dignity" that did not evolve. It is "that capital punishment is under all circumstances cruel and unusual punishment" prohibited by the Constitution. Never mind that the Eighth Amendment, which is at least a symbol of this ideal, was ratified at the same time as the Fifth Amendment, which says that no person shall "be deprived of life, liberty, or property, without due process of law." It also refers to "capital or otherwise infamous crime." If you read the Constitution, a person *can* be deprived of life, so long as it is done according to "due process of law." The only unchanging and immutable principle in the Brennan Constitution was rejected by the Constitution of 1789!

Very few Americans think they are living under government by oracle. Very few have read Justice Brennan's Georgetown speech. Even the logic is whimsical, embracing a permanent "immutable and unchangeable" principle existing in a legal universe in which the *sole* guiding rule is permutation and change. As President Lincoln argued with Senator Douglas long ago, a constitution which is based only on emergent interests is not a constitution under which people are free, and is thus not really a constitution worth having. For the judicial oracles and the academics, both far removed from the hand-soiling necessity and uncertainty of the marketplace, it is now *their* Constitution. Almost everything they now say or do betrays an abdication and abandonment of the job which most people still assume they are supposed to do. That the Supreme Court of the United States is a uniquely composed legislative branch operating with lifetime tenure, without any serious reference to a written constitution, abetted by an uncritical and supportive cortège of political journalists, surely will disappoint almost everyone interested in constitutional government.

What have been the practical results of this concept of judicial authority and constitutional government? The inward sovereignty which each judge now possess is wielded with liberality: there is simply no subject into which they will not delve and produce some detailed legislative dictate. Most remember Justice Blackmun's scientifically inspired code of rights dealing with abortion in *Roe v. Wade*. Far-ranging, scientifically-based sovereign action is not unusual and can be found in Supreme Court opinions in any area of human endeavor, whether it be racial, commercial, religious, philosophical or just plain personal.

Race

Nothing has imperiled the long-term interests of black Americans more than modern jurisprudence on this subject, though few are willing to articulate why this is so. In 1954, required separation of school children according to race was mandated by statutes in seventeen states and the District of Columbia. Four other states allowed legal segregation to be addressed by local ordinance. That year, the United States Supreme Court decided in *Brown v. Board of Education of Topeka* that laws requiring racial segregation were an unconstitutional violation of the Fourteenth Amendment and were at odds with the basic purpose of the Thirteenth, Fourteenth, and Fifteenth Amendments. The Court quoted from the case of *Strauder v. West Virginia*, decided in 1890, in which the Court, referring to the Fourteenth Amendment, declared,

> It ordains that no State shall deprive any person of life, liberty, or property, without due process of law, or deny any person within its jurisdiction the equal protection of the laws. What is this but declaring that the law in the States shall be the same for the black as for the white; that all persons, whether colored or white, shall stand equal before the laws of the States, and, in regard to the colored race, for whose protection the amendment was primarily designed, that no discrimination shall be made against them by law because of their color? The words of the amendment, it is true, are prohibitory, but they contain a necessary implication of a positive immunity, or right, most valuable to the colored race,—the right to exemption from unfriendly legislation against them distinctively as colored,—exemption from legal discriminations, implying inferiority in civil society, lessening the security of their enjoyment of the rights which others enjoy, and discriminations which are steps toward reducing them to the condition of a subject race.

Later, in 1896, the Supreme Court allowed the legal requirement of "separate but equal" accommodations for black and white, provoking a dissent from Justice John Marshall Harlan that "[o]ur Constitution is color blind."   The Court thereafter upheld laws requiring racial segregation in public schools, resolving the issue unanimously in an opinion by Chief Justice Taft in 1927.

Chief Justice Earl Warren overturned these older opinions in *Brown* in an oblique and curious way, associating the prohibition of segregation found in this equal protection guarantee of the Fourteenth Amendment more with the inward psychology of the victim than with the critical fact of segregation. The court quoted a lower court comment on the effect of segregation itself:

> Segregation of white and colored children in public schools has a detrimental effect upon the colored children. The impact is greater when it has the sanction of the law; for the policy of separating the races is usually interpreted as denoting the inferiority of the negro group. A sense of inferiority affects the motivation of a child to learn. Segregation with the sanction of law, therefore, has a tendency to [retard] the educational and mental development of negro children and to deprive them of some of the benefits they would receive in a racial[ly] integrated school system.

The court then concluded "whatever may have been the extent of psychological knowledge at the time of *Plessy v. Ferguson*, this finding is amply supported by modern authority," citing several psychological and sociological treatises. The opinion was short, less than nine full pages.

Mountains of literature have been produced in a search for the meaning of this decision, which in legal terms should have been taken to mean what it held: that legally required racial segregation is not constitutional. The decision was fair and amply justified by the language of the Constitution. Yet the scope of the decision was quickly found to concern "the motivation of a child to learn" and any matter which may affect "the educational and mental development of negro children." From then on, the federal judiciary were propelled into discovering all manner of remedies, decrees and injunctions which served this inward psychological objective, as they understood it in light of the latest available science. Their decrees went far beyond education itself and were to touch every aspect of public and private life. What happened?

Support for the original holding in *Brown* followed shortly thereafter in the passage of the Civil Rights Act of 1964. The statute required desegregation, which it defined in Title IV:

> Desegregation means the assignment of students to public schools and within such schools without regard to their race, color, religion, or national origin, but 'desegregation' shall not mean the assignment of students to public schools in order to overcome racial imbalance.

Significantly, the statute also said,

> Nothing herein shall empower any official or court of the United States to issue any order seeking to achieve a racial balance in any school by requiring the transportation of pupils or students from one school to another or one school district to another in order to achieve such racial balance.... Nothing in this title shall prohibit classification and assignment for reasons other than race, color, religion, or national origin.

Title VI of the statute dealt with education and required the elimination of discrimination in educational institutions receiving federal money, stating,

> No person in the United States shall, on the ground of race, color, or national origin, be excluded from participation in, be denied the benefits of, or be subjected to discrimination under any program or activity receiving Federal financial assistance.

The legislative history of the statute reveals vigorous arguments by its proponents that the statute went no further than to prevent racial discrimination. The proviso stating that no orders to seek racial balance were authorized was consistent with their claims and could hardly have been clearer. Indeed, the powerful support within Congress for the statute, and the general sympathy for its aims, arose precisely because it was based solidly on a fair-minded reading of the Constitution itself, and because the proposition of Justice Harlan that "our Constitution is color blind" had intrinsic appeal and wide support in and out of government.

Hubert Humphrey, the bill's floor manager, said simply that the bill imposed on public officials a "duty not to segregate or otherwise discriminate. . . . This bill cannot be attacked on its merits." To an astoundingly large group of fair-minded people, he was seen as absolutely right. During the period immediately following the passage of the Civil Rights Act of 1964, opinion polls showed that a majority of the nation supported the measure and other similar government initiatives. When asked by Senator Robert Byrd if he could give his personal assurance that he understood the bill *not* to authorize extraordinary remedies aimed at restructuring the racial balance in public schools, such as busing, Humphrey said, "I do."

Thus, the understanding was clear that neither the Constitution nor the law mandated judicial remedies to achieve some sort of ideal racial balance in public schools. It simply required that schools *not* segregate or discriminate based on race.

Senator Byrd persisted in asking if portions of Title VI would authorize the Office of Education in HEW to mandate such remedies in institutions receiving federal funds. Humphrey replied that the president would have to approve such an order and such was *not* warranted by the statute, which contained in Title IV a proviso clearly stating so, and that "the president can read." At that point Senator Javits, one of the drafters of the bill, consoled Senator Byrd that even if such an unauthorized act were undertaken by HEW and the president, the courts would not allow it to stand. Said Javits, "That is why we have judicial review."

Senator Humphrey laid the argument to rest, clearly recognizing that legal or official actions based on race were *exactly what the law prohibits*:

> In fact, if the bill were to compel it, it would be a violation, because it would be handling the matter on the basis of race and we would be transporting children because of race. The bill does not attempt to integrate the schools, but it does attempt to eliminate segregation in the school systems.

This approach was commended by an honest and defensible reading of the Constitution, comported with widely accepted standards of fairness and convictions about the equality of treatment, and honestly reflected the language of the statute itself.

America was ready for the *Brown* case as it stood. The infliction of harm or disadvantage, or the bestowal of advantage, strictly on the basis of race was something the vast majority condemned at the time. The majority of Americans would not have then, nor will they now, nor will they ever accept *either* disadvantage or benefit on a racial basis under compulsion of law. The majority correctly believed along with Justice Harlan that "the Constitution is color blind." They would, for the most part, condemn racial discrimination just as they would racial entitlement, since these were the flip sides of the same coin. Thus it came about that in 1964, the country had the opportunity to capture a broad-based, middle-class support for a common philosophical ground and to secure the legal environment it would promote.

Dr. Martin Luther King acknowledged as much in his moving speeches, which attracted growing numbers of fair-minded whites. As Dr. King had said, the long-term success of the civil rights movement would depend upon the good will of the white majority, or those who were moved by the basic fairness and rightness of King's claims for equal treatment of blacks, just as much as it would depend on the dedication of blacks. Though King's message changed toward the end of his life, which came by an assassin's bullet on April 4, 1968, he maintained his advocacy of nonviolence and Christian ethics. His message of equality, which pulled a growing number of sympathetic whites to his cause, rested on the simple conviction that color or race should not matter:

> I have a dream that some day on the red hills of Georgia the sons of former slaves and the sons of former slave owners will be able to sit down together at the table of brotherhood. I have a dream that my four children will some day live in a nation where they will not be judged by the color of their skin but by the content of their character.

King's message appealed to a principle almost everyone could understand and which most people believed (correctly) was embodied in the United States Constitution. His was a principle most people believed to be basic to the Legal Constitution. This was the message of Justice Harlan's dissent in *Plessy v. Ferguson*, and this was the most obvious meaning of *Brown v. Board of Education*. The complex jargon and regulatory schemes which, as we shall see, arose later would not have the fundamental attraction and potential for success of this simple message. King's right and forceful words merely reiterated the basic concept of the 1964 Civil Rights Act. The road to acceptance of the concept of equality—of individual equality—would in any case be difficult. It would be scarred by the violent resistance of isolated hate groups who would never accept equality. But at least the movement was founded on a principle which had the promise, even the probability, of general and widespread acceptance, precisely because it appealed to what most people believed was fair.

Opportunity had arrived at last. The philosophical appeal of *Brown* as it had been written, and of the 1964 act as it had been intended, allowed both black and white to view each other through the medium of identical, equal citizenship. This step forward of inestimable value is one which those not alive at that time do not now seem to understand or appreciate. It was a chance to build lasting progress on the common ground of the widely understood concept of fairness which "equal protection of the law" was understood by both races to mean. It was the single greatest opportunity for legal progress and institutional integrity to be preserved in the context of a *commonly* held, well understood belief in a racially neutral government conducted according to constitutional principles. It was a chance for lasting progress, for the common interest in fairness which the majority of society harbored to allow all both races to live under the shared conviction that they were, first and foremost, citizens of the United States, *equally* protected by its laws. More importantly, *Brown* and the 1964 act reflected a vision that would have prevented the dangerous realignment of the political allegiance of American voters along racial lines which has occurred since the mid-1970s, nearly destroying the Democratic Party by the late 1980s.

This vision did not prevail. In fact, it was quickly killed. The history of race as a subject of constitutional law has ever since been grounded on governmentally enforced legal entitlements based on race. These entitlements were designed to overcome the inevitable physical and material circumstances that exist in a world of neutral legal principles, or even in one without such principles. Moreover, it is a legal world from which the individual, who had been so exalted as theoretical and practical sovereign under the old common law system, finally vanished. As a legal entity, he ceased to exist, not because of direct judicial usurpation, but through strenuous executive action followed by judicial abandonment.

The time had come for "affirmative action," a concept which reversed the original goal of eliminating legalized racial discrimination. "Affirmative action" argued that discrimination, if it was the right kind, could be helpful. "Affirmative action" rejected the *Brown* court's view of the Fourteenth Amendment and the Civil Rights Act of 1964. The courts and law professors argued that the neutral constitutional principle of non-discrimination would not get them where they wanted to go; they needed, they said, inequality now to fight inequality in the past.

Where did "affirmative action" come from? How did it come to embrace the idea that discrimination based on race should be judged by its purpose and effect, or that racial discrimination was permitted by the Constitution? The 1964 Civil Rights Act clearly forbade discrimination against "any individual" concerning employment. The term "affirmative action" appears in the section of Title VII permitting the court to order such action by any employer found guilty of racial discrimination. It targets those who have intentionally discriminated.

The term "affirmative action" itself had first appeared in Executive Order No. 10925, issued by President Kennedy on March 8, 1961. There it described the actions which a contractor dealing with the federal government was supposed to take to be sure he *did not* discriminate. President Kennedy established the President's Committee on Equal Employment Opportunity (PCEEO) to carry out Executive Order No. 10925. The PCEEO drafted a program called Plan For Progress, under which employees were asked to take "affirmative steps above and beyond the Executive Order." Several companies signed the Plan For Progress, which mainly consisted of a declaration of intent *not* to discriminate. There was no mention of numerical hiring quotas. So far, the federal remedies were directed *against* discrimination.

Then Congress passed the Civil Rights Act of 1964, which, in Title VII, forbade discrimination in employment against "any individual" based on "race, color, religion, sex or national origin." Title VII did contain two references to preferential treatment. In one paragraph, Congress made it clear that an employer was *not* required to use preferences to correct any statistical imbalances between his work force and "the available work force." In other words, Congress expressly declared that having a work force with fewer women or minorities than existed in the community would *not* require the use of numerical hiring quotas.

In another paragraph in Title VII, Congress expressly allowed a relaxation of the rule *against* discrimination where religion, sex or national origin (not race), constituted a "bona fide occupational qualification." Congress had in mind employment within religious denominations and on Indian reservations.

Thereafter, on September 24, 1965, President Johnson issued Executive Order 11246. This abolished the PCEEO and transferred authority to implement the Executive Order to the secretary of labor. But this new order had a significant addition. It empowered the secretary of labor to "adopt such rules and regulations and use such orders" as would fulfill the purposes of the Executive Order itself.

In response, the secretary of labor issued new rules on May 21, 1968 to implement Executive Order 11246. These rules required employers to identify "problem areas" in their workforces, and to provide "detail for specific steps to guarantee equal employment opportunity keyed to the problems and needs of members of minority groups." The objective was still "employment opportunity," and there was no mention of numerical hiring quotas.

It was President Richard M. Nixon and his attorney general, John Mitchell, that finally gave us quotas. This development came out of the so-called "Philadelphia Plan," which became a springboard for the Nixon administration's enforcement of hiring quotas on a national scale.

The Philadelphia Plan was conceived by the Labor Department and distributed to all federal agency heads on June 27, 1969. It set forth the employment requirements for all contractors bidding on federal or federal-assisted projects in the Philadelphia area. The plan was based upon findings by the Department of Labor that several trade unions in Philadelphia had engaged in racial discrimination, resulting in low minority membership in the unions. Since employers took referrals from these unions when hiring new employees, they wound up hiring very few minorities. The plan required bidders on federal contracts to "specify the range of minority manpower utilization expected for each of the designated trades." By minority manpower utilization, the Labor Department meant the racial percentages within the work force. This was the first appearance of numerical quotas.

At this point, the principle of separation of powers actually began to work. The Nixon administration was requiring things Congress had forbidden, and Congress took notice. A Congressional reaction to the Nixon administration policies began. On August 5, 1969 the Office of the Comptroller General issued a written opinion that the Philadelphia Plan *violated* Title VII of the 1964 Civil Rights Act, since it *required* the use of race as an employment criterion.

Attorney General John Mitchell jumped into the fray, issuing a formal opinion on September 22, 1969. The opinion set forth the view that the Executive Order under which the Labor Department operated was in no way related to legislative authorization. This argument squarely raised a serious conflict between executive and congressional authority, since the Nixon administration was requiring things that Congress had forbidden.

Meanwhile, the Labor Department was ploughing ahead with the Nixon program. On September 23, 1969, the assistant secretary for wage and labor standards announced hiring "ranges" which employers had to meet to satisfy the Philadelphia Plan. The "ranges" required "filling vacancies and new jobs approximately on the basis of one minority craftsman for each non-minority craftsman " in select crafts ", which were specified as ironworkers, plumbers and pipefitters, steamfitters, sheetmetal workers, electrical workers, and elevator construction workers. In reality, employers had to immediately begin using quotas within the presented "ranges" required by the new rules.

This brought the clash with Congress to a head. On October 27, 1969, Senator Sam Ervin, chairman of the Senate Subcommittee on the Separation of Powers, convened hearings on the Nixon administration actions which conflicted with Title VII. Senator Ervin stated that, in his view, the Philadelphia Plan and the Labor Department's actions had violated this letter and spirit of Title VII. Senator Ervin declared that this executive action should be confronted immediately. As he said, in words which have since proven prophetic:

> For if we are lax today in adhering to the law, what may happen tomorrow[?]

The secretary of labor had, in fact, decided to embrace the numerical quota approach crafted by the assistant secretary for wage and labor standards for the Philadelphia situation. The secretary had decided to apply the quota principle on a national scale by incorporating it into general regulations under the Executive Order. The fuss in Congress slowed his plans down, however. The secretary approved of "Order No. 4," which applied the quota requirement of the Philadelphia Plan nationwide to all non-construction contractors with 50 or more employers and federal-assisted contracts totalling $50,000 or more. However, this order was withheld from publication in the Federal Register pending the outcome of Ervin's Congressional showdown. Congress, in its appropriations bills, had conferred authority on the comptroller general to ensure that federal law was observed in all federal contracts. The Senate picked up Senator Ervin's challenge to the Nixon administration's quota program by adding a rider to a supplemental appropriations bill that forbade dispersing funds unless the comptroller general certified the transaction receiving the funds was lawful. This rider passed the Senate unanimously, but the Senate later omitted the rider when President Nixon threatened a veto. The Senate, as Senator McClellan said at the time, "just surrendered."

After the Congressional surrender, the secretary of labor published revised Order No. 4 in the Federal Register on November 20, 1969. From then on, for all federal and federal-assisted contracts, employers were required as a practical matter to use hiring quotas. Moreover, it was not necessary for anyone to show that the employer had previously discriminated against anyone, as was the case with the Philadelphia unions. Proportional representation in the workforce, quotas, was a blanket requirement. The prohibition of discrimination against "any individual" contained in Title VII had been transcended. The concept that legal and constitutional protections extended to individuals on an equal basis was under an attack by the executive branch, and Congress had proven itself unable to resist.

This episode, which ended with Nixon facing Congress down, illustrated the separation-of-powers dynamic at work. At this point, the fulfillment of legislative as opposed to executive intent would be tested according to Senator Javits's earlier reference to the guardians of last resort: "That is why we have judicial review." Now it was up to the courts.

By the end of Nixon's first term, only the Republican party was offering the public any traditional or conservative rhetoric. The failure of the supposed opposition party to point out the non-conservative character of much of what the Republicans were doing, much of which they agreed with, placed the Democrats in an ironic position and gave the Republicans a free hand. With the public diverted by heartwarming, conservative rhetoric and promises, and with no one to call their hand, especially if there were no judicial restraint or congressional resistance, Republicans found the door wide open for just about any social program they desired. This situation foretold the 1980, 1984, and 1988 elections, in which the Democrats had moved as far away from the real issues raised by Republican action as they could.

With the die cast, the dynamics of governmental abandonment moved quickly. Congress had proven unable to insist on a constitutionally supportable remedy to racial discrimination, though it had clearly intended to exclude the far-reaching executive remedies which employed "corrective" racial discrimination. Congress had momentarily stood up for constitutional principle, as had the original opinion in *Brown*. Racial discrimination was not to be tolerated, period. But the executive transcended this principle. And Nixon now found support from a growing number of judges equally anxious as Attorney General Mitchell or the secretary of labor to enforce a plan actually at odds with constitutional principle itself, as well as the 1964 legislation. Would the judiciary ultimately restore the primacy of legislative intent and return to some basic constitutional principle, and move away from purely result-oriented administrative command?

Definitely not. The Court stepped aside just as Congress had done. In *Griggs v. Duke Power Company*, decided in 1971, the Supreme Court held unanimously that if any employment test produces a racially disparate impact, the employer must prove freedom from discriminatory intent, an essentially impossible undertaking, and show a correlation between his employment requirements and job performance. Quotas from "Order No. 4" became an appropriate tool for providing such proof.

The head of steam which the executive had built up thus increased considerably, and orders issued by the secretary of labor became more Orwellian scope and content after *Griggs*. "Revised Order No. 4," issued on December 1, 1971, stated,

> Relief for members of an "affected class" who, by virtue of past discrimination, continue to suffer the present effects of that discrimination must either be included in the contractor's affirmative action program or be embodied in a separate written "corrective action" program. An "affected class" problem must be remedied in order for a contractor to be considered in compliance.

In February 1974, six months before the end of the Nixon administration, Order No. 4 was revised again. Under the new version, past discrimination need not have been committed by the current employer, nor did the "effects of discrimination" necessarily relate to anything the employer had done.

This broadened version of Order No. 4 formed the basis for later federal Affirmative Action Guidelines of 1979. There were merely elaborations on the Nixon administration theme, and protected employers from claims by whites and males whose jobs were affected by the employer's compliance with quota requirements. Within the scope of these broad Labor Department regulations, the era of individual constitutional and legal rights was over. Thus, the executive programs which constituted the first serious assault on the concept of *individual* constitutional and legal rights were not the logical extension of the Kennedy and Johnson era. Rather, the first anti-individual numerical quota program appeared as the intentional exploitation by the Nixon administration of the divisive issue of race. It was the first full-blown appearance of abandonment at the highest levels of national government. From then on, the Republicans and the Democrats moved decisively away from the concept of common and equal citizenship and the individual nature of constitutional and legal rights. With both the executive and Congress abandoning the basic idea of individual constitutional rights, it was up to the judiciary. The quota program launched by the Nixon administration went straight to the heart of the Legal Constitution of America. It put in issue the common consensus of the majority about the nature of their constitutional and legal rights: Did we have a constitution and legal system which gave *each individual* equal Constitutional and legal rights?

The End of the Individual

The Fourteenth Amendment employed the term "person" and the 1964 Civil Rights Act forbade discrimination against "any individual." How did "individuals" as opposed to members of an "affected class" fare under these new rules? Brian Weber found out in 1979.

Weber had joined the work force at the Kaiser Aluminum & Chemical Corporation plant in Gramercy, Louisiana, in 1969. Kaiser had been under pressure from the Office of Federal Contract Compliance in 1974 to implement the new guidelines and in response adopted a complex program designed to increase minority representation in the workforce. This program had been endorsed by the union that supposedly represented Weber. As a result, Weber was passed over by a less senior black worker whose qualifications for promotion did not exceed Weber's. The previously-established seniority rights which Kaiser had followed gave way to a racially divided program in which senior blacks and senior whites were divided into two groups, and the most senior one from each group was given a promotion whenever the most senior one from the other could be promoted also—a sort of "one black, one white at a time" seniority system. Weber charged that he was then senior to some of the blacks who were promoted solely for the reason that they were segregated into the black group, rather than having their seniority considered across racial lines.

The trial court and the Fifth Circuit Court of Appeals agreed with Weber. The court of appeals held that for Kaiser to employ racial preference when it had not been shown to have engaged in racial discrimination, even if the overall effect was intended to remedy some past "societal discrimination," was not legal. The court said that to do so "has no foundation in restorative justice" and that the preference used by Kaiser thus violated Title VII. People were to be treated as "individuals" and not as members of some "affected class."

In effect, the government had attempted to tell Brian Weber that, as a non-minority employee, he had no reason to complain because any advantage (i.e., his seniority) that he had acquired must have been taken from some member of the minority employee class, to whom it would now be returned. For the government, "affected class" as opposed to individual meant that the individual citizen had acquired the legal status of an undivided part of a category of fungible (or interchangeable) goods, and could be treated as such. Though "crimes of status" are forbidden by the Constitution, civil advantages and disadvantages of status were beginning to appear under these new rules.

The decision went to the United States Supreme Court, where Justice Brennan practiced his brand of oracular justice. Whereas government lawyers and the lower courts had been unable or unwilling to evade the requirements of the Constitution and the Civil Rights Act, Justice Brennan and his comrades White, Marshall, and Stewart were up to the task.

Justice Brennan said that Brian Weber's reliance on the plain language of the law which forbade racial discrimination against any individual was "misplaced." What Congress really *meant* to say was that racial discrimination against any individual would be permissible if it actually served "efforts to abolish traditional patterns of racial segregation and hierarchy."

By this time, the individual had obviously disappeared as a constitutionally recognized entity. Also gone in the process was the majoritarian form of government based on the primacy of laws produced by a popularly elected legislature. The individual as such, and the social and governmental structure of which he was a part, ceased to exist.

Justice Blackmun concurred. He found the Court's resolution of Weber's problems "troubling" but "an acceptable one."

Chief Justice Burger issued a short dissent, in which he made reference to the institutional costs of the Court's new approach:

> What Cardozo tells us is beware the "good result," achieved by judicially unauthorized or intellectually dishonest means on the appealing notion that the desirable ends justify the improper judicial means. For there is always the danger that the seeds of precedent sown by good men will yield a rich harvest of unprincipled acts of others also aiming at "good ends."

After *Weber*, such sentiments would come only from occasional dissent, or some far corner of academia, but would *never* consistently form a ruling philosophy again. Thus the federal courts endorsed a growing body of executive guidelines as tantamount to binding minimum constitutional requirements. Yet they all contradicted the letter and spirit of the original judicial decision and legislative enactment (the 1964 Civil Rights Act) that began the process. As Professor Graglia of the University of Texas remarked, "[A] clearer illustration of administrative and judicial perversion of legislative purpose would be difficult to find."

Later, the principal spokesmen for the Court in *Weber* found themselves dissenting in the final round of the racial see-saw which the Supreme Court has ridden since 1954. In 1989, Justice O'Connor wrote for a majority in striking down a plan adopted by Richmond, Virginia, which required contractors working for the city to subcontract at least 30 percent of the dollar amount of all jobs to "minority business enterprises." However, the court's resolution did not signal a return to intelligible constitutional principle. Rather, it was a collection of nine different essays on the policy implications of what Richmond had done. The unintelligible syllabus of the official report outlines the opinion as follows:

> O'Connor, J., announced the judgment of the Court and delivered the opinion of the Court with respect to Parts I, III-B, and IV, in which Rehnquist, C.J., and White, Stevens, and Kennedy, J.J., joined, an opinion with respect to Part II, in which Rehnquist, C.J., and White, J., joined, and an opinion with respect to Parts III-A and V, in which Rehnquist, C.J., and White and Kennedy, J.J., joined. Stevens, J., and Kennedy, J., filed opinions concurring in part and

concurring in the judgment. Scalia, J., filed an opinion concurring in the judgment. Marshall, J., filed a dissenting opinion, in which Brennan and Blackmun, J.J., joined. Blackmun, J., filed a dissenting opinion, in which Brennan, J., joined.

As the syllabus reveals, the work product of nine oracles has become complex.

The background of the Richmond controversy is interesting. In 1980 the Supreme Court upheld a federal program requiring that 10 percent of certain federal construction grants be awarded to "minority contractors." Thus, in 1983 Richmond adopted its plan. The Richmond plan required that the minority contractor be a business at least "51 percent of which is owned and controlled by minority group members." The plan defined minority group members as "Blacks, Spanish-speaking, Orientals, Indians, Eskimos, or Aleuts."

Low bidders in contracts had to fill out reports identifying the 30 percent minority business entities which would be employed. The city then investigated these. At the hearings when the plan was adopted no direct evidence of racial discrimination by the city was introduced.

A contractor sued the city under Section 1983 of Title 42 of the United States Code. This law reads:

> Every person who, under color of any statute, ordinance, regulation, custom, or usage, of any State or Territory or the District of Columbia, subjects, or causes to be subjected, any citizen of the United States or other person within the jurisdiction thereof to the deprivation of any rights, privileges, or immunities secured by the Constitution and laws, shall be liable to the party injured in an action at law, suit in equity, or other proper proceeding for redress.

The trial court and the court of appeals upheld the Richmond law on the basis of prior Supreme Court precedent. The court of appeals repeated the language which had by then become typical of all such opinions. As in *Weber*, "persons" and "individuals" were simply relegated to the fungible goods category where they could be dealt with according to the "affected class" to which they belonged. The Supreme Court remanded for further consideration, and the court of appeals reversed itself, finding that the Richmond plan had not, after all, been proven to result from any "compelling governmental interest."

Richmond appealed, and back it came to the Supreme Court. Richmond argued that, as a result of prior Supreme Court pronouncements, "the city of Richmond enjoys sweeping legislative power to define and attack the effects of prior discrimination," not just individual actions against other individuals but effects on society as a whole, in which the individual had disappeared under *Weber* and its progeny.

Rather than return to the individual as the focus of constitutional rights, Justice O'Connor turned to Congress for an explanation of why the Court had previously upheld percentage requirements, as it had in 1980. Said O'Connor,

> What appellant ignores is that Congress, unlike any state or political subdivision, has a specific constitutional mandate to enforce the dictates of the Fourteenth Amendment. . . . That Congress may identify and redress the effects of society-side discrimination does not mean that, *a fortiori*, the States and their political subdivisions are free to decide that such remedies are appropriate. Section 1 of the Fourteenth Amendment is an explicit constraint on state power, and the States must undertake any remedial efforts in accordance with that provision. To hold otherwise would be to cede control over the content of the Equal Protection Clause to the 50 state legislatures and their myriad political subdivisions. The mere recitation of a benign or compensatory purpose for the use of a racial classification would essentially entitle the States to exercise the full power of Congress under § 1. We believe that such a result would be contrary to the intentions of the Framers of the Fourteenth Amendment, who desired to place clear limits on the States' use of race as a criterion for legislative action, and to have the federal courts enforce those limitations.

In fact, Justice Stevens, a Ford appointee, quickly pointed out that he disagreed with any suggestion "that a governmental decision that rests on a racial classification is never permissible except as a remedy for a past wrong." Additionally, he was concerned that a legislative body, rather than a court, had fashioned the race-based rules:

It is the judicial system, rather than the legislative process, that is best equipped to identify past wrongdoers and to fashion remedies that will create the conditions that presumably would have existed had no wrong been committed. Thus, in cases involving the review of judicial remedies imposed against persons who have been proved guilty of violations of law, I would allow the courts in racial discrimination cases the same broad discretion that chancellors enjoy in other areas of the law.

What are the "chancellors" to use as guidance in authorizing racial discrimination of an acceptable remedial nature? Justice Stevens answered,

I believe it is more constructive to try to identify the characteristics of the advantaged and disadvantaged classes that may justify their disparate treatment.

In this manner separation of power makes its reappearance under oracular government. It is relevant only to establishing the monopoly of federal control over policy and to determine which branch exercises that monopoly over the subject at hand. Justice O'Connor spoke of the need to use only racial considerations which "are strictly reserved for remedial settings," ending her opinion with a typically complex evaluation of the standard of review appropriate to scrutinize the action of a separate and non-federal governmental body. However, in this case, no factual demonstration of the remedial setting had been presented to the Supreme Court. Even Justice O'Connor noticed that on the Richmond City Council five of the nine members who had adopted the contractual code were black.

Thus the main difference between the majority and minority opinions in the *City of Richmond* case concerned the burden of proof necessary to demonstrate the utility of racial classifications in reworking the social matrix—in which the individual still remains lost—and who gets to make up the rules. That is all.

The terms Stevens used—"[c]haracteristic" and "justify"—are of course descriptive of judicial discretion and prerogative. It is they who shall decide. Recalling an earlier holding, Stevens concluded that,

> When [government] creates a special preference, or a special disability, for a class of persons, it should identify the characteristic that justifies the special treatment. When the classification is defined in racial terms, I believe that such particular identification is imperative.

In other words, it is certainly a good idea to require a legitimate reason for engaging in corrective racial discrimination.

Predictably the dissents were acrimonious and had no more to do with constitutional law than did the majority opinion. Justice Marshall plunged into the lost opportunities for reconstructing our country's deplorable social history:

> It is a welcome symbol of racial progress when the former capital of the Confederacy acts forthrightly to confront the effects of racial discrimination in its midst.

In Marshall's opinion, the fundamental principle of federalism comes to Richmond's defense as it is beleaguered by the Supreme Court, just as it once was by the Army of the Potomac:

> I find deep irony in second-guessing Richmond's judgment on this point. As much as any municipality in the United States, Richmond knows what racial discrimination is; a century of decisions by this and other federal courts has richly documented the city's disgraceful history of public and private racial discrimination.

Justice Marshall concluded with the same self-serving finality that is the mainstay of constitutional scholarship, claiming the validity of race-based laws is established by the *fact* of its former judicial approval:

> It is too late in the day to assert seriously that the Equal Protection Clause prohibits States—or for that matter, the Federal Government, to whom the equal protection guarantee has largely been applied, from enacting race-conscious remedies.

Blackmun closed the opinion with hope that the Court will assume its proper oracular role:

> So the Court today regresses. I am confident, however, that, given time, it one day again will do its best to fulfill the great promises of the Constitution's Preamble and of the guarantees embodied in the Bill of Rights—a fulfillment that would make this Nation very special.

Few understand even today that the process by which racial discrimination became an approved legal tool rather than a constitutionally prohibited activity was *not* a result of some unilateral judicial usurpation. Rather, it was produced by a collective abandonment of any real effort to preserve the structure of constitutional government and the place of the individual in it, an abandonment in which all three branches participated. When Congress refused to face executive abuses, the traditional watchdog task fell to the judiciary. As we have seen, however, their conceptual apparatus and their objectives had already moved far away from support for majoritarian government. The watchman did not awake in vain. Rather, he did not awake at all.

Now the process has come full circle. On February 7, the new Civil Rights Act of 1990 was introduced in both houses of Congress. This bill, described as an "omnibus civil rights reform law," would mandate racially determined employment quotas as a legislative requirement. Congress has joined the judiciary in remaking society according to "aggregate classes." Ironically, one of the bill's principal sponsors in the House, Augustus Hawkins, a Democrat from California, urged adoption of the bill for the reason that "[m]illions of Americans can no longer count on the courts to protect them against some of the most blatant forms of discrimination." President Bush spoke against the Democratic version of the Civil Rights Act of 1991 for twenty months, labelling it a "quota bill", which it was. On November 21, 1991, President Bush signed into law a "compromise" version of this law. It was still a quota bill. The minimal retreat which the Supreme Court had made from the principles of its 1991 decision in *Griggs v. Duke Power* was eliminated, and employees are required to show that any deviation from the prevailing social, sexual or ethnic composition of society in their workforce is a product of "business necessity". Employers will do just as they have done since quota-based affirmative action became the rule in the 1970s. They will hire by quotas. Individual rights have vanished, along with the individual himself, in a political process blending all three branches of the federal government, so that separation-of-powers considerations become interbranch dialogues about policy, but never about constitutional law or the individual.

Thomas Sowell and others have brilliantly challenged the scientific basis for such legislation as the 1990 Act. They have demonstrated that even racially neutral employment practices have never historically reproduced a society's exact racial composition in any given area of employment. Science is, however, of no concern to Congress. Nor are the enormous costs that every employer subject to this act will have to incur in order to prove the unprovable: that variations in the work force from the racial percentages reflected in society are due to "necessity." Only the obtuse and dishonest will say this law does not require quotas as a practical matter.

On June 27, 1990, the Supreme Court supported Congress in approving of race as a constitutionally permissible factor in bestowing legal privileges. In *Metro Broadcasting, Inc. v. Federal Communications Commission*, Justice Brennan's oracular powers reappeared in a decision which validated racial preferences in the award of valuable FCC radio licenses, and in the renewal of existing radio and television stations. In situations where the license of an existing station was scheduled for revocation or for a hearing pending renewal, the FCC had adopted a policy to allow transfer of the license *only* to a minority member. The new minority owner was to be given a reduced rate for the new license, which "must not exceed 25 percent of fair market value" under FCC regulations.

Justice Brennan's opinion approved of "benign racial classifications" as an appropriate tool which the federal government may use "to the extent they serve important governmental objectives." Brennan clarified the fact that, under the United States Constitution, "race-conscious classifications adopted by Congress to address racial and ethnic discrimination are subject to a different standard than such classifications preserved by state and local governments." This opinion echoed that of Justice O'Connor in the *City of Richmond* case.

Remarkably, Brennan acknowledged that the FCC policy which mandated the race-based preferences *were not* in any way related to past discrimination. Rather, they were adopted "to promote programming diversity." Thus the Court, Congress and the Executive all now agree that racially defined legal privileges and entitlements are completely detached from retributive justice, and are the proper means of achieving purely intellectual social objectives—the "proper" level of "diversity."

Federal power to enforce such intellectually crafted social agenda is enhanced by the very way in which these federal racial policies are originated and enforced: The logic is that Congress created the FCC, the FCC created the racial policies, therefore Congress has, in effect, required them. Separation of power once again makes a comeback in the form of deference which the judiciary must show as coequal federal branch in regulating the public. Says Brennan:

> With respect to the complex empirical questions, we are required to give great weight to the decisions of Congress. . . .

The vast agencies of the federal government now enforce the dictates of scientific empiricism, along with the Executive, Congress and the Courts

Preferential access to valuable FCC licenses has created a lucrative secondary market. During the 1990 North Carolina Senate race it was learned that Senator Jesse Helms's opponent, Harvey Gantt, was part of a minority investor group which acquired a television station license from the FCC and sold it a few weeks later to a white-owned media company. Gantt put up $680 and his share of the sale proceeds was $470,000. The FCC giveaway has also benefitted Ron Brown and David Dinkins. Affirmative action for the rich includes, in addition to the FCC licenses, construction contract set-asides and subsidized loans from the Small Business Administration.

Now the legislature would have to exert its lawmaking will against the judiciary, the executive, and administrative agencies to undo new nonlegislative law produced by nonlegislative government fiat, and to undo constantly proliferating legal rules contrary to Congress's own previous pronouncements in the same legal area. The proponents of judicial legislation (judicial acts superseding legislative will) have the benefit of institutional inefficiency in their struggle against the democratic settlement of issues. The legislature is relegated to the politically untenable role of confronting entitlements bestowed by other branches that have superseded its own legislative pronouncements. The legislature routinely joins the process with craftily worded statutes containing the same anti-individualistic concepts as the previous executive and judicial actions. Each branch of the federal government races with the others to achieve goals dictated by orthodox political policy, each using its own unique means, but never to restrain one another.

No doubt the probable force of public will against such things as reverse discrimination would render impossible an attempt to democratically or legislatively achieve it as a matter of law, if such attempts were widely known and understood. And in the eyes of many observers this may justify the roundabout achievement of the result. So be it. But we should openly acknowledge the appearance of a governmental consensus which has abandoned the techniques essential to maintaining our democratic and majoritarian system.

The whole sad saga thus ends with the abandonment of the most promising and widely-supported solution to what may be the nation's most serious social problem—race. A small collection of professionals has decided to bypass democratic and constitutional government to achieve a remedy they find acceptable. In the process they have abandoned the support and approval without which this remedy will, in the long run, fail. The Supreme Court, the lower federal courts and federal administrators now pursue an undifferentiated *tour de force* of sovereign action, spurred by desegregation specialists at the Civil Rights Commission and the little-known edicts of a supposedly conservative former president. The actions of the specialists on and off the bench have transcended the core principle of separation of powers upon which the legislative process depended. As Professor Nathan Glazer put it,

> The professionals, concentrating exclusively on their area of reform, may become more and more remote from public opinion, and indeed from common sense. They end up at a point that seems perfectly logical and necessary to them—but which seems perfectly outrageous to almost everyone else.

All of this has inverted the only general understanding of "equal protection" or equality of treatment that could have possibly gained acceptance throughout society. Now, the Supreme Court, other federal courts and an army of bureaucrats have to deal with the principle that the Constitution at least permits, and may even require, the establishment of racial discrimination designed to end racial discrimination, so long as the Supreme Court maintains the last word on how it is done. At once the dwindling number of legal scholars and lawyers interested in preserving the Constitution recognized this gamble with the good temper of the middle class. They realized how risky such strategic experiments in nondemocratic government could be. Writing in 1970, the late Professor Alexander Bickel observed:

> Professors in New England—and elsewhere, to be sure—will parse the glories of the Warren Court, criticize its syllogisms, reduce its purported logic to absurd consequences, disprove its factual assertions, answer the unavoidable questions it managed to leave unasked, and most often conclude by regretting its failures of method, while either welcoming its results or professing detachment from them. Historians a generation or two hence, however—other professors in New England—may barely note, and care little about, method, logic, or intellectual coherence, and may assess results in hindsight—only results, and by their own future lights.... Past historians have so dealt with the Court, as do many outside the profession, mostly contemporary observers, and one sensed that this was what the Justices of the Warren Court expected, and that they were content to take their chances. They relied on events for vindication more than on the method of reason for contemporary validation.

By the 1970s, the United States Supreme Court, followed by many lower federal courts, embraced a new idea of progress which so clearly obliterated concepts of separated powers and consent as validating principles of American law. This growing experiment in non-democratic government would gradually change even the formalities of judicial opinions themselves.

Now, Supreme Court opinions routinely set forth the highly personal convictions of each justice on any issue presented, distilled from their total arsenal of knowledge, their complete personal views of what is "reasonable." The *United States Reports* reads like some elaborately annotated newspaper account of the personal, political and moral philosophy of up to nine contributors. The reports are almost totally devoid of any rationalizing principle, and to the extent any limits on the judiciary or any other element of government are suggested, they are only viewed as optional or advisory. In short, there is now a perfect intellectual marriage between the new-age legal academic and the scientific Supreme Court. Their opinions resemble the medieval yearbook reports, in which the king's vice-regal judicial agents set forth in their opinions the position of the sovereign on any issue before them, treating statutes and other legal norms as advisory and discretionary only. In America, we have become jurisprudentially and constitutionally premodern.

Curiously, when the inward sovereign now changes its policies and behaves unsatisfactorily according to those who originally backed the nondemocratic experiment for the sake of good results, it is seen as becoming more "conservative." Even the definition of conservatism has fallen victim to result- oriented ambition. As Roger Scruton has written of traditional conservatism,

> The basic premise of conservatism is that worthwhile institutions are hard to build and easy to destroy, and that a life without institutions is seriously impoverished. Institutions are created not by plans or theories, but by the coordinated action of several generations, by a kind of pooling of human intentions in a stream which flows free of individual ambition, providing aims and values of its own.

The postdemocratic judiciary is anything but conservative in such a sense.

Thus, according to the new scholarly theory now endorsed in practice by the Court, the Court's real value should be measured by standards outside the theory of democratic government. The Court serves, so the scholars say, as a transcendent protector of individual liberty and freedom, to be called upon in those emergencies when the voice of democracy and the due course of law fail to obtain real justice.

This is what it does best, and that is why we really need it, they say. Once the Court had transcended traditional separation of powers restraints and discarded the fundamental concept of the individual, the justices could easily go beyond race in their decisions.

Beyond Race

As the Warren era progressed, the Court developed an interest in issues of personal liberty of all sorts. The Court saw itself not just as the final arbiter of racial matters but also as the indispensable final protector of personal liberty. To be fair, we should see just how well the Supreme Court performs this important job. A look at a significant and recent case will tell the story.

Frank Snepp, from Kinston, North Carolina, attended Columbia College in New York, where he majored in Elizabethan literature and graduated in 1965. In 1968, he earned a master's degree from Columbia in international affairs and joined the Central Intelligence Agency.

Prior to joining the agency, Snepp signed an agreement which contained terms requiring agency review and approval of any writing he might produce as a result of his activities in the agency. Snepp served two tours of duty in South Vietnam, the last one ending April 29, 1975, the day the last Americans able to do so left the country. As chief strategy analyst for the CIA in Vietnam, Snepp became known for his heroic eleventh-hour efforts to assist those still in Saigon during the last hours of the withdrawal. For his efforts, he won the CIA's Award for Merit. But he resigned from the agency a year later, following a number of futile attempts to interest the higher officials in the agency and the government in the details and implications of the U.S. withdrawal and the methods by which it was accomplished.

Later, Snepp wrote a book on the events leading up to the United States' withdrawal. Instantly, *Decent Interval* was received as a balanced, descriptive account of the decisive events leading to the U.S. pullout. Reviewers heralded the book as insightful and helpful in understanding why and how we hastily retreated from a country into which we had poured such vast amounts of blood and money—without so much as cleaning out the file cabinets. The book was called "[a] great service" by the *New York Times*; the *Washington Post* called it "[b]y far the richest document yet produced on the American and South Vietnamese endgame." Those reviews were typical. Indeed, reading this book today one in struck by its high literary quality, balanced style, mastery of little-known facts, and brilliant analysis.

When Random House published the book in 1976, Snepp avoided use of any classified information and matters that could compromise government personnel or security. He sought to analyze what we had done in Vietnam, now that we had evacuated it. Since he had used no classified information in the book, his observations and writings were protected speech under the First and Fifth Amendments to the United States Constitution. This protection was known at the time *Decent Interval* was published and has never been disputed since. Since any agency review could not constitutionally result in censorship of the book as written, Snepp declined to seek such review before publication. Nevertheless, the CIA brought suit, claiming that Snepp had breached his contract. The legal system was faced with the curious situation of protected speech which could not constitutionally be regulated but which had not been subject to a review process under Snepp's contract. In other words, Snepp had violated his contract in failing to seek a governmental review, which all acknowledged could not prevent the publication or alter the content of his book.

Nevertheless, Federal District Judge Oren Lewis responded favorably to a CIA request for an injunction against Snepp's publication of any information gained during his tenure at the agency without prior review as provided in his contract. But the agency could not constitutionally prevent the free exercise of Snepp's First Amendment privileges by restraining his publication of nonclassified material. It claimed a right to review, but it could not withhold approval. But because Snepp had not sought review, which would have proved meaningless, Judge Lewis issued a sweeping injunction, purporting to enjoin Snepp "and those persons in active concert or participation with him who receive actual notice of this order" from ever using any information that he "gained during the course of or as a result of his employment with the Central Intelligence Agency" without letting the CIA review it first. Judge Lewis then confiscated all profits from the book.

The terms of Judge Lewis's injunction, remarkable in and of themselves, resulted in a judicial prohibition against speech based on the use of any information Snepp had obtained, regardless of its non-classified nature. There had not been anything like this decree since the controversy over the Alien and Sedition Acts nearly two hundred years ago. The constructive trust placed over any profits Snepp was to receive from the book permitted the government to take the money. The book itself, practically speaking, was banned.

Yet, as Senator Javits remarked in 1964, "This is why we have judicial review." On Snepp's appeal to the Fourth Circuit Court of Appeals in 1979, that court issued an opinion reversing the high-handed confiscation. The court of appeals noted that Snepp's "obligation under the secrecy agreement was to submit all information as material relating to the CIA and its activities or intelligence activities generally, and not, as the defendant contends, only materials which were classified." The court held that Snepp should have submitted the book for review but of course did not challenge the basic proposition that no censorship could have resulted from a process of prepublication review of nonclassified materials. Snepp had breached his contract. Yet the government's damages were, as the Court of Appeals said, "not quantifiable." The Court thus found the confiscation of profits improper and remanded, with permission for the government to seek some other form of damages for the contractual breach which could not include censorship or confiscation.

After the court of appeals' 1979 decision, the procedural history of the case warrants special attention. First, Snepp appealed to the Supreme Court on the issue of the CIA's right of prior review. The government cross-appealed on this point and did not raise any further issue about the confiscation or damages. Under hornbook, black-letter appellate law, therefore, the Supreme Court had jurisdiction to consider *only* the issue of prior review. This they knew. This any student of federal practice knows. When the United States Supreme Court handed down its opinion in *U.S. v. Snepp* on February 9, 1980, the opinion was *Per Curiam,* or "by the Court," a practice followed when there is no desire to identify any particular member of the court with the opinion's content, such as when the matter is pro forma and has the support of the whole court. The opinion was, however, nothing short of astounding.

In an opinion that three dissenters labeled "not supported by statute, by the contract or by the common law," the nameless majority of the Court on their own motion and without any request by the government to do so, reinstated the confiscation of Snepp's then and future income from the use of information, which all conceded he had an ultimate right to publish, because he failed to ask for permission that could not have been withheld. In what is perhaps even more extraordinary than intentionally exceeding its own jurisdiction, the Court summarily denied Snepp the privilege of presenting briefs or oral argument before it announced its decision. To deny even the privilege of presenting a written brief or of being heard is inconsistent with the requirements of "fundamental fairness"—the Court's own synonym for due process of law—especially when they had decided to *reimpose* a penalty which the lower court had struck down. Since the Court began sitting in 1790, there has been nothing comparable to the judicial treatment of Frank Snepp.

Three dissenters in *United States v. Snepp* recognized that the decision involved extraordinary intervention by the high court in a manner "perhaps even beyond the Court's jurisdiction" and constituted a clear "prior restraint on free speech." Yet the decision stands. Frank Snepp walks about unable to tell us what we should know if we are to understand fully the Vietnam withdrawal. The CIA has even insisted that any fictional work written by Snepp be submitted for review. Only occasional commentary by Anthony Lewis in the *New York Times* preserves the memory of this extraordinary suspension of the First Amendment.

Alan Dershowitz's book *The Best Defense* suggests that, just before considering the Snepp case, the Court was upset by the publication of *The Brethren* by Bob Woodward and Scott Armstrong, and that the Court was out of sympathy with free speech that day. Anthony Lewis reported that a CBS documentary of these events was thwarted by the cumbersome review process set up by the CIA.

The very best commentary on the difficulty of justifying such a decision is that no one has ever tried, certainly not the Supreme Court. Any journalistic reference to the case, which is rare, meets with a stony silence from the bench.

The *Per Curiam* opinion, which revealed that no member of the majority wished to have his name associated with the opinion, deserves notice, considering the extraordinary and controversial nature of the Court's unrequested action, as well as the bitter nature of the dissent. The opinion itself abandons the very raison d'être of the First Amendment. As Justice Hugo Black wrote in a landmark opinion in the so-called "Pentagon Papers" case in 1971,

> The Government's power to censor the press was abolished so that the press would remain forever free to censor the government. The press was protected so that it could bare the secrets of government and inform the people.

The faceless justices behind the *Per Curiam* opinion in the *Snepp* case obviously consider this no longer true. Though the Court has stopped the presses, copies of Snepp's thoughtful book can still be purchased from used-book shops.

Little comfort comes from supposing that such a decision as this is atypical, or will not happen often, or that the Supreme Court suffers few provocations sufficient to produce such a response. To have a judicial body which can suspend the law and Constitution this way just once is to have neither a judicial body nor a Constitution.

In March 1989, thirty law school deans and professors met in Boston to register their protest against the *City of Richmond* case discussed above. Lawrence H. Tribe, who conducted the conference, led the group to sign a statement deploring the retreat from affirmative action. The pledge to restore momentum for this type of governmental action was signed by the deans of Harvard, Yale, Columbia, Chicago and Berkeley law schools, among others. There has been no academic requiem for Frank Snepp.

The Goodbye Music

The high court bid a last farewell to any semblance of separated governmental powers in April 1990. The case before them involved the decree of a Missouri federal district judge, Russell G. Clark, directed at the Kansas City, Missouri, School District. In response to deterioration of educational quality and to disruption caused by previous court-ordered busing within Kansas City, Missouri, many parents moved to the suburbs, a move often referred to as "white flight." The district court ordered a new sweeping desegregation remedy by which the children of the fleeing residents would be returned to a school which contained a racial mix approved by the district court. Attractive "magnet schools" would be constructed to lure them back. Unfortunately, the school district did not have to the funds to pay for this remedy. Consequently, Judge Clark ordered that school district property taxes be increased to an amount acceptable to him and sufficient to cover the costs imposed by the decree. Some law professors and journalists spoke out at once in defense of Judge Clark's actions on the theory that the district court was not *really* interfering with the power of taxation, but only ordering others to tax. Clearly the district court judge had assumed the power to levy a local tax. These specious distinctions marked only the beginning. The court of appeals for the Eighth Circuit upheld the power of the district court to levy the tax, but held that the judge should have used a "less intrusive" method, such as waiting until school district officials submitted a proposed tax plan which they were prepared to levy "voluntarily." The court of appeals thus modified the order of the district court to permit the local taxing authorities to report to the judge about their plans to levy a sufficient tax.

The Supreme Court, in an opinion entitled *Missouri v. Jenkins*, affirmed in part and reversed in part, issuing a lengthy opinion authored by Justice White. Justice White's opinion accepted the court of appeals, approach, opting for the "least intrusive" means of what is de facto the federal judicial exercise of local taxing authority. Thus the cost of the new program, estimated by the district court at $88 million, must be paid by the State of Missouri and the local school district in Kansas City.

One problem the federal courts faced was that Missouri had a state constitutional provision limiting property taxes to a maximum of $1.25 per $100 assessed value, unless a majority of district voters approved a higher rate, which could then be raised up to $3.25 per $100 assessed valuation. The state constitution required a two-thirds majority if the tax rate were to go above $3.25 per $100.

The United States Supreme Court knew that the school district had attempted to get local property owners to approve higher taxes but failed. The state constitutional provision, a local taxpayers' bill of rights known as the Hancock Amendment, thus appeared to be performing its intended function of returning taxation issues to the general population. The district court decided to enjoin the effect of this local constitutional provision so that it would not interfere with the court-ordered tax.

The Supreme Court's opinion approving the Eighth Circuit's approach also affirmed the ability of the federal courts to "set aside" provisions of a state constitution which interfere with a proper remedy for a violation of federal constitutional right.

The district court also decided to make the state of Missouri pay the bulk of the $88 million cost, adopting the principle that "the person who starts the fire has more responsibility than the person who fails to put it out." The district judge felt that a 75 percent-25 percent allocation between the state and the school district was "fair." Even with the sharing, the district judge had to require local residents to pay property taxes at a rate of $4.00 per $100 assessed valuation. On top of this, the school district was directed to issue $150,000 in capital improvement bonds to erect and maintain "magnet schools" as a part of the overall plan.

The Court held that actually levying the tax directly was going too far, stating that it was enough to enjoin the interfering Missouri constitutional provision and then monitor the supposedly compliant local taxing authority. The state argued that the resultant level of taxation would be staggering, even if conducted under a supposedly "voluntary" tax proposal submitted for federal court approval. The Supreme Court responded once again by discovering its jurisdictional limitations, the very ones it misplaced in the *Snepp* case. Justice White opined,

> We think the argument arises at the scope of the remedy rather than the manner in which the remedy is to be funded, and thus falls outside our limited grant of certiorari in this case.

Thus the Court fully supported the decree imposing the tax for funding the remedy; the resultant rule was clear. Justice White was joined by four more justices in full support of his opinion: Brennan, Marshall, Blackmun, and Stevens.

The four remaining members of the Court joined in a concurring opinion written by Justice Kennedy. Kennedy's opinion reported as "concurring in part and concurring in the judgment," was joined by Justices O'Connor and Scalia and Chief Justice Rehnquist. The language of this opinion criticized the majority. Yet, despite the fact that the majority opinion sent the case back to the district court with approval for what is de facto judicial taxing power, these "conservative" Justices *did not* actually dissent. They only *criticized* the reasoning of the Supreme Court majority. The Supreme Court opinion did reverse the district court's initial direct assessment of the taxes, but the judgment of the majority endorsed a fiction which granted the district court judge power to accomplish the same result as direct taxation by ordering local taxing authorities to impose a suitable tax.

The strange posture of the minority caused the *New York Times* to label it a "dissenting opinion," though it was not. The majority opinion stated:

> It is therefore clear that a local government with taxing authority may be ordered to levy taxes in excess of the limit set by state statute where there is reason based in the Constitution for not observing the statutory limitation.

The "reason based in the Constitution" is all that is required, whatever meaning that phrase has.

Thus, Justice Kennedy concurred in the judgment, while castigating the Court's language and reasoning. He apparently could support the judgment because he felt that any real claim that the state of Missouri had been coerced or interfered with in any way was "premature," since the state and school district had not actually collected any taxes yet. Nevertheless, Kennedy said that "the manner and methods of school finance are beyond federal judicial authority." Justice Kennedy explicitly rejected the argument that the final solution adopted by the court of appeals and Supreme Court, to review submitted "voluntary" tax proposals, was a distinction with a difference. He also rejected the sophistry that the court could order a local governmental body to do more than what the state constitution allowed. He noted that as described in Article III of the U.S. Constitution, "the judicial power nowhere includes the word 'tax' or anything that resembles it." But he *did not* dissent. The conservatives on the Court felt compelled to render an opinion critical of such blatantly unconstitutional judicial power, but could not bring themselves to openly oppose a race-related remedial program. They had to be squarely behind both sides.

The evolutions of high court politics are perhaps too much. The fact remains, however, that five members of the Court can legitimize "setting aside" the constitution of a state, ordering elected officials to perform acts defined by state law as beyond their delegated authority, and can in fact levy a tax on local citizens who have no democratic means of registering their response to it. This opinion allows the federal judge to hide behind the local tax authority under the rationale that he is only "indirectly" involved in the process of taxation, unless he actually levies the tax—whatever that means.

The strange minority opinion provided by the four "conservative," concurring justices may be the first example of "dissenting concurrence," or the "concurring dissent." The 1990 *Jenkins* opinion starkly illustrates the most significant functional difference between the pre-1965 court and that of today. In his now-famous 1955 book, *Nine Men*, Fred Rodell (a Yale law professor) summarized the essential character of the court; actions between 1790 and 1955:

> By the very nature of the way it works, the Court, for all the power its members hold, is only a negative—never an affirmative—force. It cannot create, it cannot initiate, it cannot put into action any government policy of any kind (except in the governmental sideline dealing with the mechanics of how the Court itself, and lesser courts, carry on their job). All the Justices can do is to say Yes or No to a policy or a program or a part of a policy or program that has been started by someone else in some other branch of government.

In the course of saying Yes or No—though the Justices never say it that briefly—or in the course of explaining, in legal language and commonly for the exclusive edification of lawyers, just why they are saying Yes or No, they may suggest, wittingly or unwittingly, a shift or an extension or perhaps a detour in the policies or programs of men in the affirmative branches of government.

Rodell dismissed the on-going dispute over whether the court has become more "activist" or more "restrained" during different periods in the history. For example, Rodell argued that striking down legislative regulations of business in order to support a growing economy was no different than refusing to strike down such measures when their effect was seen as economically beneficial. The reasons or motives behind the judge's actions were more important than the form it took, and both judicial nullification and its opposite, "judicial restraint", were equally "activist" in most cases.

However, the "yes or no" form of the Court's action left the initiation of governmental action to others, more democratic bodies, normally the state and federal legislatures. As Rodell pointed out, when the Court took a case involving disputed governmental action, its opinions did not merely say "yes or no", but elaborated on the constitutional issues involved, educating and instructing the lawmakers on "how to get the laws they desire in a different way which the justices will then approve." In limiting themselves to this type of review, the justices could of course be an "activist" or "restrained" as they wished in their selection of cases for review, and in the scope of their comments on the constitutional strengths or weaknesses in the law under review. However, they *would not* and *could not* originate or create the law, or issue the initial command for governmental action. As Rodell said, "they never take, nor can they take, responsibility for affirmative government action."

Since 1965, this essentially limited review function, the "yes or no" approach has radically changed, and with it the Supreme Court's relationship to democratic branches of government. The desegregation decisions drove the supreme court and lower federal courts beyond the reactive phase of adjudication, and finally made the Supreme Court one of "the affirmative branches of government." In *Jenkin's* opinion unequivocally approved the power of federal courts to initiate and affirmatively direct a traditionally local and popularly-controlled governmental power—taxation. It shattered the control of local democratic institutions as "affirmative branches of government" by not only nullifying local, democratically created limits on taxing power, but also commanding the tax levy itself, its amount, and its ultimate use.

When the supreme court actually acted as Rodell described, by saying "yes or no" to governmental action initiated by others, it gave maximum scope to the democratic processes in state and federal government by focusing debate and popular attention on what governmental action the Constitution permits, and how it should be done. The court may always have the last word, but democratic organs of government or officials executing the laws they create have the first word. They continue to have the first word until they get it right or decide to give up. However, the current Court's decision to allow federal courts to *initiate* and direct governmental action automatically removes whole areas of government from democratic control, since the court speaks with the final authority of the supreme Constitution. At this point, the court's traditional dialogue with the democracy ended, and the traditional and gradual evolution of governmental and legal rules heavily influenced by democracy was stopped by the irresistable power of an affirmative federal decree, which no longer said "yes or no", but rather said "do this or go to jail for contempt."

Rodell's perceptive analysis illustrates that a Court that can and will direct and command distinguishes the pre-1965 court from that of today. When the *Jenkins* opinion was announced, only the *New York Times'* reporter Linda Greenhouse got the point. She wrote of the opinion:

> It broke new ground for the Court, affirming a broad view of the power of Federal Judges to take active roles in the management of institutions and activities traditionally within the domain of states and localities.

This, in a nutshell, describes modern Supreme Court action. Moreover, the opinion provides a striking revelation of the essence of the abandonment process. Taxation has been one concept irrevocably and firmly rooted in consent by the United States Constitution. Indeed, imposing taxes on an unconsenting population led to the Revolution which finally resulted in a separate American Constitution. Now, however, an unelected federal judge, who is in no way subject to the popular will or in any way hindered by the requirement of consent, may creatively expand the fiscal authority of state officials by "setting aside" local limits on their power. Through them, the judiciary may reach into the pockets of local citizens "whenever there is reason based in the Constitution" for doing so. The link between democracy and taxation went out the window at the federal level, just as it had done at the state level when the New York Court of Appeals set aside the state constitution in 1975.

There is, of course, more. Much more. The Supreme Court continues to parse the finest particles of national morality in every area of life. In 1989, the Court informed the City of Pittsburgh that it could not under the First Amendment, the same one which Snepp found unavailing, display a créche on public property, *unless* it was surrounded by some secular objects such as a Santa Claus or reindeer. Again in this opinion we see the pathology of nine uncollatable essays on public morality forced into the format of judicial decision. The official reporter summary of the various opinions reveals nine differing philosophical positions disconnected by any common principle. It is literally unintelligible:

> Blackmun, J., announced the judgment of the Court and delivered the opinion of the Court with respect to Parts III-A, IV, and V, in which Brennan, Marshall, Stevens, and O'Connor, JJ., joined, an opinion with respect to Parts I and II, in which O'Connor and Stevens, JJ., joined, an opinion with respect to Part III-B, in which Stevens, J., joined and an opinion with respect to Part VI. O'Connor, J., filed an opinion concurring in part and concurring in the judgment, in Part II of which Brennan and Stevens, JJ., joined. Brennan, J., filed an opinion concurring in part and dissenting in part, in which Marshall and Stevens, JJ., joined. Stevens, J., filed an opinion concurring in part and dissenting in part, in which Brennan and Marshall, JJ., joined. Kennedy, J., filed an opinion concurring in the judgment in part and dissenting in part, in which Rehnquist, C.J., and White and Scalia, JJ., joined.

In the opinion, the Court informed Pittsburgh that Santa or something similar would be necessary to move the expression represented by the nativity scene onto a more secular level of communication, thus ridding it of any suspect motive by the state to authorize or support religion.

The city's response was realistic and practical. The manager of the city's Bureau of Cultural Programs said,

> You have to ask yourself, how much do you want to junk it up? Do you put in a reindeer and a blue smurf? I'd just as soon not do it.

So they didn't.

One lawyer in Texas advised a municipal client to display the nativity, accompanied by a "for sale" sign, to invoke the protection of commercial speech. The practical and professional community has begun to recognize a joke when they see it.

And on top of all this, the Court said that the display of a menorah on city property, as opposed to a nativity scene, was all right. One Justice, Blackmun, said that this was excusable because the menorah was erected next to a 45-foot Christmas tree and was accompanied by a printed "Salute to Liberty" which "linked" the menorah to the adjacent display of "festive lights," thereby rendering it a "secular" statement. Thus it became a communication, a form of speech, commemorating the "winter holiday season" and not advocating the establishment of any particular religion at all. It was then OK.

Crime

Perhaps the Court is not at its best concerning individual civil liberties or taxation. Perhaps their reputation of protecting liberty derives more from the criminal law than the civil. How has the Supreme Court performed concerning crime?

On December 24, 1968, Christmas Eve, ten-year old Pamela Powers went with her family to the YMCA in their home town, Des Moines, Iowa, to watch her brother participate in a wrestling tournament. During the tournament, she left her family to go to the washroom. When she did not come back, a search failed to locate her.

Shortly after her disappearance, a resident of the YMCA, Robert Williams, left the building carrying a bundle wrapped in a blanket. Williams asked a fourteen-year-old boy for help in opening the street door of the YMCA and the door of his car. The young boy assisting Williams observed the bundle as Williams dumped it into the front seat of the car. The boy said he "saw two legs in it and they were skinny and white." Williams quickly drove away. After the boy reported what he saw, a warrant was issued for Williams's arrest. Police learned that he had recently escaped from a mental hospital; then Williams's car was found abandoned 160 miles east of Des Moines.

On December 26, Des Moines attorney Henry McKnight arrived at the Des Moines police station to inform police that Williams had contacted him and wished to surrender. Williams surrendered that evening in Davenport, Iowa. He was booked and given all appropriate warnings required by the Constitution, federal, and state laws. Williams called McKnight, and McKnight told Williams that the Davenport police would bring him to Des Moines. He told Williams not to talk about the case until he got to Des Moines.

Williams was then arraigned before a Davenport judge, and given his Miranda warnings again. He talked with another lawyer in Davenport before leaving in police custody for Des Moines. The lawyer advised him to remain silent until he talked with McKnight.

Two police officers from Des Moines arrived to pick up Williams. They gave him his Miranda warnings again, and the two officers left with Williams on the 160-mile drive to Des Moines. On the way, Williams said, "[w]hen I get to Des Moines and see Mr. McKnight, I am going to tell the whole story." Shortly after leaving Davenport, one of the officers, Detective Leaming, said the following to Williams:

> I want to give you something to think about while we're traveling down the road. . . . Number one, I want you to observe the weather conditions, it's raining, it's sleeting, it's freezing, driving is very treacherous, visibility is poor, it's going to be dark early this evening.

They are predicting several inches of snow for tonight, and I feel that
you yourself are the only person that knows where this little girl's body
is, that you yourself have only been there once, and if you get a snow
on top of it you yourself may be unable to find it. And, since we will
be going right past the area on the way into Des Moines, I feel that we
could stop and locate the body, that the parents of this little girl should
be entitled to a Christian burial for the little girl who was snatched
away from them on Christmas Eve and murdered. And I feel we
should stop and locate it on the way in rather than waiting until
morning and trying to come back out after a snowstorm and possibly
not being able to find it at all.

As the car approached Mitchelville, Iowa, Williams said he would
show the officers where he had hidden the body. He did.

The evidence of the discovery of the body was introduced at
Williams's trial, over the objection from his defense counsel. The jury
found Williams guilty of murder and the Iowa Supreme Court affirmed
the conviction. Williams obtained a writ of habeas corpus from a U.S.
District Court, which held that, among other things, Williams's
statements had not been made "voluntarily" and were thus inadmissible
under governing Supreme Court precedents, in that they were made
without benefit of assistance from legal counsel.

The court of appeals affirmed and the matter came before the
United States Supreme Court. Justice Stewart delivered the Court's
opinion which addressed the admissability of the information about the
location of Pamela Powers's body. Justice Stewart held in *Brewer v.
Williams* that the use of Williams's statement violated his constitutional
guarantee of right to counsel.

Justice Marshall added his explanation of what unconstitutional
actions had been taken against Williams:

The detective demonstrated once again that the efficiency of the rack
and the thumbscrew can be matched, given the proper subject by more
sophisticated modes of 'persuasion.'

What the Court disparagingly referred to as Detective Leaming's
"Christian burial speech" thus became the constitutional equivalent of
medieval judicial torture.

Justice Powell, a "conservative" appointee of Richard Nixon, added in his concurrence an environmental element to the list of invasions of Williams's rights:

> [T]he entire setting was conducive to the psychological coercion that was successfully exploited. Williams was known by the police to be a young man with quixotic religious convictions and a history of mental disorders. The date was the day after Christmas, the weather was ominous, and the setting appropriate for Detective Leaming's talk of snow concealing the body and preventing a "Christian burial."

Chief Justice Warren Burger captured the essence of the case in the beginning of his dissent:

> The result in this case ought to be intolerable in any society which purports to call itself an organized society. It continues the Court—by the narrowest margin—on the much-criticized course of punishing the public for the mistakes and misdeeds of law enforcement officers, instead of punishing the officer directly, if in fact he is guilty of wrongdoing. . . . In so ruling the Court regresses to playing a grisly game of "hide and seek," once more exalting the sporting theory of criminal justice which has been experiencing a decline in our jurisprudence.

Williams was found guilty of the savage murder of a small child; no member of the Court contended he was not. While in custody, and after no fewer than five warnings of his rights to silence and to counsel, he led police to the concealed body of his victim. The Court concedes Williams was not threatened or coerced and that he spoke and acted voluntarily and with full awareness of his constitutional rights. In the face of all this, the Court held that because Williams was prompted by the detective's statement—not interrogation but a statement—the jury must not be told how the police found the body.

The characteristics of the majority approach to crime and individual rights are instructive. Typically, the Court subsumes every imaginable practical consideration relevant to the lives of ordinary citizens under an intellectual quest for some abstract value. It is, of course, an absurd notion that any person accused of a crime may be permitted no communication with authorities unless counsel is present. It is also absurd to argue that any innocent person would need protection against the effects of reasonable communication at all. To be told verbally of the implications of a savage murder for the victim's family in terms any reasonable compassionate person would agree with—the "Christian burial speech"—would hardly induce an innocent person to confess to anything.

More to the point, the supposed inconvenience or "violation" of that individual's rights which would allegedly result from receiving such a communication from the authorities could not possibly outweigh the value of determining guilt. Undoubtedly, the Court's abstract pursuit of a perfect world supersedes the goal of detection and conviction of crime, and actually reveals where its sympathies lie, or rather, do not lie. However much Court members might wish to seek refuge behind claims that the law or the Constitution is being protected, even if the guilty are set free, it simply will not sell.

The fact is, no ordinary citizen who is *not* guilty of serious crimes can find the slightest value in the theoretical protections the Court has constructed. They have thus evolved a truly intellectual jurisprudence in criminal law and procedure, as they have elsewhere. Moreover, the occasions from which the complex of new constitutional rights evolve are always like the ones in the *Brewer v. Williams* case. They *never* actually involve the protection of an innocent person, nor are they practically designed to do so. The guarantees such as the one in *Brewer v. Williams*—to be free from entreaties of the police unaccompanied by any suggestion of coercion—are never such that the innocent citizen would find it inconvenient to be without them. As Chief Justice Burger recognized, elaborating such rules reflects the distance which the Court has come from a "society which purports to call itself an organized society."

The protection which the Fourth Amendment afforded Robert Williams—to be free from intrusive "Christian burial speeches" by law enforcement officers—is in contrast with the protection afforded the ordinary motorist. On June 14, 1990, Chief Justice Rehnquist led a majority of the Supreme Court in holding that motorists may be stopped at will by law enforcement officers and subject to an evaluation and a chemical breath analysis administered by the officers, at their discretion.

There is no requirement for "probable cause," that is, no requirement that the arrested motorist indicate intoxication or misbehavior.

Reversing the Michigan Court of Appeals, which thought arrests without probable cause were unconstitutional, the United States Supreme Court applied its favorite method of resolving such issues. It used a "balancing test," under which the Court speaks of a metaphorical set of scales on which it places the interest of the government as it sees it on one side, and the interest of the person complaining about unconstitutional treatment on the other. These "interests" are "balanced," and the Court pretends to watch the direction in which the metaphorical scales tip. Accordingly, the Chief Justice said:

> No one can seriously dispute the magnitude of the drunk driving problem or the states' interest in eradicating it.

> Conversely, the weight bearing on the other scale—the measure of intrusion as motorists stopped briefly at sobriety checkpoints—is slight.

The Chief Justice summed up:

> In sum, the balance of the state's interest in preventing drunken driving, the extent to which this system can reasonably be said to advance that interest, and the degree of intrusion upon individual motorists who are briefly stopped, weighs in favor of the state program. We therefore hold that it is consistent with the Fourth Amendment.

Justice Blackmun supported the majority ruling, but lamented the fact that the Court's opinion might be regarded as somewhat inconsiderate by the motorists who are subject to police seizure, detainment, and scrutiny:

> By holding that no level of suspicion is necessary before the police may stop a car for the purpose of preventing drunken driving, the Court potentially subjects the general public to arbitrary or harassing conduct by the police. I would have hoped that before taking such a step, the Court would carefully explain how such a plan fits within out constitutional framework.

Blackmun ended his comments with perhaps the greatest understatement in the history of American constitutional jurisprudence saying:

> But consensus that a particular law enforcement technique serves a laudable purpose has never been the touchstone of constitutional analysis.

And strangely, the policeman who was viewed as wielding the modern equivalent of "the rack and the thumb screw" by using a "Christian burial speech" on an acknowledged murderer has become a nice guy when he randomly arrests a motorist.

No one can disagree with the Court that the death and damage caused by drunk driving is a serious problem. So is ruthless child murder. However, no one can fail to catch the irony of the difference in treatment afforded a criminal defendant who has been reasonably apprehended, warned, and prosecuted after manifesting probable cause for his arrest, such as being seen loading the body of his juvenile victim into his automobile, and an ordinary traveller who has manifest no illegal conduct or misbehavior. In the "balancing test" which comprises postdemocratic due process, the middle class is *always* on the wrong side of the scale. Even though we cannot expect perfect doctrinal consistency from the Court, the overall slant of their opinions is apparent. It will not do to argue that the Court's membership has changed since *Brewer v. Williams*, and that the current Court is now more "conservative." This only demonstrates that the "conservative" approach quickly dismantles and retracts constitutional safeguards and privileges grounded in clear precedent whenever the claimant is an ordinary citizen who has manifest no criminality or misbehavior. The established pattern of Supreme Court opinions now leaves no doubt that the intricate labyrinth of constitutional rights crafted for the demonstrably guilty are *never* extended to the law-abiding middle class. To top it all off, almost everyone concedes that these sobriety check roadblocks are a totally inefficient way to combat drunk driving. The whole thing is just a demonstrative exercise calculated to further inconvenience and propagandize the ordinary citizen.

CHAPTER THIRTEEN

"Conservatism" v. "Liberalism" on the Court

The retirement of Thurgood Marshall in June 1991 leaves only one sitting justice appointed by a Democrat—Justice Byron White, appointed by President Kennedy in 1962. President Bush's nomination of Clarence Thomas, a black federal circuit court judge from the District of Columbia, set off a storm of protest against the growing "conservatism" of the Supreme Court. Many believe that Judge Thomas does not favor quotas, or the jurisprudence of "aggregate classes," as did Marshall. Harvard Law Professor Derrick Bell laments that Thomas, although he is black, "thinks white," and is part of a growing "conservative" trend on the court. Thomas was confirmed after a spectacular televised confirmation hearing dealing with a decade-old sexual harassment charge. The accuser was a female law professor who formerly worked in Thomas's office.

Academics and journalists alike analyze recent changes in Supreme Court membership in terms of whether the court is becoming more "conservative." The *New York Times* reports that the Court's "conservative majority is solidified" by the replacement of retired Justices Brennan and Marshall by more "conservative jurists."

Political action groups also analyze new Court appoints solely in terms of the political agenda each candidate is believed to have. The National Organization for Women fought Judge Thomas's appointment to the Court. Flo Kennedy, a "feminist lawyer" vowed that "We need to kill him politically." NOW members feared that Thomas's beliefs in abortion did not match their own. In fact, everyone who discusses the Court today focuses solely on the Court's power to fulfill some "conservative" or "liberal" political agenda. The Supreme Court is treated as nothing more than an engine for political reform. The only question concerns which end of the political spectrum will get its programs enforced by the Court.

The press and the public have intuitively grasped that the Court no longer operates as a judicial institution. Even the terminology of the debate about the Court reveals this recognition—the universal use of the terms "conservative" and "liberal" to describe its members or would-be members. Both terms, "conservative" and "liberal," were historically applied to the legislature, and not to the judiciary. In fact, the term "conservative" was first applied to a political institution in the 1830s in England. In an article published by J. Wilson Croker on January 1, 1830, the term was used to describe the Tory Party. Afterwards, the term quickly became the recognized designation for that party. Croker used the term because of the tendency of the Tories to favor "measures tending to preserve cherished political conditions." The term originally described a legislative policy, not a judicial philosophy. Moreover, this application of the term began in a country—England—where prevailing constitution was based on legislative supremacy. There was no intergovernmental balance of power like the American system, with its separation of powers and federalist principles.

However, in the twentieth century, the "conservative-liberal" dialectic reappeared with a new twist. Its rebirth came on the heels of the Franklin Roosevelt's New Deal. Between 1935 and 1937, five members of the Supreme Court waged war on the Roosevelt-inspired attempts to combat the Great Depression. These five—Justices VanDevanter, McReynolds, Sutherland, and Butler voting as a solid block, joined by Justice Owen Roberts—demolished the federal legislative measures of the Roosevelt administration under the theory that they interfered with "liberties" protected by the due process clause of the Fifth Amendment. These liberties consisted of the right of large business enterprises to pursue profits and make contracts without government interference, since all such interference was viewed by the majority of the Court as a violation of due process. The NRA and the AAA were struck down. Roosevelt broke the back of the judicial obstruction by treating the Court as a legislature, threatening to pack it with new members favorable to his legislation.

The Court of the 1930s was merely continuing an established practice in striking down legislation. Before the Depression, numerous acts of both state legislatures and Congress had been nullified by the Court. The state legislation overturned by the Court from 1900 to 1930 mainly concerned the betterment of working conditions for men, women, and children. Laws regulating working hours generally, regulating wages, or regulating child labor were all overturned by the Court as violative of the due process clause of the Fourteenth Amendment, which restricts the states.

Were these Supreme Court opinions from 1900 to 1937 "conservative" or "liberal"? Writing in 1955, legal scholar Fred Rodell surveyed the opinions of the Court from 1790 to 1955. In his landmark study, *Nine Men*, Rodell made an important distinction in his use of the terms "conservative" and "liberal." Rodell distinguished between the use of that term to describe an essentially *legislative* policy-i.e., which result to you favor as a matter of policy choice—and its application to the institutional arrangement within which the judge operates. As Rodell pointed out, the *policies* supported by the Supreme Court were "conservative" of the prerogatives of business and capital, but they were not "conservative" of the institutional arrangement established by the U.S. Constitution, its separated powers and federal system. On the latter score, the opinions of the Supreme Court were decidedly "activist," since virtually every opinion struck down the considered judgment of a democratic assembly—either a state legislature or Congress. In Rodell's view, only those justices who dissented were "conservative" in an institutional sense. Justice Holmes, for example, sharply disagreed with the Court's assumption of legislative power at the expense of the state legislatures and Congress. Supporting the power of the state legislature in the face of a Supreme Court veto, Holmes declared:

> I think the proper course is to recognize that a state legislature can do whatever it sees fit to do unless it is restrained by some express prohibition in the Constitution of the United States or of the State, and that Courts should be careful not to extend such prohibitions beyond their obvious meaning by reading into them conceptions of public policy that the particular Court may happen to entertain.

For this reason, Rodell remarked on the "cool conservative clarity" of Holmes's dissents. As Rodell observed, countless observers of the Court throughout its history "have worried the problem of an active court against a passive court." The judges who struck down state or federal legislation representing the deliberate choices of democratic bodies are called "activists", and the "passive" judges who refuse to do so are praised or damned as apostles of "judicial self-denial." However, in both the court's action and inaction, deliberate governmental choices are being made. Rodell concludes:

> [T]he so-called split between the two is a silly circular self-deception on the part of those who worry and debate it.
>
> These justices after the civil war who struck down *state* efforts to regulate business because they wanted the national economy to thrive were no more activist, in so acting, there were Franklin Roosevelt's new deal justices where they passively failed to strike down *federal* efforts to regulate business—because they too wanted the economy to thrive.

A more reliable measure of the scope of the Court's power concerns the manner in which they act, rather than their decision on whether or not to act. For as Rodell observed, the Court was traditionally passive at least in one sense in the years between 1790 and 1955. This resulted from the Court's self-confinement to a "yes or no" function regarding the action of departments or officials of federal and state government, from the fact that "they never take nor can they take, responsibility for affirmative government action." The court-sanctioned federal decrees mandating local taxation and the use of resulting tax funds in the 1790 *Jenkins* case discussed above, brought an end to that distinction. The modern court may be no more or no less "activist" or autocratic than the predecessors, but by crossing the line between review of government action and affirmative promulgation of it, it has become powerful and in ways unforseen by Rodell or other pre-1955 observers of the Court.

We have now entered a completely new phase in our "conservative-liberal" analysis of the Court. Now, *all* debate concerns legislative policy—the particular policies favored by any candidate for Court membership—and *none* debate constitutional or adjudicative considerations. Everyone chooses sides solely on the basis of the policies a candidate will enforce.

In a 1990-91 term, the Court issued a series of closely divided opinions which are widely regarded as a retreat from its more liberal criminal law rulings. The Court allowed sentencing juries in criminal cases to consider the impact of the crime on the victim's family; allowed convictions to stand despite the use of coerced confessions; made second appeals in criminal cases more difficult; allowed conviction based on evidence discarded by a suspect during a police chase, despite the absence of probable cause for arrest; allowed police to detain a suspect for up to 48 hours before providing a hearing; allowing warrantless searches of containers carried in a suspect's automobile; allowed warrantless searches of luggage on buses, trains, and aircraft; upheld mandatory life imprisonment for a first-time drug offender.

On the other hand, the Court also struck down peremptory challenges based on race which excludes jurors in civil cases, and held that a suspect or police custody may not be approached or questioned by police at any time after he has asked to consult a lawyer. The Court also held that the Voting Rights Act applies to the election of state court judges under the theory that they are "representatives of the people," like members of the legislature.

It is difficult to find a consistently conservative philosophy in the policy choices contained in these opinions. For example, it is difficult to say that permitting a suspect to be jailed for 48 hours without a hearing is "conservative." It is difficult to argue that permitting warrantless arrests of motorists without probable cause is "conservative."

The analysis of the Court entirely in legislative policy terms tells us something very significant about what the Court has become. It tells us that the academics, the media and the public alike understand the fact that the Court has ceased to operate as a judicial institution. Rather, it now openly operates as an unaccountable legislative institution. Its members are now selected based upon the legislative policies they will pursue if appointed. A candidate's qualifications as a jurist or his or her judicial philosophy is unimportant. How he or she will wield legislative power or select issues is all important. The recent trend of Supreme Court rulings has been "conservative" only in the legislative policy sense and then only to a limited extent. In the exercise of its power, the 1991 Supreme Court is "liberal" and "activist."

If the name of the institution was changed from Supreme Court to Supreme Legislature, the debate about new appointments to the Court or about its recent decisions would be unaffected. Everyone has grasped the fact that they are no longer dealing with a judicial body. Observers of the court find either comfort or anguish in the policies which the changing Court will enforce on select issues such as abortion, race or crime. The concept of the Court as an adjudicative body of limited and separate powers distinct from the legislature has vanished.

What this means is that neither side, neither the liberals nor the conservatives will be happy with a Court which has abandoned the only legitimate role it can play in a true democracy. The Court's handiwork will appear to all sides to be a perplexing mixture of the very sweet and the very bitter. The inconsistency and arbitrariness which comes from legislative power without legislative accountability will ensure this result. The modern Court's capacity to do irreparable harm is now just as great as its supposed capacity to do good. There will continue to be a periodic shift in the policies which the Court pursues on select issues, and many will continue to interpret these shifts as heralding more "conservative" or "liberal" trends. The fact is, however, that the Court's power to promulgate and enforce non-democratic edicts touching every major area of national life will leave both conservatives and liberals bewildered and dissatisfied. Both sides will find that a small unelected Super Legislature which wields its enormous power selectively will be neither "conservative" nor "liberal." Rather, it will only be arbitrary in ways incompatible with democracy.

It is unlikely that the Supreme Court's recent "conservative" rulings will undo much of the damage already inflicted on the criminal justice system. Naturally the Supreme Court can not be blamed for all the defects in American criminal justice and law enforcement. A cause-and-effect relationship between these decisions and these defects can not be scientifically proven. Yet it is undeniable that the unique nation-wide scope of the Court's decisions has affected law enforcement at all levels. As we have seen, the court has taken an expansive view of the rights and privileges of the accused, often imposing extremely technical requirements on law enforcement officers, prosecutors, and courts. These requirements are in fact so technical and unpredictable that the ordinary person can find no common-sense relationship between them and basic fairness. The *Brewer v. Williams* case, discussed above, is a typical example. Additionally, these multiplying technical requirements often serve to provide the accused with powerful civil remedies under which law enforcement officers are held personally liable. Looking at the picture as a whole, many have concluded that the actions of law enforcement officers are treated more harshly and strictly than the actions of the accused criminals whom they pursue. The overall effect of the Supreme Court's new constitutional safeguards has hampered law enforcement, a predictable result after the Court's solicitude ran so far beyond common sense and the realities of everyday life.

Has the Supreme Court's new criminal jurisprudence been worth the costs? The influence of the Court's opinions and those of lower federal courts following their guidance are already evident in every major U.S. city. New York City has thus become so menacing that even the lifelong devotees of new-age criminology and constitutional theory have been affected for the first time. The Bureau of Justice Statistics reported that 24.9 percent of *all* American households experienced a violent personal crime or property crime in 1989. In their book *Chain Reaction*, Thomas and Mary Edsall report that blacks, 12 percent of the American population, committed 55.2 percent of all robberies in 1986-87 (948, 218 out of 1,717,971). Unfortunately, individuals at the bottom of the socio-economic ladder suffer the greatest damage from flourishing crime. In the past, the common attitude held by those at the uppermost rung of the economic ladder was that the effects of abandoning safeguards which the legal system provided for ordinary citizens were very remote. Intellectuals and the wealthy did feel personally the resultant increase of physical danger. This is no longer true.

In truth, the doctrinal and philosophical revolution wrought by the United States Supreme Court has seriously impaired the criminal justice system, reducing its utility to middle-class citizens, who are unable to pony up limitless new tax contributions or pay for personal protection. The physical threat created by the collapsed criminal justice system has, indeed, reached those who felt immune and secure from danger a mere decade ago. Now, only those accompanied by a bodyguard can expect a reasonable level of safety in any part of New York City after dark. The level of wealth necessary to achieve isolation from the predictable result of the abandonment of a middle-class oriented criminal justice system has escalated.

The collapse of vigorous and effective law enforcement against real crime has poured an unprecedented number of convicts onto the streets, where the judiciary and probation officials are content to let them roam. Now, two-thirds of the country's convicted criminals are on probation. Most often, this means committing a new crime. Judges now favor sentences which are in effect years of probation for serious crimes. Rape and child molestation have become crimes where probation rather than incarceration is routinely decreed.

In the atmosphere created by the United States Supreme Court, crime has flourished. Crime of all sorts resulting in a prison sentence has increased 45 percent between 1980 and 1990. The number of serious offenders on probation has increased by 75 percent. The results are as predictable as the intellectual reaction to them. In 1981, Jack Henry Abbot was placed on probation for a murder conviction due largely to the efforts of his benefactor, Norman Mailer, who popularized him as a lost genius, a "prison author." Six weeks after being released, Abbot stabbed to death a restaurant waiter named Adan for, in his words, "showing me disrespect." Mailer cavalierly chalked up Adan's death as a calculated risk which society must take. In Mailer's words:

Sometimes culture is worth the risk.

The family of Mr. Adan recovered a $7.5 million judgment in a civil action against Abbot in 1990. The judgment is, of course, largely uncollectible, and Mr. Adan is the one who has borne all the risk.

Occasionally a rare reversion to the issue of crime itself occurs. Chief Reuben M. Greenberg, Chief of Police in Charleston, South Carolina, has won fame for his tough approach to crime without regard to race. Chief Greenberg is both black and Jewish. After his first seven years as chief of police, Charleston's armed robbery rate dropped over 60 percent, homicides by 50 percent. Burglaries in 1990 have fallen to a thirty-year low. How does he do it? What is his guiding rationale? In a book explaining his approach, *Let's Take Back Our Streets*, Chief Greenberg says,

In the last quarter century or so, something has gone terribly wrong with our once-proud American way of life. It has happened in the area of values. A key ingredient is being eroded, and I think I know what it is. It's the value that belongs at the head of the list: accountability.

Yet more and more, especially in our larger cities and their suburbs, these inner restraints are loosening. Your average gang member scoffs at them. Your typical burglar has none. He considers your property his property; he takes what he wants, including your life if you cross him. The sense of guilt or remorse once associated with the commission of a felony has vanished. Now, in a stunning reversal, the criminal is considered the victim of society. He's no longer the culprit. The culprit is said to be his underprivileged upbringing; the school that didn't teach him to read, the church that failed to reach him with moral guidance, the parents who didn't provide a stable home. These, it is argued, are the causes if a hoodlum beats, robs and rapes an elderly widow. How can he be held accountable if it is not his fault?

My answer is that it is his fault. Many others in equally disadvantaged circumstances choose not to engage in criminal activities. The criminal also had a choice—and chose to be a crook. If we exempt him, even partly, from accountability, we become a society of endless excuses, where no one is prepared to accept responsibility for anything.

We in America desperately need more people who believe that the person who commits a crime is the one responsible for it, period.

Chief Greenberg, a seasoned police veteran, enforces the law "without fear or favor" and obviously still believes in the individual. However, the object of the criminal law, like that of the Constitution itself, has turned to the bestowal of some therapeutic immunity, determined by race or class, from individual responsibility—the logic of "aggregate classes." The Supreme Court's repudiation of the individual means that their supposedly "conservative" trend in recent criminal opinions should not be mistaken for a genuine revival of traditional or philosophically conservative constitutional jurisprudence.

CHAPTER FOURTEEN

The Future of the Post-Abandonment Judiciary

All these cases raise basic questions about the prospect for the success of any of the Court's actions in recent years, whether in racial discrimination, criminal law, or personal liberty. Leaving aside issues of constitutional authority, can any of the Court's postdemocratic schemes be expected to work? Does a powerful and autocratic bureaucracy enforcing a plan of material redistribution and social control over two or more races with no common constitution have as much chance of success as a common enterprise in which the participants share constitutional ideals that cut across racial lines? Does a system which relies on the coercive power of government have as good a chance as a system based on a common allegiance to principles of fairness? Can the coercive power of government easily replace consent or do as well in solving the problem of race, or any other problem? Aside from the issue of whether a coercive government should replace a consensual one, can anyone believe it will do as well at resolving problems?

The federal executive and the federal courts thought that a non-democratic solution would succeed where a constitutional system abolishing racial discrimination, which had majority support, would not. Within the common bonds of constitutional principles that could unite both races, the inward attitude of the majority would lend its force to success. The federal government's approach has given the majority a view of society so divided by race that a commonly acceptable constitutional solution appears impossible. Yet it was, and is, possible. It has been set back by a central government which forgot that it has no monopoly on the Constitution and that the Constitution actually belongs to the people. That the executive and the courts chose the approach they did reveals that they believe the average U.S. citizen is now more amenable to authority and force than to decency. As much as anything, it betrays a negative opinion, commonplace in the high reaches of

national government, of middle-class America. They view the character
and potential of the vast majority unfavorably. If they had maintained
any degree of contact with Middle America they could not hold this
view. They perceived the violent resistance on the part of some hate
groups as a badge of criminality attributable to every white citizen in the
country. It symbolized actions believed to be lurking in all their hearts.
Thus, in this case, the law was formulated to punish the good rather than
the evil and disobedient.

Yet the proponents of the legal and constitutional system regarding
race which we now have stand in a terribly unhappy and perilous
position, and will eventually awaken to their situation. They are
afflicted with a conundrum of their own making, one which is another
part of the tragedy they have wrought in this critical area. For example,
can these people acknowledge that the rights enjoyed by any racial
minority are merely a function of political decision? In other words, are
they prepared to live with the constitutional and legal principle that *no*
racial minority has achieved *any* constitutional protection for equal
citizenship and equal rights, but rather some have achieved only a
political victory in securing certain protections and advantages? The law
professors and judges have produced this result, whether or not they
acknowledge it. Apparently, they fail to realize, as Aristotle put it,

> [N]ot every action nor every passion admits of a mean . . . e.g., spite,
> shamelessness, envy, and in the case of actions adultery, theft,
> murder. . . . Nor does goodness or badness with regard to such things
> depend on committing adultery with the right woman, at the right time,
> and in the right way, but simply to do any of them is to go wrong.

If inflicting burdens or bestowing benefits strictly on the basis of race is
not wrong, then it must be left to the political process, and all such
benefits or burdens will depend on political mood, including judicial
mood. The horror is that the racial minorities will surely be the victims
of this new jurisprudence in the long run. Its creators have ensured that
race is something that *can* be used as a legal and constitutional matter to
bestow benefits and inflict burdens. Thus minorities have no genuine
constitutional protection at all. Rather than grasp the opportunity to
protect a durable principle, the perpetuation of which commands
common interest and support, the judiciary left the high ground of

constitutional principle and committed the fate of countless people to the vicissitudes of politics and the mood of the future. The low ground will surely be rockier than the sages of academe and the oracular bench can reliably predict.

Demographers have predicted that America will be mostly "non-white" by mid-21st century. Blacks and Hispanics and other immigrant groups will outnumber the predominantly Western European stock which dates to the country's first settlement. Under a normal and properly functioning constitutional system of the pre-1965 type, almost everyone would view this shift as interesting but not alarming or negative. However, under the constitutional and legal system crafted since 1965, the dominance of purely race-based political power over racially neutral principles makes these demographic changes ominous. The once generally respected legal system will surely become a battleground where racially defined political strategies, devoid of neutral constitutional restraints, will escalate, producing pointless, avoidable strife. As Thomas and Mary Edsall have brilliantly documented in their book, *Chain Reaction*, the progressive political departure from remedial legal measures based on the equal individual has Balkanized the electorate along racial lines. These governmental measures simply do not harmonize with the concept of legal equality embraced by the majority, who have progressively aligned themselves with political candidates they perceive as resisting race, sex, class, and ethnic-based governmental rules and edicts. The majority has simultaneously become hostile to the identified beneficiaries of these governmental measures, believing them to be beneficiaries of constitutionally improper privilege and solicitude. It needn't have been so.

The Framers of the Constitution understood that there is an essential relationship between the horizontal structure of constitutional government (keeping various governmental branches separated) and the vertical structure (keeping the government from overriding the constituent states or the individual). Without a horizontally separated power structure dividing government into three coequal branches, the central government becomes a threat to the states and citizens below. The common law judicial process entailed practical concepts which preserved the horizontal separation by directing judicial action away from the conscious exercise of sovereignty.

When the judiciary began its philosophical abandonment of this process, it started a revolution in American constitutional history. As to the judiciary, the process of abandonment has disproved the naive assumption that if we could just get reasonable people on the Court, all would be fine. After over twenty years, people have begun to ask how long the Republicans need to remedy something the people perceive as wrong. We are realizing that no amount of time or changing personnel will cure a system doctrinally and practically alienated from popular government, which treats the middle-class as an undepleatible asset to be milked for the benefit of groups at the extreme ends of the political spectrum.

What can be done? We will return to this question later, but for now it is good to keep in mind something a former president said. When state courts had struck down numerous statutes aimed at improving the conditions of laborers in New York and other states, Theodore Roosevelt voiced his concern with judicial abrogation of legislation. He recommended a referendum, under which the electorate would vote directly on the results of any judicial opinion which had nullified a statute passed by the popular assembly. They could reaffirm the statute or let the judicial nullification stand if they wished. For him, the ultimate possession of the Constitution remained with the people. As to the Constitution, in 1912, he said.

> It is the people, and not the judges, who are entitled to say what their constitution means, for the constitution is theirs, it belongs to them and not to their servants in office—any other theory is incompatible with the foundation principles of our government. If we, the people, choose to protect tenement-house dwellers in their homes, or women in sweat-shops and factories, or wage-earners in dangerous and unhealthy trades, or if we, the people, choose to define and regulate the conditions of corporate activity, it is for us, and not for our servants, to decide on the course we deem wise to follow. We cannot take any other position without admitting that we are less fit for self-government than the people of England, of Canada, of France, who possess and exercise this very power. But the plan I propose for our people seems to me more democratic, and from every stand-point better, than the plan in vogue in France, England, and Canada, where the legislature

is supreme over the courts. I propose to make the people supreme over
both.

We could extend the analysis of the federal courts' opinions and
of governmental actions indefinitely, to include father-son banquets,
federal judicial decrees nullifying state law which declares English the
official language of the state, issues of sexism and sexual harassment,
such as boys' choirs told to disband because their existence violates
Department of Education guidelines dealing with sex discrimination in
public education, and much, much more. But why bother? The
opinions we have reviewed characterize the pathology of today's judicial
process in the federal courts.

Every doctrine which appears in these opinions facilitates non-
democratic policies. By transcending democracy on their own since
1965, the Court assisted in similar acts by other branches of the federal
government in doing likewise. The courts have produced results
impossible in a viable, functioning democracy. Most significantly, the
relationship between the individual and his government was transformed.
The individual as a juridical entity ceased to be the focal point of
constitutional government. The philosophical leap from the individual
to aggregate classes represents the most profound shift in constitutional
philosophy since 1789.

By abandoning the individual, the central government of the
United States abandoned a cultural asset that had been building since the
collapse of the collective corporate state of feudalism which dominated
Europe until the fifteenth century. At that time, the individual began to
emerge as a distinct legal and political entity, just as the power of the
state to enforce a collective social organization collapsed with the waning
of feudalism. Those events unleashed forces in the societies of Western
Europe undreamt of before. The challenge of the individual was
enormous, as was the strain on him. As Eric Hoffer wrote of this
development:

> An autonomous existence is heavily burdened and beset with fears, and
> can be endured only when bolstered by confidence and self-esteem.
> The individual's most vital need is to prove his worth.

The modern Supreme Court jurisprudence strikes at the very constitutional foundations of the postfeudal Western world. It takes the wellspring of action necessary for both the individual and common good, and tears it to tatters. Individuals are now placed and moved about society according to "aggregate class" characteristics by the irresistible coercion of the central government. They will experience none of the self-esteem and confidence which is at the heart of individual action.

Not only have the actual holdings of the Supreme Court been destructive and counterproductive, but they have set a philosophical tone and formed an example readily emulated by the other two coordinate branches of government. The Supreme Court now sets such a poor example of what adjudication should be like in a democracy that it has become a corrosive influence on all lower court judges, both state and federal, who naturally look to the Supreme Court for guidance on the job of judging. The fact that the Supreme Court at one time set such a distinguished example has created a marvelous fund of credibility which the modern Court has just about exhausted. Thus their example has encouraged the view that the Constitution as well as the law is at most advisory, and should not restrict their search for a desirable result. This is precisely the view that medieval judges had. Thus the influence of the Supreme Court's habits has become almost as influential as their holdings, both of which have carried us back to a constitutional situation incompatible with a true democracy. Now all three branches are united in their estrangement from individual rights and in their antipathy to the interests of countless individuals subject to their authority. This attitude alone makes modern government careless of majority will.

The view of adjudication exemplified by Joseph Story's opinion in *Swift v. Tyson* was preoccupied with technique, rooted in historical inquiry, and sensitive to precedent. The new scientific approach which replaced the *Swift* concept detached itself from precedent, expanded its inquiry into non-legal data, both factual and theoretical, and looked at the future as a proving ground for judicially originated and approved policies. It opened fantastic new vistas for unrestrained experimentation by the enlightened judicial representatives of sovereign power. It promised all the great achievements which a good ruler could accomplish for society with the entire world of philosophy of science open to him, providing the raw material to generate new "reasonable" rules of law and providing a guiding hand counselled and informed by the latest and best intellectual material available. The new concept of judicial sovereignty represented the irrepressible longings of the intellect, and it presented an irresistible appeal to the combined influence of ego and progressive instinct which compels all rulers who conceive of themselves as good. Unfortunately, as alluring and intellectually seductive as it was, it did not prove compatible with democratic constitutional government in the long run.

The American federal judiciary is now the most visible sign of America's new intellectual government. The profile of the modern intellectual ruler is clear in their decisions. What are its chief features?

First, there is a willingness to experiment with people subject to their rule. Their experiments are pervaded with striking contradictions. For example, the Supreme Court has painstakingly constructed detailed limitations on law enforcement founded on the Fourth Amendment. These limitations have spared serious criminal offenders even the slightest inconvenience. But when the claimant to such protection is the middle-class motorist who has manifested no "probable cause" for arrest, he may nevertheless be arrested, detained, subject to scientific testing and eventually prosecuted for any discovered crime or misdemeanor using evidence gained from the random, warrantless, no-probable-cause arrest. The Court previously threw out such evidence as "the fruit of the poisonous tree." Now, says the Court, the middle-class citizen must eat it. The police officers who are permitted to enforce such programs are suddenly metamorphosed by the Court from a threatening Nick Nolte into a friendly Andy Griffith. The whole program is justified because of the "compelling state interest" in combatting drunk driving. The goal of ridding society of murderers, rapists and drug dealers has never had the weight of a feather in the metaphorical scales the Court pretends to use. Whimsicality and casualness are the hallmarks of the intellectual's conviction that they are far above the fray, and may experiment at will. The baffling expansion and abrupt contraction of doctrines governing the details of our everyday lives leave us dazed. The First Amendment gives flag burning constitutional protection but fails to restrain the judicial censorship of Frank Snepp, who violated no law and wished only to publish factual information in the public interest. There is no rule of law in this.

Second, the new intellectual judge is always willing and eager to rule. Indeed his willingness to rule is all-encompassing, so little confidence has he in the sensibilities of his subjects. No detail of the common man's life is too small or insignificant to merit the intellectual's attention and detailed direction. Whether the miscreant citizen and his miscreant community wish to have a crèche or menorah on the public square, or how the display should be composed, are all worthy of attention.

Third, the new intellectual rules willingly but always poorly. This has always been so with insular, intellectual rule. Centuries of Brahmin rule kept the general population of India in grinding poverty and political impotence. So it was with the mandarins of China and the ruling houses of Egypt. It was the same in ancient Greece, where rigid classifications of political and social status, including slavery, persisted down the centuries. America was not hospitable to the intellectual rule through most of its history. Today, however, the intellectual jurist has taken charge and created a sort of internal colonialism under which he may manage and direct the "aggregate classes" who compose his colonial domain. The intellectual is an unforgiving taskmaster for a country which thought it had successfully escaped colonization, and for a country which thought it had established the individual as the centerpiece of the law.

Fourth, whatever the postdemocratic, scientific judiciary undertakes is always grandiose and impossible. Rather than adjudicating some small dispute, they eagerly lay their hands on the whole of our society, forcefully reshaping the very stuff of which it is made—gender, race, family, politics, even life and death. Indeed, this is true for modern day intellectual government generally. For the impossible and the grandiose are dear to the impractical heart of the intellectual. The slow road to success pursued by the individual is, for him, a bore.

Fifth, the intellectual governor is repelled by democracy and majority rule. He hates the commonness and the vulgarity of the masses which thrive in an open society. Intellectuals have increasingly detested the way in which the collective action of the common man tends to achieve great things so naturally, and without his direction or assistance. Practically every intellectual writer of the nineteenth century was repulsed by the prospect of a populous country where the individual was motivated to work on his own, and could collectively achieve national greatness without the intellectual's sweeping plans and fiery words. Carlyle hate America for this reason. Ernest Renan, a French philosopher and historian, wrote of the "appetites of the vulgar." Freud said of America, "I regret that Columbus discovered it." More recently, Saul Bellow calls the U.S. "a pig heaven." And so it goes.

Yet the buildings and the railroads and hundreds of other expressions of popular vitality and productiveness have poured forth. Intellectuals cannot stand the idea that America does not need them. Americans are self-starters with their own internalized willingness to work and their own internalized respect for others who feel likewise. Intellectuals obstruct any plan which does not originate in their own brilliance. They thwart any plan which may produce results which are not traceable to their inspired decree. We thus are saddled with the impossible and the grandiose, when we would prefer the possible and the practical.

Sixth, the legal intellectual always treats people subject to his jurisdiction as children, and constantly stresses their waywardness and dependence on the intellectual's guidance. The citizen cannot decide to have local limitations on taxation, but must yield to judicial taxation, even though it defeats his financial and personal planning and residential preference. The limits and boundaries of local taxing authorities may be freely expanded and remodeled to catch the wandering taxpayer who desires to escape the judicial tax levy. In short, every aspect of the individual's personal preference is regulated. He may not move about or associate freely.

These are the six solidly-entrenched features of the post-Abandonment judiciary. These represent the legal present and future of the United States.

Unless the process is reversed, and government redirected away from discretionary management of "aggregate classes" and toward the protection of individuals on an equal basis, the process of Abandonment will seal the fate of the middle class in America as it did in Greece and Rome. The mounting costs of Abandonment will simply make the middle class a social and economic impossibility.

PART IV

The Academic Abandonment:
Guardians of the Grove

Custom is Most Perfect When it Beginneth in Young Years: This We Call Education.

Sir Francis Bacon, 1605

The Educational Constitution of 1965 was simple and straightforward. It included the following:

1. American colleges and universities were dedicated to educating individuals. Students were treated as individuals of equal dignity engaged in a common purpose.

2. More than ever before, universities admitted students based on demonstrated merit. Virtually everyone had adopted the Scholastic Aptitude Test by 1960, marking a victory for objective over subjective standards for university admission.

3. More than ever before, universities graded students based on demonstrated merit. Consequently, faculties sought to avoid evaluating students based on their political or philosophical orientation. Censorship or official orthodoxy was avoided. The improvement of the student's mind was more important than his or her physical characteristics. Definitions of merit focused on the mind, instead of race, creed, color, or philosophy.

4.   Most institutions encouraged free and open debate among the
       faculty and students.   College curricula were defined by a
       slowly-evolved consensus which had resulted from this open and
       tolerant atmosphere.   The faculty viewed themselves as
       conservators of a valuable cultural asset.   The legacy of Western
       society was in their custody.   Faculty not only had a favorable
       view of Western culture, but also of the society in which they
       lived.

5.   Almost everyone who could qualify could find a college that his
       or her family could afford without severe financial strain.
       Money was not a barrier to a good college education.
       Education was well on the way to being democratized and
       shared by more people than ever before.

The Educational Constitution of today is far different.   For most
institutions of higher education, it includes the following:

1.   The idea of students as individuals of equal dignity engaged in
       a common purpose has been replaced by a concept of the
       student body as a collection of dissimilar groups, each engaged
       in serving the specialized needs of its group members.   Race
       and ethnicity have replaced the common pursuit of learning.
       This reflects the educators' view of America as a Balkanized
       collection of mutually hostile interests, rather than as a joining
       of diverse groups into a common culture.

2.   The standards for university admissions reflect the educators'
       Balkanized concept of America.   These standards vary according
       to race, ethnic background, and various other factors which
       academics have chosen.

3.   More than ever, student performance is judged by subjective
       factors associated with the particular interest groups which
       academics support.   Faculties routinely evaluate students based
       on their political or philosophical orientation.   Censorship and
       official orthodoxy are common.   The student's physical or racial
       characteristics are more important than his or her mind.
       Definitions of merit focus on race, creed, color, or philosophy
       more than ever before.

4.   Most institutions discourage free and open debate on select
      forbidden issues. Curriculum is increasingly designed to serve
      racial, ethnic, or social goals.   The faculty *do not* view
      themselves as conservators of a valuable cultural asset so much
      as reformers of Western culture and the society in which they
      live.

5.   For middle-class America, good higher education is rapidly
      becoming prohibitively expensive.   More than ever before,
      money is a barrier to a good college education. Because of the
      rising money barrier, the merits and potential of the student
      often far exceed his or her practical opportunities. The very
      wealthy and the select beneficiaries of faculty-approved
      admissions policies and financial aid are crowding out the
      middle class.

Between 1965 and 1991, the Educational Constitution joined the
Economic, Political, and Legal Constitutions in the Abandonment of
middle-class America. This is how it happened.

CHAPTER FIFTEEN

The Old Groves

In ancient Athens there was a garden near the city known as *Academia*. It was a large and pleasant place with a well-known grove of handsome trees once owned by a citizen named Academos. It was there, the historian Caxton tells us, that "Plato chose his mansion and dwelling." Subsequent history shows that Plato inspired his students there, so much so that the name of the place was given to his general method of teaching. The name persists in the term *academia*, the community inhabiting the realms of higher education worldwide. In the United States the term refers to those learning and teaching at the university or collegiate level. Over the past two millennia, this worldwide community has been such a powerful perpetuator of tradition and knowledge that the university community is often referred to as "groves of academe," just as it was in Plato's day.

From the informal beginnings of Plato's teaching and conversing with his friends in his grove, there followed an amazingly persistent effort by individuals throughout the world to carry forward the concept of a sacred grove where knowledge was pursued. The universe of knowledge was explored in *academia* by members of the *facultas*, a word which in its later permutations in Western languages became identified with the characteristics or powers of the mind (mental faculties), as well as with the community whose quest was to develop those powers (the university faculty). The earliest organization still extant, Al-Hazin University, was founded in A.D. 970 in Cairo, Egypt.

The academic tradition quickly spread throughout Western Europe. In England, by the middle of the fourteenth century, the university became a corporate umbrella beneath which the various *collegia*, mostly begun by private donations from wealthy benefactors, operated as units within the university. These "colleges" became places where undergraduates, persons with no college degree, were taught by "fellows" who had already obtained a degree and wished to stay on at the university for further study. They affiliated with particular colleges as tutors or "masters" helping the undergraduates. So began in the late thirteenth and early fourteenth centuries a competitive tradition in which many different scholarly orders operated under the aegis of the university organization and were dedicated to teaching and learning.

In its earliest days, the university system had been somewhat impersonal, really nothing more than a confederation of scholars who offered lectures for a set fee. These scholars examined the undergraduates who had attended lectures for four years to see if they deserved membership in the Academy itself. If so, they conferred membership by the award of a degree. The colleges, on the other hand, provided personal help for the student. The masters and tutors at the colleges, who were former graduates continuing their studies, added a personal touch to education. Students were allowed to live within the colleges which composed the university, and a sense of loyalty to and identification with individual colleges quickly developed.

A similar system was in place in the Inns of Court in England at approximately the same time. These Inns, formerly residence halls for lawyers attending the four terms of the Central or Royal Courts held yearly at Westminster, had responded to the much publicized disarray in the field of legal education by offering lectures and personal training, conducted by members of the Inn. The move to this personalized form of education in colleges and the Inns was a smashing success, and Plato's groves bore a harvest richer than he could have dreamed. For the culture and the societies of the West, this development held the greatest possible significance, since nongovernmental, nonpolitical social institutions, along with the church, had inherited the task of conserving the knowledge of the world. Until very recently the customs and traditions of the Academy have been dedicated to performing this critical task.

The history of primary and secondary education in this country has many things in common with the history of so-called higher education, that is, education at the college or university level. In pre-Civil War America, education had been viewed traditionally as a family matter. In fact, this tradition posed the most serious obstacle to desired reform of public education. Although people saw school attendance as a tool of upward class mobility in the nineteenth century, they neverthe-less strongly opposed centralizing all decisions about what should be done with the nation's young. Those of us accustomed to universal and uniform state education have a hard time appreciating how strongly such objections were made through the first half of the last century. Nineteenth-century history abounds with conflicts between the growing legion of educational officials and families with children who objected to their jurisdiction. In particular, rural families of the Midwest, Southwest, and West found mandatory school attendance laws and truancy regulations undesirable, even though the majority of Americans eventually came to see the advantage of public school education for their own children and accepted it voluntarily. Yet parents recognized that the basis of school attendance laws was, as the political historian Thomas Fleming put it, based on the assumption that "parents do not know what is best for their children or if they know, do not care."

Vigorous opposition also arose to compulsory secondary education, not only from the extremely poor and ignorant but from skilled artisans as well. Out of the many choices the parent or child could make as to proper training and desirable education, many trained craftsmen preferred that their children seek the security of a skill or craft, largely through a well-regulated guild employing an apprenticeship system, rather than allow their children to become prepared by some general education to enter the work force as a proletarian employee of some larger enterprise. For many it was clearly a matter of individual choice or preference over mass regulation. It is equally clear that many preferred independence for themselves and their children over the growing regulation of education. These people posed an obstacle to the growth of compulsory education based not on ignorance, but rather on an alternative view of working life, its objectives and values.

In the final analysis, centralizing authority and standardizing education proved impossible without a high degree of popular support. Thus the development of modern public education was an ongoing effort to balance the desirable objectives of achieving some degree of homogenous education with the proper demands of the individual, family, and community. Few would argue even now for a perfectly centralized program unaccountable to the society and all of its various elements, including the family. To make public education standardized and mandatory, people with children had to be sold on its advantages. The successful development of secondary public education, and to a large extent both public and private collegiate education, resulted from the respect it commanded from the same growing middle-class majority which would become its greatest beneficiary as the twentieth century opened. Education had democracy on its side, and vice versa.

The middle-class majority had been enlightened enough in the nineteenth century to tolerate and eventually approve of the experiments in public primary and secondary education launched by people like Horace Mann, the first secretary of the Massachusetts Board of Education in 1837, who raised the question: "When will society like a mother take care of all her children?" In return, educators were traditionally sensible enough not to make war upon the way in which ordinary citizens conducted their lives. If the fiercely individualistic rural population was enticed to have their children accommodate the growing demands of public education, it happened because they believed public education had something to offer. The same held true for the Academy.

As a result of the accord between schools and the middle class, the content of public education in the nineteenth century did not contain anything unacceptable or obnoxious to most people. Even the extravagant zeal of Horace Mann did not produce any irreconcilable conflict between educational content in the primary and secondary schools and the values of the middle class, though his grandiose objectives may have suggested the jurisdictional assault upon the traditional family role that public education would make a century later.

Conflict did not arise largely because the content of the books chosen for school children fell in line more and more with common middle-class predilections as they became standardized. The heavily religious content of the New England primer was abandoned by the turn of the nineteenth century as education became less of a church or religious undertaking. A series of books called "readers" were prepared by men whose root and stock ran not so much to academia as to society at large. L. G. Goodrich, whose readers were begun in 1839, was a relative of Noah Webster. John Pierpont, a New England scholar, also compiled a reader, though he is recalled mainly as the grandfather and great-grandfather respectively of John Pierpont Morgan, Sr. and John

Pierpont Morgan, Jr., two of America's most famous bankers. But probably the most well-known man in the last half of the nineteenth century, though certainly not the most beloved, was William Holmes McGuffey, the author of the "Reader of Readers." As to content, his works fell solidly within the tradition of middle-class education. Henry H. Vail, an official of the American Book Company, a large publisher of textbooks, could say with all honesty that the purpose of the readers was to teach:

> [I]ntegrity, honesty, industry, temperance, true patriotism, courage, politeness, and all other moral and intellectual virtues. Readers which have been recognized as formers of good habits of action, thought, and speech for three-quarters of a century; which have taught a sound morality to millions of children without giving offense to the most violent sectarian, are surely worthy of study as to their origin, their successive changes, and their subsequent career.

Despite the profound impact McGuffey's handiwork had on children educated in the last three decades of the nineteenth century, he is not mentioned at all by the most widely read writers of American history or educational history. Vernon Parrington's *Main Currents of American Thought* misses this main current entirely: not a line on McGuffey. Charles and Mary Beard's *Rise of American Civilization* likewise does not attribute to Mr. McGuffey any important historical contribution to American culture. They do not mention his name.

The balance between popular mores and the aims of educators, which had prevailed in public primary and secondary education, also typified college and university development. American society bestowed upon the Academy the privileges necessary to its independence and creativity, most noticeably lifetime tenure. Colleges and universities were, of course, historically more independent both in their administrative operation and their activities than their lower-level counterparts. Of primary significance, universities were *not* conceived of as governmental institutions, or even as government-run institutions in a literal sense. They were social institutions. Like Thomas Jefferson's University of Virginia, such institutions may have deserved state support, but hardly anyone would have regarded such an institution as just another state agency, like the highway department or the state health department.

Because the university in America perpetuated the model of Plato's grove in its Western European form, it was pursued independent of purely secular or administrative governmental goals.

The university most closely resembled the church in the abstraction of its goals from pure politics. The difference between the functions of even the state university and the state itself was just as great as that between church and governmental undertakings. And, significantly, this difference did not result from some well-executed edict or mandate in the laws or constitution of any given state, though some contained noble words and exhortations. Rather, it developed from certain characteristics which the university had naturally inherited from a long, Western European tradition. The universities were places with an inspired mission. Above all, the educational process focused upon the individual, and considered as the measure of success the benefit of process on the individual. The focus of education in America was the same as that of the law. In this respect, it resembled American constitutional law before the jurisprudential revolution discussed in Part III. Like Plato's grove, the university was a place where an *individual* process took place, *educare* (the Latin root of *education* meaning "to bring up" or "lead out of darkness").

Thus, through a balance dependent upon the predominantly liberal and tolerant character of the American majority, modern college education eventually realized its greatest achievement and development. But like every balance, like every partnership, the arrangement continued for only so long as the partners kept their trust. Unfortunately, the Academy decided to break theirs. The seeming swiftness with which the Academy suddenly abandoned the middle class was stunning.

CHAPTER SIXTEEN

Renovation

The conditions which prevailed prior the 1960s favored the continuation of the traditional university model without any significant tinkering by the central government. There had been extensive action before then by both the state and federal government, though such action was different in nature than that appearing in the 1960s. Until then, federal aid to education appeared primarily in the form of land grants, totalling nearly 100 million acres of raw land, dedicated to the support of college education. The general population, however, had strongly resisted direct federal aid or involvement. Three bills to provide such aid were defeated in the 1870s, several more in the 1880s, and another serious effort, the Smith-Townes Act, was defeated in 1919. This pattern of Congressional crusade and eventual defeat marked the history of attempts at direct federal action past World War II. The Morrill Acts, the Smith-Lever and Smith-Hughes Acts (in 1914 and 1917) were designed to fund yet more land-grant colleges and to provide limited assistance for some vocational and home economics programs in public high schools. When World War II produced an expansion of non-taxable military facilities in many school districts, the Lanham Act authorized federal aid to offset local tax losses. The war brought the GI Bill in 1944, and later the National Science Foundation Act of 1950, followed by the National Defense Education Act of 1958.

At its most extreme, federal involvement in education was limited to categories and skills thought to be relevant to national security, particularly the hard sciences and math. But with the rise of President John F. Kennedy, the history of federal involvement in education became entwined in totally new budgetary concepts advanced by the executive branch of the federal government. A transformation in the U.S. presidency occurring in the 1960s laid the groundwork for the complete renovation of American education. This transformation began with a radically new concept of budgetary policy introduced in the early 1960s, followed by direct federal intervention in education on an unprecedented scale and by unprecedented means.

Through the Eisenhower and Truman administrations, the guiding budgetary concept of the federal government paralleled that of the prudent individual or family. As an ordinary budgetary practice, neither of these presidents believed in creating deficits. President John F. Kennedy changed this policy in 1962, announcing his new concept in a speech at Yale. His administration marked a watershed in not only budgetary policy, but also the panoply of governmental activity fed by such a policy. President Kennedy announced that the budgetary constraints which confined a family did not apply to a government. The energetic and impulsive drive to "do something" emanating from Kennedy's powerful leadership slammed great amounts of federal money behind a variety of projects. In the space program, we reversed the setbacks dealt us by Sputnik in October 1957 by launching the *Friendship 7*, a space capsule in which Colonel John Glenn orbited the earth three times on February 20, 1962. This kind of uplifting, come-from-behind impressed almost everyone. By 1962, the stage was set for a totally new type of educational reform. The national government began the attack from above.

The Blow From Above

> *The power of education is mysterious. It exerts itself through complicity and influence, rather than through coercion or control. Such power is more durable and more popular than force. Hence political movements tend to posture as the friends of education, whether or not their real purpose is to destroy or limit it.*

Roger Scruton, 1984

The inspiration Kennedy inaugurated was cut short by his assassination, but he had unwittingly prepared events for the most significant presidential figure in the transformation process, a largely misunderstood and misinterpreted contributor to the stunning changes in

American society, a man whose influence greatly assisted the Abandonment in this field: Lyndon Baines Johnson. Johnson initiated the process of transforming the universities in the 1960s. When the moment for decisive action arrived, Johnson's response, more than that of any other U.S. president, determined the degree to which this country retained the benefits of the victory of 1945, or threw them away.

Johnson's biographer, Robert Caro, documents his rise to national political prominence through the theft of the 1948 Senate race from his opponent, popular former Texas governor Coke R. Stevenson. As Caro establishes convincingly in his latest volume on Johnson, *Means of Ascent*, Johnson and his associates rigged the outcome by stuffing ballot boxes with votes for Johnson and concealing votes for Stevenson so that they could not be counted. Johnson supplanted Stevenson's vigorous belief in constitutional government, honestly run and devoted to the individual, with one of his own designs. Caro observes correctly that Johnson's illegal triumph over Stevenson represents one of the most significant turning points in modern American political history. It produced a "transformation of American politics in the middle of the twentieth century." Additionally, it left its stamp on the type of constitutional government which was to emerge after his tenure in office, and on the nation's educational system.

Johnson was above all a manipulator, bent on developing his own power, and he was a genius at doing just that. Even his closest associates in Washington never knew where he stood personally, if he stood anywhere. He had a gift for managing, steering, and building coalitions behind anything which kept him at the center of the action. This talent reflected his character better than any other feature of his engaging personality. Thus, in the principal acts of his presidency, he decided to manage, to steer, and to manipulate but not to consult the populace, whether in education or any other field. By invoking federal power in education to an unprecedented degree and in innovative ways, he disrupted the consensus between educators and the populace which had accounted for whatever degree of success education had experienced. His plan was called the "Great Society."

In his first State of the Union Address on January 8, 1964, Johnson announced the "war on poverty." In May of that year at the University of Michigan, he announced that we would all "set our course toward the Great Society," borrowing a phrase from New Dealer Henry Wallace. It soon became clear that the awesome might of the federal government would be used to expand Kennedy's grandiose but unfulfilled objectives. Moreover, not only would Johnson carry forward the Kennedy concept of deficit finance and general idea of big government as omnipotent problem-solver, but he would also give it his own stamp. He would endow it with his own specific objectives and his own view of the Great Society. Education bore the Johnson stamp more than any other project he undertook.

The devotees of Horace Mann had been building for nearly a century, but still were anchored to one degree or another to the community and thus to middle-class or majoritarian influence. The PTA or its counterpart engaged the solemn concern of most every childrearing household. Schools were governed by decentralized school boards. This made it difficult to alter the middle-class hold over education.

Thus, the innovative educators of the 1960s faced problems of curricular content and jurisdiction, and they wanted control over both. Johnson's Great Society stepped in to provide the means for obtaining such control. The Economic Opportunity Act of 1964, along with the Elementary and Secondary Education Act of 1965, started an avalanche of federal legislative and regulatory action in education, an avalanche repeated in just about every other field of human endeavor, for example, the Civil Rights Act of 1964 and the Voting Rights Act of 1965. The Higher Education Act followed, with the establishment of the National Foundation for the Arts and Humanities, which gave sizeable grants in support of the more high-brow side of public education.

The method by which Johnson encroached on education was as novel as the content of the programs that followed. It bypassed large and diffuse constituencies interested in education, thus nullifying their influence and enabling the federal government to centralize control over educational reform, including the content of its programs. The method's operational device was the "task force." Johnson employed the task force to formulate policy and legislative proposals under his direct control. In contrast, the conventional departmental procedure, under various agencies and their personnel, committees, and subcommittees, would have generated new proposals through a process of discussion and consensus. Eventually, Johnson had 135 task forces working on the Great Society.

In an incisive survey of Johnson's foray into education published in 1981, Hughes Davis Graham quotes Philip S. Hughes of the Bureau of the Budget on the significance of the new Johnson method:

> The task force was the basic tool which made much of the success of the Eighty-ninth Congress. The routine way to develop a legislative program has been to ask the Departments to generate proposals. Each agency sends its ideas through channels, which means that the ideas are limited by the imagination of the old-line agencies. They tend to be repetitive the same proposals year after year. When the ideas of the different agencies reach the departmental level, all kinds of objections are raised, especially objections that new notions may somehow infringe on the rights of some other agency in the department. By the time a legislative proposal from a department reaches the President, it's a pretty well-compromised product.

As Graham sums up,

> Thus the task force device was designed to interrupt the normal bureaucratic flow, provide for innovation, combat the inherent inertia and boundary maintenance of the agencies, and maximize the leverage of the presidential battalion of a thousand short-term political appointees over the entrenched subgovernment army of 2.5 million civil servants and their constituency and congressional subcommittee allies.

Johnson's manipulative genius broke through the impasse which had defeated Kennedy's earlier efforts at a comprehensive education bill. Congress passed the Elementary and Secondary Education Act of 1965, as Graham says, "with a whoop."

The education task forces which drove through the Great Society reforms were coordinated by Bill Moyers, Richard Goodwin, and Walter Heller. Kermit Gordon added continuity from the earlier Kennedy team. From Johnson's point of view, the great virtue of these task forces was that they were secret. Johnson could have a government representative, normally an executive secretary from the Bureau of the Budget, carry the execution of new programs directly to the schools and universities, bypassing the states as independent political entities. The local school boards and districts and the ever present PTA were rendered poor seconds to the hand of the federal government.   A considerable sweetener for the 1965 act came in the form of a $300 million grant program for assistance to both private and public schools. The process of inducing the Academy with a federal carrot was set in motion.

The genius of Johnson's federal intervention in education was that administratively and financially it operated *directly* on institutions of learning at both lower and collegiate levels.   In this manner, the intellectual fashion crafted in Washington radically altered the direction formerly set for education by lower level political entities which answered to and were controlled by the local communities nationwide. Federal regulations became directly operative and mandatory for local communities and local educators. It also provided the powerful lure of federal dollars to induce compliance with federally devised programs. The independence of educational institutions became threatened at all levels, not just in jurisdictional authority but also in the educational content and philosophy. The same thing happened to education that had happened to the individual under the federal transformation of constitutional rights we examined in Part III: as an entity distinct from federal policy, it just disappeared.   As a traditionally autonomous, social institution the university weakened rapidly.

Barry Goldwater's defeat in 1964 caused Congress to favor the Johnson methods. The Democrats obtained a 295 to 140 edge in the House and a margin of 68 to 32 in the Senate. This advantage made for swift adoption and execution of Johnson's surprising reforms. On the 1965 act, Eric Goldman remarks,

> [C]ongress had passed a billion dollar law, deeply affecting a fundamental institution of the nation, in a breath-taking eighty-seven days.

The House had approved the plan crafted by Johnson's task force with no substantive change, and the Senate, as Hughes Graham relates, "voted it through literally without a comma changed."

The policy shift and the implications for the future which all of these changes represented cannot be overstated. One professor described the result as

> [t]he abandonment of attempts to pass legislation authorizing general federal aid to elementary and secondary education and the adoption of an approach utilizing a broad range of categorical assistance programs designed to attack specific problems such as the education of economically disadvantaged children.

Under this new law, all federal aid was "categorical." It not only involved the transfer of money to existing institutions, but also required conformity to categorical requirements formulated by the central government, accompanied by the regulatory oversight of the Education Department. The burgeoning federal presence in education which the Johnson efforts began formed but a part of overall change in the central government and its approach to the individual and society, similar to the changes in the judicial process discussed earlier.

The revolution in American education had already commenced with the Supreme Court's *Brown v. Board of Education* decision in 1954. This decision addressed a serious and urgent problem. But it also marked the starting point for methods which increasingly diverged from *Brown*'s original intent. The theoretical goal of desegregation of public education, so laudably launched in *Brown*, was soon implemented in practical remedies which fell upon the only innocent parties in the whole process—the schoolchildren, the only ones who had not discriminated against anybody. The judges began the logical but destructive process of dismantling the nation's primary schools for the sake of a noble goal, what one law professor from Texas called "Disaster by Decree." The chaotic landscape left in the wake of the evolving judicial edicts carrying *Brown* to its logical extreme fed the growing educational industry and federal bureaucracy associated with it. The bigger the problem, the bigger, more costly and more forceful the solution.

It fell to President Jimmy Carter to follow up the Johnson revolution at the higher governmental levels. The Department of Education began as a non-cabinet federal agency in 1867, located in the Department of the Interior. It went through several name changes until in 1953 it became part of the newly created Department of Health

Education and Welfare. This department bore no resemblance to the new "Education Division" created as a part of HEW in 1972. By 1979 the division had grown enough to branch off as a separate department. The Department now spends over $15 billion annually pursuing an endless array of educational projects and dispensing billions to schools at every level in the nation. Its operation includes a director and staff for bilingual education and minority language affairs, an assistant secretary to ensure that government influence and participation in education is conducted with an eye to civil rights, a program for migrant education, and much, much more.

The effect of the deficit-financed expansion in higher education has been phenomenal. The number of teachers in state-supported schools doubled as their assigned activities mutated under the lure of federal money. The stipulations of the federal grants steadily transformed the traditional curriculum. The age of "values clarification" was at hand. The large influx of culturally and educationally unprepared students, largely blacks victimized by nearly a century of official segregation and public abandon, was grist for the superschool mill. Amazingly thorough, the transformation affected standards for advancement and promotion and core curriculum requirements. Here the vital link between the Johnsonian revolution and the academy was forged in this era of rising population and growing demand for education. The student population, now drawn more and more from the crass chaos of the disoriented primary and secondary institutions, nearly tripled in the 1960s. Astoundingly, the number of new students pouring into the universities during the 1960s doubled the *total* enrollment extant when John F. Kennedy was elected president.

Federal money also poured into university treasuries, until it became a significant part of the budget of almost every major university in the nation. In an article dated April 10, 1991, the *Chronicle of Higher Education* listed the federal contribution to the country's top 100 university recipients. The figures were for the 1989 fiscal year, the latest for which dates was available. The amounts are staggering. Twenty-nine schools received over $100 million each for the year, while six got over $200 million, with Johns Hopkins University at the top for a whopping $612,128 million in tax dollars. High on the list were numerous schools with a proven record of financial abuse, such as

Stanford University, the recipient of $275,781 million. Stanford, it will be recalled, and its president, Donald Kennedy, hit the news in 1990 for widespread spending abuses, such as the use of federal funds on extensive entertainment and the maintenance of a pleasure yacht. All of the leaders in the recent campus speech regulation movement, or "political correctness (PC)," (more on this later) were at the trough. The reporting institutions listed in the top 100 raked in nearly $16 billion.

Grants from foundations and corporations have also increased the independence of colleges and universities from their alumni. As the federal government, foundation and corporate giving have become the major revenue source for many institutions, the educational and philosophical views of the alumni have ceased to matter very much. For example, in addition to the nearly $16 billion in government aid, the nations top schools received $3.4 billion from foundations and corporations. Thirty-seven schools received over half of the total giving from foundations, and 40 received over half the corporate donations for 1989-90.   Coupled with federal donations, it all spells financial independence, from accountability to any broad-based social group. This, in turn, spells independence from broad-based influence, and makes the common academic hostility to the middle class feasible.

A look at the top 25 recipients of federal, foundation and corporate money for 1990 is revealed in Table 16.1, below.

Significantly, over two-thirds of the schools among the top 25 recipients of government money were also in the top 25 in *both* foundation and corporate gifts (17 out of 25). Moreover, if you expand the list of schools beyond the top 25 recipients of government money, say to the top 40 recipients, a great many more schools are *also* on the top 40 for foundation and corporate gifts. Among the top 40 are all the chief proponents of the "diversity movement" and the "PC movement". For example, the University of Texas (number 35 on the government money list) received a combined government/foundation/corporate total of $123,348,798. However, most of the PC advanced guard are in the top 25. Yale University (number 15 on the government list) received a combined total of $213,738,000. Harvard University (number 14 on the government list) received a total of $261,825,586. Duke University (number 6 on the government list) received a grand total of

$186,196,881. Stanford University (number 2 on the government list) received a total of $353,495,918. These are major trend setters in the diversity movement and PC movement. The very poorest school among the top 25, the University of Rochester, got over $100 million independent of tuition, fees or state support.

TABLE 16.1

Government and Corporate Contributions to Universities

Institution	Federal Money (Direct Grants)	Foundation Money	Corporate Money	Total Government/ Corporate
1. Johns Hopkins	612,128,000	26,293,857	11,468,122	649,889,979
2. Stanford	275,781,000	29,135,567	48,579,351	353,495,918
3. U. of Washington	246,883,000	24,057,349	31,696,958	302,637,307
4. M.I.T.	236,632,000	18,523,712	50,819,238	305,974,950
5. U. of Minnesota	203,183,000	20,776,165	38,139,780	262,098,945
6. U. of California at Los Angeles	200,090,000	44,761,695	16,316,967	261,168,662
7. U. of Michigan	198,199,000	13,220,623	15,295,245	226,714,868
8. Cornell	192,077,000	22,232,409	42,793,960	257,103,369
9. U. California at San Diego	184,633,000	13,729,120	13,102,718	211,464,838
10. U. of Wisconsin at Madison	178,913,000	31,133,094	44,634,217	254,680,311
11. Columbia Main Division	178,910,000	26,716,791	16,301,314	221,928,105
12. U. of California at San Francisco	177,273,000	15,376,732	*	192,649,732
13. Howard	175,594,000	*	*	175,594,000
14. Harvard	171,316,000	54,031,098	36,478,627	261,825,726
15. Yale	168,338,000	32,200,000	13,200,000	213,738,000
16. Penn State	166,581,000	*	31,339,015	197,920,015
17. U. of California at Berkeley	164,358,000	26,480,805	32,299,587	223,138,392
18. U. of Penn.	158,377,000	24,416,753	34,564,359	217,358,112
19. U. of Southern California	134,061,000	17,968,477	37,164,246	189,193,723

Institution	Federal Money (Direct Grants)	Foundation Money	Corporate Money	Total Government/ Corporate
20. U. of Colorado	130,430,000	*	15,553,686	145,983,686
21. Duke	122,679,000	29,469,254	34,048,627	186,196,881
22. U. of Illinois at Urbana-Champaign	120,910,000	*	23,398,690	144,308,690
23. Washington U.	120,764,000	12,644,226	*	133,408,226
24. U. of Pittsburgh	114,798,000	15,415,452	*	130,213,452
25. U. of Rochester	111,435,000	*		111,435,000
GRAND TOTAL				$5,830,120,887

*Not in top 25 in this category. Figures for federal aid are for fiscal 1989. Figures for foundation and corporate aid are for 1989-1990. The combined totals are a reliable estimate of the cash flow from these sources for a full academic year. The federal aid figures are for direct grants, and do not include other forms if aid, such as student loans. The Chronicle of Higher Education, April 10, 1991; June 5, 1991.

The financial independence of America's leading educational institutions from their alumni is another legacy of Lyndon Johnson's Great Society. It is another manifestation of the impact of America's debt-based constitution on democracy. Federal money derived from deficit financing has played a vital role in liberating higher education from its traditional partnership with middle-class democracy. Federal tax laws stimulated foundations and corporations to provide yet more money. As schools which had traditionally been tied to a broad-based constituency and committed to providing affordable education to everyone who qualified received more and more governmental money, they began to behave like the government. Getting the lion's share of their income from essentially governmental sources, they were free to tax the middle class into oblivion with skyrocketing tuition, while bestowing their favors on select beneficiaries.

As the school's financial links with middle-class democracy faded, so did their loyalties. The autocratic and regulatory regimes that have replaced older and more democratic models on the nation's campuses did not just spring up out of the blue. Money made them possible. To put it in Jeffersonian terms, these schools escaped their dependence on democracy, but predictably lost the benefits of being a part of it. When we see a college faculty behaving as arbitrarily as eighteenth-century French aristocrats, remember: now they can afford it. As Jefferson so brilliantly recognized, government money derived from perpetual debt will generally be used to destroy the influence of democracy. Thus, the Educational Constitution of the nation was transformed. Money did the same thing for colleges and universities that it did for Congress; it destroyed accountability and with it any impulse to adhere to the middle-class partnership.

It was not only the use of big money and the administrative principle of bypassing federalism which distinguished Johnson's approach. The very nature of his undertakings was different from earlier models. In the 1930s, Franklin Roosevelt's army of problem solvers were all directed to remedying some particular problem. If young people needed jobs, the CCC would put them to work. FDR was a counsellor, who feelingly persuaded people in his famous fireside chats. He opened the door to big government as no one else before could or would. It was John Kennedy who opened the door to *intellectual* big government and whose theories made it financially and administratively possible. But it was Lyndon Johnson who led the first big pack of intellectuals through the door. Johnson's undertakings differed from FDR's in both degree and kind. Unlike those of FDR, Johnson's programs were not directed at solving difficulties within some area of society; they were designed to take over *whole areas* and remake them from scratch. Why consider the particular problems of any field of endeavor, such as education, if you could remold and reconstruct the entire field itself? Instead of removing a blemish in the old statuary, Johnson's approach chiseled away enough to come up with an entirely new sculpture. It profoundly changed the very focus of government, though it grew out of FDR's changes relating to size and structure.

Lyndon Johnson fully understood the revolutionary nature of the changes he was making in government and the things subject to government control, such as education. In a 1965 interview with William E. Leuchtenburg first published in the May/June 1990 *American Heritage*, Johnson is depicted as obsessed with the power of the presidency and the idea that no previous president had used it so forcefully. He believed his background made him best able to exercise the enormous powers of the presidency: "Never was anyone so well trained for this office." Moreover, he understood that his revolutionary education policy and program would transform the nation more completely than any measure passed during the New Deal. Speaking on FDR and his New Deal programs, Johnson said,

> He did get things done. There was regulation of business, but that was unimportant. Social Security and the Wagner Act were all that really amounted to much, and none of it compares to my education act. We've added enough to the public domain to make Teddy Roosevelt ashamed of himself.

As a result of this geometric growth, the people in the Academy were increasingly replaced with an altogether new type of academic. The pre-World War II generation of college professors (many of them continuing on through the postwar era) was well-suited to secure the success of a balanced partnership between the Academy and the middle class. They were mostly men and women who had achieved success in their basic education and collegiate training. They were men and women who, despite often great opportunity for financial gain, had felt the urge for something more, something better, something greater, something which their own study and reflection had awakened during their college days. Not hostile to the society in which they existed, they did not view their job as either rationalizing some perceived injustice or social defect into a program for revolution or reform, or as executing any such program. They did not view the individuals around them, those outside the university, as some undifferentiated class of unbalanced and maladjusted sociopaths, badly needing individual counselling and personal reform. It did not occur to college professors to spend time on the project of harnessing the coercive power of the state behind any such scheme. It did not occur to them to urge the transformation of the law or its executive apparatus into an engine for enforcing their views on others. They had not yet assumed the self-appointed, governmentally authorized mantle of social policemen and high priests.

In short, the new intellectual orientation had not merged with the academic orientation before the Johnson era. When the country went to war, the members of the Academy went away to fight for it, and if they survived they came back to resume their place in a privileged invaluable order whose goals transcended those of welfare agencies and government bureaucracies. As far as their usefulness to society, these were the brightest and best we have ever had.

A new variety of intellectuals with virtues quite unlike those listed by Henry Vail began to appear. These new intellectuals, however, had never had such humanistic constraints on their powerful urge to experiment with the lives of others. As Paul Johnson develops so powerfully in his book *Intellectuals*, they are normally people "who see no incongruity in moving from their own discipline, where they are acknowledged masters, to public affairs, where they might be supposed to have no more right to a hearing than anyone else." They are, moreover, characteristically unconcerned at the human costs of their experiments. They agree with G.B. Shaw, who cautioned against anger at Stalin's murder of thousands:

> We cannot afford to give ourselves moral airs when our most enterprising neighbor . . . humanly and judiciously liquidates a handful of exploiters and speculators to make the world safe for honest men.

In the tradition of Shaw, Marx, Bertrand Russell, Steffens, Malraux, and a host of others, the intellectuals have no love for their fellow men. They have no identification with them as people experiencing human problems and human pain. They were and are, above all, casual and unmoved about the effects of their actions and the ideas of their fellow human beings. They were and are, more than any other identifiable group in modern society, personally representative of the abandonment and rejection of the humanistic knowledge.

Following the Johnsonian educational revolution, the intellectuals in the Academy began to flex their muscles. They began to proclaim their rightful places in the new order, and to assume command of the society whose tolerance had allowed them to flourish. In this, they behaved in a characteristically intellectual way, and their abandonment of the individual followed just as it had with the courts. As Eric Hoffer wrote in 1963 of the intellectual coming to power:

> There is a chronic insecurity at the core of the creative person, and he needs a milieu that will nourish his confidence and sense of uniqueness. Discerning appreciation and a modicum of deference and acclaim are probably more vital for his creative flow than freedom to fend for

himself. Thus a despotism that recognizes and subsidizes excellence might be more favorable for the performance of the intellectual than a free society that does not take him seriously....

The paradox is, then, that although the intellectual has been in the forefront of the struggle for individual freedom he can never feel wholly at home in a free society. He finds there neither an unquestioned sense of usefulness nor favorable conditions for the realization of his talents. Hence the contradiction between what the intellectual professes while he battles the status quo, and what he practices once he comes to power. At present, in every part of the world, we see how revolutionary movements initiated by idealistic intellectuals and preserved in their keeping tend to crystallize into hierarchical social orders in which an aristocratic intelligentsia commands, and the masses are expected to obey.

Despite the fact that the new intellectuals filtering into the universities were largely emigrés from the middle class, their "chronic insecurity" and the shelter of lifetime tenure provided the perfect stimulus to their defection from middle-class views. Their uniqueness could hardly be demonstrated by extolling the history of middle-American political and social beliefs, or articulating prosaic middle American values. How much more exciting to lay hold on the average American and reshape him according to some brilliant egocentric idea, for which the intellectual could take credit. For such personalities, combining the freedom from accountability afforded by tenure with their restless drive for chic one-upmanship was like putting the match to gunpowder. For all their occasional skills in any one discipline, the new-age academic personally reflects the failure of education in the truest sense, *educare*, and of the *Universitas*, to reach and improve everyone as an individual. Instead of teaching the individual more, the intellectual educator would rather have all thinking go along approved lines.

These new academics assumed an intellectual orientation similar to their counterparts on the judicial bench. They adopted a prescriptive view of society rather than a tolerant one. This view held that the institutions of the culture did not evolve out of collective action, but rather could be prescribed from above. Most important of all, the individual, the primary beneficiary of the system, was abandoned, just as he was by the law. He became merely an undifferentiated part in a centrally controlled process of reform. The partnership dissolved, and the Academy was transformed as a result. The most far-reaching result of the Great Society was, then, to intellectualize education and the governmental apparatus concerned with it.

Everything that represented or signified the traditional educational system at the lower levels or at the Academy, including its identifiable middle-class bias, was viewed as thoroughly bad by the new intellectual bureaucracy. Thus the new "intellectual" view that the middle class and the educational regime it supports is irretrievably corrupt replaced the old view, and became both the law and the curriculum of the land. Out of the cycle of expansion set up by Johnson's Great Society, a new political dynamic was about to emerge on American campuses. An alliance was being forged between a new type of faculty member, alienated from America and hostile to its traditions, and a new type of student, nurtured on the non-traditional fashion of Great Society intellects. Both the faculty and the student elements of the new alliance were still in the minority. However, beginning in the mid-1960s, they were to discover the secret to overthrowing the slow-moving tolerant democratic constitution common to American universities. Their discovery reverberates to this day. How did it happen?

The Blow From Below: The Mechanics of Revolution

The blows which shook education came first from above, in the form of the Johnsonian renovation of federal education finance, policy, and practice; the second blow, an upper cut from below, came from the student body. This blow finally put the weakened carcass of academe flat on the mat.

Perhaps the most significant fact about the student "movements" which swept and transformed the nation's campuses in the 1960's was that they never commanded anything near a majority of the student bodies or faculties anywhere. What these "movements" actually revealed for the first time was the feasibility of achieving a successful revolution with only a vocal minority as revolutionaries. The way in which colleges and universities customarily operated lent itself to the successful minority coup d'état.

The events at the University of California at Berkeley formed a pattern repeated with varied degrees of intensity across America. The pattern bears close study.

Berkeley had certain rules dealing with political activities and the solicitation of funds for their support. These rules did not allow soliciting of funds or recruiting by political activists from off campus. Therefore, an area just outside the main pedestrian gate for the Berkeley campus, Bancroft Strip, had long been used by groups for these purposes. The unrest began on September 15, 1964, when the administration began to enforce the rules in that area. Previously, the university administration had not known that the strip was technically part of the campus. By September 28, pickets had interrupted a meeting on campus where Berkeley Chancellor Edward W. Strong was speaking. On September 29, a group of students spent the night in Sproul Hall the university administration building. In response, university authorities took the names of some of the sleep-in demonstrators. The following day, the dean called in eight of the students whose names had been recorded and later announced their suspension from the university. After representatives of various student organizations were unable to change the policy against on-campus solicitation and recruiting, a group of students tried to take over Sproul Hall and the Hyde Park area, a traditional place for student oratory. On October 1, more solicitation and recruitment tables were set up. At noon, Jack Weinberg, a twenty-four-year-old member of the Congress of Racial Equality who was present as a speaker, was arrested and held by the police until 7:00 p.m. the next day. Students surrounded the police car, flattened the tires and used it as a speaking platform. Of the estimated four thousand demonstrators (many of the "hard core" according to observers) about three hundred, including Weinberg, were not students. The university decided to release Weinberg and not prosecute him for trespassing.

Thereafter, an eighteen-member student, faculty, and administration committee was set up to study relaxation of the political rules. An interlude followed during which the administration attempted to reach some sort of resolution of the student problem without further demonstrations or disruptions. However, the administration abolished this committee after recurring demonstrations on November 7 and 9.

By November 10, 1964, three hundred teaching assistants and graduate students had signed petitions supporting what the *New York Times* labelled the "free-speech movement," defying university rules forbidding on-campus political activity. The petitions were presented to Associate Dean Peter van Houten. The initial administrative position, however, held firm, and University President Clark Kerr and Chancellor Strong warned that students violating the rules "will be subject to penalties through established procedures," i.e., suspension or expulsion.

On November 15 the *Times* reported that the protest had become a noon ritual, settling into a predictable routine, taking away the emotional appeal essential to a successful demonstration. Since the week before, Weinberg had been back on a wall adjoining Sproul Hall, exhorting, according to the *Times*, "about 700 students to support the Free Speech Movement." The *Times* also reported that freedom to speak on political issues was "not directly inhibited in the university position in the dispute."

The university administration, backed now by the Board of Regents, attempted to channel the student activity along orderly and peaceful channels while still preserving the integrity of the institution itself. Accordingly, on November 20, 1964, the Regents of the University of California, following a course recommended by President Kerr, gave students the freedom to plan off-campus political activity but warned students that they would be held accountable for their actions. The university administration made its position clear that if students were convicted of breaking the law in a campus-connected demonstration, they could expect discipline by the university. In response, Mario Savio, a twenty-one-year-old philosophy student and president of the Berkeley Chapter of Friends of SNCC (Student Non-violent Coordinating Committee), called the Regents' ruling "unconstitutional" and promised a court test. Outside, 4,800 students massed as they were entertained by Joan Baez, who had found the most successful of her causes.

The level of noise and the size of the crowd continued to increase daily, and a contingent of demonstrators reoccupied the administration building. On December 3, 1964, 796 students were arrested upon the order of Governor Edmund G. Brown following their occupation of the building.

Apparently, throughout all these events, the students wanted the approval of the university for their off-campus activities, which may have been illegal under local law, with the assurance that they would not face discipline from the university should this turn out to be the case. The governor called the student activity "anarchy." In retaliation to the arrests, the Free Speech Movement (FSM) called for a strike. University reports show that the strike involved about one-third of the student population, though the protestors claimed that the figure was seventy-five percent. Then the faculty began to react formally to the firm administrative hand. Five hundred of the 1,200 faculty members met and drafted a resolution stating that the university faced a "desperate situation." These faculty favored setting up a committee to which students could appeal administration decisions on penalties for violating university rules on political action. The resolution asked that "all pending campus action against the students for acts occurring before the present date be dropped." The faculty also planned a telegram to Governor Brown condemning the use of the California Highway Patrol on campus and exclusion of the faculty from Sproul Hall. While being arrested, demonstrator Mario Savio was heard to say, "This is wonderful wonderful. We'll bring the university to our terms." Another leader, Arthur Goldburg, said, "Good! The kids have learned more about democracy here than they could have learned in forty years of classes. This is a perfect example of how the State of California plays the game."

The FSM thereafter achieved a more formal organization, with an executive committee of sixty members, each representing some campus organization. The eleven-member steering committee was dominated by representatives of the following groups: W.E.B. DuBois Club (described at that time by Department of Justice sources as being a front among college students for the Communist Party), the Young Socialist League, the Young Socialist Alliance, Slate (a student political organization) and SNCC. Initially, some conservative groups belonged to the FSM, but by the time of the arrests, they had disassociated themselves. Also, signs appeared of student opposition to the FSM, such as "Throw The Bums Out" and "Law Not Anarchy The Majority of Students Do Not Support This Demonstration."

The demonstrators, encouraged by the seriousness with which some of the faculty had taken their demands and actions, saw the opportunity to use this sympathy to create a buffer between the administration and themselves. December 5, 1964, Savio demanded the replacement of the school president and chancellor. He said, "We have promised that this university will not run, and we shall keep that promise. There is only one possible final solution: The university must be for the students and the faculty." But Savio did not speak for everyone. According to a university source, students trying to take a psychology exam got into a fistfight with picketers trying to get them to leave the class. The university news office found that 16.6 percent of the persons arrested in the occupation had no university affiliation (not as students, teaching assistants, or graduate assistants).

In front of Sproul Hall, students and a nonstudent leader rallied to push for the sacking of the president and chancellor. Sympathy began to pour in on the student-faculty side against the firmness of the administration position. For example, Michael Schneider, a director for the California Democratic Council, joined Rudy Nothenberg, a trustee, in criticizing the decision to send police to the campus. They also asked the governor for amnesty for all students and demanded the students' political freedom as well.

Press coverage increasingly sympathized with the perceived needs and message of the movement, and a new view appeared: that attendance at the university, once thought of as a privilege and a challenge, was itself a cleverly disguised form of societal oppression. Thus one reporting journalist perceived that the political issue was only a "symptom of a larger revolt against the bigness and impersonality of the 'multiversity' itself." Paul Goodman said even more clearly in an FSM pamphlet that "students—middle-class youth—are the major exploited class. . . . They have no choice but to go to college."

The movement thus began to gather the accoutrements of a significant social revolution, even though these trappings were manufactured like TV ads or billboard slogans. The FSM adopted a formal credo: "We must now begin the demand of the right to know; to know the realities of the present world-in-revolution, and to have an opportunity to think clearly in an extended manner about the world. It is ours to demand meaning; we must insist upon meaning!"

As its formal philosophy became as explicit as its credo, the most significant feature of the movement appeared. The hallmark of all student political action from that day to this, the philosophy exemplified and illuminated what the generalities of the credo meant: that the students did not come to the university to learn, but to teach. In this job, they had arrogated a position at least equal to the faculty itself.

As things dragged on, President Kerr began to waver. As the media clarified the movement's philosophy, he conceded that the decision to close off Bancroft Strip summarily from any student political activity had been, after all, a mistake, since no "consultations" between student leaders or the over-all university administration occurred before the action was taken. Kerr explained that he thought students already had the kind of political freedom they claimed to seek, since, for instance, they had the freedom to invite whomever they wanted to speak at their functions. However, the students said their freedom actually "lacked meaning." Perplexed, Kerr strove to find "meaning" in what the students were demanding, though he and other administrators concerned found great difficulty in assessing exactly what would satisfy the participants of the FSM. As for lack of meaning he said, "People can find those things which may mean something to them. They are given a choice. It would be terribly stultifying to find yourself in a place which has a single meaning, and that meaning is the same for everyone. Essentially what the FSM is saying is that they are rebelling against the freedom of choice." Later Kerr admitted, "I still don't know how we should have handled it."

The situation carried over into the new year, 1965. In January, Chancellor Strong went on sick leave, and Acting Chancellor Martin Meyerson took office. However, the protestors were unappeased, and in March they adopted a new tactic: replacing the academic-sounding jargon of the previous debates with foul language. Thus began the so-called "dirty word" campaign, much to the delight of every juvenile in the nation who could read a newspaper. Two weeks of "dirty word" protests ended on March 13, 1965.

Kerr and everyone else representing the university administration was now caught in a crossfire between dirty word activists and the increasingly bewildered Board of Regents. When the regents demanded immediate dismissal of the dirty word demonstrators, Kerr and Meyerson tendered their resignations. The Berkeley faculty expressed itself in favor of Kerr and Meyerson, voting 891 to 23 to urge the regents not to accept the resignations. In late March, President Kerr and Acting Chancellor Meyerson agreed to withdraw their resignations.

The regents did accept the resignation of Chancellor Strong, who had been on leave since January 2. On March 12, Strong explained that the reason for his departure was not sickness, as had been officially stated. He claimed that Kerr's actions had destroyed his attempts to restore order by dealing with the demonstrators quickly and vigorously. When pressed for a continuation of a strong and consistent reaction to the increasingly violent demonstrators, Kerr undercut his policy by treating the demonstrators seriously. The results, Strong said, were "further demoralizations, concessions, retreats and compromises."

A conservative block of regents had wanted to pass a resolution making participation in a sit-in grounds for dismissal, but because of a deep split on the board and Kerr's and Meyerson's threatened resignations, the resolution was withdrawn by Theodore R. Meyer, a San Francisco lawyer. Discussions became nasty and insulting at all levels, and the juvenile tendency to resort to uncivilized insults infected the regents themselves. Frederick G. Dutton, a regent opposed to the resolution, said, "This is a resolution that might be expected by the Board of Regents of the University of Alabama." So much for academic and professional courtesy.

By May 1965, the controversy reached the serious reporting and consulting stage which occurs when viable institutions evaporate in an avalanche of bureaucracy. The Board of Regents ordered a full investigative report to be prepared by an eight-member committee headed by Beverly Hills attorney Jerome C. Byrne. The following are some of the committee's findings and recommendations:

> There was no evidence that the Free Speech Movement was instigated by the Communist Party, Progressive Labor Movement or any other outside group;
> The regents and University President Kerr had failed to develop a governmental structure acceptable to the students and suited to the size of the university;
> There should be full freedom of organization by faculty and students;

There should be a revision of the university charter and shift of the university headquarters from Berkeley to San Francisco;
Each of the chancellors on the nine university campuses should be given more authority to manage his own campus;
Broadly based student governments should be encouraged.

Thus emerged a clear pattern of university reactions, a pattern in one degree or another repeated throughout American universities during the late 1960s: Initially the administration of the university conserved its monopoly over the control of the institution, only to be undercut by widespread faculty equivocation, followed by irreversible action on the part of the ultimate managing body of the university, the trustees or regents. Such wavering provided legitimacy to the demonstrators' revolutionary demands with the end result that the entire university operation was transformed by the determined actions of a minority of students, a significant number of nonstudents, and a minority of the faculty, without ever arriving at a rational or reasonable dialogue about just what the revolutionaries really wanted. Over a short period of time, an institution based on centuries of tradition decided that the university and its administration were the ones in the wrong, having "failed to develop a governmental structure acceptable to the students," and that the university administration should pick up and move to a new place. For whatever reasons, no effective conservators of university tradition were in charge. No one with institutional or administrative capability or authority made a sustained and rational presentation of the university's position. Instead of entering a rational dialogue and peaceful exchange, the guardians wound up apologizing, equivocating and running off.

Byrne's report got a cool reception from the regents. At least some recognized the implications of minority rule in the university. The chairman of the regents, Edward W. Carter said, "Particularly disturbing is what seems to be a philosophical sanction for the behavior of the relatively small proportion of students who engaged in and the minority of the faculty that actively supported civil disobedience on the Berkeley campus last fall."

By June 18, 1965, the State Senate subcommittee which had been investigating the disturbances issued its opinion. They blamed a large part of the student unrest on communists. While they acknowledged that the Free Speech Movement was born from a broadly based coalition of campus groups, they concluded "that many of the communist organizations on the executive and steering committees of the Free Speech Movement were in firm control of the situation continuously after December 3, 1964." Generally, the Senate subcommittee report criticized President Kerr, stating that the "tolerance of the radical student groups, the opening of the campus to Communist Party officials, the reluctance to curb the activities of the most brash and defiant student rebels, and the obvious distaste for adequate security measures, speak for themselves." Kerr replied that he was "proud [to be] chief proponent of the open-forum policy that has resulted in the appearance on the campus of speakers of the left, right and center to a greater extent than at any time previously in the history of the university."

By October 1965 the general unrest seemed to be settling down. The movement consolidated the focus of its complaints on the Vietnam War. By this time, the movement had developed its own bureaucracy and had a plethora of specialized action groups suitable for any political action found desirable. Thus, having no other protests or causes which seemed pertinent to campus issues, the Vietnam Day Committee (VDC), headed by nonstudents such as Jack Weinberg and Jerry Rubin, got set for an upcoming "peace march" from the campus to the Oakland Army Terminal. Once again, they asked the university for support in the form of dismissing classed during the upcoming march. The university refused.

Meanwhile, the faculty had come to enjoy its new-found photo opportunity in the excitement of a real-life political movement. The Faculty Peace Committee appeared on campus, formed in reaction to many faculty member's apparent wish to dissociate themselves from the notoriety achieved by the VDC after it had tried unsuccessfully to block some troop trains. The Faculty Peace Committee achieved the most successful rally of 1965, yet total attendance was estimated to be only six hundred, very much down from the swelling crowds of 1964.

Berkeley's prominence as a sort of national Hyde Park Corner drew a wonderfully diverse assortment of protest activity to the area. The *New York Times* reported that the plaza in front of Sproul Hall hosted a wide range of activist groups including "anarchists, socialists, conservatives, radicals and the Free Student Union, the successor to [the previous] year's wildly successful Free Speech Movement." The new chancellor, Roger W. Heynes, allowed any form of political activity in this area, provided there were no associated violent disturbances.

In 1966, the whole enterprise of political demonstrations at Berkeley entered a cycle of longevity rivalling some of the most successful Broadway shows to date. There was a microphone set up as standard equipment outside of Sproul Hall that anyone who had registered with the university could use. However, A.H. Baskin of *Time* magazine reported that, by the end of 1966, no one was using it. At any rate, the university had been chastised, and the new-age administrators who had replaced earlier hardliners readily accepted the "decrepit system" view of early student demonstrators and eagerly accepted blame for themselves and for "society," that popular villain of the 1960s.

"Constitutional" reforms achieved by the movement were few, judging by measures formally approved by student organizations representing a majority of the student body. In May 1966 *New York Times* columnist E. W. Kenworthy reported that a "new constitution, which had been framed by left wing radicals, was overwhelmingly defeated." The proposed constitution had been drafted in a convention dominated by radical delegates, who gained control of the convention because their supporters voted as a block, whereas more moderate members of the student body had divided their votes among many delegates. The new constitution would have replaced the existing Associated Students of the University of California (ASUC) with an "autonomous" student government. Kenworthy described the new system as one which "would not be associated with the administration and the Academic Senate, but would be more like a labor union in opposition." In an undergraduate vote, the new constitution had failed to receive the two-thirds majority needed for adoption by a margin of 5,053 against, 3,529 for it. Kenworthy labelled the proposed constitution's defeat as a clear message from the "vital center" of the student body.

Reasons cited for the defeat include the following: "[T]he new constitution would have foisted a radical minority government on the majority and allowed the minority to issue statements in the name of the entire campus on every public issue: . . . [and] rejection of the new radical premise that student government was not an organic part of the university structure." Kenworthy noted the view of "[Jerry] Goldstein,

[ASUC president, who] said [the majority of students] recognized that the university community could not be a political community in which confrontation between interest groups is the normal way of life. An academic community, he added, is necessarily a cooperative enterprize in learning." The week of the vote, "the radicals withdrew from ASUC in order not to give 'legitimacy' to the present structure, thus exposing their view of campus democracy."

Strangely, this vote got almost no news coverage across the nation, whereas student demands and faculty and administrative rationalizations were covered constantly and fully. At the time when the supportive and traditional forces of student opinion were largely left unnoticed by the media, conservative faculty voices were entering a twilight zone of obscurity too. The voice of the majority just did not make for a sexy headline.

The *New York Times*, however, following its long-standing tradition of detailed investigative news reporting, quickly picked up that the campus movements were not supported by a majority of either teachers or students. In December 1966, an ongoing antiwar student strike appeared to be gathering faculty support. When the university responded to the strike, led by the ever-present Mario Savio and his Student Strike Committee, by summoning the police, the *Times* reported that "significant segments of the faculty . . . indicated . . . that they were supporting the boycott of classes to join in the protest against the administration's summoning of the police to break up an antiwar sit-in earlier in the week." But the "significant segments" did not constitute a large part of faculty; the *Times* own columnist Fred M. Hechinger attributed the troubles to "small minorities." Besides, the faculty were reacting more against the police summons than supporting the strike.

The Student Strike Committee said that "the real issue is the failure of the administration to understand that a university—in the highest sense of a community of scholars, a center of learning—must have students who do not necessarily hold registration cards." On the other hand, Hechinger reported the situation as involving "small minorities of activists . . . determined to arrogate to themselves—in the name of campus democracy—the right to speak for their peers." He described how radicals "capitaliz[ed] on conflicts which temporarily rally substantial numbers of the uncommitted." Hechinger attributed the seeming usurpation of the moderate majority's view by the extremists to:

> [T]he activists contempt for analysis and theory. . . . Convinced of the infallibility of their causes, many of the activists talk about 'participatory democracy,' but rather than persuading the majority of their contemporaries to participate, they often resort to demonstrations which momentarily create the impression that they speak for the mass. . . . [T]hey ignore the fact that a greater number of professors and students are not behind them. This makes them rebels with many causes but without a strong power base. But it is also an indictment of the majority of students who still are so disinterested that they seem hardly to be aware when minority spokesmen speak for them."

The strike had been called by the Council of Campus Organizations following arrests of nonstudents who picketed a Navy recruiting table. On December 1, the strike rallied as many as 5,000 students to boycott classes. After the wavering of 1965, the university began to firm up its position again. In an effort to reduce support for the demonstrators, the regents decided to issue a warning to strikers (whose members included teaching assistants on the university payroll), stating that those "who participate in any strike or otherwise fail to meet their assigned duties in an effort to disrupt university administration, teaching, or research, would thereby be subject to termination of their employment relationship with the university, denial of re-employment, or the imposition of appropriate sanctions." Before the regents' meeting, the Senate of the Associated Students of the University of California also withdrew its support of the strike. As Chancellor Heynes refused to negotiate with nonstudents, the number of strikers dwindled to 3,000. The students wanted assurances that police would not be called in to make arrests as they had for the Navy picketers. They also wanted amnesty for the arrested picketers and students charged with university rules violations as well as changes in the discipline system.

The "warning" seemed to have been effective. An amended version of a motion prepared by President Kerr and Theodore Meyer, chairman of the Board of Regents, passed with only one dissenting vote by Los Angeles businessman, Edwin A. Pauly. Pauly had proposed a motion (voted down by the regents) which would have directed action by the administration against all who had participated in the strike. Pauly said, "If they don't know the obligations of their jobs, then we don't want them as employees." Despite being "sick and tired of law violation at the Berkeley campus," Meyer added that he was "afraid to enforce the letter of the law without delivering this warning." At last the demonstrators had been finally warned that, if they violated civil and criminal laws, these laws would be enforced against them. It had taken two years to reach this position.

In 1967, the regents decided to dismiss President Kerr. Governor-Elect Ronald Reagan met with the regents and voted for the ouster. Governor Reagan denied that his vote for Kerr's dismissal was politically motivated. His vote with the 14-8 majority to oust Kerr, he said, was "not in the political ring at all" and he had "no intention of ever trying to overrule the Regents and engaging in arm twisting." He did consider the personal intervention by former Governor Edmund G. Brown to prevent Kerr's ouster two years earlier to be "political interference." As to his ability to influence the regents' vote, Reagan stated, "I doubt if I'm that persuasive." Believing that the people of California had lost faith in the university administration because of "long embroilment" in controversy, Reagan said, "People involved in that kind of controversy outlive their usefulness," displaying his genius for evoking common morality which later put him in the White House. As for the students, he remarked,

> No one orders them with a gun at their heads to go to the university. If they cannot obey the rules they have served notice that they no longer wish to be associated with it.

Throughout late 1966 and into 1967, the fact that none of the disruptions ever commanded anything like majority support became clearer, as one organization after another withdrew support for the strikes and protests. The American Federation of Teachers voted for a suspension of the strikes in late 1966. Student organizations also began to rally behind the anti-demonstrator movement. A meeting of about half the Berkeley faculty voted 452 to 315 to label recent events as "destructive political intervention."

Thus, by mid-1967, the fervor created during the Free Speech Movement had seemingly died out. Savio married and left for Oxford. Baskin summed up the typical student response to questions concerning

campus affairs: "You don't want to talk to me; I'm just here to study."
A highly unscientific sampling indicated that the "I'm just here to study"
crowd outnumbered activists by 32 to 3. The campus appeared to have
rejected the "Filthy Speech Movement" as juvenile. The most viable
organ of protest could be found in the Vietnam Day Committee
headquarters a few blocks off-campus. But even in the VDC headquarters, which employed 12 full-time nonstudent workers for $100 per
month, there was a downcast attitude about the vitality of the protest
business. One leader said, "You can't work up too much feeling about
going to jail around here; it's sort of commonplace."

In the end it was "just too bad" for everyone concerned. The flaw
in the university which proved its undoing was not some deep-rooted
defect in "the establishment" or some uncontrollable internal
deterioration affecting the majority of students and faculty, as the
demonstrators would have us believe. Rather, the university—its
administration and faculty— was unprepared at the outset to represent
effectively the tradition of the Academy.

Unfortunately for the administration, it allowed itself to be forced
into taking a stance on the students' terms and issues. Chancellor
Strong's uncomplicated approach would have been to deal with the
students according to the rules of the university, meaning punishment for
many of the students. University President Kerr thwarted that approach,
and Strong eventually was put on "sick leave" and then retired. The
problem was not that Kerr ultimately allowed solicitation by off-campus
political activists on campus. The problem was the way in which Kerr
allowed the students to force him into making that decision. Leaving the
merits of the issue itself (whether to allow off-campus activists on
campus) aside, nothing justifies Kerr's willingness to make the decision
on that issue under the conditions then present on the Berkeley campus.
There was a rule in place that banned political activity in that area. The
administration could have continued to overlook the rule, but allegedly
Strong began to feel some heat to enforce the rule. There had been talk
before the strict enforcement began of simply deeding the strip of land
to the city. Another alternative (though probably less inviting politically)
would have been to make Bancroft Strip just another of the already
designated free speech areas on campus with a special allowance for
solicitations. At this point the administration had a chance to smooth a

potential rough spot in student relations without any apparent, real, or perceived duress by the students. Regardless of the motivations behind enforcing the rule, however, Strong should not have been faulted for the enforcement itself. Once the wall separating faculty responsibility and authority from the students had been broken, firm action later on failed to achieve much that was constructive.

Students proved at Berkeley and elsewhere that faculty were administratively incapable of defining and defending their position in any firm and instructive way. The student challenges showed the lack of effective academic consensus which could have obstructed their attempts to revolutionize the university. Thus, even though the reformers did not command majority support anywhere, they had the tool with which to remake the institution over the slow-moving majority will. They had a window of opportunity within which to strike their stronger and more numerous enemy—the majority. They seized the opportunity at Berkeley, at Harvard, at Columbia, at Cornell, at place after place.

What a minority of students, a group of nonstudents and a minority of the faculty learned was that democracy is fragile in the context of a university. Indeed, it is fragile in any context, because the majority opinion on new issues is not a readily available datum with which to combat or deal with demands for change. Even where the majority position in any given institution is clear or predictable, the majority must rely upon some executive functionaries to execute and give expression to that will as demands are made by a minority. If there is no effective executive organ in place, or if it fails to operate, a minority can work a serious transformation of the institution before the majority will is ever expressed.

This lesson was not lost on the reformist minority at Berkeley, or at many other universities. They learned that serious inroads could be made into the custodial and conservative traditions of the Academy, despite the majority support these traditions still commanded. Reformers had grasped an effective anti-majoritarian strategy: play upon the weaknesses of university administration and its basic inability to withstand and respond to the antidemocratic fashion of the reformers. In one university after another, in the offices of the president or chancellor or provost, things just got too hot to handle.

For the most part these administrators proved to be extremely poor speakers for the great traditions of the university. They found it easier and more pleasant to treat the revolutionary developments besetting the nation's campus as corporate management would treat a labor problem. The independence from the faculty and increasingly bureaucratic nature of American university administration made it singularly ineffective in representing these traditions. In effect, the fashions of the minority have slowly defeated the traditions of the already beleaguered majority. The minority within the Academy learned that the abandonment or frustration of the traditions of the majority was, after all, not really so difficult. And the metamorphosis of the Academy has continued from that day to this.

Like many other great historical events, the student movement at Berkeley began in tragedy and ended in farce. The farcical end was assisted by the fact that the academy already harbored many who had no concept of the unique mission of the university in American culture and thus had no sense of their identity with any such mission. These new guardians of the groves united their voices and influence with the student body, who, as the uninitiated, did not and could not be expected to have an understanding of the nature of the institution.

The history of the Academic Abandonment culminated in tragedy when in 1970 automatic weapons fire finally drew the line at Kent State and Jackson State College in Mississippi. It was a line which could have been drawn within the cloistered halls of the Academy with dignity and fairness in 1964, with a view to leading the students by conviction and example, rather than stimulating them to a well-deserved contempt.

Guns were pulled at Columbia and Cornell, faculty and administrators harassed, threatened, and assaulted, and university property occupied and destroyed. For every such institution where the sword was actually drawn, dozens of others teetered on the brink of violence as mounting bands of excited students probed the Academy who ran their institutions, just to see if anything was still there.

The events within these schools at all levels mirrored those in the Great Society at large. By 1968, when Johnson decided against re-election, the real world affects of the Great Society were appearing. Portions of Harlem, Brooklyn, Rochester, Los Angeles, Jersey City and Detroit were under siege or in flames. In one rally in 1965, National

Guardsmen in Los Angeles killed 34 rioters and injured 856 more. Significantly, the urban civil deterioration was imitated on the campuses and worked its way through basic education all the way down through secondary and primary levels. The rats had been pursued, but the whole barn, the whole farm was now falling in flames. The unpopular and politically managed Vietnam War became a major subject of unsettlement and dissatisfaction among college students, but it was one of many which would attract the nation's student body.

CHAPTER SEVENTEEN

The New Grove

After the upheaval at the universities in the 1960s, a new wave of changes set in during the 1970s and 1980s. The last two decades brought a revolution in the universities' mission. The universities spawned a new wave of intellectuals who discovered the way to remake the traditional disciplines of the academy, from political science to history, into a system hostile to the middle-class American and the democratic system under which he flourished. Encouraged by legal educators and led by the Supreme Court, the same philosophical detachment from middle-class America overtook the judicial system. The media followed the intellectual fashion manufactured in the academy, and also became consistently anti-middle class. The universities found themselves at the center of a social revolution of their own making. More than any other institution, the universities became the originators of intellectual fashion hostile to the political and personal values of the majority, and became responsible for the spread of this hostile fashion.

Strangest of all, the vast majority of the individuals attacking middle-class America come from the middle class itself. What accounts for this? A large part of the answer to this question is too simple and obvious to be easily noticed. It is no coincidence that both the federal judicial system and the academic establishment operate under the principle of lifetime tenure. It has become practically impossible to dislodge an incumbent if he avoids prosecution for crime. Whatever the virtues of lifetime tenure, it certainly reduces accountability.

When well-positioned intellectuals escape the restraints of accountability, they are able to lose identification with the common American citizenry, including the five principles of democratic constitutional government that Arthur Sutherland described. They forget where they came from, and lose interest in the historical processes that gave the country greatness. Our country's key social, political, and governmental institutions have become a haven for a growing group of unaccountable intellectual emigrés from the middle class.

Factors other than tenure contributed to the growth and increased influence of our estranged intelligentsia. Tenure was combined with the phenomenal growth in the numbers of faculty during the postwar years. From 1955 to 1980, the number of faculty at full time institutions of higher learning more than quadrupled. This created a vastly increased and virtually self-contained market for the academic's work product. Though academics thought and wrote more and more for themselves rather than for any larger or more diverse public, their burgeoning numbers made the insular market for their ideas a commercial success. Book publishers could profitably produce and sell things that humanities faculties had written for each other. An even greater expansion in the numbers of students in colleges and universities from 1955 to 1980 further fattened the market. The standards by which a faculty member acquired tenure demanded a prodigious volume of written material produced according to the increasingly narrow and insular outlook and fashion of the cloistered academic. Thus the orientation of the academic work product was transformed as its volume grew geometrically. The insulation provided by lifetime tenure and the insulation from general market forces resulting from the expanded student and faculty population, which created a sort of insular "tenured market," gave the academic a detachment and durability he had never had before.

But neither the near-universal adoption of lifetime tenure nor the growth in numbers was the primary factor contributing to the estrangement of the academic from the average American. Most importantly, there is the psychological question: What makes so many academics behave the way they do? Do the structural peculiarities of their industry, such as tenure, etc. inexorably make them antagonistic to the value system of the majority as they understand it? This poses a more difficult question, as sensible understanding of basic human motivation always does. What we do know, however, is that, from the 1960s onward, the academic just did not see himself as a part of mainstream America. The job itself, and the "lifestyle" it represented, attracted what Eric Hoffer called the "chronically insecure" expatriates from bourgeois America as never before. It was the 1980s that released the full force of these alienated intellects on society. The sources of university finances were revolutionized after 1965. By the 1980s, a new combination of government and government-related sources were paying the piper, and the tune changed accordingly (see Table 16.1, above).

Ironically, the very values of Western culture which the academy nurtured made it a sitting duck for the zealous intellectual reformer. These values had created an extremely slow moving, deliberative democracy in which polite tolerance for divergent views was the general rule. This sluggish and mild-mannered democratic environment could not react effectively against the assault of a strident minority, who could mobilize a sizeable part of the student body for action on short notice. After the committed minority discovered in the 1960s that democracy was a fragile thing on campus, the university was well on its way to becoming a deep mine from which the raw material for flaying bourgeois America could be profitably extracted in hugh amounts. As events at Berkeley proved, the discovery of democracy's fragility on campus was the first great step in creating an influential academic minority capable of steering the university onto a totally new course.

The freedom from accountability inherent in his office allowed the new academic to achieve the first phase of his academic revolution. In the first phase, lasting from about 1965 to 1980, a powerful anti-bourgeois fashion merged, producing an avalanche of anti-bourgeois manifestoes of all sorts. The dedicated minority inundated the academy with critical revisionist scholarship. At first, the typical post-1960s humanities academic slowly built up the antidemocratic arsenal by altering the focus and content of traditional scholarship. Historical writing and teaching shifted from a collective account of America's rise as a nation to the story of the alleged victims. Even the history of the westward expansion of Americans in the nineteenth century was revised to provide an account of how America lost its values while increasing its real estate.

The Diversity Movement

The limits of this approach were soon realized, however. If all you did was produce alternative data (or even alternative interpretations of data) for the academy and its students to analyze, the new-age scholarship might be slowly evaluated, criticized, and possibly rejected outright. Thus, to truly transcend the traditions of the academy and to revolutionize its constitution, the reformers would have to extirpate the old system.

This realization brought us to the second phase of the academic revolution. The Phase Two programs for academic revolution were inspired by the academic minority's second great discovery: that it would be necessary to proceed from objective reform to subjective reform. You could not assure the revolution against the American bourgeois value system by merely putting new material before the student audience; you had to regulate their minds. In phase two, which has revved up since 1980, enterprising faculty reformers sought to go beyond the creation of alternative scholarship and moved to eradicate the older university traditions themselves, and the focus of the new programs became almost entirely subjective. Permitting the fate of the academic revolution to be influenced by the discussion of objective facts was seen by the reformers as an unacceptable risk. Thus they were no longer concerned so much with acts as with motive. The acid test for "correctness" (a term the reformers are fond of) became entirely subjective. We were told that certain approved minorities were not capable of committing the sin of racism because of their history of deprivation and victimization. What was permissible became a function of one's identification with a growing list of officially recognized victim groups, all because the motive and thus the justification for conduct was subjective, and was irrevocably defined by that group membership.

It all became terribly complex and moved beyond rational discussion. Yet the common premise of the middle-class emigré turned academic revolutionary remained the same, whether he or she appeared under the banner of "feminist studies," "peace studies," or any of the plethora of morally superior additions to the curriculum. The premise was that anything other than unquestioning support for the program of subjective reform was very, very bad, as was any word or action supportive of the old regime. To betray any sympathy for the old middle class and its values or institutions signified a subjective flaw, and meant that a subjective reorientation was necessary. Instead of reinforcing the values of democracy by example, the university launched an oppressive regime of subjective conformity. "Political Correctness" (PC for short) was born. The entire university experience was thus transformed. The strengths and flexibility encouraged by the traditional system of open discourse was replaced by a self-conscious atmosphere in which every student and faculty member was expected to become an actor playing his assigned part to perfection at all times. By this shift to the subjective, the new academics' propaganda program cleverly laid hold upon student insecurity and naiveté, taking the moral high ground as resolutely and dogmatically as any fundamentalist religion ever could. The new code word for subjective reform became "diversity."

Recently several versions of an advertisement circulated the Yale campus, calling on the student body to unite behind efforts to eliminate "discriminatory" intellectual activity in the name of diversity. One version reads as follows:

Are You This Educated Person?
It was the first day of Yale Law School and Wilona Juanita Wong was very excited. She had consulted the Course Schedule for her first class and was satisfied that the "esteemed and respected Professor" of Criminal Law would give a thought provoking lecture. While walking to class, Wilona Juanita Wong thought about how proud she was to be at Yale. Her grandmother had been at Yale thirty-five years ago . . . serving tea. En route to class from the Dining Room no one greeted Wilona. She had been the only one admitted from her inner city high school or city college. She felt alone.
Upon entering the classroom, Wilona looked up at the Professor who looked right through her. The Professor was like no one she knew from home. . . . she saw few reflections of herself on Yale's campus. Looking over the syllabus, she recognized names of the "great" white male writers and thinkers whom she had been taught to revere. She felt excluded, alienated, negated. She wondered if her writings and thoughts would ever be considered great. Would this Law school truly train her to challenge what was ahead?
She knew something was missing.
Is Yale Law School not for *her*?

How Challenging Is Your Law School
Education?

Are We Afraid To Challenge:
(a)   The Uniformity of Legal Scholarship Here?
(b)   The Uniformity of the Faculty Here?
(c)   The Uniformity of the Student Body Here?
(d)   Is Diversity in the Academy, in Scholarship, Faculty and
       Student Body So Threatening?

Monday, October 23rd, 6 p.m. Forum on Diversity
at Yale Law School.
Student Lounge
Sponsored by Committee on Diversity

Revealingly, the second version of the ad feature the most hated
object of such reformers, a WASP, who is exposed as odious *not*
because he feels excluded but because he *does not*. This version reads:

Are You This Educated Person?
       It was the first day of Law School Classes and Worthington
Worthington Worthington III was very excited. He had consulted the
Law School Course Critique for his first class and was satisfied that the
"esteemed and respected Professor" of Criminal Law would give a
thought provoking lecture. While walking to class, Worthington
Worthington Worthington III thought about how proud he was to be at
Yale Law, the school that all the men of his family had attended. En
route to the class from the dining room, Worthington was greeted by
seven of his classmates from his New England Prep school, Ivy League
undergraduate college, and friends with whom he had "done" Europe.
He felt at home.
       Upon entering the classroom, Worthington caught the attention
of the Professor who acknowledged his presence, returning his gaze.
The Professor reminded Worthington of one of his father's friends.
Looking over the syllabus, Worthington recognized the names of all of
the great writers and thinkers whom he had always revered. He felt
inspired. One day he too could be a great writer and thinker and a
"big" lawyer.

He thought the class was all that he needed.
Is he you?
Is Yale Law School only for *him*?

These vignettes from the Academy merit careful consideration because, like many of life's little things, they are so revealing. Significantly, Wilona Juanita Wong knows just what is wrong on the very day she arrives. The transformed universities from which Wilona and all her counterparts came had been successful at replacing education and genuine curiosity with dogma and genuine intolerance. Wilona and her friends thus came with a full-blown agenda for "reform" and the will to enforce it immediately. Their minds are so conditioned to discount even the possibility of discovery and surprise that they have no doubts about the defects which the university has or the evils it contains. They have no doubt about the need for the immediate transformation of the university or graduate school, and no doubt about the central concept or theory upon which their zeal for reform is founded: "diversity."

The proponents of the views these advertisements convey are for diversity, but of what? They do not enter law school fresh from a deep inquiry into the rich and ancient tradition which forged the basic tenets and theories which comprise the ideas of the "great" white male writers and thinkers they condemn. In other words, they have not weighed and rejected their ideas. They did not arrive at Yale Law School, or at the hundreds of others, contemplative of Sir Edward Coke's advice that "[K]nowledge of the law is like a deep well," requiring a deep and tireless look before reward comes. They did not come with a conviction evolved from any analytical tradition or philosophy. They did not analyze ideas as such, because to do so may lead to some agreement threatening to diversity.

Of course, diversity represents no fully elaborated system of philosophy. How much do they want, for example? Should every idea, every person to be different? Should each speak a different language? Should there be no common concepts (any one of which would be per se non-diverse)? Just what benefit, what great pleasures or good does the diversity provide? The notions of the good, the useful and the valuable upon which the ideas of the "'great' white thinkers and writers" rest evolved over approximately seven hundred years of application and experimentation. What are the rational and empirical foundations on which the sought-after diversity and openness rest? We don't know. All we do know is that an ethos, a conviction, has replaced research and science as the highest and best means, whatever the end might be.

Thus, few better symbols for the unguided student impulses typical of today's barren educational environment can be found than the avalanche of papers, pamphlets, placards, and petitions conveying precisely the same idea as the advertisements quoted above. What such persons have sought to do for over twenty years is in fact to level and obliterate the distinction between an educated and uneducated person, and to stifle the suspicion that the question is even worth asking. It's as if the patient with appendicitis showed up at the operating theater determined to direct his own operation. Only those great ideas produced by the creative consensus of the past which are beyond the student reformer's reach remain safe. $E=MC^2$ seems to be secure, though it has certainly gained the support of a consensus of great white thinkers and writers. Unfortunately, the things which are beyond their understanding but not beyond their reach are the first victims of such reform.

Many say that resistance to modern educational reforms reflects the essentially conservative character of educators. They are right. Education *is* conservative because it has to be. It is based on conservation, just as much as it is based on experimentation with the new and untried. Traditionally, the Academy creates and conserve things of value to pass on to wayfarers in the Academy, to those passing through the groves. Significantly, the Great Society version of education, which has proven so indelible, aims not to impart anything but to release something already there. The objective is simply to "be" open, to "be" diverse, to realize the self. When this collective whim of the unguided student was imposed upon the Academy as its guiding principal, the transaction which was supposed to take place in the Academy, the *educare*, was inverted. In the tradition of the Academy, the *corpus scientiae*, the great body of knowledge which they pursued, preserved and transmitted, was supposed to be greater than the capacity of any one individual to comprehend. Now to the contrary, the commitments of the Great Society education, represented so forcefully by the Yale advertisements, are self-evident, and thus capable of immediate execution.

In the 1980s the zealous reformers and their converts, though still a minority, endeavored to obliterate ideas which ran counter to their own by aiming their regulations directly at the students' subjective condition. These ideas roughly identified with Western culture were not to be permitted to exist, even as alternatives to the new fundamentalist scholarship. Around 1980, the new academics began in earnest to eradicate the old system root and branch, and expel those who had a good word for it. A close look at the regulatory efforts and administrative apparatus dedicated to Phase Two at Duke University, Smith College, Oberlin College, Berkeley, and dozens of others will quickly convince the skeptic. It is interesting to note that, in Phase Two of the Academic Abandonment, the newly empowered tenured reformers have aimed the greater part of their efforts at the students, who are still essential in preserving the hold which the committed faculty minority has over the soul of the university.

At an astonishing number of what were formerly regarded as America's top institutions, the Phase Two programs to control the students personal and political orientation are in full swing. At such places, the very nomenclature of higher education has been transformed, reflecting the transformation in the content and its intended effect. Feminism, deconstructionism, racism, ethnocentrism, sexism, heterosexism, ableism, lookism, political correctness, and a host of other concepts sheltered under the umbrella of "diversity" has fueled a fundamentalist attack on learning itself. For example, under the "Smith Design," a thought and action code for Smith College promulgated under the authority of college president Mary Dunn, all criticism of practices that are "politically correct" per se, such as race-based admissions quotas, is forbidden. Additionally, faculty and administrative salaries are increasingly linked to demonstrated commitment to "multiculturalism." At many major institutions of higher learning in the country, mandatory "adjustment" sessions are required of students and faculty who betray any of the loathsome "isms" of Western culture. At many places, such as Duke University, they even have to take a test upon admission to disclose whether they harbor any of the horrid expanding list of "isms," which are growing in number like Topsy. If the student thinking is not quite right, some attitude adjustment sessions are in order. Every gesture, every expression, every statement is scanned under a rarified and ultrasensitive code of action, thought and behavior promulgated under university authority. The new orthodoxy finally ends by treating learning and free discourse as intrinsic evils.

The efforts at subjective control also extend to new faculty initiates. In fact, the institution of tenure itself has become an instrument for enforcing the new-age academic's anti-majoritarian code. At numerous colleges, the aspiring academic is rigorously scrutinized to be sure his or her views are "politically correct" or show the right orientation to diversity. Ken Kelsey of Penn State University advises that "faculty who fail to embrace the richness of diversity" should be informed that they will not receive tenure.

The Church of Diversity

The greatest mistake any observer of the "diversity" controversy on campus can make is to assume it is a rational movement. Admittedly, this would be a logical assumption, and would link the diversity movement to the long university tradition of rational inquiry. However, the diversity movement is something altogether new. The fact is, it is a genuine fundamentalist non-rational mass movement, entirely dependent on the non-rational elements of human psychology. It is a new fundamentalist secular church, not a rational political movement at all.

In the mid-1980s, the new-age academic realized that some form of subjective reeducation and control would be absolutely necessary if any of the other programs of the new academic, such as race-based standards and quotas, were to ever succeed. The reason for this is simple. Consider the actual effect of a race-based quota system on school admissions or membership in a professional organization. All that such a program can do is to assure a pre-determined, racially defined representation in some group. You can assure that 12 percent or 20 percent of all law students or medical students are black. With considerable effort, you can assure that a set percentage of all licensed lawyers and doctors are black. But exactly what effect does this have in a social and economic marketplace where individuals will naturally pursue some objective definition of performance? Specifically, patients do not as a rule select a physician for a specialized operation because of his race. A client with an admiralty or anti-trust problem does not look for legal services based on the ideology of diversity. The objective reality of the marketplace tends to be non-ideological. The physical reality of concrete science, concrete skills and concrete abilities is inescapable. The heart patient rests easier with a physician selected for his proven skills. The obstinate individual in the marketplace will attempt to seek out performance more verifiable by objective reality than ideology. If the individual in the marketplace—the customer, the client, or the patient—behaves this way, the result is that the profits of professional enterprise will still go to the most able, whatever their race, despite the achievement of the pre-determined racial percentage in the relevant workforce.

Thus, the shift to subjective indoctrination in phase two of academic reform was an attempt to drive the prevalent human proclivity for objective reality from the marketplace. All disciplines in which objective reality was a measure of success would henceforth be subject to subjective tests. In short, it was necessary for the proponents of the diversity movement to get themselves a fundamentalist religion rather than a rationale. You cannot convince people to handle dangerous reptiles with scientific arguments. You cannot convince a diabetic to risk his life on a minimalist microbiotic diet with scientific arguments. Thus was born the Church of Diversity.

The objective was to generate a whole new congregation of student converts who would be weaned from objective reality and inflamed with a revulsion for traditional learning. The result would be a marketplace where the consumer, the client, the customer, and the patient could comfortably act ideologically, without rationally questioning the consequences. This is why the diversity movement has all the accoutrements of Puritanism at its worst. The rigid formalism, the demand for unswerving loyalty, and the fundamental intolerance of opposition are its hallmarks. The diversity movement is a calculated departure from reason, and an abandonment of the customs and practices which accompany the pursuit of reason, such as tolerance and open dispute. It is a fundamentalism demanding blind zeal and inspired dogma. It is a secular religion where any skeptic immediately faces a modern-day Cotton Matther with a Yale Ph.D., who will send him personally and professionally straight to hell for questioning the devine message of diversity. Ask any professor who has transgressed its intricate rules, or questioned its validity.

Like all basically non-rational fundamentalist creeds, the Church of Diversity has its own Devil. His name is Discrimination, and he is greatly feared. The apostles of diversity are thus fearful of any reappearing trend or practice which would break through the treasured diversity behind which they seek freedom from the fearful power of the discriminating mind and its handiwork.

If we can choose beginning point for the evolution of the powerful antidemocratic forces we have analyzed in this book under the name of "Abandonment," the choice would be higher education. From journalism to the law, the new emancipated intellectual became dominant in the academy, and dished up a serving of anti-bourgeois concepts which astonished all observers in its volume and its intensity. It was also astonishing in its successful muting of the voice of the majority. Above all, the new-age intellectual desires to be heard, be respected and to control. Professor Stanley Fish of Duke University expresses the essence of the modern academic motive. When asked by Fred Seigel, a teacher and writer, what he wanted most, Fish answered, "I want to be able to walk into any first-rate faculty anywhere and dominate it, shape it to my will. I'm fascinated by my own will."

These, then, are the key ingredients to the academic revolution of the last thirty years: the will of the academic zealot to dominate, his discovery that the will of the majority is so vulnerable, his determination to experiment with subjective regulation, and his flight from reason. Increasingly, these factors have shaped university history since 1965.

The result is that the humanities departments and the law schools of America's major universities now are the well-insulated originators of middle class torment. Universities and law schools have thus increasingly become the factories where the tools for abusing middle America are hammered into shape. No academic has been better positioned than the law professor to directly influence the course of democratic government. His antidemocratic theorizing about judicial power has been immensely popular with the high court, which now finds that its unprecedented power has been awarded the very highest academic pedigree and approval. The legal academic has converted traditional scholarship, which induced a degree of judicial accountability and honesty, into the artful apology for unwarranted judicial power. The rigid orthodoxy of this new post-democratic fashion rules the law school as firmly as the new-age academic rules the university. The hostile detachment of the federal judiciary has proceeded along the same lines as that of the academy. No other country on earth has adopted the combined principles of lifetime tenure and final judicial review of the actions of coordinate government branches. Over the long haul, this has proven to be tailor-made for estrangement from the population at large.

Thus the academic became insulated from accountability to any constituency other than the insular club to which he belonged, and successfully escaped the discipline or influence of any generalized market for his work or his ideas. His profession also assumed a personality decidedly hostile to the fundamental beliefs by which a majority of the American public measured membership in the middle class. One may define "middle class" as that group which believes itself to be middle class, and believes that the personal and political values identified with the majority—democracy, constitutional government, and the like—are more or less good things. Likewise, the academic profession was shaped by a similar self-selection process, by which the academic adopted a conscious hostility to middle-class precepts. He now endeavors to imprint this hostile code on the mind to the student. The estranged academic intellectual perhaps still is a minority of the university's total population, and yet he is able to successfully dominate its learning environment. The democrat moves much more slowly than the anarchist, especially when the democrat is tolerant and thoughtful of others and the anarchist is intolerant and fervent. Thoughtful analysis and the amenities democracy engenders seem unable to compete with fanaticism in the short run.

All this came directly on the heels of the greatest period in the development of American higher education, and took place at a time when the respect for the academy had never been higher. The fantastic credibility of the academy at the onset of the 1960s revolution enabled the academic to mount his initial attack on the majority without much opposition. The respect which the academy enjoyed has caused the majority to listen politely if not attentively as the attack intensified over the years. This permitted the disaffected emigré academic to squander the credibility of centuries in one generation. It has transformed the image of the academic in our popular culture, and the sustained and ongoing deterioration in the credibility of the academy will make the great potential of the university even harder to realize in the future.

What, then, has been the effect of this transformation of today's university on students? What, exactly, is being done for or to them while they attend the groves of academe in the last half of the twentieth century? In the beginning of the 1960s revolution, students instinctively recognized the traditional mission of the university at the outset of the Great Society revolution. They intuitively saw it as a repository and custodian of culture and knew it had great importance and influence.

However, as the revolution progressed, students entering our colleges and universities perceived with uncanny accuracy the institutions' abandonment of any independent mission. At the moment of entering college, they were summarily left to pick among the ruins left by the previous generation's servile professors who had long since fled their posts. In a way, not much remained to attack. Today anyone glancing through a student newspaper at any institution of higher learning will notice an interesting phenomenon, one that strikes a moderately independent observer as odd and counterintuitive. For these publications show that the university now is one of the few places where those entering, those who have never resided, matriculated, or had any first-hand experience with what these once-revered institutions stood for, *arrive* with a conviction and determination to set the agenda of the institution themselves. So great has been the vacuum left by the breach of trust and flight of the Academy that the new arrivals have practically no natural respect, no curiosity, no developed instinct for discovery about that which they are supposed to encounter at the university. By some strange and efficient grapevine, they instinctively know that, for the most part, there is not much there. As Lyndon Johnson squandered national respect for the office of president, the academics threw away the residual reverence which most of society had for them.

The new-age academic's demands in the name of diversity represent the strangest part of the whole story. Reasonably and logically, a call for more diversity would be expected to *add* to the traditional university curriculum. Having more and different subjects open to students arguably makes the university more diverse, and is in fact consistent with the evolutionary tradition by which the university had developed its offerings over its long history. Yet, this was not at all what the intellectual advocates of diversity ultimately demanded. By a strange and incoherent logic, diversity required the complete repudiation of the traditional university canon and all the concepts and values upon which it was based. The reformer's argument was that the traditional university curriculum (to the extent it existed at all in any generally accepted form) had not included the newly discovered "diverse" subjects which were being developed by the dozens by the new academics. The existing curriculum was thus condemned without much of a trial as an unfair and corrupt manifestation of the oppressiveness and ethnocentricity of the society in which it had developed. One of the most amazing stories in the entire history of education is the overnight condemnation of the academic tradition by a new wave of educators, and their ability to mobilize a revolution against the traditional academy by a vocal minority, much the way a minority of Berkeley had challenged and changed the university there.

There was and is something totally new about the psychology of the reformers and their diversity platform. The most important revelation of the new and highly intellectual approach was that diversity really did not mean diversity at all. In other words, the objective of the student minority was not to diversify the established curriculum of the academy with new additions. Rather, diversity was a catch word by which the existing curricular was condemned for not *already* containing the newly popular selection of "relevant" subjects, the plethora of "studies" which has overtaken curricular everywhere. Having failed to *already* include the favored new offerings, it was tainted. The selectivity by which the curriculum had been slowly defined over the course of history had not yet included these new and worthy subjects, and revealed that the curricular content common to many colleges and universities was yet another manifestation of the bad motives of its creators. The traditional college curriculum was not so much reevaluated according to its content as it was convicted of a moral crime because of its limitations.

Significantly, this quickly moved the debate away from the utility or merit of curricular content to the moral fault in which it originated. The curriculum was viewed much the same as a convicted felon who, though he might be found to have some redeeming qualities if you looked into it, was nonetheless convicted and so must be punished. The swift takeover of the moral high ground was a brilliant rhetorical triumph. It permitted the accusing minority to prosecute and convict the university curriculum before the slow moving adherents to the traditions of the university even found out that it had been indicted. It became possible to demand the abolition of the traditions which formed the very constitution of the universities without analytical dialogue or analysis.

The new-age reformers waived the morally flawed pedigree of the university curriculum like the bloody shirt, and, as a piece of public relations strategy and propaganda, it worked. The hostility which the minority, who hated the democratically based traditions of the university, formerly directed toward the Asian war, now found a new focus in racial, ethnic, and gender terms. To these were added any other incongruous element which would permit the minority to Balkanize and weaken the Academy even further: sexual orientation, disease, weight and so on.

The Enforcement of Diversity

Most people do not realize the extreme degree of hypersensitivity and preciousness which much of the Academy and its students have achieved. Yale University is perhaps the paradigm in the newly raised consciousness. Recently, a world renowned writer and teacher of French, Pierre Capretz, was called down for "sexist" innuendo in his "French in Action" audio and visual materials, materials acknowledged to teach French with astounding efficiency and speed. The problem with Capretz's work is that it depicts various encounters between a soap-opera type of American college student, Robert; a French student, Jean-Pierre; and a French girl, Mirielle. The photography of Mirielle was faulted for visually revealing that Mirielle was, in fact, a girl (you could tell, say the critics, by her legs and her chest). Moreover, Robert appeared to be attracted to Mirielle and actually spoke to her in a way some might style "romantic." In response, a senior majoring in literature, Tracy Blackmer, initiated a formal sexual harassment complaint against Professor Capretz for portraying the fictional Mirielle as "an object of desire that gets young men to learn French." This complaint invoked the jurisdiction of a four-member faculty review committee in charge of censoring improper sexual content in university courses. The committee was highly critical of Professor Capretz's materials. One professor was disturbed that Professor Capretz had not included anything in the film which would teach students how sexist Jean-Pierre really is. The professor remarked: "Rather than having students learn to be Jean-Pierre, we could have them learn to tell him how to get lost, or talk about how the guy is a jerk, or about ways in which this is a sexist situation." Proving himself a rare man among academics, Professor Capretz said that he wouldn't change one thing about his course, "French In Action."

At Yale, Professor Capretz' intransigence has resulted in the appointment of a task force which met during the summer of 1990 to review the way in which "French In Action" is presented and to review the teaching materials that Professor Capretz will be permitted to use.

The episode is instructive. At first glance, it is curious that anyone would so willingly assert such restrictions on what traditionally has been viewed as the professor's well-guarded prerogative. Why do we have eager regulators springing forward to enforce procedures intrusively restrictive of their own freedom? The simple answer is familiar to anyone who spends time around universities and the organizations in which faculty politics transpire—conformity to sociopolitical orthodoxy is so powerful that these academic regulators never seriously consider that they need to be on the side of free expression and academic freedom. They do not see such values as useful outside their service to the orthodox causes which guide and dominate faculty politics and organization, i.e., "sexism," "racism," and all the perceived "isms" implied by behavior not meeting their approval.

If this same principle of official review were applied to the reformers to monitor and regulate the degree of sexual explicitness of a course, they would probably react with piercing howls invoking the First Amendment and academic freedom. However, the most significant subjective feature of the whole abandonment process is that most academics *never* envision that the principles of review or rules of behavior they make will be applied to them. Nothing reveals more clearly that the academic reformers do not think in terms of principles at all—only results. The unshakable conviction that official coercion will be employed only to serve their views and the related belief that the coercion will never be directed at them testify to both the extreme conformism and intolerance of such individuals. Perfectly happy to make rules outside the framework of constitutional principles, the intellectual thus remains convinced that doing so poses not the slightest risk or inconvenience to himself. This manipulative, result-oriented detachment from others and satisfaction with an orthodoxy enforced by the use of coercive procedures which do not apply to all people alike form the subjective essence of abandonment. This attitude makes the acts of abandonment possible.

The "French in Action" episode is replicated at major universities across the entire country, usually on an even broader scale. The most general manifestation of the collapse of academia is the current PC movement, shorthand for "politically correct" thinking. PC thinking seeks to abolish the traditional curriculum in its entirety, and replace it with a series of exercises designed to encourage, well, "PCness." The University of Texas has moved into the vanguard, initiating a freshman program called "Writing on Difference," in which students replace the study of literary classics with a series of assigned essays on racism, affirmative action, and so forth. Predictably, the fundamental precept of the PC movement is that the white Western male, that same old villain, has created a cultural milieu in which he is mainly occupied with repressing everyone but white Western males. The rhetoric of PC proponents is sonorous—it is soaring. White Western culture has prevented the celebration of "otherness." The result has been, according to a Stanford University PC promoter, that "We, the non-Western-Europeans, have no greatness."

The PC movement has generated its own rigid orthodoxy, removing numerous subjects altogether from debate or discussion. Those who would even raise a question about PC objectives are immediately indicted as guilty of the worst of thought crimes, the classic trilogy of sexism, racism, and homophobia. In the Church of Diversity, they have committed blasphemy. The end result, in the words of Bard College President Leon Bolstein, is that "The idea of candor and the deeper idea of all discourse is dead." Most campuses now have slid comfortably into what Roger Kendall, the author of *Tenured Radicals*, calls "liberal fascism."

The traditionalists on the faculty almost everywhere have been constructively herded off into isolation. They had better not open their mouths, as Professor Gribben at the University of Texas found out. He questioned certain parts of the new "Writing on Difference" program, and was denounced by the campus newspaper and at a student rally. "I just wanted to question a few features and my world fell apart," he remarked. Professor Gribben reflected, "In December 1987, I held up my hand and made a vote against a program for ethnic and Third World literature. That was the end of my career here." Professor Gribben resigned his position at the University of Texas in May 1991, and will take up teaching at Auburn University this fall. At least, if a parent sends a child to the University of Texas, and learns it is a joke, he can find consolation in the fact that it is a much more reasonably priced joke than Stanford or Yale.

The members of the Academy, the faculty, cannot be depended upon to revive themselves or their institutions. They have created a professional world where performance is measured more and more by philosophical orientation. It is remarkably easy. However, the students are turning out not to be so gullible and opportunistic. Remarkably, they are becoming acutely aware that their enormous tuition payments go to fund the academic joke. Many students are furious. Consequently, student opinion on campus after campus is turning to dissent from the PC orthodoxy. We are witnessing a sort of methodological return to the 1960s, but with a different message. Additionally, conservative and dissenting newspapers are springing up in campuses around the country.

Charles Horner is president of a conservative Washington, D.C.-based group which raises funds for such unorthodox campus papers called the Madison Center for Educational Affairs. Mr. Horner states that the student reaction to the transformation of the university "is the single most significant in undergraduate intellectual life in the country right now."

Mr. Horner sums up the student feeling:

> These kids have a growing sense that they are not getting their money's worth out of their college education because they feel that if they express themselves, the professors put them down as bigots or morally wrong. They have found that universities are interested in diversity, but only racially, not intellectually.

Ironically, the students are now forming the best counterbalance to new university orthodoxy.

Such phenomena as the PC Movement occur often enough today that few informed people remain who actually see the university as a place of tolerance and mutual respect among creative individuals. Such people should follow the campus news at Yale and its numerous counterparts around the country. The aggressive intolerance which they would see acted out regularly and the suffocating administrative presence that the intolerance has spawned would soon disillusion them. Sadly, the nation's universities, having abandoned their traditional calling for the most part, now produce succeeding generations of persons inured to the incessant regulatory squabbles of their intolerant mentors and teachers. The shining lights are still there, even in the regulatory landscape. But they are rare and progressively less resistant to the sexism review boards and task forces actively promoting the social orthodoxy of the university community, which has abandoned the individual.

The demand for greater "pluralism" has now worked significant change in the curriculum of almost every major university. The primary beneficiaries of the new demand have been professionals in fields emphasizing race and gender as academic subjects. Typical of the new fashion is Henry Louis Gates, Jr., W.E.B. Dubois Professor of Humanities at Harvard University. Professor Gates specializes in promoting African-American literature. He accompanies the promoting with attacks on what he describes as "the Killer Bs"—Alan Bloom and William J. Bennett. The views of both Bloom, whose best-selling *Closing Of The American Mind* criticized the modern Academy, and former Secretary of Education Bennett are regarded by Gates as part of the wrongheaded opposition which has kept the Academy from committing itself fully to satisfying student demand for pluralism. Gates intones all the right buzz-words and frequently decries "white male western culture" and its pernicious influence on good education, calling himself a "race man."

Gates launched his career in literary anthropology by finding a worn copy of the autobiography, written in 1859, of an obscure free black woman. According to critics, who are numerous, Gates published a new edition of the book, *Our Nig*, and applied to it the arcane jargon of modern technical literary criticism. One supportive Harvard professor stated that Gates had "found a way of asserting the existence of a separate black American tradition, and of asserting this in a way that places the black American tradition at the cutting edge of literary theory." Others said that "Gates has merely found a gimmick."

This kind of dialogue is neither remarkable nor wrong if it occurs in a setting which truly values pluralism. But the orientation is always adversarial, aimed at supplanting and combating what are seen not only as different cultural expressions but also as rival ones. The process reveals the degree to which the new academic regards scholarship as something akin to writing a legal brief: nothing is spared in the application of technical reasoning in order to make a point and suppress one's opponent. Because the end of the process is not to discover but to suppress, the gap between these two objectives grows large indeed.

Professor Gates could not have been clearer about his position on this issue, and for his honesty he is to be commended. As he said,

> Sure, there will be second-rate blacks hired, but it will take till eternity for the number of second-rate blacks in the university to match the number of second-rate whites.

At least we have one honest recognition that the long-term prospect of the university under the prevailing political climate will be a racially balanced workforce of second-raters.

Unfortunately, the impressive accomplishments of many black scholars and women scholars have been obscured by the predominance of such propaganda in the newly emerged race-and gender-related academic offerings. The propagandist movement retards genuine development of minorities just as surely as the destruction of common individual rights by the Supreme Court has done. Consequently, the number of black Ph.D.'s and engineering degrees has been declining in recent years, as has black enrollment in graduate and professional schools. Those most affected by the new-age scholarship will be ideologically sound according to the new lights of race and gender instruction, but professionally will be unprepared. The thrust of new-age scholarship on race and gender assumes that the primary goal of education should be the acquisition of the right mental attitude, rather than the right mental skills. The substitution of feelings for the pursuit of knowledge is thus claiming a whole new set of victims.

The conscious abandonment of principled decision making in higher education is starkly revealed in the April 1991 controversy at Georgetown Law Center over the law school's admissions policy. A third year law student named McGuire published an article in the law school newspaper which reported that the law school operates under a race-based admissions policy, which applies different standards to blacks than those applied to whites. Mr. McGuire supported his statements with data he acquired from the law school admission's records, to which he had access as a part-time employee in the admission's office.

Significantly, the immediate reaction of the law school administration was to censure Mr. McGuire, denounce his actions, and begin a disciplinary inquiry. The administration action had the support of a vocal minority of the student body. Incredibly, the dean of the law school, Judith Areen, denied that any such race-based policy existed.

Then the travails of Mr. McGuire took a more interesting turn. His disclosure attracted national attention, both from leading newspapers and from CNN Broadcasting, which featured a debate on Mr. McGuire's actions on Pat Buchanan's "Cross Fire" program on April 18, 1991. By then, the official position of Mr. McGuire's offense had altered significantly. The thrust of his offense was that he had violated certain "confidentiality" obligations relating to his position as an employee with access to student files. A representative of the law school's Black Law Students Association appeared on the Cross-Fire program, and found no hesitation in saying that, if an employee in Mr. McGuire's position had discovered an admission's policy which discriminated *against* blacks, he should be applauded for reporting it, while at the same time maintaining that Mr. McGuire should be expelled for violating the "confidentiality" rules by reporting the reverse.

The most instructive thing about the position of Dean Areen, the law school administration, and the vocal element of the student body is that the merits or truth of Mr. McGuire's assertions were deemed irrelevant. Not only irrelevant, but worthy of suppression and censure.

Ironically, no other principle or philosophy receives more lip-service in today's law school creed than freedom of speech. It harmonizes nicely with the oft-repeated platitudes which echo through the law schools just as they do through college facilities everywhere: that we are a free and open community of truth-seekers, fearlessly defending the right of mankind to have the manifold benefits of all the facts. We are told that "scholarship," the most repeated word in the faculty vocabulary, merely describes the vital work product of these bold truth-seekers, who rely on the bright light of open debate to produce their lasting treasures. Yet there will be no open discussion by these scholars on the truth or merits of what Mr. McGuire reports. When any of the sacred and non-discussable subjects arises in today's scholarly university, particularly in the law schools with their vocal free-speech credo, the reaction is *always* the invocation of some diversionary sanctions, and a refusal to debate.

Under the bright light of national press coverage, the administration at Georgetown University Law Center decided to allow Mr. McGuire to graduate, but to give him a letter of reprimand. A member of the Black Law Students Association expressed disappointment that the law school "would okay somebody's racial harassment of a group of students." McGuire's critics obviously wanted him expelled for reporting the fact that blacks are evaluated under a different standard than whites, and called for "some kind of concrete measure to prevent this type of harassment or attack."

In fact, *every* law school known to these authors practices a preferential admissions program which applies different, lower standards of admission for blacks than whites. The law school where the authors of this book teach does so. Everyone connected with legal education knows this is so.

For example, the University of Texas School of Law recently released data on the classes admitted in 1989 and 1990. The figures starkly reveal that they follow a race-based admissions system. The figures are presented in Table 17.2.

TABLE 17.2

University of Texas Law School Admissions

Academic Index (max. pts. =88)	White Applicants		Black Applicants		Mexican-American applicants	
	# admitted	# denied	# admitted	# denied	# admitted	# denied
85-88	13	—	—	—	2	—
80-84	108	—	1	—	3	—
75-89	245	40	—	—	12	—
70-74	73	302	4	—	12	—
65-69	4	323	11	—	36	1
60-64	—	168	12	4	9	13
TOTAL:	443	833	28	4	74	14

TOTAL ADMITTED: 545
TOTAL DENIED: 851

The Academic Index is computed by multiplying an applicant's undergraduate grade point average by 10, then adding the applicant's Law School Admission Test score, which ranges from 10 to 48. This produces a number which combines undergraduate performance with standardized testing. At the University of Texas Law School, the white applicant with an Academic Index of 70-74 had less than one chance in four of gaining admission. A black applicant had a 100 percent chance of acceptance. For scores of 65-69, a white applicant had a .01 percent chance of admission, while a black applicant had a 100 percent chance, if chance is the right word.

Every law school administration vigorously denies that they *actually* follow a race-based admission standard. They say that the final admission decision for each applicant is based on a host of *very* complicated factors. However, the numbers do not lie. If any law school in America has an admissions profile which differs from that at Texas, *or* if there is some other factor which correlates more readily than race with the admission decision, they should immediately send this information to the Education Watch, conducted by *The New Republic* magazine, 1220 19th Street, N.W., Washington, D.C. 20036. There is no need for any law school to suffer the unfair suspicion that they do not follow racially neutral admissions policies. Everyone can come forward with a simple chart and clear up the whole thing.

Enforcement of race-based standards is not confined to private organizations or institutions. To the contrary, college and law school accrediting associations now act in concert with the federal government. For example, the U.S. Department of Labor under the Reagan administration began a practice known as "race norming." Under this practice, state employment agencies and some departments of the federal government were told by the Labor Department to rig the scores of minority group members on standardized aptitude tests. Thirty-eight state employment agencies used the Labor Department's General Aptitude Test Battery, and then, at the insistence of the Labor Department, arbitrarily curved the scores according to race. As with the colleges, law schools, and collegiate accrediting associations, the federal government pursued its race-based practices well away from public scrutiny. Rather than have open debate in Congress, federal administrators simply began to enforce "race norming" on their own.

Colleges, law schools, and their accrediting associations have simply imitated the adjudicative posture of federal agencies like the Labor Department. They administratively create and enforce a race-based agenda that is widespread, secretive, and without any general support in society. Critical standards for everything from schooling to employment are further insulated from democracy.

Thus, the actual operative principles used by these people must be kept secret, and all efforts to articulate exactly what the operative rules are must be suppressed. Nowhere is the bad state of academic abandonment more vividly revealed than in the law faculties, with their enthusiastic public preaching about free speech, and their private censorship. Yet the eagerness of our secretive scholars to use race as a dispositive factor in bestowing valuable privileges and opportunities has proven to be political dynamite. Their furtive and dishonest behavior and its larger implications reveal why race finally became, in America's constitutional credo, different from other factors. The vast majority was finally amenable to the wisdom of excluding race as a basis for privilege or disadvantage. Now, the country and its legal system will have to dislodge the secretive monopoly which the zealous race regulators of academe have created before any lasting, respectable and successful protection of minority interests can evolve.

As its disdain for the middle class grew, the objectives of the Academy became progressively removed from the educational process. In 1989, for example, the then president of the Association of American Law Schools, Herma Kay Hill, announced her view of the main objectives of legal education (entitled "An Agenda for a Shared Future"):

> [W]e must undertake a more concrete and sustained effort to bring women, minority, and gay and lesbian law professors into the mainstream of legal education, so that these colleagues can offer our profession their unique insights without fear of being marginalized.

The Association of American Law Schools and the American Bar Association are the two principal accrediting organizations for American law schools. The Association of American Law Schools (AALS) let slip its real position on the perseverance of middle-class values in a recently released report on the effects of amendments to the federal Age Discrimination and Employment Act, which forbade the use of age as a basis for compulsory retirement policy. The report, prepared by the Executive Director of the AALS, Betsy Levin, concluded that these amendments would not likely result in law schools full of ancient incompetents, stating that "doddering professors unable to teach their classes are not likely to be a problem." What *was* a problem emerged toward the end of the report:

> However, while age is not a problem, there is a non-retiring cohort of the senior faculty members that may create some problem for the entry of young new professors, especially racial and ethnic minorities and women, into the legal teaching profession.
> The senior law faculty are, by national standards, distinctively wealthy, highly educated, white males. It is likely that they not only teach the law but also a certain way of viewing the world and an accompanying value system. This may be a problem because the present composition of the senior law faculty does not reflect the

general population, let alone that of their students in law school. This problem, of course, might be exacerbated by allowing this cohort of law professors to continue to teach indefinitely.

Here again the leaders of education have incautiously betrayed their true fears—that the hideous "way of viewing the world and accompanying value systems" of senior teachers may continue longer than it would presumably would if the institutions *could* use age discrimination to expel these members. Interestingly, there is no need to explain what makes the value system of these miscreant holdovers so vile, except that their "composition" does not "reflect" the general population and the student body.

Like virtually all mainline academic associations, the Association of American Law Schools itches to regulate and reform the character of everyone within its sphere of influence. Indeed, it has fashioned a clever scheme to extend its authority beyond member schools and to directly reach practicing members of the legal profession. One of the Association bylaws requires member schools to actively regulate the actions of all lawyers or law firms who wish to interview students from such schools, or who wish to transmit information to students about possible job openings. Interestingly, the Association's objective in doing this is *not* to ensure compliance with any applicable law touching discrimination. In Explanatory Memorandum Number 91-33, sent to member schools on April 1, 1991, the Association made it clear that the schools were expected to actively monitor and regulate discrimination "based upon the listed grounds" set forth in official Association directives, "even if that discrimination is not illegal under applicable federal, state or local law." The purpose of this procedure is to coerce the bar into conformity with social policies which go far beyond any current legal requirement. The Association of American Law Schools is retooling a formerly academic association into a social regulatory authority, much like the PC movement is doing to American colleges and universities. For example, one of the "listed grounds" in this Association directive, which the prospective employee must not transgress, is "sexual orientation." A lawyer or law firm that betrays a preference for heterosexuals is to be denied access to the school's student body, never mind what the student might want.

Moreover, the Association is so fearful that employment interviews might become occasions for conventional human communication that it encourages member schools to promulgate detailed behavioral regulations governing both the form and the content of any communication between a prospective employer and a student.   Obligingly, member schools anxious to be on the avant edge of correctness outdo each other in dishing out patronizing directives to prospective employers. The would-be employer is told in detail exactly how to avoid each contemptible "ism" which offends official Association ethic and fashion. Many law schools send their directives in the form of an agreement, which the interviewing lawyer or firm must sign on pain of being denied access to the students.   For example, Duke University School of Law admonishes the employer that "no organization will be permitted to conduct on-campus interviews without returning this form."   The purpose is to force the would-be employer to conform to practices dictated by the law professors, but not required by law.   Like most law schools, Duke actively seeks to remove "sexual preference" as a factor employers may consider.   Indeed, "sexual preference" or "sexual orientation" appears to be the principal subject of these regulatory attempts.   Harvard, Yale, Duke, Stanford, and other leaders blaze the trail, and other aspiring up-and-coming institutions, such as Washburn University School of Law in Topeka, Kansas, follow righteously along.

At many law schools, this regulatory outreach has become a primary objective.   At Stanford Law School, for example, all prospective employers are sent a "Quality of Life Questionnaire."   The questions are far ranging, and include such questions as: "In what ways, if any, do you actively recognize the value of, encourage, and seek diversity among your attorneys?"   "Do you have any openly gay or lesbian attorneys?"   Even more specifically: "For social events to which spouses, domestic partners, or guests are invited, are invitations clearly extended to those of gay and lesbian attorneys?"   In the same vein: "Have any attorneys taken same-sex partners to work-related social functions?"   These are all considered matters of obvious relevance to the educational enterprise.

Moreover, the member law schools are directed by the Association to initiate complaint procedures, which require that "students who believe the employer is violating the policy should notify the career services office." The relations and communications between a student and prospective employer which occur entirely off-campus fall under these regulations equally with those occurring on-campus.

The traditional, individualist values of freedom of contract would permit consensual agreements which do not conflict with positive law. Of course, in certain contexts, the fundamentalist leaders of academic reform would lend their full support to complete freedom among "consenting adults." Yet freedom of contract, indeed even the smallest freedoms associated with human interaction, are casually jettisoned in when the goal is to eradicate an objectionable "way of viewing the world and an accompanying value system."

The Association's approach reveals a mentality very much akin to that of many federal governmental agencies. It is a favorite tactic to deny access to a valuable resource on condition of compliance with some requirement which could be adopted in an open democratic process only with difficulty. A contractor wishing to do business with a governmental entity, for example, must contractually agree to conform to a list of requirements developed by a bureaucracy, rather than being the product of a democratic legislature. A secretive regulatory evasion of democratic processes thereby becomes routine.

The leaders of legal education leave no doubt about where they stand on the individual. Their lofty pronouncements praise intellectually inspired government control, and minimize the importance of the individual in American society. Robert A. Gorman, the current president of the Association of American Law Schools, gave a typical legal academic's view of the future in his April 1991 president's message to member schools. The Association is gearing up for the 1992 annual meeting to be held in San Antonio, Texas. The theme of the meeting will be: "Ensuring Social and Economic Justice in a Changing America: Time for a New Bill of Rights?" What these people envision is a revised U.S. Constitution which will finally be rid of its original focus on the individual. Instead, it will embody the same philosophy of "aggregate classes" which the Supreme Court now employs. In the president's message from Gorman, the individual is clearly out and intellectually managed government is in. As he said:

Today the seemingly boundless individualism and optimism of our first century and a half as a nation have been replaced by a realization that our economic "pie" is static if not shrinking, and that individual fulfillment and accomplishment is often dependent less on governmental restraint than upon affirmative governmental intervention....

Need we fashion a new Bill of Rights to shelter, to employment, to education, to health care, and to other basic elements of a dignified quality of life to prepare us for the next 200 years?

In a casual, passive voice, the individual has "been replaced by a realization" that he is obsolete. A new non-individualist postdemocratic Constitution of Entitlements materializes in his place. It matters little that the "realization" is that of the law professors, and not that of the majority.

The fundamentalist reformers easily dismiss any institutional limitations on their programs. There are no standards or rules which should obstruct the path of instant reform. As Stanley Fish, chairman of the English Department at Duke University (and also a law professor) said in a 1991 interview with Dinesh D'Souza, author of the controversial *Illiberal Education*:

The norms and standards to which our behavior conforms *are* us. They aren't a set of rules we consult.

The eagerness to purge the old guard, reflected in Ms. Hill's statement about the reform of law faculties, is everywhere apparent, and little effort is spared in hurrying the process along. As D'Souza has documented in a March 1991 *Atlantic Monthly* article, the rush of universities on the make to outdo each other in the service of what Professor Fish calls "our historicist, postmodernist, poststructuralist movement" is astonishing. The drive to out-chic others has literally transformed university policies governing admissions, student aid, scholarships, faculty recruitment, faculty perquisites, and retention and has produced fine-tuned regulations on speech at the majority of all American schools. The current wave of subjective reform has finally revealed the modern academic to public view as a tense, illiberal, and highly insecure fundamentalist. Like the reformers in collegiate and public education, these people have entered the casual and fearless phase of reform, in which they feel beyond challenge and completely in control.

CHAPTER EIGHTEEN

Scholarship in the New Grove

When the tide of the 1960s had finally run its course, the university model which was familiar before 1950 was gone. It does not exist, except as a sort of new educational diaspora, a scattered and normally unassociated band of independent thinkers operating alone. The revolution shifted the custody of the educational values tested by time and culture from an institutional setting, with its supportive natural environment, into the hands of widely scattered entrepreneurs, 'self-starters' with some divine spark of discontent. In a metamorphosis resembling the advent of the Dark Ages, the change has brought illiteracy, low productivity, and scientific and intellectual backwardness—a sort of massive devolution of one of our culture's chief assets. If only the professors had done their jobs. As reported by *U.S. News and World Report* in January 1989, the post-1960s trend has been to replace the conservators in the academy with innovators: "'60's Protestors, '80's Professors" reads the headline. Naturally, their objective is "transforming the scholarship of the 80's." As a Duke history professor reports the results "There has been a revolution in the way history is viewed."

The very format of the university was also transformed. Unfamiliar new courses crowded out the old. The unifying principle behind the drive for these changes was two-fold. First, the new offerings were supposed to be more "relevant" than the traditional ones. That is, they purported to be more directly and obviously connected with some task immediately at hand, rather than to prepare the student in a general fashion for whatever may come in later life. The idea that there was a slowly evolving core of great knowledge which students could learn and employ to their advantage in understanding and dealing with life's unpredictable future gave way to the notion of particular skills addressed to particular jobs. The quest for the fundamental principle gave way to the prescription of the particular nostrum. In this way, the unifying notion of *humanitas* and of *scientia*, knowledge, was carved up into little parts, to be dispensed like the patent cures in a drug store.

The second unifying principle was the growing antipathy toward the traditional university format. The new intellectuals reassessed and labeled the purposeful synthesizing approach of the Academy, the object of the *universitas*, as mere arbitrary and ethnocentric dogma denying the diversity of world cultures and the peoples within them. Increasingly, they viewed cultural norms as bad in themselves, no matter what their historical effect may have been, because they represented a selectivity and analytical choice associated with that worst and most hateful of human propensities: discrimination.

In carving up humanity, the new intellectual ritually employed the gross technique of tacking the suffix "studies" on the end of every segment of knowledge chosen for pursuit. Since the new intellectual felt that the traditional pursuit of universal knowledge as a whole was really a discriminatory and ethnocentric denial of any of its parts, the only logical and moral course of action would be to pursue the parts and completely abandon the whole. One could repudiate the very existence of unifying cultural and social principles, of the very idea of community itself. The centrifugal force and effect of the new intellectual movement then worked an astounding and rapid transformation of the very constitution of the Academy. Anything which could precede the term "studies" was fair game.

Perhaps the most prolific of the new endeavors is "women's studies," which produces the largest stack of unsolicited pamphlets each week on the desk of every professor in every large campus in the nation. In his penetrating collection of essays, *Untimely Tracts*, Roger Scruton gives the best summary yet of the essence of the new wave of "studies" which have beset American universities, Scruton assumes that the boomers of new-age studies naturally intend the logical consequences of their actions and understand that their programs replace education with a predetermined political agenda which they prefer to education and its predictable liberating consequences. Scruton observes,

Considerable ingenuity has been spent in inventing 'relevant' humanities. The problem has been to conserve the outward prestige of education, as an embodiment of the reasonable approach to life's problems, while persuading the uneducated that there is a learning addressed to interests which they already have. The answer has been found to lie in the word 'studies.' When added to a relevant-sounding prefix (such as 'media' or 'communications', 'black' or 'gay') this word adjoins even to the most half-baked enthusiasm an air of superior knowledge. Not only are you right, it says, to be interested in the problems of the media, of blacks, of homosexuals: there is also a way of converting enthusiasm into expertise....

But that is precisely the point. The value of such a subject is precisely that it destroys education. It keeps the student's mind so narrowly focused on his random and transient political convictions that, when he ceases to be obsessed with them, he will lack the education through which to discover what to put in their place.

In gender studies, a star who typifies the new fashion is Vivian Gornick, a widely-known feminist whose works are a centerpiece in most women's studies or "women's experience" courses at the college level. Gornick argues forcefully that the feminist movement has worked a revolution in America. Most would agree that she is right, but the evidence she cites in support of her thesis is interesting. For example, she relates,

> I was eating lunch in a crowded restaurant on Chambers Street one day while on jury duty. At the next table sat two women I recognized as secretaries from the Criminal Courts Building. One was telling the other that her husband had failed to do the laundry last night, and this morning she was late because she had to go digging for clean underwear. Her voice was tight and angry as she spoke. "He said to me, 'Why didn't you remind me, or put the laundry bag in the bedroom?' I told him division of labor means I don't have to think about the laundry. It's your job, not mine." Then, with a forkful of tuna salad halfway to her mouth and a quizzical look in her eyes, she said, "He pays lip service to feminism, but he doesn't really get it." I stopped eating. Twenty years ago that sentence was continually on my lips. At Upper West Side dinner parties, people looked puzzled when I spoke it. Now it was on the lips of someone in a fast-food

restaurant in lower Manhattan, and the person to whom she spoke was nodding her head. Who says we haven't made a revolution?

Indeed, recent years have seen some revolutionary changes in American society, American government, in our very way of life. It is refreshing that Gornick can find the telltale signs of revolutionary change at the lower Manhattan fast-food mart.

Naturally, when gender is a guiding philosophical principle, some of the intellectual insights of the movement relate to gender itself, i.e., to sex. Gornick relates another revelation:

> At a gathering of friends, all feminists who went back to 1970 with me, everyone drinking and laughing, the atmosphere, as always among feminists, one of unguarded pleasure and entertainment. I recounted the episode of the suffragist and the Columbia party.
>
> One of us, Karen I think, said with a moan, "My God, parties don't feel like that any more."
>
> "You know why, don't you," said Ann. "Because these days the most interesting people in the room are likely to be the women."
>
> "That's right," said Debra, "and can you picture the sexual charge at a party where the women are powerful, and the men hover around them?"
>
> That sobered everyone up. All heads jerked quickly from side to side. "It's never happened," said Doris, "and it's never going to happen."
>
> "Who wants it to happen?" said Alice. "Reversed positions is not what I've been working for."
>
> "Me neither," said Vera. "What we want is a roomful of people in which everyone is sexy, and everyone is powerful."
>
> "Not in my lifetime," said Karen.

Like Albert Einstein and his famous formula, Gornick finally gets to the very bottom of the whole thing with her most sweeping generalization:

> Two shall be as one is over, no matter how lonely we get.

All these "studies" urge abandonment of the deep, dark motives harbored by the student. Sentimentalities which once were left to human evolution and to the culture at large are now subject to endless manipulation and decree. No manifestation of the relations between the sexes is safe, and nowhere has the overall agenda of the new academic appeared more fickle. After a sally at Victorian morality, the new "openness" and "diversity" exhorted sexual freedom (remember the "sexual revolution"). Then in a *volte face* which stunned many slow-witted males educated in the 1950s, the uninhibited sexual freedom which we had been told was so healthy, was suddenly reinterpreted as yet another manifestation of male malfeasance. If the impulse to carnal knowledge manifested itself in deed, however slight or suggestive, it might be "sexual harassment," the second cousin and precursor to rape. Memoranda appeared informing faculties that "sexual harassment" is "such conduct that has the purpose or effect of substantially interfering with an individual's work performance or creating an intimidating, hostile or offensive working environment" according to federal law. Contrary to what everyone had been told, there *was* harm in asking. Disposition to these offenses supposedly lay deep in the psyche of all males, and their behavior became the subject of numerous lawsuits.

The nation's law schools are eager to assist the potential litigant in combatting all the hated "isms." Many have begun law journals officially dedicated to this purpose. Typical of the wide ranging goals of such schools, Stanford has recently inaugurated a Journal of Law, Gender and Sexual Orientation. The advertisements for the journal state its purpose succinctly:

> The Journal, by illuminating the ways that gender and sexual identity are socially constructed, contributes to efforts to eliminate all oppressions. We are committed to multiple explorations of the way in which society creates different identities. In our efforts to highlight the processes of social construction of identity and sexuality that underlie sexism and heterosexism, we hope to contribute to the understanding of similar processes of social construction, such as racism and classism.

In a free and open university, such undertakings could be viewed as a sign of vitality, or of actual "diversity," whatever one thought of their merits. Freedom and actual diversity are not the goals of the new-age professor, however.   "To eliminate all oppressions," such as "classism" is high on the list of objectives. Vigorous regulation in the name of grandiose generalities is one of the hallmarks of the Church of Diversity.

In fact, the new scholarship has adopted a new officially approved view of humanity. As a result, we now live in a world where most of the playful flirtations of Clark Gable and Cary Grant would be viewed as a basis for litigation. Despite many earlier reformers' lack of support for "women's concerns" (Stokely Carmichael said a woman's proper place in the revolution was "prone"), it became yet another part of the revolutionary agenda for the Academy.

The professed antipathy to the Vietnam War at the universities ended with the war. Then the hostility to the cultural foundations of the majority was simply transferred to new areas. Race and sex became new cover stories for the campaign to reform American bourgeois society. Americans have failed to grasp that a dedicated anti-middle-class minority has simply adapted itself to new tools in the same process of revolution. So it was that romance itself, a middle-class cultural concept as familiar as Fred Astaire, was given a new and gruesome aspect, the usual fate of matters subject to government regulation and prolonged litigation. Sociology, history, and science, all of which had something valuable to say on human sexual differences and their consequences, were, of course, ignored. The same a priori reformist approach produced Women's Studies, Black Studies, and Gay and Lesbian Concerns. Just about every other imaginable centrifugal project which had any potential for obscuring the conservatory and analytical tradition of the Academy was catapulted into academic prominence in the space of a decade.

The new scholarly view of humanity is accompanied by a new view of learning itself. Predictably, radical feminism and gender studies on campus have ended by repudiating knowledge and analytical thought itself, starkly revealing the non-rational fundamentalism common the Church of Diversity. For example, in a bizarre project sponsored by the State of New Jersey, "feminist scholarship guidelines" were developed for state colleges and universities. These guidelines proceed along fundamentalist paths rarely found outside Iran. In a primal metaphor which sets the tone for the "guidelines," its authors tell us that, in the beginning, "mind was male, nature was female, and knowledge was created as an act of aggression a passive nature had to be interrogated, unclothed, penetrated, and compelled by man to reveal her secrets." Or as one radical feminist put it much more succinctly, "To know is to f_ _ _." Thus the very act of analytical inquiry ought to be viewed as "the rape of nature," not a nice thing to do.

It has now come about that the latest edition of the World Book Encyclopedia, a book which pre-college students regularly consult as an elementary reference tool, says with accuracy in its entry on "University": "Today there is no set idea of what a college should be." An apparently harmless statement, it reflects the deeper uncertainty which is actually there. Formerly the Academy cultivated the capacity for critical though as something *derived from* the treasure of knowledge which it conserved. The method that the Academy practices today is a priori and derived from an a priori viewpoint. The evolution of knowledge, the relations between the sexes, romance, in fact evolution itself has been stopped dead in its tracks by a dark vision of a world brutally and hopelessly divided by race, class and gender. The vision of Elizabeth Browning has given way to that of Sylvia Plath. The new environment is often defended as being much more open to controversy, more conducive to free dialogue. Anyone who has observed the ambience of most university departments during the last twenty years knows that this new freedom applies only to orthodox challenges to older standards made on behalf of the new agenda.

Thus, the eccentric but tolerant scholar of thirty years past has been largely replaced or eclipsed by a humorless, doleful, and determined collection of new intellectuals, as distinguished from academics. For the first time in our history, the average member of the Academy is removed from the middle class, and abhors its values. The intellectual has become the academic equivalent of the United States Supreme Court. Now, for the first time, the constitution of the Academy, including its practices and people, disdains the very group which formerly gave it a strong and durable life.

Academic leaders now casually undertake countless therapeutic goals, just as the Academy has done generally. In fact, such therapy is the consciously selected primary goal of many public school curricula. The very purpose of scholarship in the New Grove is largely therapeutic.

Take for example, the recently released Sobol Report, designed to set the curriculum for New York State public schools. Entitled the "Curriculum of Inclusion," the report laments the fact that children of European descent, mainly whites, outperform others. The result according to the report has been "a damaging effect on the psyche of young people of African, Asian, Latino, and Native American descent." The principal author of the report, Professor Harry Hamilton, a teacher of atmospheric science at State University of New York at Albany, forcefully expresses his conclusion that "African Americans, Asian Americans, Puerto Ricans/Latinos, and Native Americans have all been victims of an intellectual oppression that has characterized the culture and institutions of the United States and the European American world for centuries."

Professor Hamilton offers no proof for this a priori conclusion. He has discovered that cultural norms do evolve in any productive society and has concluded that, regardless of the content of these norms, they are per se oppressive. They are bad. "Much more severe corrective action is needed to create the dynamics of change," he says. After describing the United States Constitution as the vicious "white nationalism" of a bunch of egocentric and selfish opportunists, which has permitted a thoroughly flawed political process to work injustice for two centuries, he serves up a collation of Third World propaganda that is a self-parody. This assault on middle-class conceptions of society and family has been repeated in every school touched by the Great Society movement.

Finally, in 1990, the accrediting agencies which oversee the nation's colleges began to formally acknowledge the end of the traditional university. One of the six leading college accreditation organizations, The Middle States Association of Colleges and Schools, which regulates the populous states of New York, New Jersey, Pennsylvania, and Delaware, has made the achievement of "diversity" a formal requirement for accreditation. By diversity, they mean quota hiring and admissions based on race. Though this has caused the United States secretary of education, who in turn authorizes The Middle States Association, some concern, the will of the new-age academic is undaunted. Mr. Howard L. Simmons, the director of The Middle States Association, affirmed his duty to monitor the racial and ethnic composition of colleges and universities. Enigmatically, he said there was simply no choice:

> We cannot avoid public policy issues as part of the accreditation process. . . .There is hardly any "public policy" issue which does not find some enforcement in the new education climate of the 1990s.

CHAPTER NINETEEN

The Costs of Diversity

Since the Great Society, universities have evolved along the Washington model, a large and unwieldy bureaucracy that consumed the lion's share of the resources. Increasingly, faculties benefitted from progressive abandonment of the middle class in that they were viewed as having no real job to do, and as having all privileges and no responsibilities. They were unaccountable.

Amazingly, some of the nation's well-endowed institutions could offer a first-rate education to the best and brightest *for free*. The particular sort of arbitrariness they practice in dispensing their largess is revealing. All are at odds with the middle class, who are collectively supposedly to shoulder the guilt, inconvenience, and expense attending whatever social program or agenda the university has chosen. And most such programs are virtually identical, containing a large measure of policy dictated by the central government. The middle class is supposed to pay, and pay beyond their means.

The effects of the Academy's abandonment have devastated the middle class, and permutations of the original abandonment have naturally multiplied apace. Eventually, abandonment showed up as a mounting direct cost on the middle class of escalating tuition, which they were expected to bear in full. While middle-class median family incomes were flat between 1980 and 1988, the Tax Reform Act of 1986 shifted the tax burden more completely onto the back of the middle-class taxpayer. In the same period, the average inflation-adjusted cost of attending a four-year state-supported college rose by one-third to one-half. Increases for private education were even more dramatic. The costs of tuition and room and board at Princeton, for example, shot up as shown in Table 19.3.

TABLE 19.3

PRINCETON UNIVERSITY TUITION ROOM AND BOARD

	Tuition/Fees	Room/Board	Total
1971-72	$ 2,800	$ 580/$960	$ 4,340
1975-76	$ 3,900	$ 830/$1,070	$ 5,800
1980-81	$ 6,300	$1,100/1,351	$ 8,751
1985-86	$10,960	$1,795/$2,185 + (200)*	$14,140
1990-91	$15,540	$2,283/$2,775 + (275)	$20,873

*The $200 & $275 figures represent a new cost that the university labels as a college fee, which amounts as a fee for school-related social activities.

Just as the tax burden shift of the 1980s reflected the declining government representation of the middle class, the focus of educational costs on them reflected their abandonment by the Academy. Universities reserved relief from the brunt of such artificial and staggering inflation for "aggregate" classes rather than individuals with merit or financial need. Partly the result of bureaucratic dictates accompanying governmental money, this bias was assisted by the growing independence of intellectuals from the middle-class partnership. College faculties and admissions officers naturally thought of themselves as less dependent on small or average contributors, much the same way the New York Stock Exchange has emancipated itself from the concerns of the small investor. The very rich, it was assumed, would give anyway. Both economically and intellectually, poor, and members of racial minorities were to be adopted in as wards of the state-college enterprise. The middle class had to bite the bullet.

Not only was the lion's share of the cost of shifting the university's mission from partnership to open marriage cast upon the middle class, but also the university mission itself began to predictably change. Freed from any commitment to the cultural and social values of their society, the university faculties joined in the final realization of Horace Mann's dream and became a "mother," a nagging one at that.

Now, the middle-class majority finds itself in the ironic and unenviable position of literally paying for its own punishment. Though more and more of their taxes go to the university, less and less of the benefit comes to them. The university's alignment with the government, and its already evident abandonment of concern for the majority, represent a critical blow to the middle-class majority. It has created a geometrically increasing barrier to the time-honored pursuit of a good education as a tool of upward mobility. It has made the survival of that group more and more difficult and, in fact, less and less likely.

CHAPTER TWENTY

The Aftermath

The first remarkable result of the academic revolution is that, for the first time, academics feel they are approaching perfection. They can formulate the perfect code of belief and behavior for their colleagues and their students.

Previously, no one has ever been able to define completely what an educated person should know or be. The definition of a "perfectly" educated person, or the production of one, could no more be expected than could true perfection in any other human endeavor. Yet the pursuit and the conservation of human knowledge distinguished the pre-1960 university at its best from those of today. Today's Academy has found the answer. Academics *know*, and can prescribe for society. As the good-natured tolerance and open-minded pursuit of human knowledge gave way to the new certitude, the university became less agreeable as well as less useful. By betraying its traditional independence as a social institution, it ceased to be a university in the traditional sense at all, and became a governmental instrument with no independent personality of its own. Additionally, the new reformers seem totally ignorant of any value in the system they are destroying.

The second great result of the post-1960s academics revolution is that, for the first time in modern history, the real value of all that the Academy has conserved is in danger of being seriously damaged. This is because the Academy's greatest treasures are either detested or ignored by the new fundamentalists, and because the middle class is being priced out of the market.

For example, the very consensus of values which Professor Hamilton (of the Sobol Report) abhors as oppressive has also generated much liberation. If the founders of the American Republic had accepted Professor Hamilton's innervating relativism and aversion to any course of action motivated by a cultural consensus, by their traditional training and beliefs, they would never have escaped what they regarded rightly as the rule of an unfair and oppressive government. If Abraham Lincoln had followed the Sobol Report, he would have shrunk from imposing on others the ideals which he recognized as having been inspired by cultural tradition ("Four score and seven years ago our fathers brought forth, etc."). He would have shrunk from the arrogance of abolition, since this concept embodies cultural norms. Lincoln, a self-educated man, understood education and the fact that educated people are "conceived and dedicated" to certain precepts evolved from their peculiar tradition. Yet, as the ordinary middle-class citizen has hesitated to believe, these ideals are what the intellectualized educational establishment detests. They intensely dislike education as Abe Lincoln knew it and as most of the middle-class understand it. They detest the process by which these cultural norms became identifiable, a process greatly assisted in the past by the Academy's commitment to the search for the truth, as opposed to the institutionalized relativism advocated by the Sobol Report. And the intellectuals dislike the result of education, that is, the production of an educated person who may exalt one concept or culturally evolved consensus over another. They detest education itself.

In short, the intellectual cannot accept the end product of the middle-class view of education, which is a search for the truth producing results beyond pure diversity. The intellectual cannot accept the strain on individual feelings that middle-class norms and standards produce. Introverted and therapeutic, the intellectual view of education does not lead to the progressive evolution of any concepts beyond those which assuage the individual's subjective feelings. The intellectuals cannot face the results of education, for it naturally leads to challenges which not all can meet and concepts which not all can understand, even though the concepts be true and useful to mankind. Ironically, the modern intellectual disagrees with the middle-class belief that education itself is a good thing. The intellectual who doesn't believe in it detests those who do.

Certainly there remain those in most universities who still pursue the classics, but they are few, huddled off in special programs ("Honors Colleges") which are constantly attacked as elitist and therefore harmful. Such programs now have about the same status as the similar programs for "advanced" or "gifted" students in primary and secondary schools. These latter have met the problem of preserving some semblance of education in the face of the Great Society revolution. They have moved the standards typical of the older era within the walls of a recreated Great Society institution, which of course follows a social agenda rather than the academic one. A weakened version of the old *Academia* is perpetuated as a subpart of a new and expanded "full service" enterprise.

Now, any field of knowledge which the new-age academic can vaguely associate with the cultural history and tradition of the West, bears the brand of censure, like a scarlet letter. The Church of Diversity is now a serious rival of the historic university. It is of a piece with 1960s jurisprudence, since it is anti-individualistic and thoroughly arbitrary, subjecting whole fields of scholarship and literature to a doctrinaire preemptive rejection, even nullification by a strident minority. Though Elizabeth Browning and Matthew Arnold speak to the heart of man and woman alike with words of power and beauty, we can no longer view their messages with the enlightened neutrality of the intellect. We must measure them by their degree of association with some vaguely defined subset of humanity (white Western intellectual) or with sex. Nothing more clearly reveals the basic sham which now forms the intellectual foundation of the modern university than this.

So what should the Academy have done? Over a century ago, the newly appointed president of a college in Virginia decided to change the academic calendar of the school. He reduced the Christmas holiday from a week to one day. Quickly, the students circulated a pledge to boycott classes until the old vacation was restored. The president posted a notice on campus along with a copy of the pledge:

> Any student who signs the pledge will be expelled. If every student signs this, then I will lock the college door and put the key in my pocket.
>
> Signed: Robert E. Lee, President

Five years later, they changed the name of the university to include his with the first President of the United States: It became Washington and Lee University.

The Academy should have treated the sacred groves as it would its own home. When threatened with physical destruction or defacement, it should have invoked the full force of the law without regard to the race or background of the despoilers. It should have informed those who brought demands that it would accept none. It would accept suggestions and requests, it would invite dialogue, but it alone, the Academy, held responsibility for the custody of its mission, and it would decide the merits of any proposed alteration in its custom or in its philosophy. Just as it was for the individual, this precious autonomy was the most significant factor in preserving the identity and worth of the Academy over the centuries. Once it was gone, the result would be a foregone conclusion, just as it had been at the Universities of Heidelberg and Berlin when emissaries of the Third Reich came to call. In America, the Academy risked no death or imprisonment for asserting autonomy, in support of which the middle class had bestowed the privilege of tenure for life. They should have asserted their autonomy from the Department of Education, too. If the United States Government could not transfer money to the Academy unless the Academy altered its constitution, the government should have been told to keep the money. The leaders—the presidents and provosts of the Academy —should have taken these actions or resigned. The members of the Academy should have insisted that they be done or get new presidents and provosts.

But that isn't what happened. Just as the new wave of Great Society students suspected, the fire that had once burned in the Academy had been banked down to a few dull and scattered embers. The increasingly complex administrative bureaucracy of the Academy, entwined with the Great Society regulations which accompanied the Great Society money, drifted away from the academic vision of the university. At the expense of their own traditions, university presidents became experts in public relations. The few voices in opposition to the massive abandonment of the 1960s were powerless to stem the tide. Only now are they being heard.

PART V

Conclusion

Character, in the long run, is the decisive feature in the life of an individual and of nations alike.

Theodore Roosevelt—quotation on the wall of the Entrance Hall of the Museum of Natural History in New York City.

The economic failure of the middle class means the U.S. will fundamentally change in the near future. The middle class failed because, around 1965, the country set off on an experiment with non-democratic government. This created a fatal schism between the government and the majority of the people. Now, a failed government has led this rich country into bankruptcy. A profound pessimism grips the country. So change is coming. If we continue on the present road we will get more bad change, more impoverishment, more loss of liberties. Our purpose, of course, is to turn off that road as fast as we can.

What should we do? We should do exactly what we did the last time we were ruled by a government that didn't represent us. America declared its independence from George III, July 4, 1776, before the states had agreed to any plan of confederation. During the Revolutionary War, the Continental Congress drafted the Articles of Confederation and submitted them to the states. On March 1, 1781, Maryland, the last of the thirteen states, signed the Articles. The Articles could be amended only by the unanimous consent of the states.

Congress, under the Articles, had no power to levy taxes, but could only request contributions. All important legislation needed the approval of nine states. Congress could negotiate a treaty but it had to be ratified by all the states. Finally, and most importantly, Congress had no authority to regulate foreign or interstate commerce.

On October 19, 1781, George Washington accepted the surrender of Lord Cornwallis at Yorktown. When victory relieved the colonies from the necessity for solidarity, the states began to drift into commercial warfare with each other. To favor their own citizens, the states set up customs barriers and tax burdens to discourage goods from other states. As a result, business among the states could not be conducted in an orderly way. Madison thought the situation so dangerous that the Revolution itself was at risk, particularly since the British were diligently at work to divide the states with "insidious" policies.

For the sole purpose of stopping the trade wars, the Virginia House of Delegates, on January 21, 1786, called for a convention of the states:

> [T]o take into the consideration the trade of the United States, to examine the relative situation and trade of the said states, to consider how far a uniform system in their commercial regulations may be necessary to their common interest and their permanent harmony . . .

The proposal was sent around to the legislatures of the other twelve states, and five sent delegates to Annapolis, Maryland in September 1786. The Annapolis delegates proposed that Congress call a meeting to review the Articles of Confederation and to:

> [D]evise such further provisions as shall appear to them necessary to render the constitution of the Federal Government adequate to the exigencies of the Union; and to report such an Act for that purpose to the United States in Congress assembled, as when agreed to, by them, and afterwards confirmed by the Legislatures of every State, will effectually provide for the same.

Congress, acting under the Articles of Confederation, called on the states to appoint delegates and send them to Philadelphia on the second Monday in May 1787. The Constitutional Convention was organized on May 25, 1787. For the next four months about 30 delegates met daily except for Sundays and one 10-day adjournment, from July 26 to August 6, to let the committee of detail prepare a draft of what had been agreed to up to that time. On September 17 the delegates adopted the Constitution and adjourned. Washington, in his letter transmitting the Constitution to Congress, wrote that "Individuals entering into society must give up a share of liberty to preserve the rest." Differences among the states, he continued, made it particularly difficult to draw the line "between those rights which must be surrendered and those which may be reserved." In all our deliberations, "we kept steadily in our view" that the essential matter was "the consolidation of our Union, in which is involved our prosperity, felicity, safety, perhaps our national existence." The Convention proceeded "in a spirit of amity, and of that mutual deference and concession which the peculiarity of our political situation rendered indispensable." That the Constitution, Washington concluded, "may promote the lasting welfare of that country so dear to us all, and secure her freedom and happiness, is our most ardent wish." That night the delegates met for the last time at City Tavern for dinner. Washington wrote in his diary that he "retired to meditate on the momentous work which had been executed." On April 30, 1789. George Washington was inaugurated as our first president.

The Constitution provides the means for its own revision. Early in the Convention, on July 11, Colonel George Mason of Virginia noted that amendments will be necessary "and it will be better to provide for them in an easy, regular, and constitutional way than to trust to chance and violence." Mason believed Congress should be excluded from the amendment process because "no amendments of the proper kind would ever be obtained by the people, if the government should become oppressive, as he verily believed would be the case." The convention took up Article V on September 10, 1787. James Madison submitted a draft article which authorized both the state legislatures and Congress to propose amendments. Madison's draft was adopted after some discussion. Article V authorizes a convention just like the one which

produced the original Constitution.   Article V of the Constitution
provides:

> The Congress, whenever two thirds of both houses, shall deem it
> necessary, shall propose amendments to this Constitution, or, on the
> application of the legislatures of two thirds of the several States, shall
> call a convention for proposing amendments, which, in either case,
> shall be valid to all intents and purposes, as part of this Constitution,
> when ratified by the legislatures of three fourths of the several States,
> or by conventions in three fourths thereof, as the one or the other mode
> of ratification may be proposed by the Congress.

Article V provides that Congress, by a two-thirds vote of both
houses may propose amendments. Alternatively, the legislatures of two-
thirds of the states may call for a convention for amendment. Any
amendment proposed by Congress or the convention called by the states
must be ratified by the legislatures of three-fourths of the states, or by
conventions representing three-fourths of the states. Congress is
empowered to select which method of ratification is used.

Elbridge Gerry, a delegate from Massachusetts said: "The novelty
and difficulty of the experiment requires periodical revision.   The
prospect of such a revision would also give intermediate stability to the
Government." Similarly John Dickinson, a delegate from Delaware,
who urged ratification of the Constitution, pointed out the amendment
process will allow us "by a gradual progress . . . [to] introduce every
improvement in our constitution that shall be suitable to our situation."

The legal intelligentsia hate the idea of a second constitutional
convention. They say it will be irresponsible. They say it will be a
"runaway convention." Law professors and judges, such as retired
Supreme Court Justice William Brennan, tell us the Supreme Court is
our "continuing Constitutional Convention." At the same time, they tell
us to be afraid of a real convention because it might "runaway." Where
would it runaway to? Whatever the convention does has to be ratified
by three-fourths of the states. What *are* they afraid of?

CONCLUSION

Simply this: in an Article V world it is the people who have the power. It is the people's Constitution. As Theodore Roosevelt said:

> It is the people, and not the judges, who are entitled to say what their constitution means, for the constitution is theirs, it belongs to them and not to their servants in office—any other theory is incompatible with the foundation principles of our government.

Our first Constitutional Convention of 1787 did a good job. Why should anyone fear a second one?

It's time to go back to the source of sovereignty—the people. Something must happen, as R.R. Palmer wrote about our original Revolution, "if continuing deterioration is to be avoided; some new kind or basis of community must be formed." Pat Buchanan, in *Right From the Beginning,* calls for a second constitutional convention: "[A]s our third century of constitutional government begins, there are crises that need addressing, and deformities in the balance of political power that need correcting." The call for a convention, Buchanan writes, will "reveal which of the two parties is populist, and which elitist, which trusts and which fears the people."

Congress must call the second convention upon application of two-thirds of the states. The call, like the original, should specify a time and place and direct the state legislatures to appoint delegates. In the new convention, like the original, the vote is by states with a majority, 26, required to adopt a provision. Article V does not authorize Congress or the state legislatures to limit the convention. The convention is the constitutional means of exercising popular sovereignty.

Why should Americans continue on with a political system that makes us miserable? Why should Americans do anything we don't want to? The Constitution gives Americans the means of restoring democracy. If democracy is given a chance, it will close the breach between the people's beliefs and the government's beliefs. The cleavage between real and governmental beliefs creates a terrible tension in the country.

The American majority, in the second convention, will, in all likelihood, chose to return to a world based on the individual, rather than continue with the current Orwellian management of social classes. They will display more respect for each other than the Supreme Court and Congress have shown toward them. The new convention will have unlimited power; no existing institutions or vested rights restrain it. It can change the ways things are organized in this country in any way it wants. In a convention, the people, as Mr. Livingston told the 1821 New York Constitutional Convention, "are here themselves . . . No restriction limits our proceedings. What are these *vested* rights? Sir, we are standing upon the foundations of society." The convention can alter, amend or revoke the powers presently given to the states, the national government, the judiciary, the legislature and the executive. The new government the convention recommends to the people may not resemble the old. The country is not going back to any old system; it is going to make a new one.

Americans will probably chose not to continue with a professional Congress and an overriding Supreme Court. The second convention will bring political power back under democratic control; it will restore a government which derives its just powers from the consent of the governed. Problems like debt, trade, deficits, political accountability, infectious disease, crime, and education will not be so baffling to new democratic institutions as they have been to our existing bankrupt institutions.

When all is said and done, the conflict over who controls the Constitution represents two different views of human nature, and two incompatible views of government. The new intellectual minority has no faith in the character of their fellow citizens. The majority, on the other hand, agrees with Theodore Roosevelt that the real strength of the nation lies in the character of the individuals who make it up. They agree with Thomas Jefferson who said: "The steady character of our countrymen is a rock to which we may safely moor." Our Constitution gives us the tools to bring the country back on course. Which view of human nature prevails in future America is up to us.

INDEX